HOUSING THE FAMILY

jovis

HOUSING THE FAMILY

Locating the single-family home in Germany

Christiane Cantauw
Anne Caplan
Elisabeth Timm [eds.]

jovis

INTRODUCTION

BUILT AND INHABITED: LIVING IN A SINGLE-FAMILY HOME

HOME TREASURES: MINING THE SINGLE-FAMILY HOUSE

Preface

Christiane Cantauw
Anne Caplan
Elisabeth Timm

In times when investors successfully turn inner-city housing into a commodity with prices skyrocketing under the very auspices of municipalities, urbanists, architects, anthropologists, sociologists, and critical geography for good reason focus on people's struggles with these threats. In parallel, the single-family house areas in the suburbs and in the countryside, that for a long time have been regarded as perhaps not ideal (costly infrastructure for low density) but well-functioning settlements, resurfaced on the agenda of planners and of family housing alike, and with a new topicality: an intensive and growing demand for knowledge on the transformation of suburban and rural dwelling and living in Germany in the context of demographic changes, the turn to asset-based welfare regimes, the introduction of new planning structures of the governance type, and the implementation of an ecological framework in resource use and waste management. These issues are pending in all efforts to deal with single-family houses as a vast, often problematic material heritage in German suburbia, that consists not only of a historical stock of buildings from the second half of the 20th century, but in the meantime also of single-family houses continuously spreading anew to fulfil families' wish to build a new home.

This prompted our interdisciplinary research association, in which we conducted comparative ethnographic case studies on single-family home buyers and builders in a rural, suburban, and urban field site, complemented by engineers who measured the physical substance of those houses, and by an exhibition that communicated our findings and an attitude that, other than the architectural avant-garde's critique did it since the nineteenth century, would not devaluate people's homes but question the taken-for-grantedness of this type of living and dwelling.[1] The present volume includes central results of these projects as well as further case studies, that were presented in the final conference of our research association in Münster in April 2018, to broaden the topics with further approaches to the single-family home in historical and contemporary perspectives and comparisons. Since the single-family house is researched intensively in the so-called home ownership societies worldwide (see the overview by Elisabeth Timm in this volume), this English volume could contribute to present the German case in the international debate, and to enlarge our perspective by the New Housing Studies, that fruitfully brought ethnographic and structural analyses together again.

The first section, 'Built and inhabited: living in a single-family house', opens the door to get to know the residents' views: How do couples who wish to build a new family house in suburbia, municipal administration, land market, and local politics interact? How do people organise their everyday life in a single-family home today? What do they like about their houses? What makes these houses still attractive for families? Are those areas really all the same? Urbanist Katherin Wagenknecht presents the findings of her comparative research in a village, a suburban and an urban settlement, thus taking into account the very places of these houses, and thus elucidating quite different social forms behind the always resembling facades. The artist Folke Köbberling gives families a forum for directly having their say – a simple but precise pinch to grasp the lifeworlds that generate single-family houses. Planner and architect Inken Tintemann compares inner-city and suburban family living by uncovering how they adapt in specific ways to each environment. Designer Anne Caplan and urbanist Katherin Wagenknecht tackle a question that is most pressing for municipalities that have to deal with emptying single-family house areas: What makes people prefer to buy building stock or to build a new house respectively?

The second section, 'Home treasures: mining the single-family house', addresses the materiality and economic and symbolic values of these homes: What are the economic, cultural, and ecological potentials and challenges of the materials that make up the stock of single-family houses built since the 1950s? How do people deal with the suburban single-family home as an intimate good of consumption, as an investment and/or as an inheritance? Is there any resonance between couples with small children who recently moved to a newly developed suburban area and old couples or mostly old women who spend their retirement in a large house? Architect Johannes

Warda discovered an unexpected passion for preserving old houses for family use in the centre of suburbanisation's moneylender: a magazine, with which a *Bausparkasse* advertised its products. Anthropologist Christiane Cantauw reveals why some families prefer acquiring a used single-family home, and she found out that their decisions are indeed based on a limited set of factors (like location, costs, living space), but always in a highly individual combination. Historian and anthropologist Jakob Smigla-Zywocki interviewed house buyers and asked for the cultural logic of their expenses: Although they are indebted, they feel to have gained an advantage by avoiding to pay rent – a type of living commonly regarded as economically irrational. However, there are also values in these buildings awaiting to be discovered: In waste management, the German *Kreislaufwirtschaftsgesetz* (Waste Management and Product Recycling Act) of 2012 interprets the concept of 'waste' in a new way: potentially, now all things are resources in an ideally infinite cycle. To this concept of circulation, private consumption is terra incognita and, in the meantime, has become a huge resource deposit. Engineers Sabine Flamme and Gotthard Walter dug up the single-family house and related equipment and thus can document the quantity and quality of its materials in a detailed way.

The third section, 'Detached desires: popular visions and everyday memories of the single-family house', asks for the aesthetic relations that unfold around this type of building. The rise of the single-family home throughout the twentieth century has been triggered by new and changing media technologies (printing, photography, film). Vice versa, house or home and family have been central issues to make domestic picture production a mass business. Nowadays, such pictures circulate between public housing policy, the real estate and mortgage market, prefab house manufacturers, family albums and vernacular platforms in the internet. Knowing and showing homes has always been made popular by advertising single-family homes – via the state, but also as commodities. Art historian Johanna Hartmann detects an unexpected representation of the single-family house in an exhibition that suggested an ideal home in a central section on living and housing within the reconstruction period in West Germany after the Second World War. Architect Julia Gill follows the current manifestations of the factory-made house – a vision, that social reformers and aesthetic avant-garde shared in the interwar period, and that turned into the rather uniform mass-customised appearance of suburbs since some decades. Designer Anne Caplan investigates the aesthetics and the social order of single-family houses and related carports in advertising and thus elucidates how social aspirations and a patriarchal gender order are used to sell homes.

The fourth section, 'Comparative and analytical perspectives: regional cases of the single-family home as a global form', is dedicated to the very different relations and meanings that underlie specific cases of single-family houses. Architect Carola Ebert found out how the modernist one-storey bungalow, the daydream of transparency and modern living since mid-twentieth century, were realised as a concretisation of the middle-class ontology on which the German Federal Republic was based politically. Anthropologist Sophie Chevalier looks into the French type of two-homes dwelling, which means living in a house in the countryside, often inherited, and in a city apartment as its complement. This arrangement very much documents popular inheritance practices as well as political centralism in France. Anthropologist Marcel Vellinga informs about how the Minangkabau house, a building type that became well-known globally since it was presented at World's Fairs and in anthropological exhibitions and museums, became transformed on site into single-family houses by its inhabitants, but also became an emblem of a regionalised or nationalised aesthetics that marks public as well as private buildings on Sumatra in Indonesia.
With these different perspectives that connect to the single-family house in specific cases as well as within contemporary and historical horizons, this volume aims to bring into contact the latest but dispersed research on the single-family house in Germany from different disciplinary approaches, like architecture, resource management, social history, history of the built environment, anthropology, cultural studies, planning, and urbanism.

Endnotes

1 The research network 'A House and its Objects between Family Life, Resource Management and Museum', directed by Elisabeth Timm (WWU Münster, Seminar for Folklore Studies / European Ethnology), was funded by the German Federal Ministry of Education and Research (programme 'The Language of Objects – Material Culture in the Context of Social Developments') from 2015 to 2018, funding codes 01UO1504A/B/C/D. See further information and all publications to date here: www.hausfragen.net (accessed 28 April 2019).

The single-family home between politics, consumerism, and the everyday: locating the West German case

Elisabeth Timm

Among the manifold objects of anthropological investigation, the single-family home is a very practical thing. While anthropologists often must explain their research topics wordily, everybody realises immediately what is meant when we speak of a single-family home, notwithstanding many variants of this type of dwelling and living, be it today or in past times. This clarity got the single-family home a very prominent place in German social theory and philosophy: The empirical example, with which Jürgen Habermas in his 'Theory of Communicative Action' sounded out the notion of the lifeworld as 'a basic concept of social theory' *(gesellschaftstheoretischer Grundbegriff)*, is the construction site of a single-family home: With the question of how the building labourers come to an understanding of who will fetch some beer for the upcoming midmorning snack, Habermas (1989: 121) illustrates his definition of *Lebenswelt* (lifeworld): 'From a perspective turned towards the situation, the lifeworld appears as a reservoir of taken-for-granteds, of unshaken convictions that participants in communication draw upon in cooperative processes of interpretation.' (ibid.: 124) Habermas discusses the single-family home construction site across several pages in the introduction to 'The Theory of Communicative Action'. This is his explication of the situation where an older worker asks a younger colleague to go and fetch some beer: 'the expectations the workers attach to midmorning snack, the status of a newly arrived younger co-worker, the distance of the store from the construction site, the availability of a car, and the like, belong to the elements of the situation', while the 'facts that a single-family house is going up here, that the newcomer is a foreign "guest worker" with no social security, that another co-worker has three children, and that the new building is subject to Bavarian building codes are circumstances irrelevant to the given situation' (ibid.: 123). This might change, for example, 'as soon as the homeowner shows up with a case of beer to keep the workers in a good mood, or the guest worker falls from the ladder as he is getting ready to fetch the beer, or the theme of the new government regulations concerning child subsidies comes up' (ibid.).

Habermas' explanation of the lifeworld by taking the example of a single-family home construction site is one of the very beautiful cases of crypto-empiricism of social theory and philosophy (and a typical one, too): he references a comprehensible case, with which complex theoretical approaches can be communicated, because everybody knows it. In fact, there is probably a literally concrete experience behind this crypto-empiricism, since Jürgen Habermas has been director of the *Max-Planck-Institut zur Erforschung der Lebensbedingungen der wissenschaftlich-technischen Welt* (Max Planck Institute for Social Sciences) from 1971 to 1981 in Starnberg, and that's where he was confronted with the 'Bavarian building codes' that surfaced in his magnum opus, being the builder-owner of a single-family home right there. Admittedly, the cubistic *Haus Habermas*, designed and built by *Hilmer & Sattler und Albrecht* architects in 1971/72 after considering *Haus Wittgenstein* in Vienna (1928, by Ludwig Wittgenstein and Paul Engelmann) as one of the most famous references that concreted *Neues Bauen* and philosophy alike,[1] is not of the single-family home type that comes to mind if we think of the ordinary houses that make up more popular lifeworlds around the globe. But yet Habermas could be sure that the building type as well as a figure like the builder-owner who visits the construction site of his family's home-to-be with beer as a gift for the construction workers are not explanandum but explanans. However, he paradoxically explicated his actually more general philosophical endeavour of 'The Theory of Communicative Action' with a historically and socially very specific case: the single-family home in West Germany, ordered by a male breadwinner for his family, not prefabricated, mass-customised, and offered by anonymous vendors, but built on site by craftsmen of local firms, with whom the client establishes a personal relation of the paterfamilias type (providing the construction workers with beer 'to keep them in a good mood').

It can be left undecided, how the individualistic daydream, introduced here in the Habermasian version, also in West Germany resulted in the monotonous suburbs that urbanists and architects have criticised for a long time.[2] However, unlike in the 1970s and 1980s, the single-family home is just losing its 'taken-for-grantedness', and it no longer belongs to the 'unshaken convictions' of dwelling and living. Although (rather biased) opinion polls frequently suggest that the detached single-family home still is the preferred type of housing – the 'dream of 60 % of Germans' (Interhyp n.d.) –, it is the existing vast stock of single-family homes that have been built between the 1950s and the 2000s especially at the edge of villages and small towns in rural and suburban areas, that now confronts municipal planning as well as private owners with manifold problems. Within this change from an unquestioned evidence of good family life in a sound state (see above: 'child subsidies' and 'social security', except for the 'foreign guest worker' on the construction site) to an individually as well as publicly often embarrassing heirloom, the single-family home became a new topic of interest, a new object of investigation, a new field of policy, and consequently also a new object of knowledge. So, what do we know about the single-family home in Germany, in historical perspective as well as in contemporary comparison?

The single-family home in Germany: manifestation and historical paths of a global form

The detached single-family house is a vast heritage of the Fordist decades in the 20th century. It materialises the political support of a way of living and dwelling, and it symbolises dreams of home, prosperity, and social status. This was and is a global phenomenon. Other than in the US, in West Germany living in a detached single-family home became a mass experience only after the Second World War. Although the German Democratic Republic like other state-socialist countries took another path by preferring high-rise industrialised apartment blocks, the nuclear family on both sides of the iron curtain (with some variants concerning the male breadwinner position) was the social unit that was addressed and thus produced by public housing policy. And while the single-family home in the GDR existed only in niches and living in a modern high-rise apartment block was a privilege (Hannemann 2005), West German high-rise projects (on the architectural aspects see Hnilica 2018) made a fast but short career from statements in modern architecture and social utopias pulsating with young families inhabiting them to devastated quarters needing a 24/7 social worker to maintain at least basic sociality.

For Germany, federal statistics record about 15.75 million single-family houses (in 2017), which especially in villages and medium-sized and small towns in suburban and rural areas often represent more than two thirds of all buildings

(Statista 2018; Zakrzewski et al. 2014: 253). Overall, in 2018 35.1 percent of all households in Germany are living in a single-family house (Statistisches Bundesamt 2019: 13). This means an increase of two percent since 2008 (33.0 percent), with the quota being much higher in West Germany (i.e. the old Federal Republic) with 37 percent than in the new eastern states and Berlin (27.8 percent) (ibid.). The average living area in these buildings is 129.6 square metres in 2018 (compared to 127.2 in 2008) and thus much larger than the average living area in all German households of 93.2 square metres in 2018 (and 91.7 in 2008) (ibid.). Among the households located in a single-family house, in 2018 68.8 percent belong to the inhabitants; whereas this is an increase compared to 2008 (from 65.7 percent), the rate of home ownership among households in buildings with three or more flats remained stable at about 20 percent in 2008 as well as in 2018 (ibid.: 15).

While suburbanisation based on spreading single-family houses has been the dominant spatial dynamics since the decades of prosperity after the Second World War and throughout crises like the oil shock in West Germany (and again in the East after 1990), latest research observes and debates current and complex dynamics of reurbanisation (Brake and Herfert 2012). In general, due to demographic change and booming cities that profited from intensified globalisation, a fundamental shift in the spatial development of dwellings in Germany occurred around 2000, namely from suburbanisation to reurbanisation, although there remain regions and cities that are still characterised by shrinking and/or by new developments of single-family home areas and therefore a growth in suburbia in parallel (Herfert and Osterhage 2012: 91 and 107; Krajewski 2014; Münter and Osterhage 2018).[3]

In the meantime, Germany remained a 'tenant society' (Helbrecht and Geilenkeuser 2010, Kohl 2017)[4] with a home ownership rate of only 42.1 percent (in 2018) (the EU-28 average for home ownership is 69.3 percent, with Romania and other Eastern European countries at the top with over 90 percent, and Switzerland (included as non-EU member state in this comparison) recording about 42 percent at the bottom; this data for 2017, see Statistisches Bundesamt 2019 and Eurostat n.d. – Eurostat (ibid.), documents 51.4 percent for Germany in 2017 and thus a difference compared with the national statistics that probably results from a variation in a survey method). Latest findings argue that the still comparatively low rate of home ownership in Germany mainly is an effect of a historical path of three quite stable dynamics since the nineteenth century: Urban land was not easily available for private housebuilding, public housing finance produced tenements, and the *Handwerk* tradition was an obstacle to mass production of single-family homes

(Kohl 2017). In detail, the German 'corporatist city tradition' controlled land use, whereas the very high rate of home ownership in the USA is a result of the 'private city tradition' that 'made urban land much more accessible for home ownership' there (ibid.: 77).[5] Furthermore, the German system of housing finance throughout the twentieth century 'has worked in favour of continuous additions of rental units to the German housing stock', whereas the 'rise of a specialized homeownership-finance circuit in the form of deposit banks and *Bausparkassen*' came too late to change this course (ibid: 117).[6] Finally, the strong corporatist *Handwerk* tradition in the construction sector in Germany and the tradition of using not light (e.g. wood) but heavy (e.g. bricks) materials for private housing construction already since the nineteenth century literally compounded the large-scale availability of single-family homes for private owners (ibid: 158 and 167–170). As one effect of this structure, the single-family homes built are again not mass produced but 'custom-designed' for a 'high number of private individuals acting on the construction market' (ibid.: 168f.) – like Habermas in Starnberg – and 'built on site by artisans having undergone a traditional though adapted apprenticeship program', and all in all this skilled work causes higher prices (ibid.: 170).[7] This again is related to another trait of the single-family house construction in Germany: a remarkable personal contribution by the prospective owners in the form of manual labour and in cooperation with local craftsmen (very frequent in the reconstruction period starting at the end of the Second World War, but also today). In small towns and villages, in particular, a familialist type of constructing houses is common (Rodenberg 2017; Kaspar 2011; Wagenknecht this volume). This led to a peak in workers as new home owners after the Second World War in Germany, since they had both skills and relatives with helping hands at their disposal (Kurz 2000: 31).

Different from home ownership in other countries, the single-family house in Germany has been appropriated not so much as an investment (that can be brought to the market to realise a return on investment several times), but rather as an intimised good of family consumption that is kept a whole lifetime and neither sold nor rented (Zakrzewski et al. 2014: 249). Germans are characterised as 'one-time buyers' of homes who only recently are confronted with the idea that a house is an investment that not only is sold at the end of one's lifetime or in case of inheritance, but several times during the whole lifetime to make the most of it (Helbrecht and Geilenkeuser 2010). The German preference 'to get settled once and for all in the same place' is interpreted as an effect of the 'longer waiting periods for necessary savings' to cover the comparatively high price of a single-family house in Germany (Kohl 2017:

170). This, in turn, contributes to single-family homes in Germany being a 'status good of a higher price' that is not available to broader population strata (ibid.: 190f.).

A common practice: discovering ageing single-family home areas as a field of policy and building new ones in parallel

Today, these dynamics merge and culminate in German suburbia that mainly consists of single-family homes built in the decades from 1950 to 1980, and where municipal administration and local politics are confronted almost simultaneously with emptying single-family houses at the edge of villages and small towns. This development is not only structured regionally, since emptying older quarters often neighbour new developments, and since growing cities also exhibit emptied housing stock at their edges (Bundesstiftung Baukultur 2018: 32). The inhabitants all grew old at the same time and now wonder what to do with their estates, while in parallel young families prefer and demand new buildings to realise the same dream as their parents did (Krajewski and Otto 2014, Münter 2011). 'In small cities with a population of up to 20,000 residents, the vacancy rate in single-family house areas is 11 percent.' (Bundesstiftung Baukultur 2018: 32) These developments turned those areas from 'blind spots of urban planning' (Zakrzewski et al. 2014) into 'long-term care' cases (Bundesstiftung Baukultur 2018: 58) and into spaces for experimental explorations of how to re-use these old houses and of how to motivate their owners to invest in comprehensive renovations, supported by public benefits from national and EU funds (see e.g. three projects addressing older single-family house areas in North Rhine-Westphalia in: Regionale 2016 Agentur GmbH 2016: 214-227; Bundesstiftung Baukultur 2018: 58; Simon-Philipp and Korbel 2016; Utku et al. n.d.). Developing single-family house stock became a new policy field on the municipal level (Adam et al. 2017, Köhler and Berndgen-Kaiser 2016, Köhler et al. 2016, Zakrzewski et al. 2014), not only in Germany (Berndgen-Kaiser et al. 2018).

However, public wealth is still steered into constantly renewing such dwellings, as for example with the latest federal measure named *Baukindergeld* (homeowner allowance for families with children) from 2018 that experts assess as a means to foster single-family home areas anew – against a more sustainable housing policy and countering the cut of land use (Bundesstiftung Baukultur 2018: 58f.). It is not surprising, that the efforts of municipal and regional planning until today regularly fail in their efforts to implement more flexible forms of housing, or to promote the use of adapted building stock in order to densify housing developments where infrastructure has already been financed publicly decades ago to avoid land use and infrastructure costs (Lachmann 2004).

The paradox effect of governance: funding but not accounting the single-family home

As research on planning and public administration revealed, in Germany most municipalities and/or local politicians strongly assume that 'young families' (mind the familialist social ontology behind this seemingly neutral category) who move to newly built suburbs are an advantage for the municipal coffers. Astonishingly, this assumption is not substantiated by a documented balance of accounts – neither the costs of new suburban infrastructure, nor the presumed returns from consumption and/or taxes paid by the new inhabitants are captured regularly. Full cost accounting is a tool that still needs to be invented and implemented here (Feldmann et al. 2007; Gutsche and Schiller 2009; Dieterich et al. 2006). Notwithstanding their discourse of sustainability, new EU funding policies that suggest and mobilise localities and regions to compete among each other (e.g. by the LEADER programme), paradoxically contribute to the older variant of a more spontaneous but well-established competition, especially among local policy-makers 'to fulfil people's housing preferences, irrespective of whether they are contrary to criteria of sustainability' (Feldmann et al. 2007: 57, author's translation).
These dynamics and phenomena are under intensive observation by planning research and of critical geography (e.g. Balke and Reimer 2016). While the implementation of new public management in Germany suggested (or rather, as Holtkamp 2008 documents: pretended) that this administrative and financial reform will also calculate in detail budgets that hitherto have been allocated to the municipal departments as a lump sum, deeper analyses of funding policy e.g. concerning the *Metropolregionen* yielded that this programme subordinated empirically measurable quantities to political motivations, and that researchers within this change in public funding often acted as part of an 'epistemic community' that generated the eleven German *Metropolregionen* rather than as observers and documenters of empirical facts (Hesse 2015: 362, 369). Latest research on the globally known 'suburban constellations' (Keil 2013), among them single-family home suburbs, demand for approaches that, in particular, analyse the interface between everyday life, new planning

regimes of this governance type, and, especially in Germany, the mobilisation of older '*Landschaft*' or '*Kulturlandschaft*' concepts as a strategy of revitalising suburbia within the politics of cultural heritage (Oltmanns 2016).

The single-family home as a costly passion: from consumer hub and fulfilment of social aspirations since the Second World War to responsibilisation within New Welfare

Until today, municipalities try to generate influx by offering land and infrastructure for new single-family homes (Bundesstiftung Baukultur 2018: 32) – although nobody ever recalculated whether this really pays off (Feldmann et al. 2007). This makes it necessary to look not for numbers but for tales to find out which values guarantee the individual as well as the public plausibility of this estimate: The political and popular twin-vision of family formation and building one's own house is deeply connected with ideals of growth, continuity, prosperity, freedom in one's own garden, and domestic consumption of household and consumer electronics like the parents' generation did (Staub 2014). As latest analyses yielded, working-class housing in Germany at the edge of industrialisation and urbanisation around 1900 has been characterised by the predominance of tenement buildings, other than, for example, in Great Britain and Belgium, where workers mostly inhabited small houses for one or two families (Kohl 2017: 32). It was the interwar homestead movement that lead to a small (but internationally comparatively low) increase in single-family homes (from 29.2 percent to 32.2 percent of all buildings) (ibid.: 49). After the Second World War, Germany had to face a loss of nearly a quarter (22 percent) of its housing stock (ibid.: 50). In this situation, federal housing promotion of the *Eigenheim* has been launched in West Germany to generate private property as a means of social security and as an answer to the social question, to keep the working class away from socialist orientation (in Germany since the nineteenth century: see the contributions in Harlander 2001, as a global tracking of US-driven home ownership policies in foreign aid, not only to combat communism: Kwak 2015). In the meantime, this met with the popular desire to participate in a prosperous, consumerist American way of life (Miller Lane 2007), whose roadmap in Europe led through 'hearth and home' (de Grazia 2005, but see e.g. Prinz 2016 as a critique and differentiation of Grazia's Americanisation thesis). Although the German federal housing policy has always privileged the upper middle class (Zimmermann and Bodenschatz 2001), 'the outstandingly fast development of prosperity has been the central experience of the West German population since the 1950s, in which the working class also participated' (Mooser 1984, author's translation). Together with the automobile and consumer goods industry, private households have been the engine of West German growth since the end of the 1950s. Vice versa, mass car ownership and the accelerating electrification of households have been the basis of economic growth and promised comfortable consumption and progress for all families. These developments still need deeper research. Lately, approaches that combined economic and consumption history began to bring to light in detail the relation between domestic consumption and global dynamics of resource and energy use (Gerber 2015, Wölfel 2016), with household waste becoming the source of a whole new branch of production (Köster 2017). The production of household consumer goods – refrigerators, electric stoves, food processors, etc. – and the use of these devices in the new fitted kitchens enormously increased energy use. Latest research of economic and consumer history documented and described in detail this Fordist 'alliance of waste' (Gerber 2015) between consumers, politics, energy sector, and manufacturers, its relations to a specific gender order (in the kitchen, in the house, in the labour market), and to parenting as a market for consumer goods (Gerber 2015, Oldenziel and Zachmann 2009, Taylor et al. 2004, Stokes et al. 2013). Paradoxically, the changes of this arrangement towards the new ecological framework around the private household have generated a new variant of the modernist idea of progress and growth through technology, now based on reuse and life cycle concepts (Wölfel 2016).

The vision of social advancement through building one's own detached single-family house again became a reality in the transformation of housing in East Germany after 1990, however, one that resulted in a huge transfer of wealth from East to West and from public to private ownership (Häußermann 1996: 323). That this has been possible in parallel to the already problematic situation of emptying single-family home areas in West Germany indicates how this type of dwelling could be easily functionalised politically as a promise of freedom, individuality, and democracy.

As the New Housing Studies empirically and analytically yielded, the repositioning of housing and of home ownership has been a central issue of changing welfare regimes since the 1970s, when oil-based growth policies were shaken (Graf 2014), and especially as a result of accelerating dynamics since the global financial crisis in 2008. All welfare regimes of the Fordist era that Gøsta Esping-Andersen (1990) characterised, be it conservative ones (e.g. Germany or Austria), social democratic ones (e.g. the Scandinavian type) or liberal ones (e.g. Great Britain) (in different variations), began to position, to enforce, and to normalise home ownership as a basic element of social security. Such concepts relate welfare benefits not to needs but to assets a person has. This again is linked to a market-related process to also develop low-income and poor households as customers of the mortgage market, which is discussed as a move towards 'asset-based citizenship' around 'the role of homeownership in the financing of everyday life' (Forrest and Hirayama 2015, Ronald 2012, Ronald and Elsinga 2012; Ronald et al. 2015; on ethnographic details and on homeowners as part of new protest movements in the context of austerity politics in countries with high home ownership ratios see Barbero 2015, Sabaté 2016, Keasey and Veronesi 2011, Cook and Smith 2013).

In Germany, these dynamics showed up as a dramatic withdrawal of the public sector from social housing since the 1990s, thus introducing 'responsibilisation' to the former German 'tenement society' (see above) (Heeg 2013 and 2017). It is important not to mistake this governance type of housing policy as privatisation only: Such new 'moral economies of housing' are an essential part of negotiations of citizenship, and thus they remain in the centre of public affairs (Alexander et al. 2018). This again has effects on how housing is perceived in everyday life: 'The focus on home ownership and concern with privatization in housing policy have played important roles in the commodification of the home and presenting housing as a consumer choice.' (Ronald and Elsinga 2012: 9)

This observation has been made in other welfare regimes that exhibit a longer history and higher ratios of home ownership, and these analyses very much included the sphere of consumption, following well-established approaches from the French and Anglo-Saxon tradition and poststructuralist renewal of social anthropology and sociology. For Germany, such research is rare and still waits to be carried out:[8] We do not know enough about how consumption, 'democracy', 'security', and 'freedom' became inextricably moulded in the foundations of all these houses, to the despair of urban planners who try to stop and change the still growing single-family home areas, and to the despair of everybody who hints to the rather hidden but enormous public money that is invested again and again in the infrastructure of these areas. Perhaps this blind spot is also an effect of the German tradition of looking at social phenomena. Jürgen Habermas (admittedly: as well as his contemporaries) attempted anyway to write his critical theory of modernity without even mentioning commodities and consumption (see the indexes in Habermas 1984 and 1989), although he had claimed 'good Hegelian terms' in which 'the formation of basic concepts and the treatment of substantive issues belong inseparably together' (Habermas 1984: xli). For him, capitalism theoretically worked without consumers; in his two volumes, we can only surmise them as, to use the same metaphor, natives within 'the colonization of the life-world' who suffer from 'increasing sociopsychological and cultural costs' of the 'social-welfare-state compromise (particularly impressively, perhaps, in the Federal Republic of Germany)' (ibid.: xliii). Therefore, Habermas mistook his own single-family house construction site in the Bavarian town of Starnberg for a neutral example, and consequently he mistook a male workplace communication to be representative for *Lebenswelt* and *Situation* as such – women were not even conceded the place of crypto-empirical data in his theory. In addition, he could not yet guess how popular pleasure in consumption and the (mostly hidden) public funding of expensive private purchases like a single-family house and cars to reach it would once emerge not only as a 'substantive issue' of social theory and empirical research, but also as a critical detail of the very political and philosophical concern behind his theoretical endeavour: How can the relations of production and the allocation of public wealth be regulated reasonably in a society and in a historical situation, where most people became accustomed to outfit and to enjoy their *Lebenswelt* with goods that are produced around the globe in socially and ecologically rather unreasonable circumstances – with the single-family house being one of the most vast and lasting materialisations? How can research, architecture, and urban planning address this issue, without involuntarily menacing to devalue and to tear down popular preferences of living, dwelling, and aesthetics? To elucidate this, using the German example would, of course, contribute to a deeper understanding of the current makeup of dwelling and housing as classics of the social question.

Acknowledgements

Research for this article has been done within the research network 'A House and its Objects between Family Life, Resource Management and Museum', director: Elisabeth Timm (WWU Münster, Seminar for Folklore Studies / European Ethnology), funded by the German Federal Ministry of Education and Research (programme 'The Language of Objects – Material Culture in the Context of Social Developments') 2015–2018, www.hausfragen.net (accessed 28 April 2019), funding code 01UO1504A.

References

Adam, B., Berndgen-Kaiser, A., Jochimsen, K., Münter, A., and Zakrzewski, P. (2018), 'Ältere Ein- und Zweifamilienhausbestände im Umbruch. Eine Clusteranalyse zur Identifizierung regionaler Betroffenheiten in Nordrhein-Westfalen', Raumforschung und Raumordnung | Spatial Research and Planning 76(1), 3–17.

Alexander, C., Bruun, M. H., and Koch, I. (2018), 'Political Economy Comes Home: On the Moral Economies of Housing', Critique of Anthropology 38(2), 121–139.

Balke, J. and Reimer, M. (2016), 'Zur Konstruktion einer Region. Diskursive Rationalitäten und Ambivalenzen der Regionsbildung am Beispiel Südwestfalen', pnd|online, 1–9.
Barbero, I. (2015), 'When rights need to be (re)claimed. Austerity measures, neoliberal housing policies and anti-eviction activism in Spain', Critical Social Policy 35(2), 270–280.
Berndgen-Kaiser, A., Köhler, T., Marique, A.-F., Netsch, S., Ruelle, C., and Wiechert, M. (2018), 'Approaches to handling future use of the single-family housing stock – Evidence from Belgium, Germany and the Netherlands', Open House International 43(3), 69–82.
Brake, K. and Herfert, G. (eds.) (2012), Reurbanisierung. Materialität und Diskurs in Deutschland (Wiesbaden: Springer VS).
Brettschneider, F. (2015), Macht Wohneigentum glücklich? Immobilien und Glück in Baden-Württemberg. Eine Studie im Auftrag der LBS Stiftung Bauen und Wohnen (Karlsruhe: Stiftung Bauen und Wohnen der LBS Landesbausparkasse Baden-Württemberg).
Bundesstiftung Baukultur (2018): Baukultur Report 2018/2019. Heritage – Presence – Future. Berlin: Bundesstiftung Baukultur, https://www.bundesstiftung-baukultur.de/baukulturbericht/download-201819 (accessed 22 March 2019).
Bundesstiftung Baukultur (2016): Baukultur Report 2016/2017. City and Village. Berlin: Bundesstiftung Baukultur, https://www.bundesstiftung-baukultur.de/baukulturbericht/der-baukulturbericht-auf-deutsch-englisch-franzoesisch-0 (accessed 22 March 2019).
Cook, N. and Smith, S. J. (2013), 'Debted Objects. Homemaking in an Era of Mortgage-Enabled Consumption', Housing, Theory and Society 30(3), 293–311.
Dieterich, H. et al. (2006), Jahrbuch für Bodenpolitik 2006/2007 (Berlin: VWF).
Dollinger, F., Dosch, F., and Schultz, B. (2009), 'Fatale Ähnlichkeiten? Siedlungsflächenentwicklung und Steuerungsinstrumente in Österreich, Deutschland und der Schweiz', Wissenschaft & Umwelt interdisziplinär 12, 104–135.
Esping-Andersen, G. (1990), The Three Worlds of Welfare Capitalism (Cambridge: Polity Press).
Eurostat (n.d.), Wohneigentumsquoten in ausgewählten europäischen Ländern im Jahr 2017, Statista, https://de.statista.com/statistik/daten/studie/155734/umfrage/wohneigentumsquoten-in-europa/ (accessed 27 May 2019).
Feldmann, L., Klemme, M., and Selle, K. (2007), Kommunale Planungs- und Entscheidungsprozesse in der Siedlungsflächenentwicklung. Ein Teilprojekt. Ergebnisse im Überblick über sechs Modellkommunen (Aachen: RWTH Aachen University Publications).
Forrest, R. and Hirayama, Y. (2015), 'The financialization of the social project. Embedded liberalism, neoliberalism and home ownership', Urban Studies 52(2), 233–244.
Gerber, S. (2015), Küche, Kühlschrank, Kilowatt. Zur Geschichte des privaten Energiekonsums in Deutschland, 1945–1990 (Bielefeld: transcript).
Graf, R. (2014), Öl und Souveränität. Petroknowledge und Energiepolitik in den USA und Westeuropa in den 1970er Jahren (Quellen und Darstellungen zur Zeitgeschichte 103) (Berlin: De Gruyter Oldenbourg).
Grazia, V. de (2006), 'A Model Mrs. Consumer. How Mass Commodities Settled into Hearth and Home', in V. de Grazia: Irresistible Empire. America's Advance through Twentieth-Century Europe (Cambridge, Mass., London: Harvard University Press), 416–457.
Gutsche, J.-M. and Schiller, G. (2009), 'Das Kostenparadoxon der Baulandentwicklung: Finanzstrukturelle Mechanismen, die unsere Stadtregionen teuer machen', in H. Mäding (ed.): Öffentliche Finanzströme und räumliche Entwicklung (Hannover: VSB), 199–216.
Habermas, J. (1989), Lifeworld and System: A Critique of Functionalist Reason (The Theory of Communicative Action, Vol. 2) (Boston: Beacon Press).

Habermas, J. (1984), Reason and the Rationalization of Society (The Theory of Communicative Action, Vol. 1) (Boston: Beacon Press).
Häußermann, H. (1996), 'Die Transformation des Wohnungswesens', in W. Strubelt et al. (eds.): Städte und Regionen – räumliche Folgen des Transformationsprozesses (Opladen: VS Verlag für Sozialwissenschaften), 289–325.
Hannemann, C. (2005), Die Platte. Industrialisierter Wohnungsbau in der DDR. Third, enlarged ed. (Berlin: Hans Schiler Verlag).
Harlander, T. (ed.) (2001), Villa und Eigenheim. Suburbaner Städtebau in Deutschland (Stuttgart: DVA.).
Heeg, S. (2017), 'Governing the Built Environment in European Metropolitan Regions: Financialization, Responsibilization and Urban Competition', in R. Keil et al. (eds.): Governing Cities through Regions: Canadian and European Perspectives (Waterloo: Wilfrid Laurier University Press), 65–82.
Heeg, S. (2013), 'Wohnen als Anlageform. Vom Gebrauchsgut zur Ware', Emanzipation 3(2), 5–20.
Helbrecht, I. and Geilenkeuser, T. (2010), 'Homeownership in Germany: Retirement Strategies of Households in a Tenant Society', Teorija in Praksa 47(5), 975–993.
Herfert, G. and Osterhage, F. (2012), 'Wohnen in der Stadt: Gibt es eine Trendwende zur Reurbanisierung? Ein quantitativ-analytischer Ansatz', in K. Brake and G. Herfert (eds.): Reurbanisierung. Materialität und Diskurs in Deutschland (Wiesbaden: Springer VS), 86–112.
Hesse, M. (2015), 'Wachstum, Innovation, Metropolregionen – ein epistemologischer Turn in der Raumordnungspolitik (1993–2006 ff.)?', in W. Strubelt and D. Briesen (eds.): Raumplanung nach 1945. Kontinuitäten und Neuanfänge in der Bundesrepublik Deutschland (Frankfurt/Main: Campus), 355–374.
Hnilica, S. (2018), Der Glaube an das Grosse in der Architektur der Moderne. Grossstrukturen der 1960er und 1970er Jahre (Zürich: Park Books).
Hnilica, S. and Timm, E. (2017), 'Das Einfamilienhaus als neue anonyme Architektur. Bestand und Begehren', Zeitschrift für Kulturwissenschaften 1, 15–28.
Holm, A. (2012), 'Paradoxien und Begleiterscheinungen der Reurbanisierung', in K. Brake and G. Herfert (eds.): Reurbanisierung. Materialität und Diskurs in Deutschland (Wiesbaden: Springer VS), 239–256.
Holtkamp, L. (2008), 'Das Scheitern des Neuen Steuerungsmodells', Der moderne Staat. Zeitschrift für Public Policy, Recht und Management 2, 423–446.
Interhyp AG (n.d.): Wohnträume 2016 – so möchten die Deutschen leben, https://wohntraumstudie.interhyp.de/#wohntraeume (accessed 22 March 2019).
Kaspar, F. (2011), Behelfsheime für Ausgebombte. Bewältigung des Alltäglichen im 'Totalen Krieg' – Münsters Bürger ziehen aufs Land (Einblicke – Schriften der Stiftung Kleines Bürgerhaus, 1) (Petersberg: Michael Imhof Verlag).
Keasey, K. and Veronesi, G. (2011), 'The significance and implications of being a subprime homeowner in the UK', Environment and Planning A 44, 1502–1522.
Keil, R. (ed.) (2013), Suburban Constellations. Governance, Land, and Infrastructure in the 21st Century (Berlin: jovis).
Köhler, T. and Berndgen-Kaiser, A. (2016), 'Survey Results – Pressures on Detached and Semidetached Housing Areas and Measures to Deal with them', in C. Deilmann et al. (eds.): Single-Family Homes under Pressure? Proceedings Workshop 2015, IOER Dresden (Dresden: IOER), 109–110.
Köhler, T., Jeschke, A., and Weitkamp, A. (2016), 'Akteure im Landmanagement – ein Ansatz zur spieltheoretischen Modellierung', avn – allgemeine vermessungsnachrichten 123(2), 39–49.
Kohl, S. (2017), Homeownership, Renting and Society. Historical and Comparative Perspectives (New York: Routledge).
Köster, R. (2017), Hausmüll. Abfall und Gesellschaft in Westdeutschland 1945–1990 (Göttingen: Vandenhoek & Ruprecht).

Krajewski, C. (2014), 'Entwicklungsperspektiven und -probleme eines prosperierenden ländlichen Zwischenraumes in Nordrhein-Westfalen: das Beispiel Südwestfalen', Europa Regional 19.2011(2), 3–22.
Krajewski, C. and Otto, K.-H. (eds.) (2014), Zukunftsfähige Regionalentwicklung in Südwestfalen zwischen wirtschaftlicher Prosperität, demographischen Herausforderungen und Klimawandel (Siedlung und Landschaft in Westfalen, Vol. 40) (Münster).
Kurz, K. (2000), 'Soziale Ungleichheiten beim Übergang zum Wohneigentum', Zeitschrift für Soziologie 29(1), 27–43.
Kwak, N. H. (2015), A World of Homeowners. American Power and the Politics of Housing Aid (Chicago, London: The University of Chicago Press).
Lachmann, I. (2004), Endstation Eigenheim. Zur deutschen Einfamilienhausförderung im Spannungsfeld von Raumordnungszielen und Wohnungsbaupolitik (Kassel: Kassel University Press).
Miller Lane, B. (ed.) (2007), 'Mass housing as single-family dwelling. The post-war American suburb', in B. Miller Lane: Housing and Dwelling. Perspectives on Modern Domestic Architecture (London, New York: Routledge), 272–309.
Mooser, J. (1984), Arbeiterleben in Deutschland 1900–1970. Klassenlagen, Kultur und Politik (Frankfurt/Main: Suhrkamp).
Münter, A. (2011), 'Wanderungsentscheidungen von Stadt-Umland-Wanderern in vier Stadtregionen. Regionaler Vergleich der Muster und Motive, Informations- und Wahrnehmungslücken sowie Beeinflussbarkeit der Wanderungsentscheidung', (PhD diss., Technische Universität Dortmund, Fakultät Raumplanung).
Münter, A. and Osterhage, F. (2018), Trend Reurbanisierung? Analyse der Binnenwanderungen in Deutschland 2006 bis 2015 (Gütersloh: Bertelsmann Stiftung).
Oldenziel, R. and Zachmann, K. (eds.) (2009), Cold War Kitchen. Americanization, Technology, and European Users (Cambridge/Mass, London: MIT Press).
Oltmanns, C. (2016), 'Rurality in a Society of Cities', in V.M. Carlow (ed.): Ruralism. The Future of Villages and Small Towns in an Urbanizing World (Berlin: jovis), 56–62.
Prinz, M. (2016), 'Am Ende Münster? Einsichten und offene Fragen der neueren Konsumgeschichtsschreibung', in M. Prinz (ed.): Die vielen Gesichter des Konsums. Westfalen, Deutschland und die USA 1950–2000 (Paderborn: Ferdinand Schöningh), 9–39.
Regionale 2016 Agentur GmbH (2016), ZukunftsLand. Regionale 2016 (Steinfurt: Druckhaus Tecklenborg).
Rodenberg, M. (2017), '"... früher haben die fleißig mitgeholfen...". Selbsthilfe bei Bau von Behelfsheimen und Siedlungshäusern 1943–1965', Hessische Blätter für Volks- und Kulturforschung NF 51, 233–243.
Ronald, R. (2012), Family Property Wealth and the New Welfare State (University of Amsterdam: Houwel Working Paper Series 1).
Ronald, R. and Elsinga, M. (2012), 'Beyond home ownership. An Overview', in R. Ronald and M. Elsinga (eds.): Beyond Home Ownership. Housing, Welfare and Society (London, New York: Routledge), 1–27.
Ronald, R., Kadi, J., and Lennartz, C. (2015), 'Homeownership-Based Welfare in Transition', Critical Housing Analysis 2(1), 52–64.
Sabaté, I. (2016), 'Mortgage Indebtedness and home repossessions as symptoms of the financialisation of housing provisioning in Spain', Critique of Anthropology 36(2), 197–211.
Simon-Philipp, C. and Korbel, J. (2016), Einfamilienhäuser 50/60/70. Stadtentwicklung und Revitalisierung (Ludwigsburg: Wüstenrot Stiftung).
Statista GmbH (2018), Anzahl der Einfamilienhäuser in Deutschland in den Jahren 2001 bis 2017, https://de.statista.com/statistik/daten/studie/39010/umfrage/bestand-der-einfamilienhaeuser-in-deutschland-seit-2000/ (accessed 22 March 2019).

Statistisches Bundesamt (ed.) (2019), Wirtschaftsrechnungen. Einkommens- und Verbrauchsstichprobe. Wohnverhältnisse privater Haushalte 2018 (Fachserie 15, Sonderheft 1) (Wiesbaden: Statistisches Bundesamt).

Statistisches Bundesamt (ed.) (2013), Wirtschaftsrechnungen. Einkommens- und Verbrauchsstichprobe. Wohnverhältnisse privater Haushalte (Wirtschaftsrechnungen 15, 1) (Wiesbaden: Statistisches Bundesamt).

Statistisches Bundesamt (ed.) (2009), Zuhause in Deutschland. Ausstattung und Wohnsituation privater Haushalte (Wiesbaden: Statistisches Bundesamt).

Staub, A. (2014), 'The Road to Upward Mobility: Urbanity and the Creation of a New Middle Class in Postwar West Germany', Journal of Urban History 40(3), 563–584.

Stokes, R. G. et al. (2013), The Business of Waste. Great Britain and Germany, 1945 to the Present (New York: Cambridge University Press).

Taylor, J. S., Layne, L. L., and Wozniak, D. F. (eds.), Consuming Motherhood (New Brunswick, NJ and London: Rutgers University Press).

Utku, Y. et al. (n.d.), Hausaufgaben. Bürgerschaftliches Engagement in alternden Einfamilienhausgebieten (Gelsenkirchen: Landesinitiative StadtBauKultur NRW 2020).

Wölfel, S. (2016), Weiße Ware zwischen Ökologie und Ökonomie. Umweltfreundliche Produktentwicklung für den Haushalt in der Bundesrepublik Deutschland und der DDR (München: oekom verlag).

Zakrzewski, P., Berndgen-Kaiser, A., Fox-Kämper, R., and Siedentop, S. (2014), 'Herausforderungen westdeutscher Einfamilienhausgebiete der Nachkriegszeit. Bestandsentwicklung als neues Handlungsfeld für Kommunen', Comparative Population Studies 39(2), 247–284.

Zimmermann, C. and Bodenschatz, H. (2001), 'Wohnungspolitik – Eigenheime für alle?', in T. Harlander (ed.): Villa und Eigenheim. Suburbaner Städtebau in Deutschland (Stuttgart: DVA), 330–349.

Endnotes

1 https://www.h-s-a.de/projekte/haus_habermas/1 (accessed 21 March 2019).

2 This is why we recently proposed to call these single-family houses 'new anonymous architecture' (Hnilica and Timm 2017): not appreciated like the dwellings for which Bernard Rudofsky coined the term 'architecture without architects', but like them without an identifiable designer.

3 But see Holm's (2012) argument that these processes should rather be understood as 'inner-city suburbanisation', since the social profile of gentrification conflicts shifted from 'gentrifiers against the working class' to competing middle-class factions, now demanding suburban lifestyles (e.g. social homogeneity) in city centres.

4 Biased research, charged by banks or building societies, tries to change this, see, for example, this methodologically hazardous study stating the following result: 'Homeowners are happier than tenants.' (Brettschneider 2015: 18, author's translation).

5 Bear in mind that this characterisation is true when comparing Germany with the USA. In comparison with 20th-century suburbanisation in the USA, that took place on the basis of a predominantly private or privatised infrastructure by weak municipalities and therefore developed with little control, suburbanisation in Germany has been much more planned and controlled by historically 'feudally enclosed, corporately organised social-municipal cities' (Kohl 2017: 65). But see the critique of an ongoing land use for single-family housing developments in Germany, Austria, and Switzerland that now unfolds rather uncontrolled by public authorities (Dollinger et al. 2009). Research on land use management documents that the planning experts in the building department of municipal administrations

often are outacted by local politicians who feel that promising cheap building plots earns votes, and this research also proves that the idea of a return on public infrastructure investment by the influx of young families has no documented or calculated basis (Feldmann et al. 2007).

6 On the cultural legacy of the *Bausparkassen* tradition as a popular economy of home ownership see Smigla-Zywocki in this volume.

7 On the paradox aesthetic effect of 'individualisation as standard' see Gill in this volume; on the current structure of prefab house manufacturers see Caplan in this volume.

8 But see the research referenced in Hnilica and Timm 2017 and the contributions based on empirical historical and ethnographic data in this volume.

Building a house of our own: three middle-class variants of settling and living in northwestern Germany today

Katherin Wagenknecht

Why do people prefer building a single-family home and is the family life in there still the same?

In her song 'Little boxes all the same' (1962), Malvina Reynolds satirically describes the huge suburbs of the USA that were created on a massive scale in the 1950s. She expresses the fear that the 'houses mass-produced according to industrial standards [...] would also produce standardized people and standardized middle-class biographies' (Tomkowiak 2012: 7). In the course of reconstruction after the Second World War and in the growth decades of the young Federal Republic, suburban single family house construction with social and fiscal support was not simply a 'backbone of urban development' (Simon-Philipp/Korbel 2017: 106, author's translation). The detached single-family house corresponded to the 'everyday lifestyle' (Weihrich/Voß 2002; Kudera/Voß 2000) of the male-breadwinner-and-female-homemaker family: an employed father who commuted by car to a permanent full-time job, and whose single income enabled him to make a long-term housing investment, and a mother who was not gainfully employed (or at most part-time), whose family work was also necessary because public childcare was offered for a maximum of half a day. Although this form of housing never dominated in quantitative terms, it became a symbol of respectability and prosperity in many milieus.This Fordist type of social order is undergoing fundamental changes since some years. Insecure employment relationships that at times do not guarantee a living are now experienced in many milieus. All those involved in families want a more egalitarian division of gainful employment and family work. This has been made possible by the expansion of public childcare, but also more difficult by the spatial separation of living, childcare, leisure and work in the single-family house.[1] However, people's desire for their own detached house in the countryside is still so frequently fulfilled that, in its building culture report for 2016/17, the *Bundesstiftung Baukultur* (Federal Foundation for Building Culture) devoted a separate chapter to the associated 'doughnut effect' in urban development. (Bundesstiftung Baukultur 2017: 31)

In 2016, a total of 95,509 permits for single-unit residential buildings were issued in Germany. This represents approximately one quarter of all residential buildings approved that year. (Statistisches Bundesamt n.d.) The share of single-family houses in residential developments in small towns and suburban and rural regions is particularly high. Often more than two thirds of the housing stock are single-family houses (Statistisches Bundesamt/Wissenschaftszentrum Berlin für Sozialforschung 2016: 260). Which interests and desires generate these private building activities, the results of which no longer correspond to the post-Fordist unbounding of life and work? One of the plausible theses from previous research interprets the phenomenon as part of the pluralisation of lifestyles in which values of Fordist social orders (such as nuclear families, property, social advancement, a linear, continuous career) are maintained and adapted. Thus Menzl (2014: 43) observed lifestyles that are 'postfordist in character, but consciously adhere to many aspects of suburban living'.

My research has focused on this area of tension. In contrast to previous studies, mainly from urban planning, which investigated many cases of single-family housing settlements, but hardly differentiated according to other factors, my work has been more in-depth. Even if single-family houses always produce a structurally and aesthetically identical structure,[2] the first thing that has to be examined is whether the family life taking place inside is equally uniform, whether there are any differences and, if so, how they depend on the type of residential estate, and the spatial and social environment in which the house is located. Does the single-family house in rural areas represent something different than in suburban areas? Are the ways of life associated with a town house the same as those in a village? To investigate this, I have compared the housing aspirations and lifestyles of families who have built a detached house in the last ten years: firstly, in a residential area close to a large city; secondly, in a new housing estate adjoining a small town; and thirdly, in a rural village. In this way, it can be empirically determined in depth which structures of family and residential ideas, spatial and economic conditions and social practice are realised in the building typology of a detached single-family house, depending on whether it has been built in an urban, small-town or rural environment. In a further interpretational step, these findings can then be classified in the context of social change. It will be shown that life in a single-family dwelling shows 1), striking characteristics of Fordist lifestyles (e.g. ideals of home ownership and career continuity); 2), that, depending on the type of housing estate, the expensive investment in a private home is based primarily on private-family or on privately-local socio-economic structures; and 3), that lifestyles and social forms are more strongly influenced by the type of housing estate than by building typology.

Methods and sample

The empirical starting point of this study was everyday life in a single-family home. In order to obtain information on the motives for choosing this form of living, families who have built a single-family house in the last ten years were interviewed. The sample comprises a total of 21 cases (seven in a rural village, seven in a small-town area and seven in a metropolitan estate). In my study I combine different methodological approaches. In semi-structured interviews I asked about the building process, the choice of residential location and the daily routines. The empirical data generated in this way have been analysed as information about subjective interpretations and cultural values. My analyses are thus based not only on what the respondents said, but also on how they described their life and living situation, and the arguments and justifications they used to describe their building and purchasing history.[4]

Research setting: comparing an urban, suburban and rural single-family home area

The selection of the study areas was based on statistical parameters such as population size, community size, population density and demographic development, building land prices, real estate markets and infrastructures, transport links and economic development. On the basis of the categories of settlement geography and spatial planning, a rural-agrarian, a suburban and an urban location were determined for ethnographic research.[3] Our rural-agrarian research area is located in the county of Bentheim. Ohne is a village with

587 inhabitants (data as of 2016) in southwestern Lower Saxony (Kreisverwaltung Landkreis Grafschaft Bentheim 2017). It is 45 kilometres away from the nearest major city, Münster. It is eight kilometres away from the nearest motorway access road and from daily amenities such as a supermarket, drugstore and leisure facilities. The village grew by 20 persons between 2002 and 2008 (Bürogemeinschaft Honnigfort und Brümmer 2009). The spatial layout in Ohne is characterised by agricultural economy.[5] In the last fifteen years, two new development areas with a total of 26 building plots have been put out to tender. While the first building area on the northern edge of the village has contributed to the growth of the area, the Volkers Kamp building area represents a densification of the village centre. The interviews on the topic of new buildings took place in Volkers Kamp. Here, in cooperation with the property and development company Grafschaft Bentheim (GGB)[6], eleven building plots were created, eight of which have already been sold and partially built on (as of May 2018) (GGB 2018). The small-town area under investigation is Rorup, a district of Dülmen that has been incorporated

Figure 1: View of the rural-agricultural study area: Ohne.

since 1975. Rorup has 2,270 inhabitants (Stadt Dülmen, Fachbereich 312, Bürgerbüro 2017). The administrative affiliation of Rorup is not spatially and geographically evident. Between the district and the urban area of Dülmen there are eight kilometres of road, characterised by housing estates and agricultural land. Between 2006 and 2012, the population of Dülmen fell by 1,102 people entitled to residence (Stadt Dülmen 2014). Nevertheless, new development areas were and are continuously being designated. The new development area where the interviews took place comprises a total of 47 plots. This is the third expansion area in Rorup since it was decided to build Schlüters Heide in 1980 (Stadt Dülmen 1993). The town of Dülmen offers financial benefits to households with children. The demand for building plots is not adequately covered. The municipality justifies its recent designation of a further building area for single-family homes with the continuing high demand for such building sites from young families. (Stadt Dülmen 2016) The suburban study area is a district of the city of Münster. Wolbeck has a population of 9,200 (data as of 2015) and became a district of Münster in 1975 as a

Figure 2: View of the small-town study area: Rorup.

result of the municipal area reform. Münster has a positive growth prognosis. The suburban area of Wolbeck is also growing. In 2014, 8,981 residents were registered in Wolbeck, by 2015 there were 9,213 (Stadt Münster – Amt für Stadtentwicklung, Stadtplanung Verkehrsplanung Informationsmanagement und Statistikdienststelle 2016). The city of Münster is responding with a call for tenders for new building areas. In the last ten years, several building plots have been designated on the northern edge of Wolbeck. The average price of building land for detached houses in Münster was more than 300 euros per square metre in 2015.

Out of an apartment and into a house[7]

In different ways, all the interviewees had decided in favour of a single-family house because they had opted for a family. Either there were already children in the household or the couple wanted to have a child. In the interviews,

Figure 3: View of the suburban study area: Wolbeck.

building a house and starting a family are placed in causal and temporal contexts. This connection has also been documented in older and more recent research,[8] like that of the authors Clara Mulder and Michael Wagner (2001), whose comparative quantitative study showed a connection between partnership, marriage and starting a family with home ownership.
A more recent comparative study from suburbanisation research found that families in the expansion phase (i.e. families with children under the age of seven) accounted for the largest share of urban-rural movement, 67 percent (BMVBS/BBSR 2007: 53ff., also Münter 2012).[9] The preferred (as well as the realised) form of construction was the detached single-family house: Approximately 59 percent of all urban-rural migrations involved moving from an apartment to a house (ibid.). Menzl (2007) came to similar conclusions in his study on the relocation of families from Hamburg to Henstedt-Ulzburg in the north of Germany.
When I asked the interviewees how they came to the decision to build a single-family house, they referred in one way or another to the moment when they started a family. Either they already had one or more, mostly small, children; or an integral part of their life planning was a desire to start a family. By contrast, home ownership played a subordinate role in their accounts. Bleck (2005) came to a similar conclusion in his study on 'Stadt-Umland Wanderungen in Nordrhein-Westfalen', where the focus was on personal and residential motives: the lack of space caused by setting up or expanding a family and the resulting changes in the demands placed on the domestic environment.

In rural areas, people build earlier from a bibliographical point of view

While the connection between building a house and starting a family was expressed in all interviews, there were differences between the research areas with regard to the timing of the decisions. In rural areas, the house was built first, and the couples moved in afterwards – often several years before they had children and frequently before their marriage. The fact that in the rural housing area building a family home precedes the actual establishment of a family is, on the one hand, an indication of the self-evident nature of the family's life plan, and its need for a house in Ohne. While couples in small-town and suburban areas react to an actual need by building a house (i.e. an apartment that has become too small due to family growth), in Ohne this decision is made in advance. This self-evident fact is associated with a further unformulated certainty, which became apparent during the visits to the houses in Ohne: Here, as a rule, one or two children's rooms were already fully furnished in the newly built house, and people planned not for, but with their offspring. This also corresponded to their personal life experiences. In Ohne, all the couples I interviewed grew up in a single-family house owned by their parents – a characteristic that, according to quantitative surveys, increases the probability that a young couple will also acquire residential property (Wagner/Mulder 2000: 46; however, these results do not refer to the single-family house in particular, but to residential property in general). In the interviews, this was shown by the fact that the interviewees did not even discuss the possibility of living in rented accommodation. This result corresponds to the findings of ethnographic research in many rural areas (e.g. Juel Jensen (2006) on Württemberg in southern Germany or (2010) on Upper Austria). On the one hand, the chronology of building a house first and starting a family afterwards can be interpreted as indicating a stronger or ongoing lack of standardisation in people's lives and work in rural areas – at least where the necessary level of prosperity still exists (Scherger 2007; Zimmermann 2018).[10] On the other hand, I interpret the order of house building/starting a family as a clear effect of the structures and possibilities inherent in the rural land market. On the one hand, building land is cheaper here; even larger surveys regularly confirm that in terms of costs, the desire for a home of one's own is easier to realise the further away the places are from prospering metropolitan regions and the lower the population density of the region (Vogt et al. 2015: 2). On the other hand, building land is also scarcer, as there are often more people willing to build than there is available land because municipalities have pursued a somewhat more restrictive land policy and, owing to demographic change, are becoming more reluctant to invest in infrastructure to develop building land.

Frau Müller described the situation in her place as follows:

> 'Actually it was clear almost from the start, because here you have to make the most of any opportunity which comes along. And you want to get hold of a nice piece of land. So you have to be quick and say, okay, that's it.' (Ohne, Interview 10: 1)

In Ohne, the demand for suitable building sites is greater than the available building land. This observation expressed by Frau Müller was confirmed by the mayor, to whom I also spoke. Accordingly, people thought it vital not to hesitate when the opportunities arose. In Ohne, the self-evident nature of the interviewees' family plans was also demonstrated by the fact that they hardly mentioned the issue of starting a family. Their statements were less about financial challenges or life plans. They all revolved around 'getting hold of a nice piece of land'.

The small-town variant: weighing up the costs of a house

In Rorup, on the other hand, there was a different sequence: The family either had a child already or was expecting one. In their interviews, the families who built a home in small towns described a concrete requirement. They needed more space and wanted a different, less urban living environment for their (future) child. Although the single-family house was also mentioned as an ideal way of living, there were alternative solutions to be discussed. In contrast to the surveys in rural Ohne, it is striking that the interviewees intensively considered the balance between rent and ownership. This took the form of financial calculations:

> 'And then we were faced with the choice of renting something bigger. But the fact is that we concluded that it was more sensible for us to build our own house, because although it might cost a bit more than the rent, it simply made economic sense.' (Rorup, Interview 2: 1)

The monthly rental payments are weighed up against the monthly loan repayments, the latter being assumed to make more economic sense as they serve to build up private property.[11] Decades of debt are described as being financially more prudent than monthly rental payments. This is in line with other research, which has shown the extent to which the debt incurred in building a house is not perceived as such. Nor is it seen as a risk, but as a reasonable, planned form of consumption (according to Soaita/Searle 2016 in a case study on the Netherlands, which, however, did not take into account differentiation factors according to class or the type of settlement). Compared to the couples in rural Ohne, the couples who built their house in a small town were planning in shorter biographical time spans and these were more closely oriented to concrete space requirements.

In urban areas, the house is planned on a long-term basis

Among the people surveyed in Wolbeck (which is close to a large city), the decision to build a house was less strictly linked to starting a family. Although in most cases starting a family prompted a change in their housing situation, families often decided to rent a single-family house first. In Wolbeck, the view that a single-family house is the ideal form of family housing was not directly linked to the form of ownership. This was mainly due to higher occupational mobility and insecure job conditions, i.e. fixed-term contracts. One of the interviewees explained,

'I was also involved in a project where it was clear from the start that this was temporary. I have now returned with a permanent position and a long-term perspective of staying in one place.' (Wolbeck, Interview 17: 11)

Unlike the other two research areas, the interviewees in Wolbeck regard long-term income security as a central factor in their decision to build a house. In contrast to the other research areas, families in Münster who want to build their own home have to raise more than seven times their annual net income to buy a detached house. On the other hand, in the district of Coesfeld (research location Rorup) and the county of Bentheim (research location, Ohne), the cost is on average four to five times the annual net income (IW Consult and IfD Allensbach 2017: 10). Higher property prices, higher rent levels, expensive building land and the scarcity of suitable building land delay the decision to acquire property until the financial situation is judged to be sustainable. Some of the respondents reported that this was why it took several years between their decision to build a house and their doing so. On top of that, they had to wait for the possibility to buy a plot of land.

Over the past ten years, the price of new houses has risen by more than half of their original value. In 2007, potential buyers spent an average of 210,000 euros on a newly built single-family house, but by 2017 they had to pay 330,000 euros (NRW.Bank 2017: 34). Between 2006 and 2017, prices for building land for detached and semi-detached houses in North Rhine-Westphalia rose by an average of almost six percent. Regional differences are becoming apparent. In the Münster region, prices rose by more than 15 percent between 2007 and 2017. In the Coesfeld region, on the other hand, prices only rose by up to 5 percent (NRW.Bank 2017: 47).

Nevertheless, it was not an option for the families in Münster-Wolbeck to look around for building land in other towns and villages because they were not prepared to give up the social relationships they had established locally: Moving into one's own four walls should not mean a change in social or everyday relationships.

At this point, it can be seen that for all interviewees the decision to buy a single-family home has the same prerequisites but is nonetheless not the same. The mass purchase of suburban homes in West Germany since the 1950s was linked and stabilised by the calculable framework conditions of a prosperous economy: 'Permanently secure incomes, low biographical mobility pressure and clearly structured patterns of everyday life' (Menzl 2007: 409). That these preconditions are made explicitly in the interviews, especially in the single-family home area close to the city, has to do with the fact that they are no longer self-evident for the social milieus living there. The different timings in people's lives for building a house result from the specific interplay between the socio-economic structure of the locations and the professional situation in the milieus of those people who want to build a house. The connection between social and material conditions, which was clearly formulated in all the interviews, was interpreted and implemented in different ways. For childless couples in rural areas, it was the desire to start a family that provided planning security with regard to building their own home, although here the desire to have children was so self-evident that it was clearly not worth mentioning in the interview. Indeed, it was necessary for the researcher to question the issue of family planning in order to explicitly address and thematise it in the interviews. Here, the plans for starting a family were clear and concrete. Thus, when I asked Herr Klaas what would happen if the couple had more than the planned two children, he replied tersely, 'We won't.' (Ohne, Interview 13: 51) Financial aspects were not primarily addressed: on the one hand, this had to do with the lower costs, but on the other hand, it was also because people who wanted to build here could mobilise many more resources via local and family networks (see below). In the small-town context and in the vicinity of the large town, building a house came after the couples had started a family. Moreover, in the small town the financial investment was so high that it was necessary to make a specific calculation based on rental costs, potential resources and personal contributions. In the metropolitan area, people needed to establish themselves professionally with a secure, long-term income. At the same time, another prerequisite for building a house was putting an end to professional mobility.

The single-family home as materialisation and temporalisation of the family

The popularisation of the single-family home as a form of housing since the Second World War was closely linked to the idea of a family life spanning several generations in one place. Hence (using France as an example), Bourdieu et al. (2006: 51, author's translation) characterised living in one's own single-family home as a shared 'wager on the future' of the family, 'i.e. on its cohesion, its integration or, if you like, on its resistance to break-up and dispersion'. By building a single-family home, owners ideally stabilise their social relations over generations (Bourdieu 2006: 50). Comparative research has shown that this attitude has had a particularly strong influence on Germans' approach to purchasing their own single-family home. Unlike, for example, in Great Britain, where buying and selling residential property several times in the course of a lifetime is much more common, single-family homes in Germany are generally the result of a once-in-a-lifetime decision (Mulder/ Wagner 2001: 141). The decision is usually final and is maintained into old age. The fact that so-called 'ageing single-family housing areas' (Zakrzewski 2011; Zakrzewski et al. 2014) have become a new topic of urban planning in recent years is a result of these many one-off investments since the 1950s. In quantitative terms, this is reflected in the fact that 47 percent of the properties inherited nationwide are detached single-family homes (as of 2015) (Deutsches Institut für Altersvorsorge GmbH 2015: 33).

In the interviews conducted for this study, it was striking that the interviewees in all research areas exclusively addressed the family use of the newly built house rather than its sale. A possible move on grounds of changing housing needs or for reasons of age played no part in their thinking and future perspectives. They rather expressed, albeit ironically, an idea or wish to stay in the house 'until the bitter end' (Ohne, Interview 8: 6).

Herr Schroer put it in concrete terms:

> 'Well, you can't really put it precisely in those terms. Looked at the other way around, you say to yourself that you have built this house with your own hands and well, you can't leave it just like that, can you? No. It contains a lot of memories, too.' (Rorup, Interview 1: 21)

In all interviews, this kind of emotionally attached attitude towards the house can be found as part of the recent family history. This moment of narrative emotionalisation turns the house into a personal object of remembrance, which has been invested in with a view to the future, but which at the same time is not for sale. The intimisation of the house and the family is strikingly documented in the popular wish for the children to take over the house and thus keep it in the family's possession. This was also the case with the Meier family:

> 'So this house is sort of meant for a family, you know what I mean [...] it's meant for a household. Of course, the children can live in this household as long as they want and as long as it works for them [...] obviously you have your own ideas about it, but no decisions have been taken yet. Only time will tell. Maybe you could also say that when I'm eighty or so, and you too... And it's not working any more, then you have to think about whether one of the children should take it over. We can talk about it then.' (Rorup, Interview 2: 21)

The statement at the beginning of the interview that the house was intended for a family supports Herr Meier's plan for one of his children to live in the single-family house later. Frau Lutz could also imagine that one of her children would take over the house in time. In return, she would even accept a move into an owner-occupied flat.

> 'Oh, we would like to – I could imagine living here until the bitter end, but I could also imagine that if one of the children wants to take it over ... because I think, well, when we're old, if we can – if

> we can still get up the stairs ((laughs)). So, I don't know [. . .] but maybe at that point we could move into a flat of our own or [. . .] something like that and let the children get on with it here . . .' (Ohne, Interview 8: 6)

Both house owners wanted to hand over their house to their children at the appropriate time. So, if the Lutz couple were no longer able to live in their own house due to age-related restrictions, they would suggest an internal family solution and the children would take over the single-family home. Such single-family houses are not merely residential buildings but highly personal materialisations of their respective families as a social group. They do not simply fulfil a specific need for space pragmatically but also temporalise the family over several generations into the future. Although the interviewees also admitted that it was not certain how their own family life and the real estate market would develop, selling up would not be their preferred option. To put it in a nutshell, a self-built house that has been inhabited by the family for years is less perceived as a mere building than as a member of the family. Hence, it is only logical that in their minds they view a house as a sort of capital investment that can be turned into something of worth to the family (security for their children/heirs) and not simply as an object on an anonymous economic market.[12]

The single-family house as a life-time success

Regardless of the time when the decision is made to build a house of one's own (or when it is actually built), all the interviewees interpreted a home of their own as a progressive step in their lives. In their biographies, moving into their own four walls was seen as an event in the family's success. Thus Frau Müller relates:

> 'Well, we got married in 2010 and then we thought, okay let's have a think about how things can move on from here. [. . .] And in 2011, we came to a decision. In January 2012 we began to build, and in February 2013 we moved in.' (Ohne, Interview 10: 1)

The way Frau Müller tells her story in terms of its chronology strengthens the impression that this is a stringent biographical development, within which building a house has a plausible position. A house of one's own becomes a status symbol within a natural development, something which has already been shown in previous studies (e.g. Gill 2010: 40).

The newly built detached house is of particular importance here. The hierarchy is clear, as a construction and real estate entrepreneur from the Münsterland region explained: 'Everything that is newly built has the best reputation.' Then again, a detached single-family house has a higher value than a semi-detached or terraced house. The acquisition of second-hand real estate for residential purposes ranked last (again in the same order) (Münster, Interview 23). Some of the families interviewed for this study also visited second-hand properties, but 'not really with great enthusiasm and more out of despair' (Wolbeck, Interview 17: 1). In none of the interviews was second-hand real estate perceived as an alternative to a newly built single-family home. Even when the fraught, high-priced land market in the urban and suburban settlement makes it more complicated to find an appropriate plot of land, a second-hand house is not regarded as a possible alternative to a newly built home. The empirical data make it clear that people's preference for newly built single-family houses (both narrated and in practice) is independent of the local real estate and land market. New construction is clearly preferred, both in rural Ohne, where the supply of second-hand residential property is restricted and would mean moving to another town, and in Wolbeck, where the purchase of an old property could be implemented more quickly than finding a building site. My question as to whether a second-hand property would have been an alternative received similar answers in all the research areas. The reasons were also the same: adapting a second-hand house was firstly considered to be more complicated in terms of construction, financing and time; secondly, it was a question of the intimate connection of the family with its house as described above; the family did not want to acquire other people's history (the previous owners or tenants) but wanted to make its own start.

First: second-hand homes are regarded as being more complicated

The families and couples interviewed often equated the purchase of a second-hand property with considerable additional expenditure. In concrete terms, families saw it as being more complicated in terms of the additional efforts the building required, the time and money involved. Herr Meurer explained it as follows:

> 'That's what I said to myself, before we even move in [into the used property, author's note], we will have to do it up before we even start, we'll have to rip out so much, order so many containers and everything, it'll take up so much time and energy.' (Rorup, Interview 6: 5)

For Herr Meurer, there was no question that a second-hand property would only be renovated, not completely rebuilt. A second-hand property would be unable to satisfy the expectations and demands of the buyer and it would be impossible to modify it at a reasonable cost. In the eyes of Herr Meurer, the purchase of a second-hand property would mean a long detour: instead of building a single-family house tailored to one's own needs and expectations, the first thing that needed to be done with a second-hand property was to create the same freedom of design. As other research has shown, the idea of being able to have a completely individualised design is paradoxically an integral component, especially in the ready-made house sector, where suppliers and customers alike agree that it is structural and aesthetic decisions that make a house unique. Another reason for mistrust was people's speculation about the structural defects that might be hidden behind the facade. Admittedly, many houses might 'look in some way or another totally attractive from the outside but there'd be so much to do inside' (Ohne, Interview 8: 7).

Frau Lutz was less concerned with the necessary alterations, as described by Herr Meurer. Instead, she pointed out the potential risks of buying an old property. For her, buying a second-hand property involved uncertainties with regard to the building substance and the condition of the house. By contrast, the interviewees were sure that a newly built home would give them comprehensive information on the building fabric, materials and condition as well as a transparent cost situation. Herr Drein also justified his decision to build a new house with the unforeseeable costs that a second-hand property might entail.

> 'It was an important point for me that I would hear more and more often that when someone bought a second-hand property he would very soon have to pay a lot for the renovation of the water pipes, gas pipes and all those things.' (Wolbeck, Interview 19: 5)

At this point it has to be emphasised that, even retrospectively, the interviewees gave plausible arguments for their decisions, and that there were certainly no less daunting stories about new buildings that turned out to be structural and financial fiascos. In contrast to new buildings, however, when it comes to the use of ordinary second-hand single-family homes, the information provided by sellers/agents has not been popularised. Here there is hardly any knowledge, apart from the publication of outstanding individual projects in specialist journals for architecture and urban planning.[13] True, the public sector has acknowledged the infrastructural and material resources in these buildings,[14] but their potentials have hitherto not been included in municipal information for people interested in converting a house.

Second: the unease about second-hand property

Some of the interviewees explicitly stated that it was very important for them to move into the house first. For example, when Herr Meurer commented on his first occupancy: 'Maybe it sounds a bit strange, but no one else has lived in it before, [...] when you build a new house, [...] nobody was in it, so to speak, and somehow that's gratifying to me.' (Rorup, Interview 6: 5) For him, this sense of satisfaction more than compensated for the advantages of alternatives he visited; an existing building on a larger site and one with a lower purchase price. On the other hand, the Kanich family from Wolbeck bought a second-hand property in order to build a new one on the same site. Naturally, the old property was demolished. The building substance and other features of the property they had purchased played no role in Frau Kanich's remarks. The decisive factor for the purchase was the motivation to stay in the current neighbourhood. Whether or not the plot was built on (and, if so, how), played a subordinate role in the decision-making process. Right from the start the family did not even consider renovating or converting the existing property. It was all about the plot of land on which the old house was located.

Who builds the house?

Much of the interviews were devoted to stories about the building process. The accounts tell of extra assignments before and after they went to work, of weekends spent on the building site, of spontaneous visits to clean up and tidy up, and of months of strain until the owners were finally able to move into their own four walls. The central theme of all these narratives revolved around the interviewees' personal contributions and the help and support provided by acquaintances, relatives and neighbours. These might include simple visits to the building site, monitoring the contractors, daily cleaning up and airing, as well as roofing, laying electrical cables and concreting the base plates. There were not only differences with respect to what they meant by 'personal contributions', but also site-specific forms of social networks.

The rural site: housebuilding as a local matter (family, friends and neighbours)

In the interviews, the central narrative in the stories of the families in Ohne were the personal contributions made by friends, family and neighbours. In their tales, their own personal contributions were closely linked to the work and support they received from their friends, acquaintances and family. All the couples I interviewed here had a family and a biographical connection to the place. At least one partner had been born in Ohne and had relatives there. For example, mountains of sand had been removed from the property of acquaintances with the help of agricultural vehicles, a friend's earth mover had transported bricks, and a large number of friends and neighbours had helped the family with the roofing. In their stories, the houses would not have been built without the support of both the family and the local community. Here, building a house is a family business.

'I tell you, the roof, the wooden construction, was made by my father-in-law, bricked by my brother-in-law, he's a bricklayer, indeed, and ourselves [...] my uncle did the wallpapering, yeah, and my father-in-law

> installed the windows, [. . .] so everything was done on a family basis [. . .] even the electrics, my brother did that, he's an electrician, together with my brother-in-law, they did it together.' (Ohne, Interview 8: 2)

Here, Frau Lutz talked about a somewhat more differentiated network: each family member was assigned certain tasks and competencies for which he or she was responsible during the building of the house. At the same time, it became clear how much personal work was involved in building the house. Her father-in-law had made the wooden constructions and the windows, her uncle had wallpapered the house, her brother-in-law had done the brickwork, her husband had shifted rocks, her father had installed the underfloor heating, and her brother, an electrician, had taken over the electricity installations. Here, not only the high proportion of personal contribution was impressive, but also the fact that the Lutz family was able to mobilise the skills and abilities of the various trades in the wider family. Frau Lutz explained that 'everything was done on a family basis', thereby formulating the central features of the building process. For the Lutz family, building a house was a family affair involving all family members according to their abilities.

The decisive factor was not about one-off, spontaneous support but about elements in a permanent and reliable structure of relationships. The owners were thus able to position themselves as current and future participants in local networks in the best possible manner. During the entire construction period, personal networks were referred to in different ways. Moreover, building a house integrated the family into the locality, since many local people had contributed to building a young family's home. Nonetheless, the various forms of support retain the character of spontaneity and voluntary work and generate a duty to return the favour as described by Mauss (1990) in his analysis of gift exchange. A brother lends his agricultural equipment in a seemingly selfless and spontaneous, voluntary and altruistic manner, and helps with tips and advice; or a father invests his know-how and time. By contrast with the services of a paid craftsman this reciprocal help establishes and maintains relationships in such a way that in principle they can be called up as a resource at any time. The crucial factor is that it is not a form of stopgap help. Thus house building itself becomes a resource for accumulating social capital in barter processes, and home owners position themselves in the best possible way as current and future participants in local networks.

Multiple but separate networks in a small-town area

Even in small towns, personal and private support plays a major role in building a house. 'We wouldn't have been able to do it alone,' said Herr Schroer, and his wife, emphatically confirming this, added: 'No […] We wouldn't have been able to do it all, at all. […] all this was really a family business.' (Rorup, Interview 1: 22) Without the support of family, friends and acquaintances, the single-family house they live in today would never have been built in the way it was. Family support in the form of personal work is a prerequisite for construction. Without the help and support that the family can rely on, Herr Schroer considered that the only feasible alternative would have been a terraced house, which would have been less expensive to build. Frau Schroer's concluding statement that building a detached house was a family business emphasises the importance of family support. However, unlike in Ohne, there was no mention of alternative networks in their stories, nor was the assistance location-based. No friends or acquaintances provided help and support in any form whatsoever during the building phase. The Schroer family asked for help exclusively from relatives and turned down any other offers. In contrast to Ohne, where an individual family's home generated both family, neighbourly, and local integration, the home of the Schroer family was a family matter. Although the family built the house and organised itself in the mode of gift exchange, it all remained within the family.

There are also differences in the organisation of the various social networks that are mobilised in small towns. In Ohne, for example, not only family members but also friends and acquaintances did the roofing work. In Rorup, there was an exclusive concentration on one network only. Family and friendly networks were cultivated separately from each other. Although all social areas, such as family, colleagues, friends, etc. were organised according to the same principle of interaction, in all fields of social communication and relationship the principle of gift exchange prevailed, and buyers moderated these fields in such a way that they existed independently of each other. This finding provides interesting information about local social life. True, although Rorup has a social life, unlike Ohne, it is not the place of a specific social intersection that exists exclusively there.

House building as an anonymous market activity in an urban environment

In Wolbeck, there was yet another picture. Most of the houses on sale were ready to move into. The building process was organised with the help of a general contractor. The contributions of the couples themselves, 'sweat equity' and their involvement on the construction site, as observed as a structural moment in the other two research areas, played a subordinate role in the suburban area. With the exception of one family, the couples interviewed in Wolbeck built their homes with a general contractor. The relationship between the buyers and the general contractor was regulated by a contract. Building a house in Wolbeck was not a medium for family or local integration, but rather something that was undertaken in a basically anonymous market situation. Conversely, this also meant that these families were unable to use building a house as an investment in local networks. It was a matter solely for the family who wanted to build and who acted as a client.

Everyday life in a single-family house

A central topic in the interviews was the organisation of everyday life, in particular the provision for and care of children. As shown above, the families/couples in rural areas were in their mid to late 20s, considerably younger than in the other two research areas. Their children were usually only a few months (or years) old at the time of the survey. In the small-town area, on the other hand, the interviewed families were older when they moved into their own house. The average age of the interviewed owner-builders in Rorup was mid to late 30, and their children were attending primary school. In urban areas, the couples were somewhat older when they moved in, and most of their children were already attending secondary schools.
Despite these differences, all the research areas had one thing in common: In all families, looking after the children was predominantly a woman's job. Similarly, all the women interviewed worked full-time until the birth of their first child, after which they reduced their weekly working hours in different ways, but mostly to a maximum of 20 hours a week. Men, on the other hand, continued to work full-time and thus without exception took on the role of the families' principal wage earner. This modernised bourgeois family model, in which the man works full-time and the woman part-time, was evident in rural, small-town and urban areas, as has been demonstrated many times with respect to the Federal Republic of Germany (i.e. West Germany) (Statistisches Bundesamt (Destatis) and Wissenschaftszentrum Berlin für Sozialforschung (WZB) 2016: 55; Wirtschafts- und Sozialwissenschaftliches Institut 2017: 17ff.). In the county of Bentheim and the district of Coesfeld, three quarters of the children between the ages of one and two were cared for at home. In Münster, the proportion of children of this age who were looked after in day-care facilities was significantly higher: 37 percent (Statistische Ämter des Bundes und der Länder 2016: 27ff.; Bundesministerium für Familie, Senioren, Frauen und Jugend 2018: 8). The following section describes the different and site-specific ways in which families organised the necessary childcare services.

Children as a medium of family integration in a rural area

The provision for and care of children in rural areas was a task to be managed within the family and performed by women. The necessary time capacities and knowledge about small children were proven and legitimised by the personal experience of being a mother. A special feature of the business of looking after children was that it was taken on and offered as a matter of course. Close relatives, more precisely the mothers-in-law of the young parents, played a major role in caring for the children. The support they provided was less a matter of exceptions and emergencies than of permanent and reliable arrangements, which could be called upon at very short notice and which no longer had to be specifically agreed but was almost a natural part of everyday life. This exclusive concentration on family networks and resources was justified by the interviewees on the one hand by the children's age, and on the other hand by inadequate infrastructures in the locality. The day nursery in Ohne which had opened in 1994 had to be closed again in 2014 for lack of children. Travelling to other day care facilities in the surrounding communities was described as too expensive. For this reason, the municipality of Ohne has joined forces with two surrounding municipalities to find a joint solution (Gemeinde Ohne 2016: 2). At the time of the interviews, however, the nearest day care centre was in the next but one town, a ten-minute drive away.

Family childcare, on the other hand, was flexible and could be organised at short notice. Frau Mueller explained how her mother looked after the children when she had an appointment with a doctor or wanted to take part in leisure activities.

> 'Yes, in that case my mother and parents-in-law would have to take care of them [the children, note kw], wouldn't they? Exactly, if we have to go out in an evening, like for example tonight when we have a regular meet-up in the local bar. [...] then my mum comes and she looks after the children for a bit until my husband comes home and she can also stay the night, if he's not so late – I mean, if he comes home later, but now it's all taken care of, now she's looking after them here.' (Ohne, Interview 10: 25)

At the same time, Frau Mueller described her situation as special when she said:

> 'Well, times have simply changed [...] Then money had to be earned. Then money really had to be earned, and if the mothers had to go out to work, then the children had to be cared for; but it's no longer the case that parents or grandmas and grandpas live with them in the same house. Everyone is left to their own devices. I have my mother here. No question about it. But many of them still go out to work because they have to.' (Ohne, Interview 10: 11)

Frau Mueller categorised her life as a double privilege: She was able to reduce her weekly working hours and could also count on her mother to support her with childcare and household chores. The unspoken prerequisite for this was of course low mobility between the generations, a factor which had played a major role when building a house. Only if grandparents lived on the spot were they able to help out in this way.

Family support remains the exception in small-town areas

The situation was different in Rorup, a small town. Here, too, the children were cared for and looked after mostly within small families. When help was needed, the neighbourhood would step in.

> 'Yes, I mean, on an estate, a new housing estate, you have to admit that everyone is in the same boat. They're all young families, that's simply the way it is here – we all have the same problems, I'd say.' (Rorup, Interview 1: 8)

Where the Schroer family lives, the neighbourhood consists mainly of families in a similar situation. Their house was built and the move to Rorup was completed some years previously, the two children are two and seven years old and visit the relevant care facilities in Rorup or Dülmen. Here, Frau Schroer describes one aspect of the 'homogeneity effects' of suburban living (Menzl 2010: 152), which has also been delineated in other research on suburban family life. Since people were sitting 'in the same boat' and knew the concerns of others, there was a low inhibition threshold to spontaneously accept help at short notice. Childcare help was only asked for in exceptional cases, but this also had to do with the fact that grandparents lived further away. Knowing that your neighbours have similar experiences and problems, you can call on neighbourly help when necessary. But this is meant and openly spoken of as an exception. Frau Sattler summed up this ideal as follows: 'But we have always handled it in such a way that it's only on a voluntary basis, i.e. that there's always one of us for the children around the clock.' (Rorup, Interview 5: 57) This documents the ideal of the nuclear family that exists and functions as a self-contained organisational unit. Asking for help is regarded as an exception to be only used in emergencies, like sickness and accidents.

Privately paid support in an urban environment

Even in Wolbeck, childcare was mostly a matter for the women. As in small town areas, women reduced their weekly working hours or interrupted their employment. However, in contrast to rural families, who have biographical and kinship connections to their place of residence along with the associated social resources, families in urban areas lack this locally close kinship network. In addition, no homogeneous and resilient neighbourhood evolves, as was observed in small-town areas. Homeowners living in urban areas must therefore find and establish alternative solutions for coping with everyday life and childcare. The families in Wolbeck organise themselves without the support of private networks. Instead, they fall back on permanent, paid professional support. The Grube family employs an au-pair who lives in the family house and helps the family with shopping, cleaning and childcare.

This kind of support enables the wife to stay working part-time, but at the same time, the second (half) income is also necessary to finance the au-pair (payment, accommodation). Since, as in this case, au-pairs mainly come from countries with very low wage levels compared to Germany, these families become part of the 'world market private household' (Hess and Lenz 2001; Hess 2002). Here too, it was not a question of men having to step out of the job market for a time. Frau Grube clearly described the everyday difficulties:

> 'That's why we have her [the au-pair, author's note] here now, otherwise it wouldn't have worked at all the last few years. Well, we don't have a grandma, and a grandpa, not real ones. [...] so it's not possible to look after children without any support from third parties. Absolutely impossible. [...] On the one hand, it's the times that are involved, on the other hand, when small children get really ill in winter quite a lot. You can't keep arriving at work and saying, uh, my child is ill, I'm not coming. Then there are three months of school holidays a year that have to be managed somehow. But that's not possible with six weeks of leave. Then the kindergarten is closed for further training and this and that. And last year, my kindergarten went on strike for four weeks. And similar things. So there's always something. And without help you can't cope, so it's – it's frightening how many, how many problems can crop up to wreck your life when you've got to look after the children.' (Wolbeck, Interview 21: 31)

Differences between the research areas can be observed in the field of childcare and nursing. Similar to building a house, the care of children in rural areas is also organised on a family basis. And similar to house building, this is based on all participants reducing their biographical and spatial mobility. In the small-town environment, on the other hand, the dominant idea is for everyday organisation to be carried out by the nuclear family. Any recourse to family or private or neighbourhood networks remains an exception. Here it is not clear whether the family's attitude towards outside help is a reaction to the residential location, or whether it already existed before and contributed to placing the family in such a situation. After all, the families in suburban Wolbeck rarely had family connections nearby. Thus, daily routines were designed to meet these deficits by resorting to paid services – an au-pair or help from neighbours, both of which took on family features.

Summary

The above analyses have shown that both similarities and differences are concealed behind the uniform appearance of single-family houses. The results show that everyday practices and values in single-family houses do not result solely from the typology of buildings, but are also markedly influenced by the type of residential settlement. Depending on the type of settlement, families face different conditions and prerequisites when it comes to moving into their own four walls. Each location has its own specific cultural and economic structures. In rural areas, it is the desire to have children that provides planning security with regard to building a home. Extensive local and private resources guarantee that families will be able to build their own homes. In both small and large towns, building a house is primarily considered a financial investment. Accordingly, financial planning security is a prerequisite for building a house.

In rural areas, house construction and the organisation of everyday life is a communal project in which relatives, acquaintances and neighbours play their part: Together, roofing work is dealt with and birthdays are celebrated, the children are cared for and differences only become apparent in the way the house is built, i.e. in rural areas, as a joint local activity amongst relatives, friends and neighbours, as a result of mobilising specific network resources or as an anonymous exchange of goods. Whereas a house in a village becomes an instrument for the accumulation of social capital, in an urban context it is a self contained, anonymous transaction without a community-building dynamic.

Housework and child care are the responsibility of wives and mothers in both rural, small-town and metropolitan areas. They generate time resources by reducing their paid employment. On the other hand, there are differences in the concrete arrangements for balancing child care and paid work. In rural areas, everyday life is organised through family networks that are not only locally available but also naturally and permanently integrated. In small-town areas, the maxim is that private support services are the exception rather than the rule. Here it is not clear whether this is a result of mobility (most of the people interviewed in Rorup do not have a family in the area) or whether, conversely, the choice of where to live is also the consequence of a highly intimate idea of what a family should be. Whatever the case, everyday life here is almost exclusively organised by the nuclear family. In urban areas, on the other hand, paid services are used, whereby the income levels of the couples permit them to have financial and spatial resources (e.g. a room for an au-pair) to take advantage of global wage differences. In Wolbeck, families have less social capital at their disposal, in the form of local family networks to organise their own everyday life. Instead of local family resources, as shown in Ohne, the interviewees in Wolbeck talked about casual acquaintances that are sporadically deepened, but usually exist superficially and without any commitments. The results clearly show that life in a single-family home displays striking features of Fordist lifestyles: The ideal of home ownership as a symbol of status and family success and the associated notion of a continuity in family life are central motives in family decisions. Choosing one's own four walls is a unique, very costly investment that results from a specific interplay of the type of residential settlement, local socio-economic structures and family ideals. Here, it is impossible to determine which element might be the temporal cause and which might be the logical cause. In rural areas, families primarily mobilise private-family resources. Even in small towns, families primarily rely on private resources. The striking feature here is the strict separation of networks into family, acquaintances, friends and neighbours. In contrast, in a metropolitan context people build their own homes, not with private support but as commodities. This finding on the different resources that vary according to settlement type illustrates the third thesis of the article; namely that social and cultural lifestyles are structured and organised more strongly by the place of residence than by building typology. Little boxes, but not the same.

Acknowledgements

This article summarises the initial results of my current dissertation research, 'Gebaute Familie'. The study was developed in project A, Ein Haus für uns bauen: eine Ethnografie tradierter Familienideale im Wandel (Building a House for Us: An Ethnography of Traditional Family Ideals in Change) in the research network 'A House and its Objects between Family Life, Resource Management and Museum', director: Elisabeth Timm (WWU Münster, Seminar for Folklore Studies/European Ethnology), funded by the Federal Ministry of Education and Research programme (The Language of Objects – Material Culture in the Context of Social Developments), www.hausfragen.net, funding code 01UO1504A. In a further project within this network, families who acquired a second-hand detached house in the last five years were interviewed. See the article by Cantauw and the comparative study by Caplan/Wagenknecht in this volume.

References

Bleck, M. (2005), 'Stadt-Umland-Wanderungen in Nordrhein-Westfalen. Eine Meta-Analyse', (Master's thesis, Universität zu Köln, Köln).

BMVBS/BBSR (2007), Akteure, Beweggründe, Triebkräfte der Suburbanisierung. Motive des Wegzugs – Einfluss der Verkehrsinfrastruktur auf Ansiedlungs- und Mobilitätsverhalten, (Bonn: BBSR Online-Publikation 21), https://www.bbsr.bund.de/BBSR/DE/Veroeffentlichungen/BBSROnline/2007/DL_ON212007.pdf?__blob=publicationFile&v=2 (accessed 25 July 2018).

Bourdieu, P. et al. (2006), 'Eine sichere Geldanlage für die Familie. Das Einfamilienhaus: Produktspezifik und Logik des Produktionsfeldes', in P. Bourdieu et al., Der Einzige und sein Eigenheim (Hamburg: VSA), 49–106.
Deutsches Institut für Altersvorsorge GmbH (eds.) (2015), Erben in Deutschland 2015–2024: Volumen, Verteilung und Verwendung (Berlin).
Driessen, K. (2010), 'Akteure, Beweggründe, Triebkräfte der Suburbanisierung. Motive des Wegzugs, Einfluss der Verkehrsinfrastruktur auf Ansiedlungs- und Mobilitätsverhalten', in H. Pechlaner and M. Bachinger (eds.): Lebensqualität und Standortattraktivität. Kultur, Mobilität und regionale Marken als Erfolgsfaktoren (Berlin: Erich Schmidt Verlag), 215–228.
Driessen, K. (2010), Verkehrliche Konsequenzen des Suburbanisierungsprozesses und deren volkswirtschaftliche Bewertung am Beispiel der Region Köln (Aachen: Institut für Stadtbauwesen und Stadtverkehr) (Berichte Stadt Region Land des Instituts für Stadtbauwesen und Stadtverkehr der RWTH Aachen University 54).
Heinemann, I., Nienhaus, S., Pande, M., and Wagenknecht, K. (2019), Heirat, Hausbau, Kinder. Narrationen von Familienentscheidungen, in U. Pfister (ed.): Kulturen des Entscheidens. Narrative – Praktiken – Ressourcen (Göttingen: Vandenhoeck & Ruprecht), 90–115.
Helbrecht, I. and Geilenkeuser, T. (2010), 'Homeownership in Germany. Retirement Strategies of Households in a Tenant Society', Teorija in Praksa 47(5), 975–993.
Hess, S. (2002), 'Au Pairs als informalisierte Hausarbeiterinnen – Flexibilisierung und Ethnisierung der Versorgungsarbeiten', in C. Geissler, C. Gather and M. Rerrich (eds.): Weltmarkt Privathaushalt. Bezahlte Hausarbeit im globalen Wandel (Münster: Westfälisches Dampfboot), 103–120.
Hess, S. and Lenz, R. (2001), 'Das Comeback der Dienstmädchen', in S. Hess and R. Lenz, (eds.): Geschlecht und Globalisierung. Ein kulturwissenschaftlicher Streifzug durch transnationale Räume (Königstein/Taunus: Ulrike Heimer), 128–165.
Juel Jensen, A. (2006), Mutterpflicht und Mütterwünsche. Eine ethnographische Studie in einer schwäbischen Kleinstadt (Tübingen: Ivv Verlag).
Kudera, W. and Voß, G. (eds.) (2000), Lebensführung und Gesellschaft. Beiträge zu Konzept und Empirie alltäglicher Lebensführung (Opladen: Leske + Budrich).
Mauss, M. (1990 [1950]), The Gift. The Form and Reason for Exchange in Archaic Societies, translated by W. D. Halls (London: Routledge).
Menzl, M. (2007), Leben in Suburbia. Raumstrukturen und Alltagspraktiken am Rand von Hamburg (Frankfurt/Main: Campus).
Menzl, M. (2010), 'Zwischen langgeplanter Selbstverwirklichung und ungeahnten Kontexteffekten – Wohnen im suburbanen Eigenheim', in A. Dittrich-Wesbuer / W. Knapp and F. Osterhage (eds.): Postsuburbanisierung und die „Renaissance der (Innen-)städte": Neue Entwicklungen in der Stadtregion (Detmold: Rohn), 141–157.
Menzl, M. (2014), 'Urbanisierungsprozesse in Suburbia? Überlegungen zur Ubiquität der urbanen Lebensweise', in F. Roost et al. (eds.): Jahrbuch StadtRegion 2013/2014 Schwerpunktthema Urbane Peripherien (Opladen: Verlag Barbara Budrich), 43–60.
Münter, A. (2012), Wanderungsentscheidungen von Stadt-Umland-Wanderern in vier Stadtregionen – Regionaler Vergleich der Muster und Motive, Informations- und Wahrnehmungslücken sowie Beeinflussbarkeit der Wanderungsentscheidung in vier Stadtregionen (Münster: MV-Verlag).
Mulder, C. H. (2013), 'Family dynamics and housing. Conceptual issues and empirical findings', Demographic Research 29, 355–378.
Mulder, C. H. and Wagner, M. (1998), 'First-time Home-Ownership in the Family Life Course: A West German-Dutch Comparison', Urban Studies 35(4), 687–713.
Mulder, C. H. and Wagner, M. (2001), 'The Connection between Family Formation and First-time Home Ownership in the Context of West Germany and the Netherlands', European Journal of Population 17(2), 137–164.

Scherger, S. (2007), Destandardisierung, Differenzierung und Individualisierung. Westdeutsche Lebensläufe im Wandel (Wiesbaden: Verlag für Sozialwissenschaften).
Schweitzer, P., Seiser, G., and Strasser, E. (2010), 'Houses, families, and the making of community: the Austrian rural case', in P. Heady and P. Schweitzer (eds.): Family, Kinship and State in Contemporary Europe. Vol. 2, The View from Below: Nineteen Localities (Frankfurt/New York: Campus), 91–127.
Simon-Philipp, C. and Korbel, J. (2017), 'Einfamilienhausgebiete als Gegenstand der Stadtentwicklung und Stadtforschung', in disP – The Planning Review 53(1), 106–113.
Soaita, A. and Searle, B. (2016), 'Debt amnesia: Homeowners' discourses on the financial costs and gains of homebuying', Environment and Planning 48(6), 1087–1106.
Tomkowiak, I. (2012), Little Boxes All the Same? Suburbia: gelebt – gedacht – inszeniert (Zürich: Institut für Populäre Kulturen).
Vogt, L., Biernatzki, R., Kriszan, M. and Lorleberg, W. (2015), Ländliche Lebensverhältnisse im Wandel. 1952, 1972, 1993, 2012. Dörfer als Wohnstandorte. Thünen Report 32(1) (Braunschweig: Johann Heinrich von Thünen-Institut), https://www.thuenen.de/media/publikationen/thuenen-report/Thuenen-Report_32-1.pdf (accessed 10 August 2018).
Wagner, M. and Mulder, C. H. (2000), 'Wohneigentum im Lebenslauf', Zeitschrift für Soziologie 29(1), 44–59.
Weihrich, M. and Voß, G. (eds.) (2002), tag für tag, Alltag als Problem – Lebensführung als Lösung? Neue Beiträge zur Soziologie der Lebensführung 2 (Chemnitz: Hampp Verlag).
Zakrzewski, P. (2011), 'In der Übergangszone: Alternde Einfamilienhausgebiete zwischen Revitalisierung, Stagnation und Schrumpfung', in O. Schnur and M. Dilling (eds.): Quartiere im demografischen Umbruch. Beiträge aus der Forschungspraxis (Wiesbaden: Verlag für Sozialwissenschaften), 47–67.
Zakrzewski, P., Berndgen-Kaiser, A., Fox-Kämper, R., and Siedentop, S. (2014), 'Herausforderungen westdeutscher Einfamilienhausgebiete der Nachkriegszeit. Bestandsentwicklung als neues Handlungsfeld für Kommunen', Comparative Population Studies 39(2), 247–284.
Zimmermann, O. (2018), 'Dimensionen von Destandardisierung. Eine differenzierte sequenzanalytische Betrachtung der Familiengründung', (PhD diss.,Technische Universität Braunschweig, Braunschweig).

Sources

Bundesministerium für Familie, Senioren, Frauen und Jugend (ed.) (2018), 'Kindertagesbetreuung Kompakt. Ausbaustand und Bedarf 2017. Ausgabe 03' (Berlin), https://www.bmfsfj.de/blob/126672/b3269db29ac336a256ac863802957533/kindertagesbetreuung-kompakt-ausbaustand-und-bedarf-2017-ausgabe-3-data.pdf (accessed 26 July 2018).
Bundesstiftung Baukultur (ed.) (2017), Baukulturbericht. Stadt und Land 2016/17 (Berlin: Medialis), https://www.bundesstiftung-baukultur.de/sites/default/files/medien/78/downloads/bbk_bkb-2016_17_low_1.pdf (accessed 8 August 2018).
Bürogemeinschaft Honnigfort und Brümmer im Auftrag der Gemeinde Ohne (2009), 'Dorferneuerung. Gemeinde Ohne', Entwurf April 2009, (Haren an der Ems).
Gemeinde Ohne (ed.) (2016), 'Haushaltssatzung und Haushaltsplan 2017' (Ohne), http://www.schuettorf.de/pics/medien/1_1493881349/Haushaltsplan_Ohne_2017_komplett.pdf (accessed 26 July 2018).
GGB Grundstücks- und Entwicklungsgesellschaft Landkreis Grafschaft Bentheim mbH (ed.) (2016), 'Bauen und Wohnen in Ohne' (Bad Bentheim), http://www.ggb-grafschaft.de/pics/medien/1_1449146227/Verk-Daten-VolkersKamp.pdf (accessed 6 September 2017).

GGB Grundstücks- und Entwicklungsgesellschaft Landkreis Grafschaft Bentheim mbH (ed.) (n.d.), 'Wohnbaugebiete. Ohne. Volkers Kamp', https://ggb.grafschaft-bentheim.de/staticsite/staticsite2.php?menuid=1179&topmenu=1012 (accessed 8 August 2018).

Information und Technik Nordrhein-Westfalen, Pressestelle (ed.) (2017), Primäreinkommen und verfügbares Einkommen der privaten Haushalte in NRW (Düsseldorf), https://www.it.nrw/sites/default/files/atoms/files/257_17.pdf (accessed 9 August 2018).

Interhyp Gruppe (ed.) (2018), 'Wohnträume 2018. So möchten die Deutschen leben' (München), https://wohntraumstudie.interhyp.de/download/interhyp-wohntraumstudie-2018.pdf (accessed 6 June 2018).

IW Consult and IfD Allensbach (2017), 'Sparda-Studie "Wohnen in Deutschland 2017"', https://www.iwkoeln.de/studien/gutachten/beitrag/hanno-kempermann-agnes-millack-wohnen-in-deutschland-2017-332561.html (accessed 15 September 2019).

Kreisverwaltung Landkreis Grafschaft Bentheim (ed.) (2017), 'Zahlen Daten Fakten 2017/2018' (Nordhorn), http://www.grafschaft-bentheim.de/pics/medien/1_1501837457/Zahlenspiegel_2017.pdf (accessed 4 September 2017).

Landesamt für Statistik Niedersachsen (ed.) (2010), Statistische Berichte Niedersachsen. Einkommen der Lohn- und Einkommensteuerpflichtigen und seine Besteuerung 2010, (Hannover), https://www.statistik.niedersachsen.de/download/97826 (accessed 28 September 2017).

Landesamt für Statistik Niedersachsen (ed.) (2014), Statistische Monatshefte Niedersachsen 12/2014 (Hannover), https://www.statistik.niedersachsen.de/veroeffentlichungen/statistische_monatshefte/statistische-monatshefte-niedersachsen-87704.html (accessed 9 August 2018).

NRW Bank (ed.) (2017), Wohnungsmarktbericht NRW 2017. Wie entwickeln sich Wohnungsnachfrage und Marktanspannung? Was wird gebaut? (Düsseldorf), https://www.nrwbank.de/export/sites/nrwbank/de/corporate/downloads/presse/publikationen/publikationen-wohnungsmarktbeobachtung/aktuelle-ergebnisse/WEB_Doppelseiten_Wohnungsmarktbericht-2017.pdf (accessed 7 August 2018).

NRW Bank (ed.) (2016), 'Wohnungsmarktbericht NRW 2016. Sonderthema: Wird dort genug gebaut, wo neue Wohnungen gebraucht werden?' (Düsseldorf), http://www.kas.de/wf/doc/21233-1442-1-30.pdf (accessed 6 September 2017).

Stadt Dülmen, Fachbereich 312, Bürgerbüro (ed.) (2017), 'Einwohnerstatistik für den Monat Juli 2017', Stand 29.08.2017 (Dülmen), https://www.duelmen.de/fileadmin/user_upload/allgemein/medien/buergerbuero/aktuelle_einwohnerstatistik.pdf (accessed 4 September 2017).

Stadt Dülmen, 010 Zentrales Controlling (ed.) (2014), 'Strukturdatenbericht der Stadt Dülmen', Stand April 2014, 2. Auflage (Dülmen), https://www.duelmen.de/fileadmin/user_upload/duelmen.de/stadtportrait/strukturdatenbericht_stand_2014.pdf (accessed 6 September 2017).

Stadt Dülmen (ed.) (1993), 'Bebauungsplan Nr. 'Schlüters Heide – Erweiterung, Teil II', Gemarkung Rorup, Stadtbezirk Dülmen-Rorup, Flur 5', 1993, www.o-sp.de/download/duelmen/7738 (accessed 4 September 2017).

Stadt Dülmen (ed.) (2016), 'Begründung des Bebauungsplan Nr. 235 'Pastor-Rück-Straße'', www.o-sp.de/download/duelmen/122601 (accessed 21 August 2017).

Stadt Münster, Amt für Stadtentwicklung, Stadtplanung, Verkehrsplanung, Informationsmanagement und Statistikdienststelle (ed.) (2016), 'Stadtteilsteckbrief 2015, 87 Wolbeck' (Münster), http://www.stadt-muenster.de/fileadmin//user_upload/stadt-muenster/61_stadtentwicklung/pdf/steckbriefe/Stadtteilsteckbrief_87_Wolbeck.pdf (accessed 4 September 2017).

Statistische Ämter des Bundes und der Länder (ed.) (2016), 'Kindertagesbetreuung regional 2016. Ein Vergleich aller 402 Kreise in Deutschland', https://www.destatis.de/DE/Publikationen/Thematisch/Soziales/KinderJugendhilfe/KindertagesbetreuungRegional5225405167004.pdf?__blob=publicationFile (accessed 26 July 2018).

Statistisches Bundesamt (Destatis) (ed.) (2015), 'Wie die Zeit vergeht. Ergebnisse der Zeitverwendung in Deutschland 2012/2013' (Wiesbaden), https://www.destatis.de/DE/PresseService/Presse/Pressekonferenzen/2015/zeitverwendung/Pressebroschuere_zeitverwendung.pdf?__blob=publicationFile (accessed 30 July 2018).

Statistisches Bundesamt (Destatis) (ed.) (2013), 'Wirtschaftsrechnungen. Einkommens- und Verbrauchsstichprobe Wohnverhältnisse privater Haushalte', (Wiesbaden), https://www.destatis.de/DE/Publikationen/Thematisch/EinkommenKonsum Lebensbedingungen/Wohnen/EVS_HausGrundbesitzWohnverhaeltnisHaushalte 2152591139004.pdf?__blob=publicationFile (accessed 4 September 2017).

Statistisches Bundesamt (Destatis) (ed.) (n.d.), 'Genesis-Online Datenbank, Baugenehmigungen im Hochbau: Deutschland, Jahre, Bautätigkeiten, Gebäudeart/Bauherr, 31111-0001', https://www-genesis.destatis.de/genesis/online;jsessionid=0AE3006E8042970EBB089583FE85D57C.tomcat_GO_1_1?operation=previous&levelindex=3&levelid=1504861424420&step=3 (accessed 7 September 2017).

Statistisches Bundesamt (Destatis) und Wissenschaftszentrum Berlin für Sozialforschung (WZB) in cooperation with Das Sozio-ökonomische Panel (SOEP) am Deutschen Institut für Wirtschaftsforschung (DIW Berlin) (eds.) (2016), 'Datenreport 2016. Ein Sozialbericht für die Bundesrepublik Deutschland', (Bonn), https://www.destatis.de/DE/Publikationen/Datenreport/Downloads/Datenreport2016.pdf?__blob=publicationFile (accessed 26 July 2018).

Wirtschafts- und Sozialwissenschaftliches Institut (ed.) (2017), 'Wer leistet unbezahlte Arbeit. Report Nr. 35', https://www.boeckler.de/pdf/p_wsi_report_35_2017.pdf (accessed 26 July 2018).

Interviews

Rorup, Interview 1, Schroer family, 12.11.2015
Rorup, Interview 2, Meier family, 18.11.2015
Rorup, Interview 5, Sattler family, 19.12.2015
Rorup, Interview 6, Meurer family, 4.12.2015
Ohne, Interview 10, Müller family, 11.3.2016
Ohne, Interview 8, Lutz family, 15.3.2016
Ohne, Interview 13, Klaas family, 12.4.2016
Wolbeck, Interview 17, Schmidt family, 6.10.2016
Wolbeck, Interview 19, Drein family, 8.9.2016
Wolbeck, Interview 20, Kanich family, 9.2016
Wolbeck, Interview 21, Grube family, 4.10.2016
Münster, Interview 23, Bau- und Immobilienunternehmer Münsterland, 2.11.2016

Endnotes

1 For details on these developments see the introduction by Elisabeth Timm in this volume.
2 See the contributions of Anne Caplan and Julia Gill in this volume.
3 See the table in Caplan/Wagenknecht, Build or buy?, in this volume.
4 In addition, I undertook visits to houses, by which I mean guided tours of residents' own homes, during which I asked about typical household routines, and residents documented the tour photographically. Since this material cannot be published for personal privacy and copyright reasons, it is used as a supplement for the

evaluation and can only be represented in a descriptive manner. Finally, I used a field diary to record the research relationship, which serves as further data for an ethnographic study. These materials are evaluated in the dissertation research. The current presentation of some of the results is limited to the analysis of the interviews.

5 Due to its high natural potential, the entire area of the municipality of Ohne has been designated as a special area for agriculture. See also the draft document on village renewal in the municipality of Ohne (April 2009), prepared by the Bürogemeinschaft Honnigfort und Brümmer for the municipality of Ohne, 15.67 percent of the total area in the district of Bentheim is used for agriculture, however, this is still below the national average of 53 percent, cf. Landesamt für Statistik Niedersachsen (ed.): Landkreis Grafschaft Bentheim, https://www.statistik.niedersachsen.de/download/49200 (accessed 28 August 2017).

6 This company is the Grundstücks- und Entwicklungsgesellschaft Landkreis Grafschaft Bentheim mbH.

7 I published an earlier and shorter version of this section together with colleagues in German (Heinemann et al., 2019).

8 See also the article by Inken Tintemann in this volume.

9 Both studies are based on an empirical qualitative and quantitative survey of 1,000 households using the regions of Cologne, Leipzig, Münster and Magdeburg as examples. The data were collected in 2006/2007.

10 However, it is an open question as to whether this finding is about clinging to traditional lifestyles or about a twofold migration effect (because those who have different lifestyles move to urban centres, and those who want to have a house and then a family move to rural areas to fulfil their wish).

11 See the article by Jakob Smigla-Zywocki in this volume.

12 See, as a contrast, the study by Caplan/Wagenknecht in this volume, comparing families who built new houses with those who bought them second-hand.

13 See the article by Johannes Warda in this volume.

14 See the article by Sabine Flamme and Gotthard Walter in this volume.

'Young family with child' or 'where is it the greenest'?

Folke Köbberling

The Kling Family, Blankenfelde, two children, previously living in Berlin-Neukölln and Berlin-Lichtenrade

Why did you move here?

The trigger was that we had a flat that was also very nice, but relatively speaking it was not much cheaper than the whole house we are now living in. Then we thought, well, it's daft, if for just the same as for a four-room flat you can have a six-room house, paying 500 DM a month extra. And that's basically why we decided to buy a house.
You can also describe it a bit geographically or, in principle, it was like we moved out of the city in stages after the children were born. Previously, we were in Neukölln, in a very densely populated area, near Sonnenallee, Harzer Straße there were relatively few green spaces, narrow streets, a lot of traffic. A social mixture with a relatively high percentage of foreigners, a high percentage of workers, dirty streets, even people who are sometimes difficult to deal with, so to speak. And we thought that it would be better for the children if we looked for a better environment. Then we moved to Lichtenrade. The first step towards suburbanisation. Then after three years the step from Lichtenrade to a very nice but very expensive flat – and it came to the point that we said that we can also move out to the surrounding area, to the countryside, and we are also very satisfied with that. Because here you have a lot of open space and live surrounded by the greenery.

Could you briefly describe where you live here?

This is pretty much on the periphery. The town centre of Blankenfelde with the church is rather a long way back there. The railway station is a second centre, and five or six years ago, these were all fields that belonged to the Protestant church. Then the idea was brought up of various companies building residential estates here. Now 2000 people live in this area. We think it's quite good. It is still one of the main roads through Mahlow to Lichtenrade that we have here. I mainly go by rail, so the connection is quite good.

That was also a very important aspect, depending on where you work, that you can get there without a car. Especially later for the children, that you don't have to drive backwards and forwards by car all the time. So the children can definitely grow up much more freely. They can get out of the garden back there, and the footpath is a good mile long. There are two playgrounds, a roller-skating rink – you don't have to worry about anything.

Here they can go out unattended, here we let them go out without worrying. Of course, they are not allowed on the road, they are still too young for that, nine and five years old, but if they go in that direction there will be nothing else except the nearby woods. We don't have to worry about that anymore, because they are relatively responsible. We couldn't have done that in Berlin. Not in Neukölln, because there are busy roads and there was so much conflict potential in the social fabric that you can't just let children go out, and in Lichtenrade, the Lichtenrader Damm was right next to us, and that's a main road with constant traffic from morning till night.

Do you have contact with the neighbours?

The neighbours that we have here are all very nice; they have children too, some have none. We get along quite well with our closest neighbours, because we live on the edge of the residential estate, we don't get to see much either – in the middle it gets pretty cramped, I have to say. We wouldn't have liked that so much. But here on the edge you are also a bit less disturbed and some of the neighbours have become real friends of ours. They look after our house. The neighbours are also all from Berlin.

How long does it take you to get to work or the children to get to school?

I need an hour to get to work, the children and my wife need half an hour by car. They go to school in Berlin. In principle, there were two reasons for going to school in Berlin. First, they were already there anyway, in rooted structures so to speak, then you leave the children there. If you let the children go to school here – we are both teachers in state schools – then Berlin has its own school holidays and Brandenburg partly has different school holidays. This is of course a big problem for a family, if the children have school holidays sooner or later than the parents, if

Baufeld
der
GEHAG-
Aktiengesellschaft
Schutt abladen verboten
Ballspielen nicht erlaubt

you're planning a longer trip. This is a big point – failure of politicians in Berlin and Brandenburg – that there is still such a divergence. But the second point is that there is also an educational barrier. There are still a lot of old Brandenburgers working in Brandenburg who certainly have a different idea of teaching, of education than we do if we were to call ourselves youngish, middle-aged, somewhat open-minded teachers. We would have been a little concerned about sending the children to school here.

To put it pointedly, can you describe it as a "ghetto"?

It is a ghetto. You can say this, first of all, it didn't grow, it was stamped out of the ground into a landscape that was completely different ten years ago, fields – the "old GDR" – yes, those are all old owners. There are also new people who have bought houses, but here you can call it a ghetto in the most extreme sense, in the sense that very many West Berliners with children have moved out here, older people who want to enjoy their retirement in a small terraced house. Social housing has also been built at the end of the street, so there is not only a middle class here, but a mixture. Originally it was planned to build a small shop on the site of the residential estate, with a kindergarten and so on, but then cost reasons I supposed meant that all that didn't happen. There is less money in that than in putting up houses. I think that's a big disadvantage, because although we officially live here, we do live more or less in Berlin.

What is the economic situation with buying a house?

We got subsidies to buy a house, because back then I wasn't working yet, and so it was quite affordable. Though it has changed in the meantime, and I have been working again for three years and now, there is always a review, and in the end, even with such a mid-terrace house, I think, without two halfway decent incomes it is not affordable. You are led to believe – all the tax savings are deducted – just when something really happens: washing machine breaks down, car needs a major repair, then it doesn't work out. It's not cheap. Let's say that with just one income it wouldn't be possible. It costs 3000 DM with all the extras. Of course, it's also part of it that we will own the house when we have paid it off sometime. We could also imagine living in the city, but that's just too expensive. This one cost 450,000 DM and for the same house there you pay 600,000 DM.

What about exclusion here?

One can say that right-wing radicalism is a problem in Blankenfelde. Of course, with the long-established young people here in Mahlow, that forms a joint municipality together with Blankenfelde, right-wing radicalism is very widespread. They meet at the Blankenfelde railway station or in Mahlow – known throughout Brandenburg – to beat some people up. But also here in the residential estate, where mostly children of former West Berlin families live, they make a joke of making right-wing radical jokes, xenophobic agitation. I myself was in the playground and experienced how after I told young people off for throwing their cigarette butts into the sand pit, bothering the little children, they started shouting antisemitic jokes and about gassing Jews etc., only to provoke. That's not funny. Those were 15-16-year-olds who should know better by now.

The Krahne Family, Berlin-Frohnau, three children, previously living in Berlin-Moabit

Why did you move here?

We lived in the city, in Moabit. Simon had problems with his asthma and we really wanted to move to the edge of town. We were looking for something in the north because the air is supposed to be the best in the north. I was telling a colleague what it's like to look for a flat. And she lives above us and said that there would be a flat free here in the house. We took a look at it and then we were immediately so enthusiastic about the area. That was actually the reason we moved here.
The asthma, but also the living situation on Lüneburger Straße. That is opposite the government quarter and it had already been a big building site for three years. That's connected, there's dust, but it wasn't just the dust, there was an incredible amount of noise. They were working day and night, they were totally under stress. The railway tracks were also being renovated, they were at it day and night; the gravel was being removed. It was difficult because we always sleep with the window open.

Could you briefly describe your housing situation?

The housing situation is especially nice, because we are living together with the family above us. We share everyday life, eat together, so each adult cooks once a week and looks after the others' children, practically a shared flat, only in two flats. That is what is especially nice, and then there is light, the children have so much space, everyone has their own room. Then the area here. In the beginning we always said, we're doing it for the children, but now we enjoy it ourselves. I often go for walks, ride my bike to work. We're out of town and in the woods in two minutes and that's great; the peace. We like living here very much, there are animals here that you never see in Moabit.

What is the infrastructure like?

It is five minutes by bike to the railway station. Shopping is no longer the same as it was in Moabit. Everything was nearby; we had a big Turkish shop where we went a lot. Fresh vegetables are a problem; they are also

more expensive here, much more expensive. There are also a number of supermarkets; there is Reichelt, Aldi and Spar and everything is easily accessible, but there is still a difference in prices. It's like when we're in the city, we often bring something back.
I still like to buy in Turkish shops – in the Tegelcenter there is a market hall and sometimes we shop there. That's a long way, you can only do that after work.

How do you get around?

We don't have a car, but logistically it's more difficult. In Moabit, we walked 40 metres, then we always went up into the flat with a shopping trolley. Up in the lift. Here, there is nothing comparable. And you can't get here with a shopping trolley. That means we now have to carry it all by bike. But that is the price, we gladly accept that, but it is an attraction to go shopping on foot here. People already look. Especially in Frohnau there is nobody apart from us who goes shopping with a granny trolley. At the parents' evening two to three parents come by bike, the other parents come by car, even if they live only one street away. They are used to the car. Most families have two or more. They even drive to the railway station by car, or they drive down the motorway to work.

What's the difference for the children to Moabit?

In Moabit, the children were only allowed in to the courtyard of the residential complex. There was dog shit everywhere on the street.
That's Miri's third word after mum and dad – dog shit – that was a bit embarrassing. Here, the children can leave the house and be gone for three hours – a big relief.
In Moabit it was really different. When we sent the children out, we were afraid. There were discussions with parents about what to teach the children, what they are allowed to do and what not to. True, everything was closer, they were allowed to go to the gymnastics club alone, but we were more afraid than here. And here with the garden, they are there very often. Or they go out alone. Meanwhile, the big ones also go to the border strip.

With Miri it is not quite clear whether she likes it better here, because she grew up in Moabit. The kindergarten, her friends. Of course, she also has nice memories of schoolmates. It's not the same with the others. Miri doesn't want to move back either; she wants her friends to come here.

What's your economic situation in the new flat?

We pay 2,000 DM. Of course, in Moabit everyone says we're paying a fortune. For these circumstances it is a bargain. For this location here, the size of the flat. It is 140 square metres. Then again, we pay half of our salary. Nevertheless, we still have more than before and don't need anything big.

What is the new school environment like? Is there criminality?

Of course, the primary school has completely different conditions here than in Moabit. Criminality does not play the same role in primary school here as it did in Moabit. That was a problem. In Moabit, children were already withdrawn from primary school. It started in primary school, and in the other schools it is even more extreme. And here, the children come from relatively sheltered homes, the parents have a lot of time and money. They make offers for leisure time that the parents in Moabit did not. They take great care of their children. If something is lacking at school, the teacher asks us if we would like a CD player and a cassette recorder and then one of the parents immediately contacts her, no problem at all. The difference in the learning level is almost extreme. It makes a difference whether half of them don't understand it linguistically or don't care. For example, the first maths test of Miri, our eldest, was given a six. The teacher marked it strictly. She said that the children must know where the line is.
Usually only one parent here goes out to work, so there is more time. That was not the case in Moabit. In our surroundings everybody worked, including shift work. The people here are mainly teachers, artists and actors. They live quite differently, have more money, and it is a different level of education. They also have a different aspiration to educate their children; they also do it much more consciously – sometimes I find it a bit intense – because they are always afraid that their children are not being encouraged enough. Which, of course, is not the case at all. They do violin lessons and ballet and then the parents drive them everywhere by

car, because the children usually can't walk there. They walk 20 minutes to school. Here, the parents have such an influence. They are high earners, people who in turn know others who earn a lot; i.e. you have relationships with companies. Of course, the school has computers because you have the right relationships. It's just a different type of parent, people that have influence, and so the schools have more money.

For that rent you could have got your own home in the affluent suburbs, couldn't you?

The new settlers in the affluent suburbs are still trying to get their children into Berlin schools. The east-west conflict still plays an important role. In Miri's class, children have also moved away, but they haven't changed schools because of it.

And then there is no greenery. There are no trees and a lot of cars. Everybody has their car and there is a lot of traffic. The gardens are very small. Everybody has their chain-link fence and then there's the next one. Here, the children have much more space in a common garden. We now have a bigger garden than if we had a terraced house.

Frau Waniek, Berlin-Marzahn, two sons, married, previously living in Berlin-Prenzlauer Berg

Why did you move here?

Yes, we live in Marzahn, but not where you would think when I say Marzahn, not in a prefabricated block, but in a semi-detached house. Although you can see the tower blocks all around, it is very quiet and very cosy and more like a small village.
We actually moved here from a large prefabricated high-rise in Prenzlauer Berg, but there it was just too noisy for us. We were living on a main road which was busy day and night, the ambulances and the police. And some of the neighbours weren't so nice any more. Many people we knew well had moved away, and we didn't like the new neighbours so much. Also the children who were living there, who were our children's friends had moved away, many good friends anyway. Only the bullies were left. Always. That's why we didn't like it so much any more. And we also simply wanted our own house so that we could change anything we wanted. The flat was also too small.

Can you briefly describe your housing situation?

Marzahn is an estate where you are closest to the city and where you can still build detached houses. It is very close to the centre, 20 minutes to Alex [Alexanderplatz, translator's note]. Marzahn is very green. My husband has to go to work in the city, my son has to go to school. We didn't want to move so far away from the city. We made enquiries at a construction company, and they said they had something in Marzahn. That's right near the school, and so we said, yes that's it. And in the house we planned everything ourselves, the house was not finished. That means that now all the rooms are as we wanted them to be, that we have enough space. In the past, we didn't have a proper cellar, only a storage room. Now we have a real cellar, and the children can make something out of it.

What's the infrastructure like here?

Marzahn is nicer than its reputation at any rate. It's relatively green now after the 20 years that we have had the new buildings. The houses have been refurbished quite well in the meantime, and there is the infrastructure for shopping. It's not too expensive out here, but of course there isn't everything you need, so you have to drive into town to do some shopping. You get what you need every day. There are enough schools. Actually, meanwhile there are old people's homes as well. I go to school by bike, the little one by bus to Biesdorf, a village near Marzahn. My husband and my other son take the train, underground and tram. We have a car, now we don't need it regularly any more. I used to need it regularly.

What is the difference to Prenzlauer Berg?

You have more room in the house to store everything and a cellar where you can do more. It's quieter, but it's harder for the children because their friends are so far away. With the little one, because he goes to school in Biesdorf and all his friends live there. Even if you lived in Biesdorf, it would be a long way to a friend. So, they can't just say, 'I'm popping over to my friend's place.' The friend lives at least a quarter of an hour away on foot. Because of this rural situation, the children have a long way to school. Five minutes by bus, that's four or five bus stops, and they also visit each other, so they have to take the bus. This is bad for small children. There are children here in Marzahn, too, but not as many as there used to be. Since he doesn't go to school with them, he doesn't know most of the children here either. And the big one has his friends in Berlin, he has almost no friends here. But he didn't have that many friends in Prenzlauer Berg either.

He goes to a school that has pupils from all over Berlin, they just like to keep to themselves, such a special school, they have special interests and they are together in their spare time a lot. They can't do so much with others. They play chess or go to competitions.

It was about the fact that we needed a bigger place to live, and if you want a flat that's bigger than 100 square metres, it's almost as expensive as renting a house. So we decided to take a house, a bit of garden, a bit of patio. It is more for us than for the children. We bought it, but even if you would rent it, it's not that much more expensive than a flat. And if you buy it, you get a loan from the state of Berlin, and with children it's not much more expensive than paying rent. It's just nicer.

What's your relationship with your neighbours like?

With the neighbours there are sometimes petty quarrels because of building work. We had a lot of trouble with the construction companies. We're not together that much; we have other friends than the neighbours.

What kind of people live here?

Mixed. Recently, many families have moved into single-family houses. But mostly with older children, because earlier you can't afford it. Our youngest is the youngest child here.
There are hardly any small children in the whole district. You find children in the high-rise blocks, but still not many. The average age is supposed to be 40, but there are not as many children as before. Previously, Marzahn was full of children.

Is there criminality here?

Like everywhere else, there's crime here, too. Some people get beaten up, you hear that again and again. I also had cases in school. The children have also had trouble with others, but it was no better at Prenzlauer Berg. I don't know if there are districts where it's really better. I don't see any difference there.
There is no right-wing radicalism in our school, but there are also schools, comprehensive schools, where this is more pronounced. It depends very much on the school environment where it occurs. In my private surroundings, we have graffiti, but in principle, right-wing radicalism is not so excessive. Just like in the city. It's not becoming more or less. We have little contact with it, I have to say. We started living in Friedrichshain in 1984, it was really difficult there – we did have nice neighbours though, old people who took care of the children, and young families. But it was really very difficult, because a backyard like that is very dirty.
The children couldn't play in the yards. They had to go to playgrounds, there was a nice one nearby, but you always had to go with them. The children had to cross the roads; everything was full of parked cars. They could never cross the road alone. That was the most difficult part, especially if they wanted to play with a friend, we had to take the child there and pick them up. Later at Prenzlauer Berg it was easier. It was the new development area, a big prefab block, a kindergarten in the middle,

a large field and a playground. The children could always go out alone and it was much easier. When my son was three years old, he always went out to his friends on his own, to the kindergarten, which is much nicer. In this respect, the prefab block is quite practical. If there are lots of children everywhere, the children's facility is there, and the children know each other, you know the children. If anything happens, you know where the children belong. Actually not bad, and it used to be the same in Marzahn. With many children and everyone knowing them, not much actually happened, and it was nice for the children.

Jana Büttner, Berlin-Rahnsdorf, one son, divorced

Why did you move here?

I moved in here a year and a half ago. My husband at that time wanted to build a house. An estate agent showed us this plot and we immediately liked it a lot. I never want to move to the city again.

What is the infrastructure like?

The public transport connections are not so good. There is only a bus every 20 minutes, you are dependent on a car.
Shopping is still possible, a chemist's, what you need, a drinks shop is not far away, you can also go on foot. It's OK. Otherwise, if I do something, it's going into the city, cinema, bars or discotheques. That's an hour's drive by car, that's fine.

Where do your friends live?

I don't have any friends nearby, because most of the people who moved here are more like 40-50, I guess. I'm 30. The neighbourliness has really developed with the people who live at the back. They have a smaller child and a bigger one, that's really, really nice. It's quite good.

Do you feel lonely living in your situation?

I don't feel lonely at all, there's far too little time for that because I'm busy all day long. Then the driving. Then I'm happy when I'm at home and have my peace. Otherwise it's a phone call and then someone comes by. I just call the babysitter. My sister-in-law then comes by, she thinks it's nice here, she lives in the city, and in summer she always calls, oh Jana, can I just drop by.

What kind of people live here?

I think there are still a lot of old people who live here occasionally. The generation in their forties and fifties. It's well mixed here, we also have a home for asylum seekers. Probably it's like in the city, but it's not so concentrated.

Where do you spend your spare time?

Mostly I spend my spare time in the city, then I get in my car and drive to friends. I would never move back to the city again. It cramps me. Before I moved here, I thought I would find it too stuffy like that in a single-family house. Now I just feel freer, open the door and there is at least a little space until the next one. There are no more stairs, no lift and people I can't stand.

What financial impact does such a house have?

Oh, when it was planned, so to speak as a threesome, if you still have someone who is earning it works. It has a financial impact when you are the sole earner. If you are alone, it is quite a burden. If you're paying it off alone, then most of the income is spent on the house, that's clear. I go to work for the house. And the beneficiary will be Ramon at some point, I think. And that's what I'm actually doing it for.
Sometimes when I was doing night duty and drove home, when you live in the city, you don't even notice the surroundings, the countryside anymore, you look around, just some concrete, the horizon is relatively cramped, and it's not like that here at all. And then after the night duty, I make a small trip to the Müggelsee lake and watch the sunrise, and if sometimes you are not feeling so good, then that's my place where I go. I look at the sun and always tell myself, maybe it looks different every day, everybody is different, too, but the sun always rises, no matter what happened last night.

How long does it take you to get to work every day?

I did a management course and the employer financed it for me for a year. That was on condition that I would work there for at least a year, until next April, and then I have to see what I'm going to do. Because there is simply not enough time for Ramon and me, because three hours a day are lost.
I get up at half past four, at five I wake Ramon, at half past five we set off for kindergarten. I pick him up there at half past four, and if we're lucky, we'll be home by half past five.
After that I think I'm more tired than Ramon; he's still bouncing around here and I ask myself, where does he get the energy from?
That's the price.

The size of the house. If you lived somewhere else, then you just have state support or something like that, and then it is just 80 or 90 square metres, and then I feel somehow restricted; it's built up everywhere, everywhere so cramped, and that's not on.
The 130 square metres are just right now, completely OK. At that time, I said to my husband, because I knew how important the house was to him, that as far as I'm concerned he could keep the house, it wasn't so important to me and it's just material things and I don't want that. The only thing I want is Ramon and my stuff and then I go too. And then we talked about it in peace and who could keep up the house at all, and then we agreed on why we had been doing it in the first place.
Namely, for Ramon, and then we calculated back and forth and it turned out that I was actually the one who in principle also has support from my friend.It was more reasonable, although I didn't actually want the house at first. Now I'm actually very happy about it, now I don't want to miss it any more.

What will Ramon's school situation be like?

I tried the school because he will be six in August. Then he would have been able to go to school next year, and that didn't work, because I wanted him to go to preschool, and preschool in that school is only from seven until one o'clock, and that doesn't work. And I didn't want him to go to school with me in the Wedding district either.
You actually go to school where you live, not where your mother works. So, I initially just put it off, perhaps it's also better like that. It doesn't really bother me, even if he would start in Wedding, I honestly have to say. Here in Erkner, there is the asylum-seekers' home and there are a lot of Albanians in the school. It doesn't bother me at all. Now if it were only Albanians and he was the only German, that would bother me.

Is there criminality here?

One and a half years ago, there was a wave of break-ins here, but only in all the new houses, and I remember I was a bit scared, we had just moved in and settled. Every evening, the police now drive by, and I haven't heard anything more. They drive past not just because of burglars, but also because of the wild boars, because here a wild boar attacked an eight-year-old child. The police are often here and chase away the boars.

The Eike family, Berlin-Zehlendorf, two children

Why do you live here?

It's my husband's parents' house. He grew up here. During his studies, we were in the Wedding district and then the house here became free because his father had moved out.

Can you briefly describe how you live here?

It's a terraced house, built in 1928/29 by Bruno Taut. It has a small garden. We live on an estate of similar houses. It's a listed building. It has very many and very small rooms. 120 square metres and three floors. We like living here very much.

What is the infrastructure like?

We have everything nearby that we need or would like, e.g. the Krumme Lanke is a ten-minute walk away, the Grunewald is five minutes away. In 20 minutes, you can get to the city centre by underground. There is a shopping mall, church and kindergarten five minutes away, everything is within walking distance.

How do you get around?

By bike, underground and car. I need the car because I'm working and sometimes have to go to the doctor with my children and then to pottery. Sometimes you can't do that without a car.

Are there good neighbourly relations?

The neighbourly relations are very good.

Where do your friends live?

Most of them live in the area. Very good friends live only 40 metres away.

What is the difference to city or country life?

I think this estate combines the advantages of the countryside with the advantages of a city. The estate itself is like a village. You're not watched, however, as I imagine it would be in a village. There is no social control.

Is there a mix of people?

No. Of course there are many groups that can't live here because they can't afford it. There are not many students, there are not many unemployed, there are very few foreigners compared to Kreuzberg. Young and old are very mixed. There are a lot of children, but also a lot of old people.

What is your children's environment like, are there dangers?

There is car traffic here on the estate – speed limit 30 – so relatively little. There is a big road in front, Argentine Avenue, there are traffic lights, we always train the children how to cross there. Here in the estate they are allowed to walk alone, the older one also goes further.

What is the school situation like?

I think it's good. The older one likes going. The little one has just started, he has only been going to school for one and a half weeks.
Other families thought that Zehlendorf is better supported financially by the Senate than Neukölln, for example.
I don't have any comparison. But I don't think that the schools here get more money from the Senate. The schools are in a structurally dilapidated state. I am also a teacher in Zehlendorf. Our school, for example, has been surrounded by scaffolding for three years. Perhaps the parents are more committed than in other districts.

What about the financial side of buying a house?

We didn't inherit the house, we bought it. We lived in it for a while and then bought it from my husband's father. It's still a big financial burden, but it would be worth more to me.

The ------- family, bought a villa in Potsdam/Babelsberg, currently still living in a 150-square-metre flat with a rooftop terrace in Berlin-Schöneberg, three children

Can you briefly describe why you're moving?

We will soon be moving from Schöneberg to Potsdam-Babelsberg, because we wanted it to be close, beautiful and green. We bought a house there. We absolutely wanted a house with a garden, we wanted to go into the surrounding area, and we wanted to have Berlin within reach. And that fulfilled all the requirements, and we wanted it close to water.

Can you describe your living situation there?

The house is relatively large. We have enough space there, an area of over 200 square metres is enough for all of us. The garden is about 1,000 square metres. We hope to move in there before Christmas. The change of government determined our plan, because afterwards the prices rose. We bought the house before the change of government – in the expectation that everything would become more expensive afterwards, and that's how it was. So, to that extent the calculation paid off. Otherwise we might have waited a few more years. We bought it just under a year and a half ago. Yes, until we were through with the building authorities.

What is the infrastructure like there?

There is everything you need in terms of infrastructure.

How will you get around?

There it will either be by car or by train.

What will the difference be for the children?

We wanted to be able to open the door and for the children to be in the garden. So we save time, so the children can keep themselves busy, basically. Here in the city this is relatively limited. In the city, there are not so many grasshoppers and beetles and you can't so easily go back and forth to the third floor and the garden with a heavy door in between – that's just different – when you just open the door and you're in the garden.

Where do your friends live?

Our friends all live in the city, but it's not that far away, half an hour by car, a little longer by train.

What sort of expectations did you have for your house?

The house we are moving into now fulfils all our needs, is large, has a large garden, the lake is nearby. Indeed, it fulfils all our wishes.
There is little traffic, crime I don't know – I have heard of break-ins, thefts in the area, but we won't be affected by it, and otherwise it all seems quite tranquil. We have already seen a nice children's shop. That's nice.

Why didn't you have a new house built for that money?

We didn't want a new building, I don't know why, we just didn't want it. We wanted an established area. There are also new single-family houses, but no new building development area.

Isn't a villa like that very expensive?

Economically a house like that is a big burden. Otherwise we have to limit ourselves very much. We reckoned with that. At the moment only one of us is working, my husband.

Your son is 15, will he miss his friends when he moves to Babelsberg?

They have to arrange it anyway, as they are spread all over the city. Most of them now live towards Zehlendorf, and it doesn't matter if he sits in the train for a quarter of an hour longer.
We have chosen the house so that he can still go to the same school. He only has to cycle to the train station. He now goes to school in Tiergarten and he'll stay there. That was a condition for our search. We didn't want to accept that for a house it works out badly for the good school situation. In Tiergarten it's a good school. For the small children the primary school situation there is certainly better than here, and at secondary-school age you can choose everything in Potsdam and Berlin. I don't expect any worsening.

Comparing family housing in Düsseldorf and Neuss-Allerheiligen: new aspects, stable qualities, and increasing challenges regarding everyday life in the suburb and the city

Inken Tintemann

In West Germany since the reconstruction after the Second World War and, after reunification, in the whole of Germany, housing and dwelling until the 2000s has been determined by suburbanisation, mainly performed by young families moving to the peripheries (Beckmann et al. 2007, Menzl 2007). Since then, the spatial development in Germany has additionally unfolded in different variants of reurbanisation with a socioeconomic profile that also includes those young families that for decades have been the protagonists of suburbanisation (Brake and Herfert 2012). Although statistics still indicate that it's mainly young families who are moving to the outskirt, first qualitative and quantitative evidences prove that they also contribute to the current reurbanisation (Ehrenbrusthoff 2005). This development is a hopeful trend and worthy of support – for ecological reasons it is urgent to reduce the land use caused by suburbanisation as much as it is important to stabilise the cities by rejuvenation. In this situation it is highly relevant for spatial planning to have detailed knowledge of the motives that shape the families' decision making. In a qualitative study, I therefore compared housing choices of families who moved to a suburb with those who preferred (to stay in) the city (Tintemann 2015).

Taking the suburb of Neuss-Allerheiligen and the Düsseldorf inner-city districts of Pempelfort and Bilk as research sites, I focused on one of the big cities in Germany (the second biggest in North Rhine-Westphalia, following Cologne) that is characterised by an ongoing suburbanisation with a simultaneously ongoing reurbanisation. Düsseldorf is the state capital of North Rhine-Westphalia and a growing and prospering city with 639,407 inhabitants (effective

31 December 2017, Amt für Statistik und Wahlen der Landeshauptstadt Düsseldorf 2017). Neuss is a city nearby, belonging to the Rhein-Kreis Neuss district. Including rural areas, it has 159,122 inhabitants (effective 1 January 2018, Stadt Neuss 2018). The village of Allerheiligen is part of this city and is only about 10 kilometres away from the centre of Düsseldorf.

My main research question is how contemporary family needs and housing options interfere. To answer this, I generated detailed data on everyday family routines and management strategies of parents and children on the basis of qualitative interviews. I asked about their motivation when choosing the areas and places they lived in at that time and reconstructed different ways in which families organise their daily needs in the city and in the suburb. All in all, this comparison leads to surprising results that demonstrate how families cope with and use the always specific facilities in the city centre and at the outskirts. As a planner, and with the well-known criticism of the single-family home in mind, it is important to me to know the strengths and weaknesses of the urban and suburban structures families are nowadays confronted with. It is important to identify the driving forces that support reurbanisation and the associated opportunities to stop land consumption. Urban sociologists assume that aspects of social change, especially concerning the organisation of employment and gender roles, are one main reason for the new interest of families in urban areas. To investigate this thesis, I analysed the daily routines in the context that has been characterised as late modernity: with new communication technologies at hand, flexibilisation of employment, increasing job mobility, pluralisation of family structures, the trend towards an organised and isolated childhood, the development from a class society to a lifestyle society, and especially a change of gender roles.

In (West) Germany of the Fordist decades, family life has been characterised by the male-breadwinner-and-female-homemaker model, with a sharp distinction between employment and leisure. For decades, suburban dwelling has been the dominant pattern of housing for families with children. However, especially due to more equal gender ideals of young couples, the model of one parent (in most cases: the mother) staying at home or working part-time nearby in order to be able to manage the family, while the other parent (in most cases: the father) commutes to work is no longer adequate. Besides, it never did exist for single parents whose number is increasing. Now, urban environments are increasingly chosen as suitable options for families, also with the argument that their spatial density provides better timeframes for combining child care and employment. All in all, urban sociologists expect that especially the changing gender orders will have an effect on the future of urban planning and housing in a way that inner-city areas will become interesting for families again: 'Since the female homemaker as we knew her nowadays no longer exists, career-oriented women and men alike need the modern urban machine that organises everything as a commodity, i.e. as a public service, what was formerly supplied informally in private households mainly by women' (Siebel 2010, 49, author's translation).

Walter Siebel's thesis implicates the hope that this development might perhaps direct the families back to the cities and thus reduce the ever-expanding land use for suburbs. In the long run, this change could make cities more attractive, while the demand for suburban single-family homes would decrease. Unfortunately, this perspective does not include the special situation families live in, which also has to be examined for any kind of conclusion.

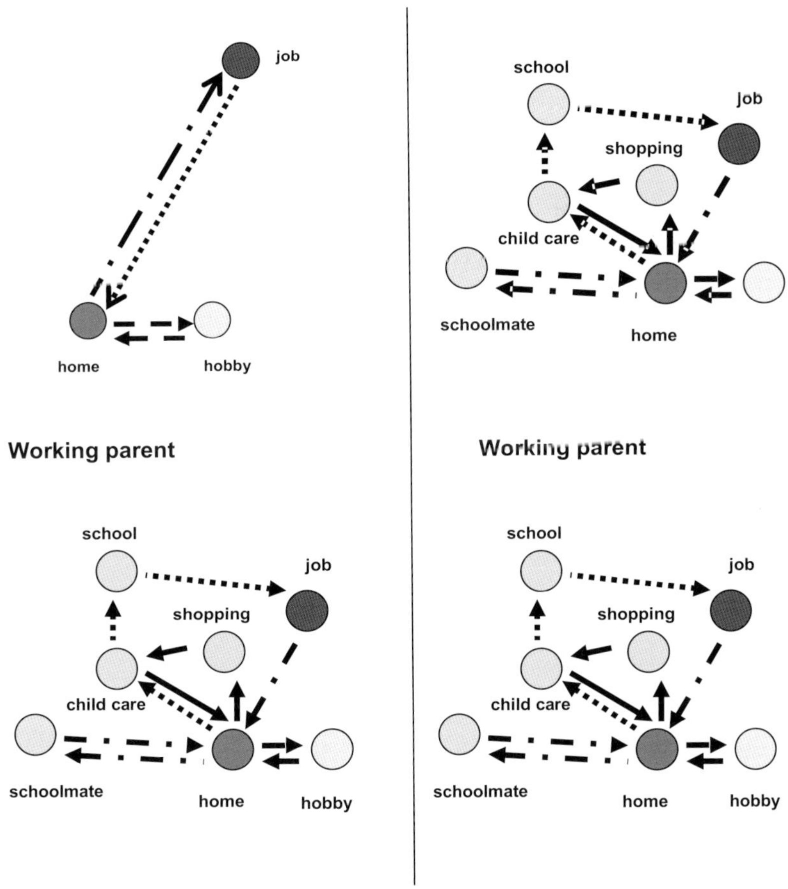

Figure 1: Role models in families: type "breadwinner" and equal role model (source: Spitzner 2001, modified by Inken Tintemann).

To investigate this, my research started with the assumption that the spatial and biographical mobility of families is not determined by uniform, dominant social patterns, but that dwelling choices rather unfold as a result of the household types' needs and the individual lifestyle preferences that each specifically combine employment, schooling, leisure activities of the parents and the children, child care, and supply. In the following paragraphs I will compare the different ways in which families living in a suburban home and those living in an urban flat do this.

By analysing the spatial and temporal dimensions of daily family life in general and the needs of individual family members in specific, I differentiate between qualitative (e.g. space for children playing outside safely), quantitative (e.g. number of rooms), and time-management aspects (e.g. local supply structures that enable saving time, possibilities to externalise child care, or rationalisation of activities). The results lead to a catalogue of requirements. With this I generated a matrix to compare the different types of housing estate structures and how they fit the families' needs.

needs caused by size and heterogeneity of families	good ratio of sqm/rent, adequate number and dimension of rooms, storage for the children's toys and clothes, retreat in the housing unit for individuals
needs of parents taking care of their child(ren)	easy access to the housing unit, easy care and comfortable living conditions, traffic-calmed and child-safe environment within sight, child care and educational facilities nearby, tolerant and homogeneous neighbourhood
needs of boys and girls at different ages	areas for playing outside for children at various ages, environment that supports the subjective impression of feeling safe, good infrastructure for individual mobility (public transport, cycle path network)
needs of parents as working adults	modern and prestigious housing conditions (including atmosphere), acquisition of property, good infrastructure for individual mobility (mainly by car), proximity to parking areas, supply with convenience goods, workplaces, and facilities for recreation as well as cultural and administrative infrastructure, availability of family and friends

Table 1: Needs of family members (source: Tintemann 2015, with reference to Danielzyk et al. 2012 and Faller et al. 2009).

In the following context, 'family' describes the social form of two generations living together in one household consisting of adults responsible for care and having parental authority as well as their underage children. Because of their special social relevance, their heterogeneous structure and the high dynamic of internal change, families are – compared to other types of households – different. The biography of family households shows a permanent ongoing change.

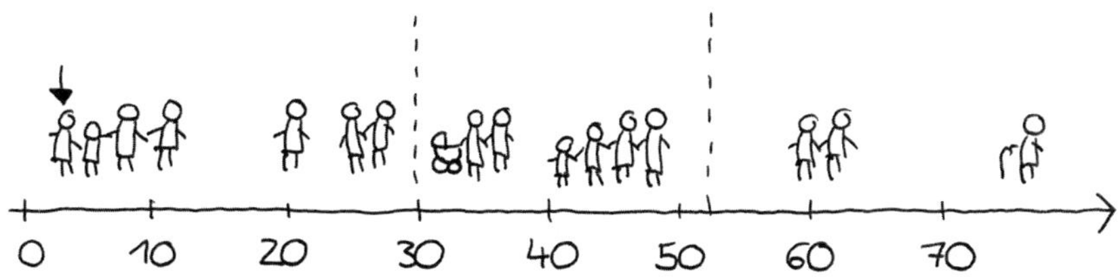

Figure 2: Biography of family households (author's illustration).

Since the main effect of changing gender orders is an increasing employment of mothers, saving or rather gaining time to integrate the different trajectories in the course of the day is the parents' main task. While the Fordist household arrangement had implied the mother-housewife as temporally fully flexible resource to coordinate every need that came up, women are now subject to their own employment structure and thus no longer available without restrictions. The same restrictions are valid for single parents, too.

Strategy	Effect	Example
proximity	reducing time for commuting	A shop near the workplace saves time to go on errands.
flexibility	optimising time lapse with the aim to integrate more activities in one timeslot	Longer opening hours of shops make it possible to shop supplies after work.
externalisation	delegating activities to save time and to synchronise several duties	Catering saves time for buying and cooking food.
rationalisation	reducing activities	Bulk buying and stockpiling minimise the number of trips to shops.
boundary-extending behaviour	multifunctional places help avoid commuting.	Eating at the workplace reduces commuting time and work at home.

Table 2: Time saving strategies of employed parents (source: based on Ludwig et al. 2000).

Families' everyday life in the urban and suburban setting

So, how do families in the two different settings organise these issues? Which strategies are possible? How does this relate with their lifestyle preference on the one hand and with the spatial specificities of an inner-city flat and those of a suburban single-family home on the other hand?
As usual, the first contact with the interviewees already generated differences that had to do with the social structures of the localities: In the suburb of Neuss-Allerheiligen, the contact to the families was easy to make because everybody seemed to know each other and the first interviewed family organised further interview contacts. Via such snowballing the sample could be established smoothly.
Against this, a personal approach was not successful in the inner-city district of Düsseldorf-Pempelfort. Thus, I approached this setting via an institution as intermediary, namely the head of a kindergarten and the developer corporation Interboden who contacted families that might be interested in taking part.

Figure 3: Places for interviews: private and calm on the outskirts, public and lively in the city (author's illustration).

I left it up to the families to choose the place for the interviews. It is telling that ultimately all interviews in the suburb took place at the homes of the families, whereas I met the families in the inner-city district at public places (like cafés) of their choice. The only exception were the families I interviewed in the new flats of the corporation *Interboden*. This can be interpreted as information on the basic communicative and social structures in question: While families in the suburb know each other and the households act together towards me as a stranger addressing them, in the inner-city district this integrative dynamic comes from such different institutions as a kindergarten (public). On top of that, the families in new habitations seemed to be proud to show me their homes and abundance of space.

The interviews then provided information about how families live in and around their homes and how they find solutions for fulfilling their needs concerning space and time. Since it is evident that requested qualities like space, safety requirements for children's mobility, and a greener environment are rather found in suburban areas, it is interesting to concentrate on the families' time

Figure 4: Neuss-Allerheiligen (Photo: Inken Tintemann).

Figure 5: Düsseldorf-Pempelfort (Photo: Inken Tintemann).

saving strategies and their connection with the place of living. Here, the urban area is supposed to offer better conditions and more possibilities due to its dense structure. Externalisation or delegation is one strategy to save time. As Siebel (2010) stated, the urban areas seem to offer many opportunities for this. Though also the suburb benefits from attributes that support externalisation caused by the socioeconomically homogeneous milieu and the safe environment of newly built estates.

Parents trust in the child-safe environment with reduced car traffic and the converging interests of neighbours who all have children, too. The close contact among families, among each other and, furthermore, the relationship with their grandparents is of great importance. Surprisingly, families often emphasise that they move back to the place of their childhood in a suburban area where the grandparents still live. While in the suburb the high costs for a home and the high number of family homes generate a certain homogeneity of the residential area that again makes the parents trust in each other, families in the city integrate into a kind of community by meeting at special public places like greens and playgrounds. The families' terms for these places are 'Kontakthöfe' (literally: contact yards) and 'Oasen' (literally: oases).

It is surprising that such different structures like the play street in the suburban case and a playground in the inner city both bear a similar social form: families who trust each other and act together. The following quotes from the interviews illustrate these specificities of externalisation.

Nordpol family,[1] Düsseldorf-Pempelfort (inner-city)

'The Service-Point (a facility in the residential complex) accepts parcels when you are not at home at daytime. And they organise everything – your whole life if you want to: they arrange a house or window cleaner, they take you to the airport or to the doctor. They offer a huge portfolio. We have a cleaner.'

Dora family, Düsseldorf-Pempelfort (inner-city)

'The local playground is a big reason to live here. It was a monastery garden before. It's so beautiful! And it has only one entrance. You have a good overview and even small children can move freely. It even has a small coffee bar and a toilet [...]. It's the place where everybody meets, one parent takes care of the children and the others can do some purchase.'

Paul family, Allerheiligen (suburb)

'The really positive side effect is the nice neighbourhood. The children can move freely. Sure, sometimes you put your head out of the window. There's always somebody. Everybody keeps an eye on every child. Whenever there is a car approaching, everybody shouts "Attention!".'

Julius family, Allerheiligen (suburb)

'My mother already told me years ago that they will build another new single-family house nearby. At first that was not interesting for us. But then we said: Why not! And now, when a child is ill, I always think: Wow! What a good decision. I'm so lucky! I drive my kid to its grandma, and they both love it.'

Another way to save time is to cross the boundaries of the mono-functional space. Thanks to a comfortable number of rooms and square metres in suburban single-family houses, families can in many cases afford to work and live under the same roof. So, parents can set up a home office or a workshop. In the city, it seems to be the other way round. Here, the function of the living room is transferred to the public space outside. Restaurants and cafés are not only places for consumption but also for meeting people instead of meeting them at home, where the rooms are comparatively small. As mentioned above, these practices already revealed themselves to me when I arranged the interviews; here are some more concrete examples that have been told:

Julius family, Allerheiligen (suburb)

'I work in my workroom. Every client has a folder. I need to build towers with these folders, something I would never do in the living room. Furthermore, my children have priority. If one of them is ill, it's ok. Then it stays at home and I work less.'

Dora family, Düsseldorf-Pempelfort (inner-city)

'For more than half of the year you can stay outside in front of some nice cafés, soup kitchens, bars, restaurants and chill out with your friends.'

Flexibility helps organising life, too. Flexibility means arranging the tasks of the day in a ranking that makes everything fit in. In the suburb, commuting time is a problem. If the employment allows you to start work very early in the morning, the risk of traffic jams is reduced, and as a result of an earlier return home, parents gain time for family duties or leisure activities. In the urban area, families benefit from extended opening hours of public institutions and suppliers like supermarkets, medical and child care institutions. As the families reported:

Paula family, Allerheiligen (suburb)

'My husband works in Leverkusen. He drives about half an hour every day. He starts very early. Usually, he leaves home around 6:00 a.m.'

Ludwig family, Düsseldorf-Pempelfort (inner-city)

'Nearby are many shops with extended opening hours. From organic bread to cocaine – you are supplied with everything 24 hours, seven days a week [...]. You don't have to plan what to do next [...]. Everything I want is next door.'

The typical advantage of the city is proximity to an abundance of facilities and offers thanks to its dense and multifunctional structure, while for suburban families, travelling long distances between different functional structures is common. In this context, saving time is possible thanks to the car-friendly infrastructure and the strategy of rationalisation, e.g. bulk buying. While families in the urban environment have the opportunity to go on errand as a joyful activity in the near vicinity or at the market, those in the suburbs tend to buy all goods for the family household for the whole week at a place where everything is available at once in order to reduce trips and save time. It depends on the individual lifestyle if this practice is considered a joyful activity as well.

Ida family, Düsseldorf-Pempelfort (inner-city)

'We live in the middle of the quarter: In this direction it is five minutes by bike to the nursery and in that direction, it is five minutes to the nanny. That means that I can pick up both kids within ten minutes. Perfect!'

Julius family, Allerheiligen (suburb)

'I have no time for shopping. I only drive to the "Moselstraße". There is Deichmann, Intersport, dm, Strauss, Media Markt, and Toys'R'Us as well as an Edeka supermarket. There are car parks, so you can just pop in. The children love it. It's easy to reach. I drive through the countryside. It's not near, but it's practical. I never thought I would go for it like that.'

Friedrich family, Allerheiligen (suburb)

'Time with my children is important to me, especially since I am employed. So, we have all standard products in stock. I freeze cold meals. Only cheese I do not freeze. But everything else is frozen and defrosted if needed. Everything – even vegetables. Only fruit is difficult. That's where we have to restrain ourselves. Well, Saturdays are for bulk buying.'

Conclusion: single-family homes – there's life in the old dog yet!

In sum, the comparison underlines how families in the urban as well as in the suburban housing developments each make the most of the specific structures. With regard to the strong presence of Fordist ideals of family life, it has to be underlined that the families are no longer following a single pattern or ideology but satisfy their needs quite pragmatically. That Fordist ideals are no longer hegemonic could be detected in the interviews with the families living in inner-city areas as well as in the suburbs. Families are interpreting spaces in new ways, modify their functions, make them fit, and organise their everyday life. The cultural significance of individual lifestyles seems to be increasing, whereas strong cultural patterns like the homestead ideology lose their binding force. More than suburban settlements do, urban areas benefit from this trend, because they offer various possibilities to modify the use of the surroundings. Single-family homes in suburban areas, however, comply more with today's family needs than expected (or hoped for), but for other reasons. Compared with urban dwellings, the possibilities for new technical or design standards and more living space are better, and there are also possibilities for combining child care and employment. As the research shows, families need to externalise. In the suburban setting, the practice of extending networks was very common: As many of the parents in the study grew up in this very suburban setting themselves, they were able to build a well-organised supporting network (old friends and grandparents). Some even ventured into establishing 'multi-generational' households in a development area where individual living concepts can be realised made-to-measure. Many positive effects like informal circles of support grow out of the homogeneity in newly built housing estates. All families are in a similar stage of life with similar challenges and needs. They recognise each other as like-minded and trust each other. Parents tend to share responsibility in this ambiance. In inner-city residential areas, this need is increasingly satisfied by specialised locations where like-minded persons meet, tie social networks, and where everyday life can be extended into public space.

Figure 6: Places with social control to supervise playing children: suburban play street and urban 'Kontakthof' (author's illustration).

The public space has an importance in any sense for those living in the cities. Many activities are possible here, but there is no alternative anyway. Caused by the decrease of private space, families share public spaces, e.g. to set up washing machines in the basement, to meet friends, enjoy green ambiance. Besides its advantages of more variety and diversion, the transfer of daily routines into the public space requires compromises and frequent change of location, while the single-family home provides space for many daily tasks and needs in only one integrated space unit.
An advantage of the urban setting is its density, which allows parents to enlarge the time slots in their daily schedules and gives them more opportunities for their multiple activities. Shops and other infrastructural facilities like gyms, hospitals, and even for child care are open up to 24 hours and reachable in a short time.
So, more activities can be fitted into the day without time constraints. Consequently, more leisure time is available for extra activities and less activities

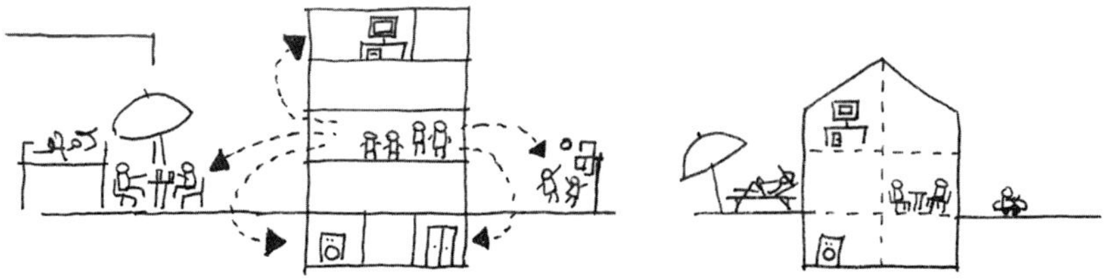

Figure 7: Private garden/'living space miracle' in suburban areas – 'oasis'/unlimited functions in urban areas (author's illustration).

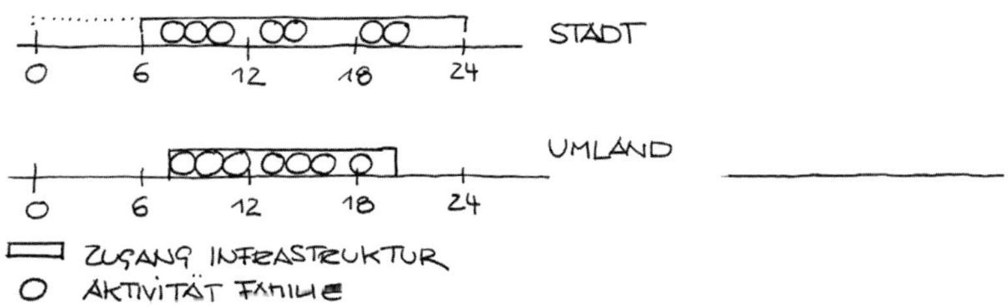

Figure 8: Daytime with access to infrastructure for family activities in city/suburb areas (author's illustration).

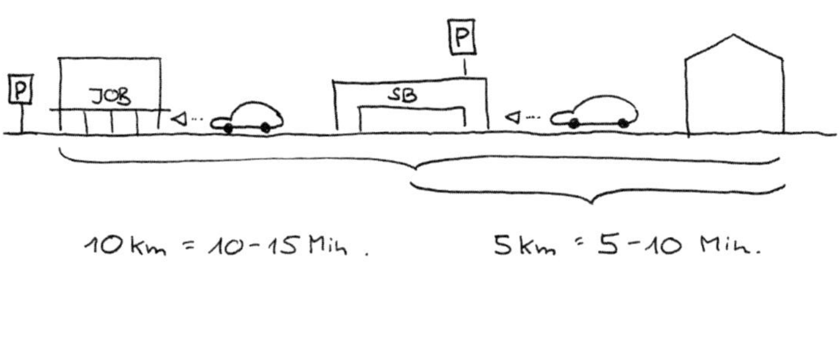

Figure 9: Optimised individual motor traffic in suburban areas (author's illustration).

overlap. The motorcar-adapted infrastructure of the suburbs allows saving time due to fast reachability. It won't be easy to exceed this advantage.
As the individual strategies of families living in the suburban setting underline, especially new single-family housing estates are still attractive for families: There is a high chance for parents to find other people who live in a similar situation they can cooperate with and who tolerate their living situation with noisy and lively children. There are stable advantages of achieving a suitable and affordable life. More than expected, time saving strategies can be identified, that solve the problems of combining employment of both partners with family life.
This evidence proves that planners have to expect that the demand for residential areas will probably persist and be renewed with every generation. Although this type of living emerged and spread in the Fordist decades, families adapt it to new types of everyday routines that are typical for a more flexible relationship of employment, care work, and leisure. This means that the challenge of reducing land use for housing estates and its negative consequences has not been solved yet. Another problem are the ageing suburban family houses. Every new plot of a single-family home will lose attractiveness as soon as the first homogenous cohort has grown up. A big challenge will be to keep older existing suburbs alive and attractive. First exploratory research is occupied with this. Possibly, the changing self-conception of families nowadays will generate new forms. While for a long time leaving the single-family home, which had become a sort of intimate consumer good, was unthinkable,[2] there is a trend towards reorganising social life with friends and changing the living space. For these changes, old suburban areas have to be adapted and are recently perceived anew as a structural and material resource.[3]
All in all, the good news is that more and more dense inner-city quarters are an accepted alternative for families who prefer to stay in an urban area. Their structures offer a growing number of possibilities for families, like a good infrastructure that allows to save time and to optimise compatibility of job and family. However, with housing prices skyrocketing, it is up to the public sector to conceive it as its task to establish a framework that finally supports the reurbanisation of families. While public infrastructure investments in areas for suburban detached houses have been paid for decades in Germany as a matter of course, public expenses for inner-city environments with a special focus on families are far from being self-evident.
Thus, as the last conclusion of this comparative research, I would recommend municipal planning and municipal politics to provide attractive and suitable inner-city living spaces – especially for families. As an example, infrastructure

for families has to be optimised especially regarding facilities in public spaces that can substitute the lack of private space. In parallel, we have to keep an eye on the old suburban single-family housing areas. As the biography of the family (fig. 2) shows, the need of a family home only exists for a short period in life, but it generates an enduring architectural structure. Very soon, new family homes lose their original function, because they don't accommodate the family of the first generation anymore. The advantage of a homogenous population in these housing estates turns into a demographic problem. To make them as attractive for families as new housing developments, strategies are necessary to signalise a second and third generation of families that older estates can be family homes, too. Attributes like heterogeneity and the lack of being 'new' are comparable to urban places. Successful developments like 'Kontakthöfe' and castling concepts transferred from solutions we find in the cities could be feasible answers.

References

Amt für Statistik und Wahlen der Landeshauptstadt Düsseldorf (ed.) (2017), 'Düsseldorf kompakt', https://www.duesseldorf.de/fileadmin/Amt12/statistik/stadtforschung/download/stadtbezirke/Duesseldorf_kompakt.pdf (accessed August 2018).

Beckmann, K. J. et al. (2007), 'Akteure, Beweggründe, Triebkräfte der Suburbanisierung', BBR Online Publikationen 21 (accessed 7 February 2019).

Brake, K. and Herfert, G. (eds.) (2012), Reurbanisierung. Materialität und Diskurs in Deutschland (Wiesbaden: Springer VS).

Danielzyk, R.et al. (2012), 'Wohnstandortentscheidungen von Familien mit Kindern. Trendverschiebungen im Zuge der Spätmoderne', in N. Weixlbaumer (ed.): Anthologie zur Sozialgeographie. Wien (Abhandlungen zur Geographie und Regionalforschung, 16), 9–34.

Ehrenbrusthof, N. (2005) 'Die Innenstadt als Wohnort für Familien. Eine Fallstudie am Beispiel von Familien im Berliner Stadtteil Prenzlauer Berg', (PhD diss., Humboldt-Universität zu Berlin), unpublished.

Faller, Bernhard et al. (2009), Stadt als Wohnort für Familien. Ergebnisse der ExWoSt Studie "Strategien und Aktionsfelder für städtisches Wohnen von Familien" (Bonn: BMVBS/BBSR).

Ludwig, I. et al. (2002), Managerinnen des Alltags. Strategien erwerbstätiger Mütter in Ost- und Westdeutschland (Düsseldorf: edition sigma).

Menzl, M. (2007), Leben in Suburbia. Raumstrukturen und Alltagspraktiken am Rand von Hamburg (Frankfurt/Main: Campus).

Schork, C. and Weeber, R. (2011), 'Umzugsmobilität und Bildungswanderung. Städte gewinnen durch Zuwanderung von jungen Erwachsenen', Planerin, 52–53.

Siebel, W. (2010), 'Impulsvortrag zum Thema Stadt', in Landesinitiative StadtBauKultur NRW (ed.): Stadt:Mensch:Heimat: Die Zukunft unserer Städte: Kongress des Ministeriums für Bauen und Verkehr des Landes Nordrhein-Westfalen Bonn, 25. Januar 2010, Dokumentation, https://stadtbaukultur-nrw.de/projekte/stadt-mensch-heimat/ (accessed 7 February 2019).

Stadt Neuss (2018) 'Eckdaten zur Bevölkerung', https://www.neuss.de/wirtschaft/statistiken/bevoelkerung/eckdaten-zur-bevoelkerung (accessed August 2018).

Tintemann, I. (2015) City oder Suburb. Wohnoptionen für Familien im gesellschaftlichen Wandel, untersucht in Düsseldorf-Innenstadt und Neuss-Allerheiligen, http://www.pt.rwth-aachen.de/files/dokumente/pt_materialien/city%20oder%20suburb%20pt-materialien_35.pdf (accessed August 2018).

Umweltbundesamt (2018) 'Flächen sparen. Böden, Landschaften erhalten', https://www.umweltbundesamt.de/themen/boden-landwirtschaft/flaechensparen-boeden-landschaften-erhalten#textpart-1 (accessed August 2018).

Endnotes

1 All names have been changed for anonymisation.

2 See the contributions by Caplan/Wagenknecht and by Wagenknecht in this volume.

3 See the articles by Cantauw and by Flamme/Walter in this volume.

Build or buy? A qualitative comparison of housing preferences in single-family home areas in northwestern Germany

Anne Caplan
Katherin Wagenknecht

In recent years, scholars and urban planners have devoted increasing attention to single-family home developments of the 1950s to 1980s (for example, Adam et al. 2017; Lachmann 2004; Feldmann et al. 2007). A distinct field of knowledge and action has emerged from the combination of a widespread desire among families (especially young families) for new-build homes and the efforts of municipalities to minimise land use, exploit existing building stock within the locality, and repurpose areas of ageing single-family housing.[1] Studies initially set out to document and examine the extent and nature of the existing stock and of migration decisions (for example, Menzl 2007; Driessen 2010, Münter 2011; from a broader historical perspective with an outline of the issues also Harlander 2001; Hnilica and Timm 2017). More recent research on planning has frequently shown that municipal authorities are confronted with value judgements – coming from both local politicians and individual residents – that favour new-build homes, making it more difficult to encourage other, more flexible forms of housing and the utilisation of existing building stock (Schiller et al. 2009; Dieterich et al. 2006). The present chapter adds depth and nuance to this field of research by using qualitative and comparative methods to examine the building of new single-family homes and the purchase of existing (or 'second-hand') single-family homes. Our focus is on the family lifestyles and cultural values that are associated with the different types of housing, in a more fine-grained analysis of the different desires for old and new buildings that may provide particularly important knowledge for the domain of municipal planning. Our study also takes account of three different types of locality: a rural village shaped by agriculture, a housing development in a medium-sized town, and a suburban district of a larger city. The qualitative investigation covered a total of forty cases, all families living in detached, single-family houses. In each of the areas studied, we interviewed families who had built a single-family house in the preceding ten years and families or couples who had purchased an existing building in the same locality.[2]

In the following, we briefly present the areas under investigation as contextual information, although the distinctions between them are not the main focus of our analysis.[3] Our chosen rural, agricultural locality is Ohne, a village with a population of 587 in 2016.[4] Ohne is part of the county of Bentheim, located in the south of Lower Saxony on the border with North Rhine-Westphalia. Its nearest city is Münster, 45 km away. The autobahn and the amenities of daily life are 8 km away. The village grew by twenty individuals in the years between 2003 and 2008.[5] In the past ten years, two new housing developments in Ohne have been put out for tender. One of them is on the northern edge of the village, and extends its surface area; the second, Volkers Kamp, is more central, part of a project to develop the south of the locality, and densifies the village.[6] At Volkers Kamp, eleven building plots, between 389 und 936 square metres in size,[7] were created in collaboration with Bentheim's land and development corporation GGB.[8] The price per square metre is €67.50.[9] According to the owner-builders themselves, each had to raise between €150,000 and €250,000 to finance their new-build single-family homes. The prices of existing homes were – again according to the owners – between €55,000 and €200,000. In the county of Bentheim, the average annual taxable income in 2010 was €27,500.[10]

Our investigation in a mid-sized town took place in Rorup, a community of 2,270 people that was incorporated into Dülmen in 1975.[11] Dülmen is a medium-sized town with a population of 46,000.[12] Rorup's administrative status as part of Dülmen is not reflected in its geography: the district is located 8 km away from the main part of the town. In the period from 2006 to 2012, Dülmen's population dropped by 1,102.[13] The new housing area where the interviews were carried out has a total of forty-seven plots. It is Rorup's third expansion area since 1980, when the 'Schlüters Heide' development was launched.[14] The plots are sized between 400 and 600 square metres. The price of building land was €160 per square metre in Dülmen and €130 in the Rorup district;[15] the municipality of Dülmen offers price reductions for households with children.[16] According to our interviews, the new single-family houses in Rorup cost each owner-builder between €180,000 and €290,000. The need for building plots is not yet satisfied, and due to the continuing high demand of young families for plots of this kind, the municipality recently identified a further area for constructing single-family homes.[17] Existing single-family houses in Rorup, built in the 1960s to 1990s, are priced at between €155,000 and €250,000. According to the buyers, improvements to these homes cost between €30,000 and €200,000. The average annual income per taxpayer in Dülmen in 2010 was €33,732.[18] The suburban area investigated in our study is Wolbeck, a district numbering 9,200 residents in the south-east of Münster, northern North Rhine-Westphalia.[19] Wolbeck was incorporated into Münster, a city of currently 310,039 residents, in the course of local government restructuring in 1975.[20] By 2040, Münster's population is predicted to rise by 16.6 percent,[21] and the suburb of Wolbeck is growing as well: in 2014, 8,981 residents were registered in Wolbeck, but by 2015 the figure had already risen to 9,213.[22] In the past ten

Ohne/County of Bentheim (rural area)	**Rorup/Dülmen (small town)**	**Wolbeck/Münster (suburban area)**
587 inhabitants	2,270 inhabitants (Dülmen: 46,000 inhabitants)	9,200 inhabitants (Münster: 310,000 inhabitants)
Increase 2003-2008: 20 persons	Decrease 2006-2012: 1,100 persons	Increase 2014-2015: 232 persons (forecast Münster till 2040 +16.6 percent)
Distance to Münster: 45 km	Distance to Dülmen: 8 km	Distance to Münster: 11 km
2 development areas in the last 10 years	3rd extension since the development of the construction site in 1980	Several development areas in the last 10 years (northern fringe of Wolbeck)
Price per square metre: 67.50 €	Price per square metre: 130.00 €	Price per square metre: 300.00 €
Average plot size (new): 390-940 sq m	Average plot size (new): 400-600 sq m	Average plot size (new): 300-500 sq m
Average costs for new buildings: 150-250,000 €	Average costs for new buildings: 180-290,000 €	Average costs for new buildings: 185-330,000 €
Average costs for existing buildings: 55-200,000 €	Average costs for existing buildings: 155-250,000 €	Average costs for existing buildings: 200-410,000 €
Average taxable income (in 2010): 27,500 €	Average taxable income (in 2010): 33,700 €	Average taxable income (in 2010): 37,100 €

Table 1: Socio-economic profile of the research areas, sources: see p. 121.

years, several development plots have been put out to tender on the northern edge of Wolbeck. In 2015, the average price of building land for single-family homes in Münster was more than €300 per square metre. The average taxable income for the city in 2010 was €37,105.[23]

The dream of your own home is the dream of a new build

Our qualitative analysis of the interviews in Northwest Germany shows that living in a home of one's own is essentially equated with building a new house. This becomes particularly clear in the statements of those homeowners who decided to buy a 'second-hand' building: they always reference their decision against the new-build option. Many of these owners of older buildings denigrate the home they have purchased or describe it as a compromise reached because a new build would have been unaffordable.

In 2011, the Flasberg family bought a house built in 1997 in the village of Ohne. As their narrative indicates, the Flasbergs believe that a new build would have cost more, and that the expenses associated with an existing building are more stable or at least more manageable and predictable:

bw24: 'So, in your case, the costs didn't get out of hand?' // Herr Flasberg: 'Yes, that's the great advantage when you buy a finished house or let's say an older existing house, you know exactly: this and this will cost this and this, and if I want to alter something, I can calculate it better than if I was building a whole new house.'

Herr Flasberg's idea of the second-hand single-family home combines the possibility of individualising the house with greater control over costs. For the Reißner family, too, the assumed higher cost of a new build was the reason to choose an existing property. The home that the family really envisaged was not feasible within their financial constraints. Instead, the Reißners bought a single-family house in Rorup, built in 1975, for €135,000. Since the purchase in 2012, they have invested a total of €30,000 in conversion and modernisation work. Herr Reißner is a master craftsman in a plumbing company; Frau Reißner works part-time as a bookkeeper. They have two sons. Frau Reißner describes the decision to buy an existing home and the search for a suitable house to buy as circuitous. First, the family had to face the fact that their dream house was unaffordable:

Frau Reißner: 'Yeah, and then, via a few detours, we arrived at this house here, and in the end [...] we made it our house, because actually it's not really our dream house in the way we would have liked. You can't afford it. [. . .] No, that's a bit mean, but I thought, well, that's not my house, no. It's not – it's nice, it's a, what's it called, a heritable leasehold, that's it, it's nice. It's a nice house, but it's not really my dream, right? And that's why I wouldn't really say, look, this is exactly what I wanted. I think the basement will be just as I'd like it to be, because we rebuilt it completely, and I think – but it's not that I'm saying. Some people might build a home themselves or really, really care about it. It's not our plan to grow old here.'

Frau Reißner takes a rational approach to her financial options: a new-build home in the desired location was not affordable, so the family bought an existing building as a compromise. In terms of cultural values, it is relevant that the new build remains virtually unquestioned as the reference point for the family's decision. Frau Reißner equates a dream home with a newly build home – it is only the basement of her own, second-hand house that fulfils her expectations, because it has been 'rebuilt completely'. Here we see that second-hand house, unlike a newly built one, cannot be a dream home.

The cultural ideal of private homeowners is a new build, designed according to their own ideas and wishes, which they assume would be perfectly adapted to their needs. Purchasing an existing home, in contrast, seems to be just a second choice. In the interview, Frau Reißner dissociates herself from her property, an effect reinforced by her implication that a person would 'care about' a new build more, having built it themselves. Being less attached to her second-hand house, she plans to seek a different home for her old age, possibly even leaving the area. The second-hand house features here as a useful commodity for a particular phase of life. Frau Reißner comments that it is 'not my house'. This is partly due to the legal situation: the plot is subject to a heritable building right (*Erbbaurecht*),[25] so that the family does not own the land but leases it. For Frau Reißner, a house can only be a dream home if it is built on land that one owns. 'Nice' is as far as she is willing to go in her evaluation of the second-hand single-family house on leased land. The Reißners' attitude also indicates that freehold property serves as a cultural demarcation vis-à-vis families who do not own land outright. For them, both land ownership and the house as property are means of distinction.

Newly built owner-occupied homes are considered projects of self-realisation that, as such, can only be brought to fruition on one's own land with the freedom for creativity that this bestows. The Meiers, who built their own home, attach particular importance to this aspect:

Herr Meier: 'Well, even so, we did have another look at existing houses beforehand. A couple here in Rorup, but somehow' // Frau Meier: 'There's no point' // Herr Meier: 'the advantage is that you have a big plot, but you don't have the house the way you want it. That's why we built our own.' // Frau Meier: 'And I think, if you, if we'd had to buy an existing house, and then you have to start renovating it, then you end up paying the same as for a new build, I'd say.'

The Meier family began building their home in Rorup in March 2011. They carried out much of the work themselves, accepting that this would slow down the building process. The overall cost, including the land, was €300,000. For the Meiers, a second-hand home cannot be 'the way you want it'; the desire for a maximally individualised house can only be satisfied by a new build. Frau Lutz gives financial reasons for her and her husband's decision to build a house in Ohne:

kw:26 'Did you also look at existing buildings?' // Frau Lutz: 'We didn't look at them properly, but of course we did have a look on the internet to see what was on the market. But we moved away from that idea quite quickly, because even houses that looked really great from the outside and so on, on the inside you would've had to do so much work, and in Ohne there weren't that many on offer – we would've had to move further away and then you'd have to ask yourself: is it affordable, because the plots are expensive everywhere, aren't they.'

Like Frau Meier, Frau Lutz considers the expense of adapting an existing house to be too high. She also cites the locally specific situation, a dearth of second-hand single-family homes on sale in Ohne.

Overall, it seems that building one's own home is more highly valued than buying an existing building, a judgement shared by both owners of a newly built single-family house and purchasers of a second-hand one. This is indicated on the one hand by the dismissive descriptions of their home provided by the buyers of a second-hand house, who represent their purchase as a second-best solution, and on the other by the owner-builders' categorical rejection of the option of buying an existing house.

Sweat equity and lifestyle: building and modernising a single-family home

Once the future owners have decided whether to build or buy, the process of realisation can begin. The owners' own labour – their 'sweat equity' – proves to play a crucial role for both house types and the construction work associated with them. Our analysis shows that these personal contributions are more than just a way of saving money. Rather, the rationale of the owners' own labour unfolds within two different social and cultural contexts: as an exchange of gifts favouring social integration and investment in the network of local relationships,[27] and as the expression of a particular lifestyle. Personal contributions to construction work that are regularly mentioned in the interviews are manual jobs such as wallpapering, plastering, tiling, and bricklaying. Work of this kind carried out by the homeowner has an additional cultural value in Germany because it is biographically and historically associated with new beginnings in the period of reconstruction after the Second World War – an experience that forms part of personal memories (Rodenberg 2017). Our investigations show that do-it-yourself in an owner-occupied home has a very special significance in the present day as well.

Personal support as a social investment

When they were planning and carrying out their own contributions to the building work, all the families we interviewed made use of available opportunities to mobilise labour and other forms of support, though in different ways:[28]

Frau Müller: 'So a lot of our friends were, um, farmers, they helped us with tractors if we had a huge pile of sand to move or if the stones had to be shifted somewhere, then friends came by with their tractor or with one of those farm loaders. They usually had one of those, too. And they helped with the roof. Because we did the roof ourselves, you see. So, the basic framework of the roof was done by a carpenter, a friend. And then, when it came to the roofing we had all our friends over on one day, and in the evening, we had a barbecue and, well, everyone got sunburnt because it was one of the hottest days of the year, and then, we still have photos of it, our friends took photos of their sunburns.'

The Müllers built a single-family house in Ohne in 2014 and were able to draw on support from friends and relations. Whether they needed a tractor, a trailer, sand or just more helping hands, they first asked around in their familial network. For the most part, according to the Schroer family's account, that network answered the call. The Schroers found their help and support – including, but not restricted to, the loan of machinery or supply of building materials – exclusively in the circle of their relatives. The family built the house and organised itself in the form of an exchange of gifts among relations. This was also the case for the Wiedmanns in the small town of Rorup:

Herr Wiedmann: 'That's how it's always been. Within a family, everyone helps out every now and again, and then you know very well that you're going to help that person another time, and so you don't even think about whether you somehow owe them something or anything like that. You just do it without thinking much about it. That's how it works here.'

The self-evidence that Herr Wiedmann attributes to mutual assistance in these networks shows that the exchange of support circulates within the extended family over a timeframe of many years. Herr Wiedmann's comments describe the functioning of a gift exchange with great clarity. Unlike commodities, the services offered and received in this case are not quantified, immediately paid off or documented as an account to be settled in future; instead, the participants can rest assured that in principle their own contributions will always be answered by gifts in return at some point in the future. The assistance with various construction projects that the Wiedmanns have offered in the past obligates the recipients of those gifts to return the favour, without this having to be put into words. The principle of reciprocal support within the wider family network is self-evident and is fulfilled without further reflection. In this way, the house-building process becomes an element of social integration into a personal network. Through participation in the construction, relationships are created and renewed. The house to be built is thus also an investment in the social capital of the family concerned, in a local setting. As qualitative studies in comparable localities have shown, a relatively low degree of mobility is a significant factor in such networks, because in a more widely dispersed family the 'sweat equity' contributed can be neither invested nor cashed in (see Seiser and Schweitzer 2010 on private house building in a rural area of Upper Austria).

DIY as the actualisation of a lifestyle

In some of the accounts of families who have built their own single-family house in the past ten years, we find another facet of personal contributions to the construction: carrying out building work oneself is part of a lifestyle choice (see Honer 1993: 178; 2011: 155). This exemplified by the case of Herr Meier. Asked how he managed to find the time for his very extensive participation in the construction work alongside a full-time job, Herr Meier replied:

'Well, whenever it fitted in, right? In other words, I did see it as a bit of a hobby as well. You have to, I think, because otherwise it'll break you and maybe that does happen. I don't know, but for me it was fun. Because I'm someone who likes to do a lot myself, and the other option, let's say, we said we want to build a house, and that's why we actually built it. Other people buy one, or they have one built, but I'm not the type who could stand there behind the fence and watch what they're doing, no, that's not me.'

Herr Meier is a scaffolder and describes himself as someone who likes to pitch in rather than just watch other people work – a person who would like to do a lot of the work himself rather than buy something. Building his own home became his hobby and remains so.[29] His own labour forms part of his lifestyle as an owner-builder. He perceives the building of his home as a crucial life project to which he devotes a large amount of time.

Herr Schmidt and his family built a single-family house in Wolbeck in 2010.[30] In his comments, Herr Schmidt stresses his DIY skills, which enabled him to build his own home, and makes the construction sound like a task he set himself as a mechanical engineer. He describes in detail the labour that he contributed to the construction:

'It was obvious to me, I mean, I am a mechanical engineer. What I wanted was to absolutely build it myself, so not to buy a second-hand house. We – partly because we waited quite a long time for this building area. [...] So there haven't been any painters working in this house, we've done it all ourselves. We did the levelling, I helped with the cutting work on the walls. I also did all the [various building tasks] and stuff like that. [. . .] the things you could do with screwing in the OSB panels and stuff like that, I did that myself.'

Unlike the speakers discussed above, Herr Schmidt does not elaborate on the 'we' that he mentions early on, and his narrative soon switches to the first person singular. If the accounts quoted in the previous section always, in terms of both causality and narrative, tie personal contributions to private networks and support, for Herr Schmidt external support plays no role at all. We may conclude that in his case, building his own home does not function primarily as an investment in local networks, but is above all the expression of a DIY habitus as a lifestyle (see Voges 2017b). This particular attribution of meaning to DIY in one's own home can also generate cultural distinction, by demarcating the speaker from those families who buy an existing house or have one built. Frau Reißner, for example, explains:

'Um, it's really surprising, we got rid of this ugly glass partition, the previous owner put that in, and you could open it. He was really proud of it, actually, it really reminded me of a caravan. When you have an old house, and this is an old house, there are just going to be things, and the previous owner did a lot of DIY, and he didn't care that much about some things that my husband does care about.'

To explain the alterations the family has made to the house, Frau Reißner cites divergent tastes and values. The owners of a second-hand house find themselves in constant dialogue with what is already there. By stressing that, in contrast to the previous owner, the Reißners *care* about certain things, Frau Reißner produces an element of distinction. She likens the state of the house when they bought it to a camper van or mobile home, not to a proper house. Another interviewee, Herr Goll, devalorises in a similar way. Finding the features of his 1960s house (incidentally the largest single-family house in our sample, with a living area of 189 square metres) inadequate, he explains this by the period when it was built:

'It's an old house, isn't it, but we're making it new for ourselves and modern and fit for the future. That's right. And that was enough for the most part. What there was downstairs was just, for example, these bathrooms that were built in 1967, 1969, they were really small, they were 2 x 2 m, well we can have a look at that in a minute because what we now have as a guest toilet, that used to be the bathroom.'

The Goll family's budget of €200,000 for renovations and remodelling was intended to modernise the house. Herr Goll gives less weight than Frau Reißner to the individual taste of the previous owner, perhaps in part because the house belonged to a member of his own family, and instead contextualises it historically. The family converted the bathrooms, regarded as too small, into guest toilets, translating them into a new function that symbolises both modernity and affluence. In other words, whereas the Reißners are concerned with adapting the house to their individual taste and values, Herr Goll describes the alterations as necessary adaptations to present-day standards and trends, a move that simultaneously just happens to mark him out as an affluent homeowner: what used to be a whole bathroom is now a mere WC.

An invisible burden and ordeal: financial and practical consequences of the construction phase

One immediate consequence of buying or building a house is a new set of financial and personal burdens. We have already indicated that many purchasers regard second-hand homes as a compromise; they hope this compromise will pay off by imposing fewer daily financial constraints. This attitude is manifested in the way the interviewees portray the process of obtaining the necessary money: those buying existing single-family homes make a point of emphasising that even in their new, larger house they do not experience any restrictions on day-to-day consumption, whereas the owners of new-build homes tend not to discuss financial consequences in detail, stressing instead the great physical and personal efforts and sacrifices they have made in order to build their individual dream home.

The second-hand single-family house in use: functional orientation

When the owners of second-hand homes talk about their loan arrangements and mortgage payments, they accord great importance to calculations that offset their 'second-best' choice, in terms of the financial burden or their own personal input. Either they perceive no financial burden at all in their everyday life or, as in the case of the Borbach family, that burden is attributed to paying off the mortgage faster and thus making far higher payments than would otherwise be necessary:

Herr Borbach: 'So, at the moment we pay out a very high proportion of our salary for the house, more than you should really, based on what you read in finance...' // Frau Borbach: 'But we just want to pay it off relatively fast // but I just want to have it over and done with quickly, and after all, we can still live perfectly well, we can go on holiday, none of us have starved.'

Financial pressures resulting from the house purchase are played down here; after all, nobody has 'starved'. The day-to-day consequences are defined as tolerable and are subordinated to the advantages of quickly becoming debt-free. The owners' desire to minimise the financial burden is typical of the narratives on purchasing second-hand homes. Frau Großkötter, who lives with her family in a house in Wolbeck, explicitly remarks that she did not want to make any sacrifices because of her purchase of a second-hand home:

bw: 'But it makes itself felt, doesn't it, for example that you might have to do without a holiday?' Frau Großkötter: 'No, we don't really have to do without anything, but then we worked all that out in advance, because we both, because we do like to travel, and neither of us wanted to do without that. We somehow managed to budget things so we can still travel.'

Frau Großkötter indicates that the monthly payments for the house were calculated in such a way that the couple would be able to continue taking their usual vacations. Frau Reißner likewise wished to retain some financial scope for everyday consumption despite her house purchase:

'But it was important to us to keep up the same standard of living, you know? That's to say, if we buy a house, we don't want to get into debt or not in a way that means we have to do without anything. We have expensive hobbies and we do very much like living with plenty of money, and we just didn't feel like doing without that.'

Frau Reißner thus insists that a second-hand home must not result in debt, or not in too much debt. Here, debt is seen not as a permanent liability, but as a limit on financial freedom in daily life. Asked to elaborate, Frau Reißner added that despite having taken out a top-up loan, her monthly payments were still lower than the rent she had paid before.

Overall, those families who have bought an existing property say less about restricting their everyday consumption. Their new, second-hand house fits seamlessly into the course of their life. It does not really mark a rupture in their lifestyle, and they do not intend it to constrict or even change that lifestyle – aside from fulfilling their desire for more space.

The new build as a central life project

Unlike the purchasers of second-hand properties, the owner-builders talk about their house as a central life project, one that changes their everyday routines through many different kinds of sacrifice. Frau Schulz stresses the time invested in the house. Her account once again reveals the rejection of compromise as a cultural value held by those favouring the new build:

kw: 'What does that look like in practice, because I suppose you have to choose a lot of things when you build a house like this?' // Frau Schulz: 'That took a lot of travelling around. As you just asked about the plots, no, about the houses. I was looking at this and that and looked at really a lot of houses and facing bricks. My husband and I were on the move a lot, we spent a lot of Sundays, Saturdays, when we said, Oh look at that, and this, and that, and how about that style and that brick, and then I was determined to have this type of brick, the one we have now. Then you had to start thinking about the painting, first it was too white, no I don't like that, then it was too yellow, because the outside windowsills are sandstone and I wanted it exactly that colour, like the sandstone sills, the mortar, you see? So we drove around a lot and we were busy, busy, busy.'

Frau Schulz's comments show how much detail work the construction required. From the facing brick to the mortar to the windowsills, every choice was weighed up separately and compared with other houses. Many weekends, according to the family, were spent just gathering inspiration for the design of their own new home. The Sattlers also emphasised the great demands on their time:

Herr Sattler: 'The problem is simply that you really have absolutely no free time for a year, and you're just either at the building site or at work, and then you're finished, well, put that in quotes. You move in, and then you – then you've run out of steam, then it's – then you can't do any more, that's how it is. And that's just how it is, you know, when...' // Frau Sattler: 'But ok, on the other hand, that means we finished it, doesn't it.'

In this account, the newly built home becomes a project that dominates daily life, absorbing all energy and potential leisure activities. The Sattlers' life during the construction phase was a matter of commuting between his workplace and the building site. Home was only for eating or sleeping, and family chats or short phases of relaxation fell by the wayside. Remarks such as 'you're finished' – in the sense that 'you've run out of steam' and 'can't do any more' – distinguish these accounts from the comments of those buying a second-hand house, who downplay the family's own effort. Instead, the building phase is portrayed as a whole chapter in the family's life, marked by self-denial and constant overwork up to the point of complete exhaustion.[31] For the Müllers in Ohne, too, the building site became almost a temporary home:

Frau Müller: 'I work shifts, and every now and again I had a day off. So and perhaps, when you finished a night shift for example, then you went to the building site. My husband always did that after work. We always met up here, so for a whole year, this was where we spent our life together. Yes, you can say that, that's right.'

Frau Müller explains how she integrated visits to the building site into the rhythm of her shift work. Until the couple finally moved in, the building site was their meeting place. Frau Lutz, who built a house in Ohne with her husband, recounts how the couple organised the construction work to fit around their working days:

Frau Lutz: 'It has really stuck in my memory that we spent every spare moment here at the site. That's because we did a lot ourselves [...]. Exactly, yes, we always went to the building site after work. My husband always went after work or maybe if he had to let someone in or something like that, then he let them in and then went off to work. I sometimes had late shifts and then either I was here before I went to work, and maybe I could do a few small things, maybe tidy up and so on. And otherwise, after work, that's right.'

Unlike the purchasers of an existing house, these interviewees regard their own investment of both time and money as very great and arduous, and they say so unambiguously. For these property owners, the new build has such high value that many other things become less relevant.

The single-family house as retirement plan or family seat

In the homebuilding legislation of the 1950s, the Federal Republic of Germany's policy on owner-occupied homes laid special stress on their contribution to wealth formation (Zimmermann 2001). The period since the 1980s has seen a restructuring of the German welfare state towards responsibilisation. In the context of asset-based welfare in this regime, the habit of equating security with home ownership acquired a new accentuation (see Helbrecht and Geilenkeuser 2010: 976). The notion that property may provide security for old age also finds expression in our interviews. Both the owner builders and the purchasers of 'second-hand' houses contemplate making use of their home in their old age, but they aim to realise this goal in different ways, the distinction being between financial retirement planning and an actual residence for retirement. Whereas the second-hand home is viewed more as a present-day place to live and as available capital, the new build is emotionalised as a home for old age, as a collective family achievement associated with long-term hopes for the owners' residential situation.[32] The preference for a new build is intertwined with the idea of being able to live rent-free and debt-free in one's old age;[33] the owners of second-hand homes expect a financial benefit that will materialise later when the house is sold. While owner-builders view their home as a rent-free residence for their old age, the owners of second-hand houses imagine that in their old age they will sell the house and move into a smaller apartment. The Golls, for example, are thinking of selling their modernised home when they reach retirement:

bw: 'Can you imagine selling it one day?' // Herr Goll: 'We might do in the long run, sure! When you're let's say in your mid-sixties or so, then the garden and all that, to be completely honest, I have to say I probably won't be wanting to do it, well then I could really imagine' // Frau Goll: 'Either it gets sold or one of the children would get it.'

The owners of second-hand homes not only make compromises with their purchase, but also show greater flexibility with regard to the use of their house and a greater willingness for geographical mobility. They can well imagine selling their house and moving to a different area. In addition, our material shows quite concrete reflections on how much will be fetched by the second-hand home, which serves its owners as a financial retirement policy:

Herr Goll: 'We are at – we're currently valued at 240,000 including the land and the house, but I should say that I wouldn't sell it for that. So now we should, if you tot it up, at some point we should get 300,000, over 300,000 euros.'

The example of Herr Goll indicates that in the owner's mind, the value of the house rises with the work put into it, including the owners' own labour, which is why homeowners believe they will obtain a higher price for the house than the one indicated by the mortgage valuation. Here, we begin to see one of the reasons why the development of ageing single-family home areas faces more than merely the financial calculations of the homeowners: the owners' material and immaterial investments, and their personal attributions of value, are articulated in exaggerated ideas of the properties' market value.

In 2009, the Eckert family bought a detached single-family house in Wolbeck built in 1963. In view of rising prices in Münster, they describe their property as 'a good deal':

bw: 'Have you thought at all about possibly selling the house when you get older?' // Herr Eckert: 'I mean, what are you going to do when you reach retirement age, you do have time to do the cleaning, but is that self-fulfilment? No, of course it isn't. I'm not quite as easy-going as my wife is, but I would still say, 'ok, it's had its day', and the way things are looking now it would be a pretty clever decision from a financial point of view as well, and to say 'Everything I'm improving here, everything I'm putting into the house, I'll get it back one day', looking at what's happened to land prices around here and what our neighbours paid for their house, for example. Phew, it's a good deal, no problem.'

The Eckerts see the purchase of their single-family house as a financially 'clever decision'. Their prime concern is not the desire for a place to live for several generations, but rather the prospect of making a good profit when they sell. In this case, the house as an investment good is inextricable from the flourishing property market in Münster. A contrasting situation is found in the case of Herr Ellwanger, who bought a 1930s house in Ohne in 2006. He spent €180,000 on the house purchase and describes this as an investment despite the fact that, even now, he already expects to be able to sell the house for only €100,000 to €150,000, which in fact means the property is a loss-maker:

bw: 'So you definitely hope that to a certain extent the house is an investment for you?' // Herr Ellwanger: 'Yes, if you can get rid of the pile of shit for €100,000 or for €150,000, then you can put it off another ten years, if you keep your head. As an old person, a really small car and somewhere to live, you don't need much more than that.'

Herr Ellwanger does not reflect on the current property market in rural Germany but hopes that selling the house in his old age will enable him to afford a small rented apartment in the region. In the further course of the interview, he explains that he has already decided to move out of the house aged sixty to sixty-five, on the grounds that then he will not need so much space and he does not wish to leave it half-empty. The owners of second-hand homes, then, make quite dynamic plans for the future, including selling the house and moving away in their old age. The owners of new builds, in contrast, tend to emotionalise the building and add an intimate dimension, seeing their property as part of the family's history (Druta and Ronald 2016: 7–10):

Herr Schroer: 'And when I get older, well you don't exactly get fitter, do you, one day. Or because, you can't really say, that's why. On the other hand you think to yourself that you built this yourself, the house, and can you really just simply leave it behind. It's full of so many memories.'

The Schroer family shows a personal attachment to the house because of having built it themselves and imbued it with 'so many memories'. Accordingly, it is very difficult for them to think about alternatives: it remains an open question what will happen to the house when they grow old, how long the house will be inhabited by its first owners. What is certain for the Schroers is that they can't 'just simply leave it behind'. Frau Schmeling, too, sees little reason to leave the home she built in rural Ohne:

kw: 'Do you know how long you want to stay in your house?' // Frau Schmeling: 'Yes, hopefully until we – yes, until we're old, I think, when you really are old, then you have to remodel the house a bit and then maybe convert it for old age, because with a stairlift you can do all sorts of things, we've already got a floor-level shower upstairs, so that won't stop us. With the stairlift, you can probably do something about the stairs as well. Until we're old, really.'

For the Schmelings, the physical ageing process is no reason to leave their owner-occupied home. Rather, they consider adjustments to the building that would make it easier to use. The Meiers from Rorup, too, refer to the physical circumstances of growing old. But Herr Meier notes that because every person grows old differently, it is almost impossible to make plans that would apply across the board:

Frau Meier: 'Oh' // Herr Meier: 'How long. I'm now forty, over forty' // Frau Meier: 'Sixty years.' // Herr Meier: 'Yes, perhaps. Sixty years, that would be good. Yes, well I don't know why I would move out. Of course, it could happen one day. Every person grows old differently, and you'd have to decide when you get to that stage, but now, for the time being, I wouldn't say I plan to move out at this or that time.' // Frau Meier: 'We have neighbours who say 'no, I'm not going to grow old here.' They want to move away one day. But we haven't yet – we haven't thought about it as yet.'

The Meiers jokingly connect living in a single-family house with the dream of being able to stay there to the ripe old age of one hundred. The assertion that 'every person grows old differently' evokes the hope that they may turn out to be part of a spry and mentally alert generation of old people who have no reason to move out of the home they built for themselves. Both the purchase of second-hand properties and the building of new ones involve a 'collective bet on the future' (Bourdieu et al. 1990: 8). The examples we have discussed show that although ideas about the usage of the single-family house in the owners' old age respond to the property and land market situation in each particular case, that is not all: they also convey different cultural evaluations of the commodity nature of one's own four walls. The tendency is for the second-hand property to be a temporarily advantageous object of use, whereas the new-build home is an intimate family possession.

Conclusions

Our study reveals clear differences between the two types of owners in values and attitudes concerning their houses. The new build is portrayed as a lifelong project that changes everyday routine. The 'sweat equity' contributed during construction work has plausibility for the participants as a lifestyle or a project of self-realisation. The newly built house is valued as an intimate, familial, personally configured good. All the owner-builders' resources – whether personal effort, time, or finances – are oriented on this life project, described by the owners as an exhausting and all-absorbing process. The new-build owners feel a close personal tie to the building, also expressed in the fact that they think of their house as a family residence for their old age. The second-hand house, in contrast, is portrayed by its owners as a compromise. The personal efforts rendered are less a means of self-realisation than a necessary expedient in order to adapt the existing building to the owners' requirements. Being a compromise, the property must pay its way financially, and the owners take it for granted that they will invest their own labour. The tribulations of such efforts are accepted as a matter of course and integrated into daily routines. These owners think of their house not as a place to live in their old age, but as a form of financial retirement plan that may entail geographical mobility.

Finally, our data reveal distinctions between different types of location, most importantly between urban and rural areas, that will require more detailed analysis in future research. For example, assistance in the building or conversion of a house was often sourced from the family or neighbours (Menzl 2007: 263–284); however, this finding applies primarily to rural areas, far less so to urban areas. Furthermore, homeowners in the urban setting showed more willingness to compromise in response to rising land and house prices at their place of residence, something that has also been noted for other regions (Münter 2011).

Acknowledgements

This chapter was written as part of the research association 'The Flow of Things or Private Property? A House and Its Objects between Family Life, Resource Management and Museum', led by Elisabeth Timm (WWU Münster, Seminar for Folklore Studies/European Ethnology), funded by the Federal Ministry of Education and Research (BMBF) programme 'The Language of Objects: Conservation, Research and Knowledge Transfer in Cultural Heritage', www.hausfragen.net, funding code 01UO1504A. The empirical data on the newly built single-family homes in the areas investigated come from the subproject 'Building a House for Us: An Ethnography of Family Ideals in Transition'. The empirical data on the second-hand single-family homes in the areas investigated come from the subproject 'As If Made for Us?! Second-Hand Property and Family-Specific Conceptions of Housing and Living', led by Christiane Cantauw (The Folklore Commission for Westphalia at the Regional Association of Westphalia-Lippe LWL), funding code 01UO1504B.

Translated from German by Kate Sturge.

References

Adam, B., Berndgen-Kaiser, A., Jochimsen, K., Münter, A., and Zakrzewski, P. (2017), 'Ältere Ein- und Zweifamilienhausbestände im Umbruch. Eine Clusteranalyse zur Identifizierung regionaler Betroffenheiten in Nordrhein-Westfalen', Raumforschung und Raumordung OnlineFirst. DOI: 10.1007/s13147-017-0479-y.

Bourdieu, P., with Bouhedja, S., Christin, R., and Givry, C. (1990), 'Un placement de père de famille: La maison individuelle: spécificité du produit et logique du champ de production', Actes de la Recherche en Sciences Sociales 81–82, 6–33.

Dieterich, H., Lohr, D., and Tomerius, S. (eds.) (2006), 'Flächenneuinanspruchnahme, demographische Entwicklung und kommunale Finanzen. Auswege aus der Leerkostenfalle?', Jahrbuch für Bodenpolitik 2006/2007.

Driessen, K. (2010), 'Verkehrliche Konsequenzen des Suburbanisierungsprozesses und deren volkswirtschaftliche Bewertung am Beispiel der Region Köln' (PhD diss., RWTH Aachen University).

Druta, O. and Ronald, R. (2016), 'Young adults' pathways into homeownership and the negotiation of intra-family support: A home, the ideal gift', Sociology 51(4), 1–17.

Feldmann, L., Klemme, M, and Selle, K. (2007), Kommunale Planungs- und Entscheidungsprozesse in der Siedlungsflächenentwicklung. Ein Teilprojekt. Ergebnisse im Überblick über sechs Modellkommunen (Aachen: Universitätsbibliothek der RWTH Aachen).

Harlander, T. (ed.) (2001), Villa und Eigenheim. Suburbaner Städtebau in Deutschland (Stuttgart: Deutsche Verlags-Anstalt).

Helbrecht, I. and Geilenkeuser, T. (2010), 'Homeownership in Germany. Retirement strategies of households in a tenant society', Teorija in Praksa 47(5), 975–993.

Hnilica, S. and Timm, E. (2017), 'Das Einfamilienhaus als neue anonyme Architektur. Bestand und Begehren', Zeitschrift für Kulturwissenschaften (1): 15–28.

Honer, A. (1993), Lebensweltliche Ethnographie. Ein explorativ-interpretativer Forschungsansatz am Beispiel von Heimwerker-Wissen (Wiesbaden: Deutsche Universitäts-Verlag).
Honer, A. (2011), Kleine Leiblichkeiten. Erkundungen in Lebenswelten (Wiesbaden: VS Verlag für Sozialwissenschaften).
Lachmann, I. (2004), Endstation Eigenheim. Zur deutschen Einfamilienhausförderung im Spannungsfeld von Raumordnungszielen und Wohnungsbaupolitik (Kassel: Universität Kassel).
Mauss, M. (1990 [1950]), The Gift. The Form and Reason for Exchange in Archaic Societies, translated by W. D. Halls (London: Routledge).
Menzl, M. (2007), Leben in Suburbia. Raumstrukturen und Alltagspraktiken am Rand von Hamburg (Frankfurt am Main: Campus).
Miller, D. (2011), 'Alienable gifts and inalienable commodities', in F. R. Myers (ed.): The Empire of Things. Regimes of Value and Material Culture (Santa Fe: School of American Research Press), 91–115.
Münter, A. H. C. (2011), 'Wanderungsentscheidungen von Stadt-Umland-Wanderern in vier Stadtregionen. Regionaler Vergleich der Muster und Motive, Informations- und Wahrnehmungslücken sowie Beeinflussbarkeit der Wanderungsentscheidung' (PhD diss., Technische Universität Dortmund).
Rodenberg, M. (2017), '"… früher haben die fleißig mitgeholfen …" Selbsthilfe beim Bau von Behelfsheimen und Siedlungshäusern 1943–1965', Hessische Blätter für Volks- und Kulturforschung n.s. 51/2017, 233–243.
Schiller, G., Gutsche, J. M., Siedentop, S., and Deilmann, C. (2009), Von der Außen- zur Innenentwicklung in Städten und Gemeinden. Das Kostenparadoxon der Baulandentwicklung, Dessau-Roßlau. http://www.umweltbundesamt.de/uba-info-medien/mysql_medien.php?anfrage=Kennummer&Suchwort=3858 (accessed 28 August 2017).
Schulze, M. (2012), 'FreiZeitArbeit. Zum Verhältnis von Freizeit und Arbeit anhand der Entstehung des Heimwerkens in Deutschland von 1918 bis 1970', sinnprovinz. Kultursoziologische working papers 1. http://www.sinnprovinz.uni-leipzig.de/tl_files/papers/Sinnprovinz_01_M_Schulze.pdf. (accessed 21 August 2017).
Seiser, G. and Schweitzer, P. (2010), 'Houses, families, and the making of community: the Austrian rural case', in P. Heady and P. Schweitzer (eds.): The View from Below. Nineteen Localities (Frankfurt/Main: Campus), 109–127.
Simon-Philipp, C. (2001), 'Suburbane Wohngebiete. Konzepte zur städtebaulichen Qualifizierung des Ein- und Zweifamilienhauses in der Bundesrepublik Deutschland 1949–1999' (PhD diss., Universität Stuttgart).
Spiritova, M. (2014), 'Narrative interviews', in C. Bischoff, K. Oehme-Jüngling, and W. Leimgruber (eds.): Methoden der Kulturanthropologie (Bern: Haupt), 117–130.
Voges, J. (2017a), '"Mit Geschmack und wenig Geld". Heimwerken als Aneignungspraxis des Einfamilienhauses von den 1950er bis in die 1980er Jahre', Zeitschrift für Kulturwissenschaften (1), 97–115.
Voges, J. (2017b), '"Gut hat's Familie Selbermann, weil sie alles selber kann." Die "Do-it-yourself-Bewegung" in der Bundesrepublik Deutschland als soziales, kulturelles und ökonomisches Phänomen', Hessische Blätter für Volks- und Kulturforschung, n.s. 51/2017, 245–250.
Zimmermann, C. (2001), 'Wohnungspolitik – Eigenheime für alle?', in T. Harlander (ed.): Villa und Eigenheim. Suburbaner Städtebau in Deutschland (Stuttgart: Deutsche Verlags-Anstalt), 330–349.

Sources

Bürogemeinschaft Honnigfort und Brümmer, im Auftrag der Gemeinde Ohne (2009), Dorferneuerung. Gemeinde Ohne, draft April 2009. Haren/Ems.

Information und Technik Nordrhein-Westfalen (IT.NRW) (2010), Einkommen der Lohn- und Einkommensteuerpflichtigen in NRW 2010, https://www.it.nrw.de/presse/pressemitteilungen/2014/pdf/172_14.pdf (accessed 28 September 2017).

Information und Technik Nordrhein-Westfalen (IT.NRW) (2015), Pressemitteilung: Neue Vorausberechnung zur Bevölkerungsentwicklung in Nordrhein-Westfalen: Bevölkerungszahl steigt bis 2025 um ein Prozent, https://www.it.nrw.de/presse/pressemitteilungen/2015/pres_101_15.html (accessed 28 August 2017).

Information und Technik Nordrhein-Westfalen (IT.NRW), Geschäftsbereich Statistik (ed.) (2017), Kommunalprofil Dülmen, Stadt Kreis Coesfeld, Regierungsbezirk Münster, Gemeindetyp: Kleine Mittelstadt, 31 May 2017, Düsseldorf. https://www.it.nrw.de/kommunalprofil/l05558016.pdf (accessed 14 August 2017).

Kreisverwaltung Landkreis Grafschaft Bentheim (2017), Zahlen Daten Fakten 2017/2018. Nordhorn, http://www.grafschaft-bentheim.de/pics/medien/1_1501837457/Zahlenspiegel_2017.pdf (accessed 30 August 2017).

Landesamt für Statistik Niedersachsen (ed.) (2010), Statistische Berichte Niedersachsen. Einkommen der Lohn- und Einkommensteuerpflichtigen und seine Besteuerung 2010, Hannover. https://www.statistik.niedersachsen.de/download/97826 (accessed 28 September 2017).

Landesdatenbank NRW (ed.) (2017), Kommunalprofil Münster, krfr. Stadt, https://www.it.nrw.de/kommunalprofil/l05515.pdf (accessed 22 August 2017).

Landkreis Grafschaft Bentheim, Fachbereich 2, Kreisentwicklung (2013), Der demografische Wandel im Landkreis Grafschaft Bentheim. Nordhorn, http://www.grafschaft-bentheim.de/pics/medien/1_1377684963/Anlage_11_Demografischer_Wandel_in_der_Grafschaft_Bentheim.pdf (accessed 28 August 2017).

NRW Bank (2016), Wohnungsmarktbericht NRW 2016 (Sonderthema: Wird dort genug gebaut, wo neue Wohnungen gebraucht werden?). Düsseldorf, 49, http://www.kas.de/wf/doc/21233-1442-1-30.pdf (accessed 28 August 2017).

Stadt Dülmen (1993), Bebauungsplan Nr. 'Schlüters Heide – Erweiterung, Teil II', Gemarkung Rorup, Stadtbezirk Dülmen-Rorup, Flur 5, www.o-sp.de/download/duelmen/7738 (accessed 28 August 2017).

Stadt Dülmen (2016), Begründung zum Bebauungsplan Nr. 235 'Pastor-Rück-Straße' Gemarkung Rorup, Flur 34, www.o-sp.de/download/duelmen/122601 (accessed 21 August 2017).

Stadt Dülmen, 010 Zentrales Controlling (2014), Strukturdatenbericht der Stadt Dülmen, April 2014, 2. Ed, https://www.duelmen.de/fileadmin/user_upload/duelmen.de/stadtportrait/strukturdatenbericht_stand_2014.pdf (accessed 28 August 2017).

2Stadt Dülmen, Fachbereich 312, Bürgerbüro (2017), Einwohnerstatistik für den Monat Juli 2017, 29 August 2017, https://www.duelmen.de/fileadmin/user_upload/allgemein/medien/buergerbuero/aktuelle_einwohnerstatistik.pdf (accessed 30 August 2017).

Stadt Münster, Amt für Stadtentwicklung, Stadtplanung, Verkehrsplanung, Informationsmanagement und Statistikdienststelle (ed.) (2016), Jahres-Statistik 2016 Bevölkerung, http://www.stadt-muenster.de/fileadmin//user_upload/stadt-muenster/61_stadtentwicklung/pdf/jahr/Jahres-Statistik_2016_Bevoelkerung.pdf (accessed 28 August 2017).

Interviews

New-build homes, interviews carried out by Katherin Wagenknecht

Rorup, Dülmen

Interview Schroer family, 12 November 2015
Interview Meier family, 18 November 2015
Interview Schulz family, 24 November 2015
Interview Sattler family, 19 November 2015

Ohne, Bentheim county

Interview Lutz family, 15 March 2016
Interview Schmeling family, 21 March 2016
Interview Müller family, 11 March 2016

Wolbeck, southeast of Münster

Interview Schmidt family, 6 October 2016
Interview Mahler family, 14 September 2016
Interview Kanichs family, 23 September 2016

'Second-hand' homes, interviews carried out by Benjamin Widholm

Rorup, Dülmen

Interview Reißner family, 7 January 2016
Interview Lehmann family, 30 June 2015
Interview Wiedmann family, 17 December 2015
Interview Goll family, 4 November 2015
Interview Borbach family, 19 November 2015

Ohne, Bentheim county

Interview Ellwanger family, 7 April 2016
Interview Flasberg family, 15 March 2016

Wolbeck, southeast of Münster

Interview Eckert family, 7 September 2016
Interview Großkötter family, 5 December 2016

Endnotes

1 There are currently numerous structural development initiatives in Northwest Germany, such as the project 'Jung kauft alt' ('Young buys old', started in 2007) in the municipality of Hiddenhausen. Funded by the state of North Rhine-Westphalia, this aims to develop the potential of the single-family house estates of the 1950s to 1980s and conserve the buildings' grey energy (see http://www2.hiddenhausen.de/Hiddenhausen/Wohnen/Jung-kauft-Alt, accessed 28 August 2017). Other examples are projects to redevelop ageing single-family housing under the umbrella of the North Rhine-Westphalian 'Regionale 2016' initiative (see http://www.regionale2016.de/de/projekte/projekte/projektkategorie-heimat-landschaft-freizeit/quartiersanpassung-wulfen-barkenberg.html; http://www.regionale2016.de/de/projekte/projekte/projektkategorie-heimat-landschaft-freizeit/wohnzukunft-suedkirchen.html, both accessed 28 August 2017). On the options with recommendations for action, see also Simon-Philipp 2001.

2 We used open, semi-structured interviews, not working through a standardised list but facilitating narratives about the interviewees' everyday life and their choice of a place to live. Accordingly, we do not (or at least not primarily) analyse these data as documenting quantitatively measurable facts, but as illuminating subjective interpretations and cultural values. We base our analyses and conclusions not only on what the respondents said, but also on how they said it – the argumentation and rationales that emerged in their accounts of building or buying their homes. With the exception of place names, all material has been anonymised. On the narrative interview in cultural anthropology, see Spiritova 2014.

3 Other publications by the research association address the specific aspects of life in single-family homes in the various districts (see especially the doctoral research in progress by Katherin Wagenknecht, 'Gebaute Familie').

4 Kreisverwaltung Landkreis Grafschaft Bentheim 2017.

5 See Bürogemeinschaft Honnigfort und Brümmer 2009: 28. The average age in the county of Bentheim was 41 in 2008; it is expected to rise to 47 by 2030. Landkreis Grafschaft Bentheim, Fachbereich 2, Kreisentwicklung 2013.

6 Bürogemeinschaft Honnigfort und Brümmer 2009: 20.

7 Illustrative plot sizes, Grundstücks- und Entwicklungsgesellschaft Landkreis Grafschaft Bentheim mbH 2019.

8 The GGB's full name is 'Grundstücks- und Entwicklungsgesellschaft Landkreis Grafschaft Bentheim mbH'.

9 Sales data on the Volkers Kamp construction area, http://www.ggb-grafschaft.de/pics/medien/1_1449146227/Verk-Daten-VolkersKamp.pdf (accessed 22 August 2017).

10 Landesamt für Statistik Niedersachsen 2010.

11 Stadt Dülmen, Fachbereich 312, Bürgerbüro 2017.

12 The largest age group in the town of Dülmen is sixty-five or above (19.7 percent), the second largest is fifty to sixty (17 percent). Information und Technik Nordrhein-Westfalen, Geschäftsbereich Statistik 2017.

13 See Stadt Dülmen, 010 Zentrales Controlling 2014.

14 Stadt Dülmen 1993.

15 The average price across the state of North Rhine-Westphalia was €142 per square metre in 2016. NRW Bank 2016.

16 https://www.duelmen.de/1588.html (accessed 14 August 2017).

17 Stadt Dülmen 2016.

18 Information und Technik Nordrhein-Westfalen 2015.

19 The largest increase in net immigration to Münster is found in the age group eighteen to twenty-five (mainly students). The disposable income of private households was €22,000 per inhabitant in 2014. Landesdatenbank NRW 2017.

20 Figures dated 30 June 2017, http://www.stadt-muenster.de/stadtentwicklung/zahlen-daten-fakten.html#c36301 (accessed 28 August 2017). Between 2010 and 30 June 2017, Münster's population rose by 30,236. Stadt Münster, Amt für Stadtentwicklung, Stadtplanung, Verkehrsplanung, Informationsmanagement und Statistikdienststelle 2016.

21 See Information und Technik Nordrhein-Westfalen 2015.

22 See Stadt Münster, Amt für Stadtentwicklung, Stadtplanung, Verkehrsplanung, Informationsmanagement und Statistikdienststelle 2016.

23 See Information und Technik Nordrhein-Westfalen 2015.

24 'bw' is the interviewer Benjamin Widholm. A note on the transcripts: the excerpts from the interviews have been translated in a more streamlined form than the original German, which is marked by frequent repetitions, hesitations, and fragmented syntax.

25 In the German *Erbbaurecht*, somewhat similar to leasehold in the UK system, the lessee acquires the right to build a property on land that does not belong to him. Instead of a one-off purchase price, the lessee pays an agreed monthly ground rent. The details and value of this rent are set down in the land register as if the *Erbbaurecht* were itself a property. The right to use the leased land may be sold and bequeathed. The relevant German law, 'ErbbauRG', can be found at https://www.gesetze-im-internet.de/erbbauv/BJNR000720919.html (accessed 18 July 2017).

26 'kw' is the interviewer Katherin Wagenknecht.

27 Following Marcel Mauss theory of the gift, our observations of reciprocal help in construction work may be analysed as follows. All social relationships are structured by particular forms of the exchange of gifts. Mauss noted 'the so to speak voluntary character of these total services, apparently free and disinterested but nevertheless constrained and self-interested. Almost always such services have taken the form of the gift, the present generously given even when, in the gesture accompanying the transaction, there is only a polite fiction, formalism, and social deceit, and when really there is obligation and economic self-interest' (Mauss 1990 [1950]: 4). The gift form does not exist in isolation from the principle of the commodity, and may be embedded in commodity- and market-like relationships. For more detail, see Miller 2011.

28 Personal support for others as a social investment was found primarily in the rural and small-town areas investigated, Ohne and Rorup. In Wolbeck, a suburb of a larger city, it was more of an exception or a marginal phenomenon: the majority of homes belonging to the families interviewed in Wolbeck were built by a construction company and handed over ready for occupancy. The owners' own contribution, or rather their participation in the process of construction, was restricted to regularly inspecting the progress of work.

29 In an article on leisure and work, Mario Schulze (2012) offers a historical view of German DIY, which became established as a private activity or hobby after the First World War. See also Voges 2017a.

30 Unlike the other areas studied, Wolbeck does not show a clear tendency in favour of new construction. Most of the interviewees would have considered buying a second-hand house. This probably reflects a very specific situation in the Münster region: rising land and property prices increase the willingness for compromise among people who want to stay in the region with their family and are seeking a detached home.

31 The construction phase in suburban Wolbeck took a very different form. Whereas some of the families from Rorup and Ohne visited the building site every day, to inspect progress or perform their own manual labour, many Wolbeck families delegated this responsibility to the construction company. Some did not visit the building site of their future home for several weeks at a time.

32 The cultural dispositif of home ownership as a built, familial vision of the future was discussed by Bourdieu in his study of the housing property market in 1980s France. In this account, the house is 'the central element of a *patrimony* which is expected to survive at least as long as its owner, and even to outlive him as a transmissible inheritance'(Bourdieu et al. 1990: 6).

33 Unlike mortgage payments, which indirectly lead to the building up of assets, rent payments (even if they are lower) are represented by the interviewees as 'money lost'. As the financial crisis of 2007/2008 showed, however, this apparently mathematical consideration in fact involves a cultural assumption about the value of owner-occupied homes, which may be countered by market developments. The certainties of supposedly 'wasted' rent and supposedly 'secure' investment in property themselves articulate a cultural order and a particular historical situation.

Old houses become single-family homes: *Bausparkassen*, *Denkmalpflege* and conversion architecture, 1977–2002

Johannes Warda

Among the great German home loan banks, *the Schwäbisch Hall* bank is the most popular. With its iconic brick logo, the smart fox, and the well-known slogan 'Auf diese Steine können Sie bauen – *Schwäbisch Hall*', which roughly translates as 'you can build on these bricks'[1], the bank's name has become the German byword for financing the *Eigenheim*.[2] While popular memory as well as urban history for a long time equated the West German system of financing homeownership by *Bausparkassen* with sprawling suburban areas made up of newly built single-family homes, I will elucidate a hitherto unknown part of these banks' vision of housing.

In 1977, the bank introduced another marketing feature that helped consolidate the brand's popularity: *mosaik*, a customer magazine. From 1977 until 2002, it appeared four times a year. The number of distributed copies ranged between 2.3 and 3.4 million per annum. The magazine was mailed to all bank customers and was available to take away in the branches of the *Genossenschaftsbanken* [German cooperative bank association], located in city centres as well as in small villages. The very first issue featured the historic Eltz Castle on the Moselle River as Germany's 'most beautiful' and 'best preserved' high medieval castle (N.N. 1977). The Eltz Castle article served as the overture to *Schwäbisch Hall*'s love affair with *Denkmalpflege*, *Altbauerneuerung*, and *Stadtsanierung* [historic preservation, refurbishment, and urban renewal]. The home loan bank did not just publish recommendations for recreational outings to heritage sites. Soon, it seems, *mosaik* became a special interest magazine for renovation-related topics. In almost every issue it provided its readers with feature articles about historical buildings and old towns – and thus articulated the general leaning towards different forms of nostalgia at that time. Based on these findings, this chapter seeks to challenge the dominant narrative of the West German home loan policy as resulting in consumerist attitudes forgetful of the environment.

This said, a couple of questions arise as to the entanglement of homeownership and historical buildings and the existing building stock in general: In how far did the concept of the detached single-family home relate to the socio-cultural changes in the 1970s and 1980s? How did the boom of the historic city and the growing interest in old buildings interfere with the popular making of the single-family home as a financial product? The analysis departs from a micro study of refurbishments of single-family dwelling featured in *Schwäbisch Hall's mosaik* magazine: How did the magazine reconcile the topics of old houses and building new homes? What were the editorial strategies of presenting old buildings in *mosaik*? Which topics emerged alongside the introduction of the old building theme? And why was *Schwäbisch Hall* interested in old buildings at all? This chapter presents a close reading of architectural reality edited by *mosaik* magazine between its first issue in 1977 and its relaunch in 2002, when the magazine was renamed *house and more*, unveiling a multifaceted story of home loan banks, conversion architecture and diversifying lifestyles.

Financing and popularising renewal and conversion: endeavours in 1970s and 1980s lifestyles

The fact that *mosaik* began to appear in 1977 coincides with fiscal regulations which were important for financial products offered by *Bausparkassen*. Following a growing general interest in urban renewal, West German federal legislation from then on promoted the renovation and purchase of old buildings. The *Gesetz zur Förderung der Modernisierung von Wohnungen* (WoModG 1976, or housing modernisation act) was introduced, which subsidised housing renovation and retrofitting of new routines and functions concerning layouts, heating, sanitarian and kitchen facilities etc. Additionally, the income tax regulations were revised to allow tax deductions for building renovation costs. Two years earlier, in 1975, the European Cultural Heritage Year marked a peak in the popular and political awareness of the many threats modernist renewal policy of that time meant for the built heritage (Petzet 1975). Grassroots movements in many European cities took issue with the prevailing practice of replacing historic inner-city quarters with mass housing and commercial buildings (Baumeister et al. 2017).

The arising movements ranged from anti-demolition protests to house squatting to experimenting with alternative and participatory planning processes. In cases such as the International Building Exhibition Berlin (IBA) in the 1980s, DIY renovation projects and cooperation with house squatters even became part of the official municipal renewal policy. The obsession with old buildings at that time went far beyond the common cause of historic preservation. Moreover, a growing awareness of the transformative capacity of old buildings in general developed, which is expressed in numerous publications on architectural conversion, ranging from one of the first coffee-table books (Cantacuzino 1975) to Claus Arendt's (1977) 'Altbau-Erneuerung', the first German language DIY guideline of its kind. Right away, the first issue of *mosaik* published in early 1977 informed its readers about the new tax benefits for their investments in old building upgrades, featuring an interview with West Germany's secretary of finance (N.N. 1977a and c). The legal criterion for the tax incentives supporting modernisation projects referred to buildings as 'old' after a life span of 20 years, which is a common period of time for regular modernisation work. Yet soon, *mosaik* went even further and turned to much older buildings. The magazine portrayed *Schwäbisch Hall* clients and their renovation projects, covered urban renewal campaigns in small and medium-sized West German cities, and featured home stories with celebrities of the time.

The magazine premiered with a cover story about popular German actor Gustav Knuth and his wife (who actually lived in Switzerland). Knuth was famous for playing down-to-earth characters at the *Ohnsorg Theater* in Hamburg (which stages plays in Low German) and in 1970s German TV series with local colour. The second issue featured a story about actress and author Barbara Rutting's renovation project, an old farmhouse in the foothills of the Salzburg Alps. Rütting and her husband, Lutz Hochstraate, then director at the *Schauspielhaus Salzburg*, bought the run-down farmhouse in the late 1960s and made it their new home. During the hard work of renovating, Rütting says, she became a farmer: 'The farm has changed our life' (Recht 1977: 13, 15). Apparently so, Rütting also became a pioneer of the postmodern whole-food movement. Her organic cuisine cookbook, in which she shared the experience of living in the countryside, soon became a bestseller (Rütting 1976). She continued to advocate for a lifestyle of health and sustainability, resulting in her becoming a member of the Bavarian Parliament for the Green Party in the 2000s. Here, just as with the Eltz Castle article, *mosaik* was perfectly in tune with the *Zeitgeist* of the 1970s and early 1980s. Alternative lifestyles became mainstream, and a notion of nostalgia and the longing for the old town were widely shared (Fischer 1980; Becker 2017: 101).

Suburban dreams meet inner-city reality

Under the title of 'At home in the middle of the old town', a 1978 feature article portrayed the inhabitants of a newly renovated building in the historic centre of the City of Sindelfingen (N.N. 1978), located in south-western Germany near Stuttgart. Unanimously, as the article stated, they couldn't imagine to live anywhere else (6). 'I had everything I wanted in my professional career,' said Jürgen Wald, a former engineer. 'Money, lots of business travel. But at some point, I realised that I was just a consumer and didn't live the life I wanted.' Together with his wife, Wald revitalised the store and workshop on the ground floor of the old house, once used to manufacture spinning wheels and bleach wool. The mayor of Sindelfingen described the case of this house as the initial moment of revitalising the entire historic town. 'Our inhabitants are extremely

Celle

In der Altstadt ist kein Zimmer frei

Die Celler verdanken ihre schöne und lebendige Altstadt zwei wichtigen Dingen: dem Traditionsbewußtsein ihrer Geschäftsleute und, so meinen sie, der „Verwandtschaft" zum englischen Königshaus.

Das mit dem englischen Königshaus muß man erklären: Die englischen Könige Georg I. und Georg II. stammen direkt von dem letzten Celler Herzog ab. Und in Celle ist man fest davon überzeugt, daß deshalb während des Zweiten Weltkrieges keine Bomben auf Celle fielen.

Doch es gibt in Deutschland viele Altstädte, die den Krieg zwar heil überstanden, die Nachkriegszeit aber nicht. Und hier kommt das Traditionsbewußtsein der Celler Bürger und Geschäftsleute ins Spiel. Die dachten nämlich nicht daran, aus ihren Fachwerkhäusern in der Altstadt auszuziehen, sondern sie blieben da wohnen, weil es eben Tradition ist, daß ein Geschäftsmann über seinem Laden wohnt. Das war schon bei der Stadtgründung im 13. Jahrhundert so – und so ist es noch heute.

Noch etwas begünstigte die Erhaltung der Celler Altstadt: Sie ist samt Schloß und Französischem Garten rings vom Stadtgraben umschlossen. So war es praktisch gar nicht möglich, daß sich von außen her Modernes in Beton und Plastik einschleichen konnte.

Nun ist die Celler Altstadt aber ganz und gar kein Freilichtmuseum. Im Gegenteil. Sie ist ein quicklebendiger Stadtteil mit einer gesunden Bevölkerungsstruktur. Fast alle alten Häuser haben im Erdgeschoß ein Geschäft – vom Tante-Emma-Laden bis zur schicken Boutique. Viele Gaststätten und Cafés kommen den Touristen entgegen, die zu Tausenden die Altstadt besuchen.

Sie ist nämlich sehenswert, die Celler Altstadt. Die ältest datierten Fachwerkhäuser sind aus dem 16. Jahrhundert. Sie sind im typischen niedersächsischen Stil gebaut und wunderschön bemalt. Sinnige Sprüche in Latein und Platt schmücken die Fassaden. Selbst die Barockbauten sind in Fachwerk ausgeführt, denn Steine gibt es nun mal nicht in dieser Gegend. Aber: Das Fachwerk der Barockbauten ist rein konstruktiv und farblich der Ausfachung angeglichen, die Fassaden sind durch Giebel und reich gegliederte Eingangszonen geschmückt.

Die Altstadt von Celle wird von den Bürgern als Mittelpunkt ihrer Stadt akzeptiert, die Wohnqualität ist beachtlich. Wohl haben viele Häuser keine Zentralheizung,

Lebendiger Stadtteil mit historischen Fassaden in Celle. Oben von links: Stilreine Erker am Rathaus – das Renaissance-Rathau[s] mit dem Turm der Stadtkirche im Hintergrund – die Fußgängerzone in de[r] Zöllnerstraße – der Gartenhof hinter der Ratsapotheke. Darunter: Hinter drei alten Fassaden hat di[e] Volksbank ihren Sitz. Links: Schönes Fachwerkhaus aus dem Jahr 1600.

mosaik

Figure 1: Half-timbered houses, an epitome of the historical city (1979).

interested in old buildings,' he added. Responding to the demand, according to the article, it was common practice for many municipalities in south-western Germany to buy up old houses in order to restore them. *mosaik* presented a variety of reasons for living in the old town. An article about Freiburg, also located in south-western Germany, summed up the most important ones: 'a car-free inner city, the vibrant street life of students and locals mixing and mingling, the picturesque old town' (Recht 1980: 6). Freiburg, which had been vastly destroyed during the Second World War, appears as a perfect example of post-war city planning and careful renewal where 'people matter, not cars'. Urban density and the variety of leisure activities, as goes the message between the lines, offer a high standard of living. Apart from promoting the image of avantgarde urban lifestyles in the shell of the old town, the magazine also catered to a rather conservative and nostalgic fascination with old cities. In a 1979 report about Celle, a small city in Lower Saxony, a number of pictures of the iconic half-timbered buildings (fig. 1) epitomised the ideal of a well-preserved German historic town (Plate 2013).

Throughout the magazine's existence, the old town reoccurred frequently as a topic and was a cover story more than once. In the 1970s, the city of Marburg became a well-received example of careful urban renewal, withdrawing plans to demolish old buildings in the inner city (Klotz 1978: 113ff.). 'Marburg's historic old town has been saved', a 1978 *mosaik* cover exclaimed (fig. 2). Until well into the 1990s, the magazine celebrated historic cities, presenting them as an 'oasis' (1999a: 14) or following the track record of their renewal, for example in the case of Ettlingen in south-western Germany. Praised as the 'most beautiful historic town' (N.N. 1991a: 52), the article tried to look behind the scenes of a success story and find out what it takes to keep the process of urban renewal alive for more than 20 years. According to the architects and planning officials in charge, Ettlingen took the wise decision to stick to the pedestrian scale of the old streets and alleys, not allowing cars in the inner city. Likewise, plots of land designated for new buildings were kept in a size similar to the city's medieval footprint (54f.).

Blatantly absent from the editorial content is the contested counterpart from the 1970s and 80s nostalgic discourse of the old town, namely the so-called anonymous mass housing projects and satellite cities at the urban periphery. *mosaik* did not employ the juxtaposition of 'old' and 'new' (as 'good' and 'bad'), which has been a common strategy of heritage publications since the 19th century (Petzet 1975: 28f.). One prominent exception was the *Gropiusstadt*. The district in the south of West Berlin served as the setting for Christiane F.'s '*Wir Kinder vom Bahnhof Zoo*' (1979), an autobiographic report about a

Magazin der Bausparkasse Schwäbisch Hall
1/
mosaik
Bauen Wohnen Freizeit
Alles über
• Die Wohnungsbauprämie '78
• Die Risikolebensversicherung
Energiesparen groß geschrieben
Marburg: Die Altstadt ist gerettet!

Figure 2: A 1970's issue: Saving the 'old' town (1979).

lost generation living in the modernist satellite city, winding up in drugs and prostitution. *mosaik* picked up this topic in its youth section on the occasion of the book launch (N.N. 1980: 38; this being the only example of a negative account of mass housing. The topic has never been brought up again in the years after).

Although the single-family home as a particular Western typology is by and large a suburban phenomenon (Harlander 2001), its context – suburbia and the suburban infrastructure – was hardly addressed in the popular discourse of the time. The editorial coverage in the *mosaik* magazine depicts the single-family home as an autonomous entity without a particular place and time. This impression is supported by the many full-page advertisements for prefabricated single-family houses in every issue. Except for a certain variety of regional architectural designs attributed to the homes offered, they could be commissioned and built everywhere in Germany.[3] The detached single-family home as an easy-to-consume and customisable product strikingly contrasts with *mosaik*'s editorial strategies to introduce the historic city centres with their dense neighbourhoods as a place worth to be considered for family living: Each portrayed city and its historic centre is treated as a particular place with its own history and a tradition everybody can choose to be part of. Most importantly, the articles open up the perspective for the material strategies behind the creation of an urban atmosphere and particular flair, which is framed historically but points towards a sustainable, urban future.

Old houses become single-family homes

Not only presented *mosaik* the old town, and thus inner-city dwelling as a young, fashionable and desirable lifestyle. The very act of converting old houses into private homes was also granted ample editorial space. The topic of new life in old buildings was addressed in almost every issue. Under varying headlines – *'Modernes Wohnen in alten Mauern'* (*Modern living within old walls*, Recht 1988: 6f.), 'Neuer Glanz in alten Mauern' (*New splendour within old walls*, cover 1/1997), 'Frischer Wind in alten Mauern' (*Wind of change within old walls*, cover 4/1999), for example – mosaik reported about the experience of families buying old houses, renovating and living in them. The 1978 story 'Das Ulmer Haus' (*The Ulm house*), referring to the city of Ulm in south-western Germany, was the first portrait of a *Schwäbisch Hall* client and her project of refurbishing a medieval town house (Recht 1978). Although quite costly (400,000 *Deutsche Mark*), owner Anna Burgmayer set

Wenn aus Mietern Eigentümer werden

Vom Fabrikhof zum Wohnhof

Mitten in Darmstadts Stadtteil Bessungen liegt „Die Fabrik“: Klotzige Backsteingebäude, hoher Kamin, die Nachbarhäuser direkt angebaut. In dieser Fabrik wohnen 24 Menschen – junge, alte, acht Kinder; Familien, Singles, Alleinerziehende. Es ist keine Wohngemeinschaft im üblichen Sinne und doch ist es eine.

Denn die Familien, die diese Fabrik mit hohem Einsatz an Geld und Eigenarbeit zu einem ungewöhnlichen Wohnhaus umgebaut haben, leben für sich – in komfortablen Eigentums- oder Mietwohnungen. Aber sie leben auch zusammen in einer Gemeinschaft, in der man immer jemand findet, der einem zuhört, der hilft. In der die Kinder überall offene Türen und freundliche Zuwendung finden, in der keiner allein sein muß, aber jeder allein sein kann, wenn er will.

Vor mehr als hundert Jahren wurde die „Fabrik“ gebaut – allerdings war es niemals eine Fabrik im üblichen Sinne, sondern eine Großwäscherei. Im Laufe der Jahre wurde ein Gebäude nach dem anderen in die enge Bausituation des ländlichen Stadtteils buchstäblich „eingeschoben“, so daß eine sehr dichte Bebauung entstand. Die Fabrik steht auf einem Grundstück von nur etwas weniger als 900 Quadratmetern, überbaut sind davon 550 Quadratmeter.

Diese Fabrik schloß 1969 – für Wäschereien dieser Art gab es keinen Bedarf mehr. Um die Gebäude nicht ganz verkommen zu lassen, wurden sie vermietet – stückweise sozusagen. Eine Jugendorganisation zog ein, ein kleiner Gewerbebetrieb und eine Handvoll Studenten, die hier primitive, aber billige Unterkünfte fanden.

Bitte blättern Sie um

Hier arbeiteten jahrzehntelang Männer und Frauen – heute wird in der „Fabrik“ gewohnt. Und zwar bequem, modern und individuell. „Man hat hier immer Gesellschaft, wenn man will und kann alleine sein, wenn man das möchte“, freuen sich die Bewohner der ehemaligen Wäscherei in Darmstadt-Bessungen.

22 mosaik

Figure 3: New forms of family dwelling: conversions of a factory (1984).

out to restore the building, which turned out to be of outstanding heritage value. Burgmayer said she wanted to give back to her native city the house's former beauty. The article presents the preservation authorities as helpful pool of experts and informs about the renovation funds available there. Up to 50 percent of the extra building costs caused by the status as a listed landmark, according to the article, are likely to be reimbursed by public funds. Among the individual persons or single families devoted to renovating old buildings, the high number of collaborative projects *mosaik* reported about stands out. Whereas *Baugruppen* (building communities) have become more popular in Germany only over the course of the last two decades, the mere fact of starting a renovation project as a group was discussed in *mosaik* long before that. The magazine portrayed a group of families who bought an old laundry facility in suburban Darmstadt, located in the State of Hesse, and converted the building into a multi-family dwelling (Recht: 1984).[4] The inner courtyard was kept as a common area designed by all inhabitants, while the apartments built into the shell of the factory building were planned individually (fig. 3). The article emphasised the simultaneity of private space, where people can retreat to, and a sense of community that manifests in daily practices, such as eating together outside or children playing in the courtyard. Most notably, 'Oma Else', grandmother to one of the families moving into the factory, remarked, 'I used to live by myself in a detached single-family home and felt very lonely. Here, with my veranda facing the courtyard, I meet people all the time.'

In the context of the rather siloed concept of the single-family home as a living environment, moving into an old building, or converting a factory into a family dwelling, does stand out as unconventional. While younger people are explicitly addressed, the variety of editorial content simultaneously included the needs and interests of a larger audience, speaking of new, more liberal forms of living. The articles sought to address a particular generation and milieu. While the main target audience of the bank selling building saving plans remained young families and their spatial needs, the feature stories of new home owners in old buildings introduced yet another, more unconventional way of life and its protagonists: sort of the 'creative class' (Florida 2002), as one would call it nowadays. This finding is supported by the fact that most of the portrayed owners of old buildings were architects who took on the task of building an unconventional home for themselves.

Material appropriation

The editorial themes of renovation and the old town introduced the readers to the field of historical and natural building materials, a thoughtful management of architectural resources and the advantages of urban living. A step further into details, the magazine did not only encourage the bank clients to buy old homes but also to engage in their renovation hands-on. The section *'Modernisieren und Renovieren'* (modernisation and renovation) with how-to advice columns was part of the editorial concept of *mosaik* from the first issue onwards. Next to financial advice as mentioned above, dealing physically with historical buildings is treated as a manageable task for prospective homeowners: *'Keine Angst vor Denkmälern'* (Don't be afraid of listed buildings) (N.N. 1994). The practical topics resonated with a general receptiveness of Germans of the post-war, boom years generation for the DIY movement (Voges 2017). DIY and sustainable lifestyles came together in the issue of environmentally sound materials and building physics. Up to date with the discourse of the 1980s, *mosaik* introduced the theme labelled as *'Baubiologie'* (building biology) (Neubeck 1989). In mainstream architecture, the awareness for this issue grew around new buildings, whereas refurbishment projects

Figure 4: Do it yourself: heritage conservation (1982).

were handled rather pragmatically, using a toxic mix of materials for energetic retrofitting. An outspoken yet subtle critique of the building industry and its materials is conveyed in the 1982 story of a catholic youth association-rehabilitation collective (fig. 4) in a small town in south-western Germany. The group began its career of saving Rottweil's built heritage in the late 1970s when the 17th century barn house of the parish was slated for demolition. The group informed the preservation authorities and began restoring the building, using traditional building techniques and materials (Recht 1982: 6). After this initial success, the group took on the role of a local preservation task force. Craftsmen and building experts shared their knowledge with the group who stepped in to consult owners of old buildings about the question whether the buildings could be saved or not. The goal was to convince the owners to restore the buildings carefully and to use local building materials only. For its practice, the group imposed the 10-kilometres rule: Only building materials such as clay, brick, and wood, new or reused from demolished buildings, that could be acquired within this radius were considered suitable for the group's projects (Recht 1982: 10). 'Old houses are built from stone, wood, chalk, and clay which makes them very elastic and thus durable,' a leader of the group summed up their building philosophy, 'concrete and iron, added later on, caused much of the damage old buildings suffer from today.' (Recht 1982: 11) Thus prepared for the challenge of architectural recycling, *mosaik* started to include conversion case studies of houses that had already been built as single-family homes in the post-war period. Articles about the transformation of buildings from the1950s and 60s appeared in the 1990s (N.N. 1991b; N.N. 1993). Just before the 2000s, the iconic prefabricated single-family home, the *'Fertighaus'*, had become the object of transformation (fig. 5). *mosaik*'s efforts to promote the conversion of old buildings and thus to acquire a new group of saving plan clients, culminated in a competition among the readers for the best refurbishment project (N.N. 1999b).

Figure 5: As time goes by: transforming a 1970s prefabricated single-family home (1999).

A postmodern material practice: The home loan bank and preservationism as unexpected twins

Browsing through just one of the many popular magazines that have mushroomed around the single-family home in post-war Germany has turned out an astonishingly high number of articles dedicated to presenting good examples of adapting building stock for use as single-family homes. The infinite history of the single-family home provides us with countless examples of transformations – be it out of life course-related necessities, since families grow or shrink, be it as a practice of cultural and artistic expression. Any piece of architecture, as we have seen, can become a single-family home. And sometimes, the single-family home itself is the object of material transformation. Surprisingly, if one considers the modernisation paradigm and the discourse on urban decay at that time, historical buildings were, without exception, presented as something positive and desirable. Unsurprisingly so, if one considers the intentions behind the *Schwäbisch Hall* magazine: to make money by keeping people building.

The attitude of *mosaik* could be characterised as postmodern and inclusive. While directed at the typical target audience of their products – young families about to build their own home – the magazine addressed a multitude of issues revolving around single and family life and sought to include different models of living and dwelling. In doing so, the magazine en passant promoted particular, more unconventional lifestyles. All featured stories dealt with the overall question, 'What does it mean to young people to live in an old house?'. In the magazine, the juxtaposition of old and new as an architectural style functions as a synonym for unconventional or avant-garde lifestyles. A bit exoticised in the early years, evoking forms of communal housing such as collectively renovating and living in an old factory, all practices of dwelling, from single households to family homes are presented as equal options of a variety of multiple ways to choose from with the help of a *Schwäbisch Hall* saving plan. Individualism is the message, yet framed by a postmodern sense of plurivalence and the idea of a free choice between different offers.[5]

The above-described material practices of making an alternative kind of not detached single-family home can be understood as part of general architectural trends in the second half of the 20th century. Typically, concepts of architectural recycling are closely linked to 'historical' buildings and the design issues of reconstruction, contrast and contemporary competitiveness (Corboz 1976). A closer look at the history of architecture reveals a wide range of much older motivations for keeping existing buildings (and not demolishing them). The economics of preserving architecture include concepts such as cultural memory and heritage as well as the pre-modern, sustainable practices of repairing, reusing and recycling whole buildings or parts of them for the sake of saving resources. From the post-war boom era until well into the 1970s, these material practices were limited to the field of cultural heritage preservation. Meanwhile, preservation knowledge and reusing old buildings has become a paradigm in architectural design. It has almost become a style of its own (Braae, Riesto 2011). The overlapping concepts of architectural recycling and historic preservation both share the material resource paradigm, i.e. they are interested in the material value of architecture, appropriate materials (and not so much in its artistic qualities or its mere appearance). As I have argued previously, the appreciation for old buildings and the rising interest in historic preservation strategies among architects has developed as a critical reaction to the urban renewal policies during the 1960s and 70s (Warda 2015; 2016). *mosaik* magazine was part of the wave of nostalgia at the time. It promoted recycling architecture, inner-city revival and densification and presented a multifaceted image of historic preservation: one that is about beautiful old cities – which makes the magazine yet another medium of the modernist imagination of the 'old town' (Vinken 2010). However, most of all, *mosaik* presented historic preservation as a material practice of appropriating and adapting historical buildings to new uses. The magazine went even further, applying the notion of material transformation to any piece of architecture that has the potential to become a single-family home. Thus, writing on the (cultural and architectural) history of the single-family home, I conclude that it transcends the concept of building new shells for new families. Architecturally, the single-family home goes far beyond the post-war homes and prefabricated houses in suburban housing estates becoming part of the desire for self-fashioning and individual opportunity instead. What remains probably the key element in this is the concept of ownership and the home loan banks' determination to establish property.[6]

References

Arendt, C. (1977), Altbau-Erneuerung. Leitfaden zur Erhaltung und Modernisierung alter Häuser (Stuttgart: DVA).

Baumeister, M., Bonomo, B., and Schott, D. (eds.) (2017), Cities contested: Urban politics, heritage and social movements in Italy and West Germany in the 1970s (Frankfurt/Main, New York: Campus).

Becker, T. (2017), 'Rückkehr der Geschichte? Die "Nostalgie-Welle"in den 1970er und 1980er Jahren', in F. Espositio (ed.): Zeitenwandel. Transformationen geschichtlicher Zeitlichkeit nach dem Boom (Göttingen: Wallstein), 93–117.

Braae, E., and Riesto, S. (2011), 'As found. A New Design Paradigm', Nordic Journal of Architecture (1), 8–9.

Cantacuzino, S. (1976), New uses for old buildings (New York: Whitney Library of Design).
Corboz, A. (1976), 'Old Buildings and Modern Functions', Lotus International 13, 69–79.
F., C. (1978), Wir Kinder vom Bahnhof Zoo (Hamburg: Gruner+Jahr).
Florida, R. (2002), The rise of the creative class: and how it's transforming work, leisure community and everyday life (New York: Basic Books).
Fischer, V. (1980), Nostalgie. Geschichte und Kultur als Trödelmarkt (Luzern, Frankfurt/Main: Bucher).
Harlander, T. (ed.) (2001), Villa und Eigenheim. Suburbaner Städtebau in Deutschland (Stuttgart: DVA).
Klotz, H. (1978), Gestaltung einer neuen Umwelt. Kritische Essays zur Architektur der Gegenwart (Luzern, Frankfurt/Main: Bucher).
Krichbaum, J. (ed.) (1995), Deutsche Standards. Produkte und Objekte in Deutschland, die als prominenter Teil für das Ganze stehen. Namen und Begriffe, von Aspirin bis Zeiss in Bild und Wort (Köln: Edition Acrum).
Müller, M. (1999), Bausparen in Deutschland zwischen Inflation und Währungsreform 1924–1948. Wohnungsbaufinanzierung im Spannungsfeld zwischen Staat und privaten und öffentlichen Bausparunternehmen (München: Beck).
Petzet, M. (ed.) (1975), Eine Zukunft für unsere Vergangenheit. Denkmalschutz und Denkmalpflege in der Bundesrepublik Deutschland (München: Prestel).
Vinken, G. (2010), Zone Heimat. Altstadt im modernen Städtebau (München, Berlin: Deutscher Kunstverlag).
Voges, J. (2017), "Selbst ist der Mann." Do-it-yourself und Heimwerken in der Bundesrepublik Deutschland (Göttingen: Wallstein).
Warda, J. (2015), 'Architektur reparieren in der „Wegwerfgesellschaft". Zur ressourcenökonomischen Dimension des Denkmalbegriffs', in M. Grewe, M. Tauschek (eds.): Knappheit, Mangel, Überfluss. Kulturwissenschaftliche Positionen zum Umgang mit begrenzten Ressourcen (Frankfurt/Main, New York: Campus), 309–326.
Warda, J. (2016), 'Architektur aufbewahren. Zur Ideengeschichte des Gebäuderecycling', in C. Lewe, T. Othold and N. Oxen (eds.): Müll. Interdisziplinäre Perspektiven auf das Übrig-Gebliebene (Bielefeld: transcript), 227–245.
Winkelmann, A. (2007), Kulturfabriken. Zeichenwandel der Fabrik in der freien Kulturarbeit (Berlin: Humboldt-Universität), urn:nbn:de:kobv:11-10081094 (accessed 15 August 2018).

Illustration credits

Figure 1: N.N. 1979: 12f.
Figure 2: mosaik 3(1): 1.
Figure 3: Recht 1984: 22f.
Figure 4: Recht 1982: 6f.
Figure 5: N.N. 1999b: 28f.
All illustrations courtesy of Bausparkasse Schwäbisch Hall AG

Sources

N.N. (1977a), 'Die Vorteile im Erwerb von Altbauten', mosaik 1(1), 64f.
N.N. (1977b), 'Burg Eltz', mosaik 1(1), 81.
N.N. (1977c), 'Bei der Modernisierung hilft der Staat', mosaik 1(2), 35.
N.N. (1978), 'Zuhause mitten in der alten Stadt', mosaik 2(4), 4–8.
N.N. (1979), 'Celle. In der Altstadt ist kein Zimmer frei', mosaik 3(3), 12–14 and 17.
N.N. (1980), 'Achtung Drogen Lebensgefahr!', mosaik 4(3), 38.
N.N. (1991a), 'Die schönste Altstadt', mosaik 15(1), 52–56.
N.N. (1991b), 'Von den Sechzigern in die Neunziger', mosaik 15(4), 6–10.
N.N. (1993), 'Entdecken Sie die 50er Jahre', mosaik 17(3), 14–18.

N.N. (1994), 'Keine Angst vor Denkmälern', mosaik 18(2), 40.
N.N. (1999a), 'Oase mitten in der Stadt', mosaik 23(1), 14–16.
N.N. (1999b), 'Fertighaus: Erstaunliche Verwandlung', mosaik 23(4), 28–30.
N.N. (2002), 'Mehr Haus auf kleinem Grund', mosaik 26(2), 8–24.
Neubeck, M. (1989), 'Baubiologie: So kann man alte Häuser sanieren', mosaik 13(2), 70–72.
Plate, U. (2013), 'Fachwerk gut, alles gut? Denkmalpflegerisches Handeln im Umgang mit Fachwerk', Forum Stadt 40(4), 327–338.
Recht, C. (1977), 'Jetzt ist es unser Hof', mosaik 1(2), 12–16 and 77.
Recht, C. (1978), 'Das Ulmer Haus', mosaik 2(1), 4–7 and 89.
Recht, C. (1980), '... Und fahren kann man mit der Straßenbahn', mosaik 4(3), 6–11 and 111.
Recht, C. (1982), 'Fantastisch, was in Rottweil geschieht, wir finden: Jungens, das hat Zukunft', mosaik 6(3), 6–11.
Recht, C. (1984), 'Vom Fabrikhof zum Wohnhof', mosaik 8(4), 22–26 and 89.
Recht, C. (1988), 'Neues Wohnen in alten Mauern', mosaik 12(3), 6–9 and 79.
Recht, C. (1988), 'Wohnen in der alten Werkstatt', mosaik 12(4), 6–10.
Rütting, B. (1976), Mein Kochbuch. Naturgesunde Köstlichkeiten aus aller Welt (München: Mosaik).
WoModG (1976), Entwurf eines Gesetzes zur Verbesserung der Wohnverhältnisse (Wohnungsmodernisierungsgesetz – WoModG), Bundestagsdrucksache 7/4551.

Endnotes

1 All translations from German are by the author.

2 Yet from the perspective of the history of brands, the Wüstenrot home loan bank is regarded a German standard. Founded in 1921 as a means to deal with the housing shortage after World War I, Wüstenrot was Germany's first home loan bank (Krichbaum 1988: 28).

3 Yet in some municipalities, local building codes may impose restrictions on the actual design.

4 On the transformation of factories into cultural spaces see Winkelmann 2007.

5 See the article by Julia Gill in this volume.

6 See the article by Jakob Smigla-Zywocki on the issue of ownership in this volume.

‘Of course, it’s not all finished.’ The conversion of existing real estate between networking, appropriation practice and long-term project work

Christiane Cantauw

73.7 percent of the approximately 15,000,000 single- and two-family houses counted in Germany according to the 2011 census (Statistische Ämter des Bundes und der Länder 2014: 8) are properties built between 1949 and 1990 (Effenberger 2015: 4). A national comparison within Germany shows that the average age of single-family houses in East Germany is higher than in West Germany, where the years 1949 to 1978 (especially the 1960s and 1970s) proved to be a period of increased building activity in the single-family and two-family housing sector (Statistische Ämter des Bundes und der Länder 2014: 11). In North Rhine-Westphalia, for example, 54.6 percent of the 2011 single-family house stock was built between 1949 and 1990; in Lower Saxony the figure was 14.4 percent (Effenberger 2015: 4). In view of these figures, it is justifiable to say that older single-family houses built before 1990, solely in terms of numbers, are the main feature of building stock in German towns and cities. How they are dealt with is often perceived, discussed and problematised in the media (Friedrichs and Leeks 2014; Schieritz 2016; Matzig 2014; Fabricius 2018) and in the academic world (Hnilica and Timm 2017; Krajewski 2015; Menzl 2007; de Temple 2006), as well as in the political arena at municipal and supra-municipal level. In view of dwindling resources, climate change and drastic demographic changes, older single-family housing areas have been identified as a field of action for environmental technology, urban development and (municipal) politics.[1] Accordingly, the relevant publications focus on issues like energy and urban development sustainability of existing properties[2], modernisation potentials (Zakrzewski et al. 2014), marketing opportunities[3] and price declines.[4] Not so long ago, the Regionale 2016 and StadtBauKultur NRW used a number of project studies in North Rhine-Westphalia (Utku et al. 2017; Hausaufgaben in Barkenberg)[5] to sound out ways in which civic engagement in this field can be stimulated and used to develop the relevant residential areas. Here, as well as in a pertinent human geography study,[6] questions were also asked about the attitudes of owners of existing real estate, primarily with a view to assessing the potential for change.

That said, there still lacks a more intensive discussion of why people decide to buy an existing property, how they deal with its material state, how they adapt to it or how they change it. This article, which deals with the conversion of existing properties after a change of ownership, aims to make a first step in this direction.

The article is based on 20 qualitative, guideline-based interviews with purchasers of existing properties in rural, small-town and suburban areas conducted in the municipalities of Ohne (Grafschaft Bentheim district, Lower Saxony), Dülmen-Rorup (a district of Coesfeld, NRW) and Münster-Southeast (NRW). Ohne is part of the municipality of Schüttorf and is located in southern Lower Saxony. In 2017, the population of Ohne was 595.[7] Münster is the closest major city, 45 kilometres away. Ohne has one small village shop.[8] Larger supermarkets and other shopping facilities are located in Schüttorf, about eight kilometres away, or in Wettringen, Neuenkirchen and Bad Bentheim, each of which is roughly ten kilometres away. Ohne has neither a kindergarten nor a primary school. The schools in Schüttorf or Bad Bentheim (primary and secondary schools) can be reached by school bus. In addition, there is a 'citizen's bus' that travels to the nearby larger towns once an hour. In the joint municipality of Schüttorf, new building plots with a size of about 900 square metres are currently being offered at a price of 60 euros per square metre (plus development).[9] According to the interview partners, existing properties are traded at prices between 55,000 euros and 200,000 euros[10], whereby the supply is very limited.

Dülmen is a small town in the south of Münsterland. 2,271 inhabitants currently live in the district of Rorup (March 2019), which was incorporated in 1974 following municipal restructuring.[11] In view of the continuing demand for building land, the municipality has put out to tender a new development area.[12] As a result, the population is expected to increase in the near future. The plots there will be marketed at a price of 160 euros per square metre.[13] Dülmen-Rorup has a good connection to the motorway. In Rorup there is a kindergarten and a primary school. The centre of Dülmen with its supermarkets, other shopping facilities and secondary schools is eight kilometres away and is served by a school bus. The standard land value[14] in Dülmen-Rorup in 2018 was between 105 and 180 euros per square metre.[15] The supply of existing properties is currently very limited.

The districts of Münster-Wolbeck, Münster-Angelmodde and Münster-Gremmendorf are located southeast of Münster. A total of 30,117 people live here (as of 2018).[16] An annual increase of 1,600 persons is forecast for the entire urban area of Münster, which currently has around 310,488 inhabitants (Baumeister 2016).[17] The three districts mentioned above will record significant population growth over the next five years due to new construction sites[18] and the conversion of a barracks.[19] According to a 2018 property market report, the average selling price for existing properties in the Münster-Southeast district ranges between 1,440 and 3,860 euros per square metre.[20] However, prices have risen sharply over the past 20 years, both in the market for new building land and in the existing real estate market.[21] Münster-Southeast is located about 10 kilometres from the city centre, which can be reached by bus every 20 minutes. There are supermarkets and other shopping facilities in all three districts. Münster-Wolbeck also has a school centre with all three types of schools. Primary schools and day-care facilities for children are provided in all three districts.

The houses in the sample (project B) were built between 1880 and 1999.[22] Broken down according to survey location, the oldest existing properties in the sample can be found in Münster-Southeast (built between 1880 and 1960). In Ohne, the sample covers the years of construction from 1930 to 1999, and in Rorup the years of construction from 1967 to 1997. According to the interviewees, the plot sizes in the sample are between 250 and 2,200 square metres, with the largest plots being located in rural areas. The living spaces reported by the interviewees are between 115 and 300 square metres. Here, too, the rural area stands out with the largest living spaces.

According to the buyers, the costs of buying the properties ranged between 50,000 euros (Ohne) and 500,000 euros (Münster-Southeast). Costs for the conversion work they have carried out so far[23] range between 5,500 and 200,000 euros. All interview partners in the sample described the conversion of their newly acquired single-family houses as a matter of course and indispensable. This attitude is to be taken as the starting point for further considerations. The first question that arises is how the interviewees organised the conversion of their existing property: How much time and what financial and family resources did they have recourse to? It is also important to ask what social and cultural functions the conversion work fulfilled (and continues to fulfil). How were the personal and financial burdens of the conversion process dealt with argumentatively? What did they see as a success with regard to their own efforts?

The planning and execution of conversion/renovation work

Immediately after purchasing their property, the buyers of existing real estate began conversion and/or renovation work. None of the respondents questioned the necessity of this work. Even the buyers of comparatively new properties (built between 1997 and 1999) had made conversion plans a few weeks or months in advance before moving in:

'Beforehand, we painted the place and started renovating. We had something like three months, we had given ourselves time.' (interview Fischer family, Ohne, 12 April 2016)

During the conversion, the Fischer family had laid parquet on the upper floor. In addition, a solar system was installed on the roof, a painter was commissioned and a new fitted kitchen was purchased.

Interviews with purchasers of houses built between the 1950s and 1970s quickly reveal that conversion work on older properties is far more complex:

'We then started, yes, directly on 2 November. November 1st was a public holiday. [...] and we moved in at the end of the year, at the end of last year. So we had a tight, tight schedule. [...] of course, it's not all finished yet, but we had given notice that we wanted to leave our flat at the end of the year and yes, that's the way it came to be that when we moved in, it wasn't quite finished.' (interview Krause family, Rorup, 13 January 2016)

In the case of existing properties, it was necessary for the owners to evaluate energy, technical and aesthetic construction measures against each other. This was not always easy, because considerations with regard to the maintenance of the building and living comfort had to be weighed against each other. For financial reasons most interviewees did not want to spend too long on renovation work before moving in. Frau Reißner explained this as follows:

'For financial reasons we decided to overlap the rent for only one month, because otherwise we would be blowing a month's rent, in principle, you know what I mean? And that was actually the crucial point. On top of that, my husband builds everything himself. We do it all without, completely without companies and it would have taken him five years [...] before we could move in here.' (interview Reißner family, Rorup, 7 January 2016)

Other property buyers in the sample also indicated that they wanted to avoid the twin financial burden of rent and mortgage. In return, like the Eckert family for example, they were prepared to accept some serious restrictions on their comfort:

'in the mistaken belief that we'd get a bathroom and two rooms ready in a month. One bathroom, well, that was finished in December, four months later. We had a roof over our head here, so to speak. So that was very funny. We were practically showering (laughs) in the food, with a hot water pipe.' (interview Klein family, Münster-Southeast, 4 October 2016)

Like the Klein family, the Eckert family had only planned four weeks for the renovation of their newly acquired second-hand property:

'So the [children] found it awful here, too. It really was, it was all in absolute chaos, because after four weeks you simply can't expect to bring a house built in nineteen hundred and, and mm sixty-two to the point where you can move in here.' (interview Eckert family, Münster-Southeast, 7 October 2016)

All in all, it can be seen that the periods planned for conversion measures were too tightly calculated for a variety of reasons. These included a lack of experience, limited financial resources or overestimating the proportion of their own contribution. The result was that many families planned or were forced to move into a house that was not fully habitable.

That said, renovations and conversions do not simply place demands on a family's physical, financial and social abilities. Many of the interviewees also addressed the demands resulting from the unfamiliar situation: the temporal momentum of rebuilding processes that repeatedly required rapid decisions, and the financial burden that had to be recalculated time and time again.

Herr Goll, for example, described internal removals in terms of reconstruction demands and the process of redevelopment:

'And then, after we had the upstairs rooms as good as completed, the interior work almost finished, and the bathrooms too, everything was ready for use, my little son was born. Exactly, then the little one came along, I had finished the children's room upstairs last April. So we had the upstairs children's room finished, our bedroom finished, the bathroom finished and then I started… I sort of came down here, and we cleared everything out, the things down here, from the bottom to the top. […] then tore down everything out here. And here everything was basically open during the building phase. Complete, yes.' (interview Goll family, Rorup, 4 November 2015) In the further course of the interview, Herr Goll added, 'But I must say, it was a real adventure, it was exciting. Exactly, we moved from the bottom to the top, practically lived at the top and turned everything inside out down here.'[24]

The Goll family moved into Herr Goll's parental home and, among other things, completely redesigned and extended the front of the house. The fact that the Golls moved back and forth with their newborn son between the floors of the house during the conversion phase and renovated and cleaned up the house on each floor also challenged their creativity. During conversions the family had to do without a kitchen, and cooking was done on a stove mounted on castors, as were some of the cupboards and the sink, in order to allow the 'mobile kitchen' to be used wherever and whenever possible. The whole process was not described as a burden, but more as an adventure and a challenge. The fact that many years later the old kitchen cupboards, mounted on castors, are still in the basement of the house demonstrates their importance for the owners. The Goll family is a good example of how the available space can be used creatively, and how its use is subject to constant change during renovations. The single-family house became an interim space during the conversion process. The furniture and household effects had not yet found their final place, and living in this interim space lacked the everyday routines associated with certain walking distances between rooms and work processes; it's all 'unfamiliar' (Schinkel 2013: 16). With regard to the relationship between people and things, the material changes (kitchen furniture on wheels) also show how the owners adjusted to the 'obstinacy of things' (Depner 2015: 38ff.) and adapted things to suit their (in this case) temporary needs.[25]

Many interviewees also addressed the need to deal with 'surprises' that only become visible during construction. Herr Flasberg lives with his family in a single-family house built at the end of the 1990s. He had to do less modernisation work on the house and, during the inspection of the house, aptly described the difference between a new building and an existing one:

'How the previous owner did it, I don't know, but I think that everything fitted somehow (clears his throat). That [is] always the case, if you haven't built it yourself, you can only get a vague idea.' (interview family Flasberg, Ohne, 15 March 2016) Frau Klein, who bought an existing property in poor structural condition, explained: 'Yes, of course it's a little bit of a surprise when you buy an old house like this, because in the end everything is basically faulty, you don't notice it because it's all hidden behind the walls, you know what I mean?' (interview Klein family, Münster-Southeast, 4 October 2016)

Both excerpts make it clear that at the time of purchase the condition of existing properties was not clearly apparent. This also makes it difficult for new owners to calculate the time required for the conversion, and explains why they described their experience as an open process.

Networks

Before, during and after moving into their own home, the interviewees were able to fall back on a variety of unpaid support from third parties. Almost every interviewee mentioned family members, friends, acquaintances and relatives who were involved in the work on or in the new home. The example of the Wiedmann family from Rorup will be used to illustrate how this was done in individual cases. The family lives in Frau Wiedmann's parental home, which was built in the mid-1970s. It has recently been converted into a two-family house to enable three generations to live in two households under a single roof. Frau Wiedmann grew up in Rorup and has a large family as well as many friends and acquaintances in the surrounding area. Herr Wiedmann does not come from the region. During the rebuilding, the family received help from a lot of Frau Wiedmann's relatives and friends. Many of the helpers were skilled craftsmen, whose support was particularly valuable. When asked whether his relatives had also helped with the conversion, Herr Wiedmann replied: 'Well, they live a bit far away, you know what I mean?' In response to Frau Wiedmann's objection that 'none of them are craftsmen', he continued, 'If they drive here, the journey takes two and a half hours, three hours actually. And none of them are craftsmen, exactly. They all come from a big town and they're not used to working with their hands.' Frau Wiedmann summed it up like this: 'They're all office workers rather. Office workers, yes.' (interview Wiedmann family, Rorup, 17 December 2015)

Here, the reason for the lack of family support was the distance to the building site and the lack of the necessary expertise ('none of them are craftsmen'). Nor did Herr Wiedmann's family, with the exception of his mother, help with the move. By contrast, Frau Wiedmann's family lived in the neighbourhood, had the necessary skills and was large enough to be able to spread the work amongst a great number of potential helpers. Here there is a recognisable difference between relatives who did and did not provide any help. The latter were categorised as 'townspeople' and 'office workers' whose support was not needed and perhaps even not asked for.[26] At an earlier point in the interview, Herr Wiedmann had already explained the reasons why local people helped each other:

> 'That's always the case. Everyone in the family helps and people know exactly that other people will help them later, too. And it crosses no one's mind to think whether you owe them a favour, or something like that. You just do it, yes, without having to think about it. That's the way it works here.' (interview Wiedmann family, Rorup, 17 December 2017)

Herr Wiedmann explains mutual help as a form of 'sweat equity' from relatives, which will be 'repaid' by returning your help at a later point. Here it is clear that family bonds exist in a structure of giving and returning.[27] Thus, on the one hand, the family (resp. the extended family) integrates and confirms itself among its members; at the same time, it initiates and/or strengthens bonds of friendship in the neighbourhood.[28] Herr Wiedmann ended his statement with the unmistakable words: 'That's the way it works here' to emphasise that he understood the social components in mutual family help and felt duty-bound to adhere to them.

The practice of mutual help ist not restricted to any specific area of study. Friends and neighbours had even helped to renovate the house that the Klein family had bought in Münster-Southeast. All in all, the family said that the close circle of helpers comprised around 20 persons. For example, friends would cook for them during the work and/or they were able to go for a shower in their own homes or at the neighbours. Here, help was not simply restricted to work on conversions, moving house and financial support, but extended to everyday life in the family.

In this case, relatives outside the core family played no role whatsoever. Frau Klein's reasons for this were that 'everyone does their particular thing in the family. That way, it would be impossible to return favours in the form of active support, you could not be certain of reciprocity and people would remain owing something to those who helped them out (interview Klein family, Münster-Southeast, 4 October 2016).

This was different in the case of neighbours and friends who lived nearby. Here it seemed likely that people would repay others at a later date for their support. In the case of both the Wiedmanns and the Kleins, it was clear that geographical distance was as equally important a precondition for the formation of a network of support as were family relationships. By contrast, mobility proved to be a hindrance because geographical distance made it difficult or practically impossible to return a favour. Almost all owners of used houses described family networks and/or neighbourly support as important. This support implied both active help in moving furniture and also expert craftwork tips and advice, for example when renovating the bathroom or with electrical problems in the house. This can be shown by the following examples[29]:

- A brother-in-law has a carpenter's shop.
- There are plumbers in the family.
- An uncle has a heating company.
- A brother-in-law is a painter.
- A cousin works in a carpenter's shop.
- A brother-in-law is an electrician.
- There's a carpenter in the circle of friends.
- A brother-in-law is a master carpenter.
- An uncle works in a bank.
- Advice on financing was given through private contacts.
- There's a woman architect/valuation expert in the circle of friends.
- There's a structural engineer in the circle of friends.

The social networks of buyers of existing real estate are an important resource which can partially compensate for the lack of financial resources. On the other hand, it is difficult to use third-party support to compensate for an inadequate time budget. Social relationships are also confirmed by working together, in that both helpers and the people they support spend time together.[30] Time is doubly important in this context, because it combines the gift of work as a form of trust for future reciprocity. Supporters must trust that their help will pay off sometime in the future. Direct reciprocity is usually not possible. Adloff/Mau reduce this cultural technique to a nice denominator by pointing out, with reference to Diego Gambetta, that the 'granting of trust and the giving of a gift [...] can produce precisely those forms of behaviour which, logically speaking, appear to be their condition' (Adloff and Mau 2005: 44; see also Gambetta 2001: 236).

Working in and on the house: do-it-yourself activities[31]

Contemporary historical studies show that the popularity of do-it-yourself is on the one hand closely linked to residential property and house ownership. On the other hand, it is an expression of a specific variant of consumer-oriented everyday life as it has developed in the Federal Republic of Germany since the 1950s.[32] In the context of this article, the question arises as to how the owners of existing real estate specifically justify their independent renovation, conversion and modernisation work, how they acquire the necessary know-how and when and why they fall back on professional services.

An important aspect of doing independent repairs and renovation work on your existing property is the potential cost savings. Do-it-yourself work is meant to keep the cost of conversion work low:

> 'The architect gave us an estimate for having it done by someone else, just the house as it stands here now, without outside facilities, without paving, without a garage. [...] like that, it would cost between 280,000 and 290,000 euros. So, and then of course we both gaped and we told him to sharpen his pencil a bit and see where we could do some of the work ourselves. And then he finally came up with a total of 220,000 euros and with these 220,000 euros, I reckoned, we'd have the garage and the outside facilities and so on, everything included, even though he hadn't planned it that way. But, let me tell you, all our own efforts alone took much longer than if we had handed it over to outside companies.' (interview Schulz family, Ohne, 6 April 2016)

According to their own calculations, the Schulz family saved more than 70,000 euros by doing it themselves. The fact that the work required a larger time budget ('took ... considerably longer') was no problem for Herr Schulz. In an interview with Frau Reißner, she also emphasised the savings made through DIY. If a craftsman had been hired, the costs for the tiling work in the guest WC would have been just as high as upgrading a large bathroom on one's own. At the same time, Frau Reißner also stressed that craftsmen would have completed the work more quickly. Nevertheless, the argument for cost saving still held. 'But the bottom line is, of course, the financial side. If I want it to be the way I want it to be, I can't afford it.[33] That's just the way it is.' (interview Reißner family, Rorup, 7 January 2016) Some of the money saved was obviously invested in higher quality equipment, which could not have been afforded if outside workers had been hired.

In their interview, the Goll family also referred to the savings made through being prepared to do it themselves. The family was actively involved in the conversion work performed by skilled craftsmen, because family members carried out all the simple work and/or the manual labour. In this way, according to their own calculations, they were able to save around 36,000 euros. In this case, too, there are reports of significant cost savings through personal contributions or DIY on conversion work in the house.[34]

The interviewees' pride in their own contributions, expressed in terms of the saving of a quantifiable sum, was clear, especially when a lot of the work was done personally. In addition, since the 1950s working on your own home has been socially accepted as a meaningful leisure activity. Seen from this perspective, working on one's own home is not only regarded as a meaningful occupation, but also pays off financially (Voges 2017a: 60).

Although cost saving was mentioned as the most important reason for renovating a residential property yourself,[35] other considerations also played a role. For example, Herr Eckert pointed out that if there had been a problem with the heating system, 'common sense' and self-confidence would have been enough to solve it: 'I somehow bought a bunch of books and mastered it myself.' (interview Eckert family, Münster-Southeast, 7 October 2016) From this example it can be seen that dealing theoretically and practically with a handicraft problem and finding a solution to it makes it possible for people to experience self-efficacy. Buck Clifford Rosenberg contrasts the resulting (self-) security with Late Modern experiences of uncertainty and risk, when he writes: 'DIY home improvement is one such technique, through which enterprising citizens seek to improve and take control of their lives in a late modern world of uncertainty and risk. [...] [It] is central to neoliberal processes of self production in late modernity.' (Rosenberg 2011: 175)

In the case of homeowners who are talented or trained in manual work, personal contributions also help to distinguish them from others:

'Yes, and many people simply say, "We never imagined you could make something like this out of the house, that you've got there, or just out of the shape of the rooms." And they respect the fact that by and large we did everything ourselves. "What! You can do that? You could do that?

How did you do it?" Yes, how do you do it then... "I don't know anything about laying your own floor, doing your own tiling, ceilings and everything like that."' (interview Schulz family, Ohne, 6 April 2016)

Here, the house is used as proof of the knowledge and skills of its owner,[36] which amateurs are not able to distinguish visually from the work of experienced craftsmen. This is why this was explicitly pointed out in the interview.

House owners basically see personal contributions to the conversion process as a joint task. Nevertheless, in DIY there is a division of labour between the sexes. Overall, the interviews show that men are more closely and intensively involved in the renovation of their own homes. Without exception, men were responsible for carrying out physically and technically demanding work. What the women did exactly was rarely discussed in the interviews.[37] The proportion of time taken up by men when talking about conversion work, and DIY was significantly higher than that of the women, who left this area of communication to their husbands. The methods used by the media to represent the topic ('Self do, self have.') are not the only way in which DIY appears to be a male-dominated activity.[38]

Appropriation practices

Refurbishment and renovation work require a mental and – as has been shown – often practical examination of the property. The interviews showed that this can be read as an appropriation practice. Frau Klein, for example, described this in an interview as follows:

'Well, I think it's great and of course it's something very special if you've filled every joint with acrylic yourself and painted every ceiling yourself and above all, to see how it's slowly growing, you keep wishing for more. "Oh, can you imagine what this would look like?". Or the other day, we sat here and said "Wow, do you remember a year ago?" Well, you have a completely different relationship to it than if you're sitting in an apartment that has already been renovated, where all you had to do was put in the furniture. So here you love every corner ((laughs)) in such a house, it's really crazy. I couldn't have imagined it that way either, but ((laughs)), but that's how it is, yeah yeah.' (interview Klein family, Münster-Southeast, 4 October 2016)

Appropriation is described here as a process that is influenced by experiencing self-efficacy and the possibility of creatively reshaping the interior of the building.[39]

When asked about the refurbishment and renovation work that had been carried out, the interviewees often made an aesthetic evaluation of the house/

furnishings of the previous owners/occupants. The value judgements were usually rather negative. In contrast to the previous owners' furnishing and design, which was often described as tasteless or lacking in style, the interviewees presented their own interior design and renovation activities as an aesthetically significant improvement. For example, Frau Fischer commented on the appearance of her single-family home at the time of buying it, as follows: 'It also looked quite awful, it was quite unpleasant. It was terrible on the outside and it just wasn't pretty. But then we had sufficient imagination to see how it might look nice.' (interview Fischer family, Ohne, 12 April 2016)

The furnishings and fixtures of previous owners were at best taken over on a temporary or transitional basis. They clearly made it more difficult for new owners to settle into their own home. For that reason, the Heuerding family immediately asked for the house to be completely cleared out: 'We wanted the house to be completely empty.' (interview Heuerding family, Rorup, 1 December 2015)

Dissociation from previous owners can also be read as an appropriation practice. In contrast to historical, listed buildings, where the owners usually aim to restore the original condition, the interviewees also used their renovations to conceal the past history of the property. Their own renovation activities were intended to wipe out the current state of affairs and create a target for which there may also be (unattainable) prototypes: 'You never get to the point where everything really looks like it does in *Schöner Wohnen* magazine.' (interview Eckert family, Münster-Southeast, 7 October 2016)

'It lasted very much longer'. Time as a factor

The older existing properties (built before 1980) all needed updating in terms of their energy requirements/costs. Typical deficiencies reported by respondents include a lack of or inadequate insulation, outdated heating technology, poor energy efficiency (open fireplace, single glazing), lack of drainage and out-of-date pipes and lines. Furthermore, older single-family houses did not always live up to the buyers' expectations in terms of aesthetics and living comfort: floor coverings and tiles, wall designs (panels), bathroom furnishings and the layout of the rooms often failed to meet the new owners' expectations. In order to bring the properties into line with these expectations, they felt it was essential to carry out a more or less comprehensive conversion.

It is evident that time is an important factor in many respects when it comes to converting existing properties: Although interviewees began conversion work

immediately after buying their houses, for a number of reasons they needed far more time than initially estimated. As a result, they often described their renovation work as not yet completed. That said, they regarded the 'unfinished' part of their property less as a problem and more as a challenge and an opportunity to examine the property and its materials and adapt them to their own requirements. In this respect, conversion work begins with a period of more or less intensive theoretical (acquiring the necessary know-how) and, above all, practical examination of the existing property.
This analysis also includes the modifications made by purchasers of existing real estate. Be it that they have to adjust their ideas to living on and with a building site, or that they have to deal with solving unexpected structural and/or energy problems. From this perspective, conversion is a process of relating to a house that was not built for the purchasers. It plays an important role in the appropriation of the house as a (family) domicile, because dealing with its current state and involving themselves in more or less serious renovations gives new owners the time and opportunity to make their own mark on their house. Time also plays an important role with regard to the formation and confirmation of support networks, as social networks are established and expanded by working together. Before, during and after moving in, numerous support services are requested and called up by family members, neighbours and/or friends. In this way, the participants create or confirm social, reciprocal ties that extend beyond the present and prove to be a social glue that encourages people to settle into their new place of residence.
Whether it be the result of the participants' limited time quota or a lack of know-how, renovation work on existing real estate requires time as well as financial expenditure. The actors justify the investment of leisure time in carrying out do-it-yourself work primarily with a quantifiable cost saving. This can, however, also be categorised as an experience of personal efficacy that initiates a process of attachment to the property.
Overall, the descriptions of the conversion work show that the potential that buyers see in their respective properties plays an important role in the purchase decision. From this point of view, the potential offered by the existing property is evaluated by the players during the renovation work. They initiate a process of transformation in which the existing property is changed into 'our house'. It seems obvious that the time factor plays an important role here.

Acknowledgements

Research for this article has been done within the research network 'A House and its Objects between Family Life, Resource Management and Museum', director: Elisabeth Timm (WWU Münster, Seminar for Folklore Studies/European Ethnology), funded by the German Federal Ministry of Education and Research (programme 'The Language of Objects – Material Culture in the Context of Social Developments') 2015–2018, www.hausfragen.net (accessed 28 April 2019), funding code 01UO1504B.

References

Adloff, F. and Mau, S. (2005), 'Zur Theorie der Gabe und Reziprozität', in F. Adloff and S. Mau (eds.): Vom Geben und Nehmen. Zur Soziologie der Reziprozität (Frankfurt/New York: Campus), 9–57.

Baumeister, K. (2016), 'Prognose. Münster wächst bis 2025 auf 321.608 Einwohner', Westfälische Nachrichten, 23 November, https://www.wn.de/Muenster/2016/11/2609986-Prognose-Muenster-waechst-bis-2025-auf-321.-608-Einwohner (accessed 27 March 2019).

Caplan, A. and Wagenknecht, K. (2018), 'Bauen oder kaufen? Eine qualitativ-vergleichende Studie zu Wohnpräferenzen in Einfamilienhausgebieten in Nordwestdeutschland', Forum Stadt. Vierteljahreszeitschrift für Stadtgeschichte, Stadtsoziologie, Denkmalpflege und Stadtentwicklung 49(3), 259–273.

Clarke, A. J. (2001), 'The Aesthetics of Social Aspiration', in D. Miller (ed.): Home Possessions. Material Culture behind Closed Doors (Oxford: Berg), 23–45.

Depner, A. (2015), Dinge in Bewegung. Zum Rollenwandel materieller Objekte. Eine ethnographische Studie über den Umzug ins Altenheim (Bielefeld: transcript).

de Temple, N. (2006), '"In die Jahre gekommen…". Einfamilienhaussiedlungen im soziodemografischen Wandel', Die alte Stadt 2, 123–138.

Druta, O. and Ronald, R. (2016): 'Young Adults' Pathways into Homeownership and the Negotiation of Intra-Family Support. A Home, the Ideal Gift', Sociology 50, 1–17.

Effenberger, K.-H. (2015), Projektbericht Entwicklungsdynamik EFH, Arbeitsbaustein 4: Differenzierung der EFH-Bestände, Dresden (Leibniz-Institut für ökologische Raumentwicklung).

Fabricius, M. (2018), 'Immobilienblase kurz vor dem Platzen', Die Welt, 21 February, https://www.welt.de/print/die_welt/finanzen/article173796074/Immobilienblase-kurz-vor-dem-Platzen.html (accessed 19 October 2018).

Friedrichs, J. and Leeks, J. (2014), 'Verlassen und verramscht – wenn keiner Omas Haus will', 45 min. (Köln: WDR).

Gambetta, D. (2001), 'Kann man dem Vertrauen vertrauen?', in M. Hartmann and C. Offe (eds.): Vertrauen. Die Grundlage des sozialen Zusammenhangs (Frankfurt/New York: Campus), 204–237.

Hausaufgaben in Barkenberg (2015), Dokumentation der Auftaktwerkstatt zur Zukunft von Einfamilienhausgebieten der 1950er bis 1970er Jahre (o.O.) (Kooperationsprojekt der Stadt Dorsten, der Regionale 2016 und StadtBauKultur NRW).

Hitzler, R. and Honer, A. (1988), 'Reparatur und Repräsentation. Zur Inszenierung des Alltags durch Do-It-Yourself', Soziale Welt Sonderband, 267–283.

Hnilica, S. and Timm, E. (2017), 'Debatte: Altbauten in der Vorstadt. Eine Debatte zu Gestaltungsrealität und Nutzungsutopien', Zeitschrift für Kulturwissenschaften 2017, 141–142.

Korff, G. (2005), 'Sieben Fragen zu den Alltagsdingen', in G. M. König (ed.): Alltagsdinge. Erkundungen der materiellen Kultur (Tübingen: Tübinger Vereinigung für Volkskunde), 29–42.

Krajewski, C. (ed.) (2015), Was wird aus den Traumhäusern? Teil 1: Zum Umgang mit Einfamilienhaussiedlungen. Analysiert am Beispiel von Altena und Finnentrop in Südwestfalen (Münster: Institut für Geographie der Westfälischen

Wilhelms-Universität Münster), https://www.uni-muenster.de/imperia/md/content/geographiea/publikationen/workingpapaers/wp14.pdf, (accessed 19 October 2018).
Matzig, G. (2014), 'Neues Deutschland', Süddeutsche Zeitung, 22 September.
Mauss, M. (1990), The gift: form and reason for exchange in archaic societies (New York / London: Norton).
Menzl, M. (2007), Leben in Suburbia. Raumstrukturen und Alltagspraktiken am Rand von Hamburg (Frankfurt/New York: Campus).
Miller, D. (n.d.), 'What is a Relationship? Kinship as Negotiated Experience', https://www.ucl.ac.uk/anthropology/people/academic-and-teaching-staff/daniel-miller/what-relationship-kinship-negotiated-experience (accessed 25 March 2019).
Rosenberg, B. C. (2011), 'The Our House DIY Club. Amateurs, leisure knowledge and lifestyle media', International Journal of Cultural Studies 14(2), 173–190.
Schieritz, M. (2016), 'Hausgeträumt', Die Zeit, 4 January, https://www.zeit.de/2015/51/immobilien-eigentum-wirtschaft-investition-berlin (accessed 19 October 2018).
Schinkel, S. (2013), Familiäre Räume. Eine Ethnographie des 'gewohnten' Zusammenlebens als Familie (Bielefeld: transcript).
Statistische Ämter des Bundes und der Länder (ed.) (2014), Census 2011. Gebäude und Wohnungsbestand in Deutschland. Erste Ergebnisse der Gebäude- und Wohnungszählung, Hannover.
Utku, Y., Gudewer, S., Krüger-Willim, C., and Bölting, T. (2017), Hausaufgaben. Bürgerschaftliches Engagement in alternden Einfamilienhausgebieten, edited by the Landesinitiative StadtBauKultur NRW 2020, Bottrop.
Voges, J. (2017a), Selbst ist der Mann. Do-it-yourself und Heimwerken in der Bundesrepublik Deutschland (Göttingen: Wallstein).
Voges, J. (2017b), 'Mit Geschmack und wenig Geld. Heimwerken als Aneignungspraxis des Einfamilienhauses von den 1950er bis in die 1980er Jahre', Zeitschrift für Kulturwissenschaften 2017(1), 97–116.
Zakrzewski, P., Berndgen-Kaiser, A., Fox-Kämper, R. and Siedentop, S. (2014), 'Herausforderungen westdeutscher Einfamilienhausgebiete der Nachkriegszeit. Bestandsentwicklung als neues Handlungsfeld für Kommunen', Comparative Population Studies 39(2), 247–284.

Interviews

Ohne, Fischer family, 12 April 2016
Ohne, Flasberg family, 15 March 2016
Ohne, Schulz family, 6 April 2016

Münster-Southeast, Klein family, 4 October 2016
Münster-Southeast, Eckert family, 7 October 2016

Rorup, Krause family, 13 January 2016
Rorup, Reißner family, 7 January 2016
Rorup, Goll family, 4 November 2016
Rorup, Wiedmann family, 17 December 2015
Rorup, Heuerding family, 1 December 2015

Endnotes

1 See https://www.bmi.bund.de/SharedDocs/downloads/DE/veroeffentlichungen/2018/ergebnisse-wohngipfel.pdf?__blob=publicationFile&v=3 (accessed 4 April 2019); on municipal projects see for example: StadtBauKultur NRW, 'Projekt Hausaufgaben' (Information on: https://stadtbaukultur-nrw.de/neues/jung-kauft-alt/, accessed 18 October 2018), the regional project 'Innen leben –

Neue Qualitäten entwickeln!', 2016, and also the municipal authority promotion programme 'Jung kauft alt' (Information can be obtained, for example, on the website of StadtBauKultur NRW: https://stadtbaukultur-nrw.de/neues/jung-kauft-alt/, accessed 22 October 2018); also summarised by Zakrzewski et al. 2014.

2 See e.g. https://ratsinformation.stadt-koeln.de/getfile.asp?id=357875&type=do& (accessed 10 April 2019); https://www.fona.de/mediathek/pdf/Zukunftsstadt.pdf (accessed 25 March 2019).

3 See e.g. https://stadtbaukultur-nrw.de/neues/jung-kauft-alt/ (accessed 22 October 2018).

4 This aspect has been particularly emphasised in the media.

5 See also the regional project *WohnZukunft Südkirchen*: http://www.regionale2016.de/de/regionale-projekte/projekt-datailseiten/wohnzukunft-suedkirchen.html (accessed 25 March 2019).

6 In a study published by Christian Krajewski (Krajewski 2015), which examines how two communities in the Sauerland region deal with older single-family dwellings, residents and owners of existing real estate were asked, among other things (within the framework of a quantitative household survey), to assess their housing situation, the generation change in the houses and their civic commitment.

7 Landesamt für Statistik Niedersachsen, LSN-Online Regionaldatenbank, Tabelle 12411: Fortschreibung des Bevölkerungsstandes, as of 31 December 2017 (accessed 26 March 2019).

8 https://www.ohner-dorfladen.de/ (accessed 26 March 2019).

9 http://www.schuettorf.de/staticsite/staticsite.php?menuid=13&topmenu=2 (accessed 4 April 2019).

10 See Archiv Volkskundliche Kommission für Westfalen, *Bestand 'Hausfragen'*. The data were obtained from interviews with the Fischer, Flasberg, Schulz, Krause, Reißner, Goll, Wiedmann, Heuerding, Klein and Ecker families.

11 https://www.duelmen.de/fileadmin/user_upload/allgemein/medien/buergerbuero/altersp_rorup.pdf (accessed 26 March 2019).

12 Construction area Pastor-Rück-Straße: 26 single-family homes, three apartment buildings and eight semi-detached houses are planned there, see https://www.duelmen.de/4057.html (accessed 4 April 2019).

13 https://www.duelmen.de/4057.html (accessed 4 April 2019).

14 The land guideline value is an average land value per square metre determined from purchase prices, based on a fictitious property typical of the area. It is determined by expert committees., see https://www.boris.nrw.de/borisplus/?lang=de (accessed 5 April 2019).

15 https://www.duelmen.de/4057.html (accessed 4 April 2019).

16 https://www.stadt-muenster.de/fileadmin//user_upload/stadt-muenster/61_stadtentwicklung/pdf/karten/Statistische_Gebietsgliederung_Schematische_Darstellungen_Bevoelkerung.pdf (accessed 4 April 2019).

17 https://www.stadt-muenster.de/stadtentwicklung/zahlen-daten-fakten.html (accessed 27 March 2019).

18 For current building areas see https://www.stadt-muenster.de/stadtplanung/aktuelle-baugebiete.html#c38194 (accessed 25 March 2019).

19 http://www.staedtestatistik.de/fileadmin/vdst/Aachen2017/FJT2017_0314-10Muenster_01.pdf (accessed 25 March 2019).

20 https://www.stadt-muenster.de/fileadmin//user_upload/stadt-muenster/62_gutachter/pdf/GMB_119_2018_pflichtig.pdf (accessed 26 March 2019).

21 Between 2011 and 2018, the standard land value in Münster-Southeast almost doubled. In 2011, it was around 220 to 280 euros per square metre. (see www.boris.nrw.de, accessed 25 March 2019); for the valuation of real estate see also https://www.stadt-muenster.de/fileadmin//user_upload/stadt-muenster/62_gutachter/pdf/GMB_119_2018_pflichtig.pdf (accessed 26 March 2019).

22 The duration of the interviews followed by an inspection of the house in project B was between 1.5 and 3.5 hours. The interview partners were recruited via mayors, local leaders, advertisements, direct mail and the snowball system, which has produced good results especially in small towns. A comparative study of projects A and B from the joint research project can be found in this volume and elsewhere: cf. Caplan and Wagenknecht 2018.

23 Under reconstruction work, both energetic-technical modernisations and extensions and aesthetic adaptations are summarised here.

24 In the quotation Herr Goll speaks of an 'adventure', suggesting that this was an 'exciting' experience. Specific differences to this point of view based on gender are not explicitly reflected in the sample: It is not clear whether the conversion is more of an adventure for men and a burden for women.

25 How people introduce and adapt their products into their new environment is a fundamental and important question for European ethnology. (cf. Korff 2005: 40).

26 Whether the Wiedmann family asked Herr Wiedmann's relatives for help at all cannot be ascertained from the interview.

27 See basically on this theme Mauss 1990.

28 Cultural and social-anthropological researchers on the concept and manifestations of the exchange of gifts (which Marcel Mauss strictly contrasted with modern socialisation in general and the commodity form in particular) have documented and researched the flexibility of this social and economic form, particularly in the context of the family, consumer society and urban situations (e.g. Miller: undated).

29 In order to ensure anonymity, the names and places of investigation are not mentioned here.

30 Miller interprets such behaviour as a way of overcoming the discrepancy between a normative ideal of the relationship and the actual state (Miller (undated): 17). With regard to an intra-family context, Oana Druta and Richard Ronald point out that intergenerational support, i.e. financial and practical help in converting/building a house, which parents grant their children, also helps them to agree on a common cosmos of values and to make long-term provisions for the family (Druta and Ronald 2016: 9f.).

31 According to Jonathan Voges, this includes 'activities of a manual nature' which 'are carried out by unskilled persons – do-it-yourselfers – on and in their own house or apartment'. Voges points out that in addition to the actual outcomes, these practices 'also have added social and mental value' (Voges 2017a. 17). The term DIY, which has been used in the Federal Republic of Germany since the 1960s, is to be used synonymously here.

32 Voges names the framework conditions for the DIY movement in the Federal Republic of Germany: 'the reduction in working hours, the additional space gained through larger dwellings and the construction of owner-occupied homes, and finally an increase in disposable income' (Voges 2017a: 61). See also: Voges 2017b; Hitzler and Honer 1988.

33 This statement refers to the performance of all the work done by a professional craftsman. The interview uses the example of tiling by referring to 'great tiles' from a local shop.

34 With regard to the bricklaying work, Herr Goll explained: 'The first offers were all around seventy to eighty thousand euros. So in the end, we did it all ourselves through our own efforts. Here with bricklayers, material and hourly wages, it came to around thirty-four thousand euros.' (interview Goll family, Rorup, 4 November 2015) The following applies to all the cost details: it was not possible to check how precise these details were in the discussions, as no invoices or building documents were submitted.

35 At least in part, this can also be seen as a plausibility strategy (cf. Voges 2017a: 70).

36 However, the architect had rarely visited the construction site, 'because I basically

knew it myself, can do it myself. I just wasn't allowed to sign myself ((laughs)).' (interview Schulz family, Ohne, 6 April 2016).

37 Frau Klein is an exception here. She refurbishes old furniture and was actively involved in the renovation of the house, e.g. making the backsplash in the kitchen. In the interview, however, she usually spoke in plural ('we tore out all the floors') when describing the renovation work, so it is difficult to say who carried out this work in each individual case. All in all, however, Frau Klein showed that she was extremely interested and well informed when it came to the work that had been carried out or was still to be done in and around the house (interview Klein family, Münster-Southeast, 4 October 2016).

38 The problem of gender-specific role assignment in DIY is addressed, for example, in the American sitcom 'Home Improvement' (1991–1999). In Germany, the series was shown on ARD under the title 'Die Heimwerker' (from 1992, two episodes), 'Der Dünnbrettbohrer' (from 1993) and again in 1994 as 'Der Heimwerker'. From 1996, the sitcom was broadcast in a new dubbed version as 'Hör mal, wer da hämmert' on RTL. On the theme of DIY as a TV format see with reference to Australia: Rosenberg 2011.

39 Rosenberg (2011: 186f.), for example, takes this perspective, and interprets the Australian example of the new public mobilisation of do-it-yourself as an element of people presenting themselves as 'productive citizens' who also work in their spare time. Alison J. Clarke also stresses the dynamics of social distinction in home and flat-related do-it-yourself work using an English example (Clarke 2001). In contrast, Jonathan Voges (2017a: 13) suggests that DIY should also be interpreted as an attempt to partially reverse the change in the world of work, where the actors 'return to a state of handicraft, holistic and self-responsible activity'. From this perspective, DIY could be understood as a retreat into the private sphere and as compensation for alienated, meaningless gainful employment.

Renting is wasting: on the popular economy of home ownership in Germany

Jakob Smigla-Zywocki

Introduction

In 'La poétique de l'espace', Gaston Bachelard described 'the house as a tool for analysis of the human soul' (Bachelard 1994: XXXVII). Consequentially, the analysis of the hidden meaning and symbolism of the house has a significant position in his work. Within this, Bachelard (1994: 17) measures housing quality in relation to the verticality of the house. Concerning urban housing, he notes pejoratively:

> 'The inhabitants of the big city live in superimposed boxes. [. . .] The number of the street and the floor give the location of our "conventional hole", but our abode has neither space around it nor verticality inside it. [. . .] Home has become mere horizontality. [. . .] For here, where houses are no longer set in natural surroundings, the relationship between house and space becomes an artificial one. Everything about it is mechanical and, on every side, intimate living flees.' (Bachelard 1994: 26 f.)

Thus, Bachelard states, real living takes place in a house. Additionally, good housing is linked to 'nature'. Housing in a city, on the other hand, is described as living in boxes placed one above the other. A similar position is represented by German philosopher Otto Friedrich Bollnow, who dedicated the third chapter of his fundamental work on special experiences of human life to the secureness of the house:

> 'In order to survive in the world and be able to fulfil his tasks there, man needs a space providing security and peace, to which he can retreat, in which he can unwind and become his normal self again, when he has worn himself out in battle with the outside world. [...] Only as a dweller, only

> in possession of a house, only in having at one's disposal such a "private" domain separated from public life can man fulfil his nature and be fully human.' (Bollnow 2011: 130)

For Bollnow, the ownership of a house, or more precisely of a private area, is one of the prerequisites of being human. The anthropological function of a house is to be a retreat. The possession of such a home is indispensable to become human to the full extent. Both Bachelard and Bollnow make the detached house the focal point of their consideration. For both philosophers, inhabiting mainly takes place in a self-owned home. Living in a rented accommodation is hereby being devalued in comparison with living in a house you own. It is obvious, that the ideas of these two philosophers are not so much about the *conditio humana*, but highly culturally specific, inextricably tied to a seemingly natural order, i.e. bourgeois society with the type of domesticity being privacy, as it developed since the eighteenth century, and based on the possibility to turn land into private property for this purpose. These philosophers' observations have a historical tradition in German-speaking countries. During the late nineteenth and the early twentieth century, migration to the industrialising and growing urban centres led to the 'housing question' (Wohnungsfrage). Quite different political factions understood densified cities with miserable living quarters as a cause of social tension and political upheaval.

Against that, the detached small house, located in the garden city of reform architecture planning, and owned by its upright and modest inhabitants (Redensek 2017), enjoyed an excellent reputation. Housing reformers propagated home ownership as appropriate also for working class families and believed that this would reduce their vulnerability towards economic crises (Schulz 2006: 370). Thus, house ownership was even understood as a guarantee of an economically stable and politically calm working class, which was believed to be more loyal towards the state (Wischermann 1997: 362 f.). In advertising, the motif of a happy childhood in the garden of one's parents' house became popular (Wagner-Douglas 2005: 104 ff.). The dichotomy between urban and rural areas became articulated by the dichotomy of renting vs. home ownership, e.g. as a major theme in the Nazi propaganda commercial *Menschen im Schatten, Menschen im Licht* (literally: 'People in the shadow, people in the light') from 1934. It tells the story of a worker in Berlin, who lives his life in dark barracks and visits a befriended couple (also working class) in their new home in the suburbs at the weekend (Ziereis 2005: 114 f.). The message is clear: renting accommodation is presented as low-quality living, while living in one's own property symbolises health, happiness, and freedom. After the Second World War, West German reconstruction policy with the Cold War on the horizon again supported a preference of home ownership, financially as well as politically: Subsidies or tax regulation that facilitated home ownership were announced as the working class' share in post-war prosperity, as a democratisation of the bourgeois privilege of owning a house, as contribution to asset accumulation that for the time being would prevent these households from turning into political radicals. Emerging consumerism made the household in general and the one located in a detached house surrounded by a garden in particular the main place of consumption, leisure, and prosperity.

Today, the Federal Foundation *Baukultur* observes that the residence desired by the majority of the German population is to be located in a small rural community:

> 'However the desire for a life in a small municipality is not connected with the idea of village life and work. Rather, the country is equated with "green living", [...]. [...] Those who usually choose – from the age of about 30 – a less urban residential location are mostly drawn to urban expansion areas in the affluent suburbs of cities. Thus they connect the hope for "a piece of green" with simultaneous accessibility to their workplace.' (Bundesstiftung Baukultur 2017: 36 f.)

Further examples are periodically published housing market reports of banks, in which either the development of the housing supply, the demand, and fundamental observations of the housing field are being addressed (NRW.Bank 2014), or reports of local authority districts, which focus on regional developments on district and city levels (RegioWoB OWL 2011). German building societies, in particular, with accumulated savings of remarkable 876.6 billion euros in 2015 (Statista 2016: 8), act as a big player on the housing and house market and have established their business model on the desire of home ownership of potential buyers.

Accordingly, it is not surprising that German building societies have their own studies carried out to determine the reasons for the house purchase request of their customers – or rather: to promote them, since it is in their interest to sell houses or to profit from private households who finance a property. In their 2013 home ownership study, the LBS (Landesbausparkasse) asked for the motives of first-time buyers of property. 79 percent of those surveyed answered (multiple answers where possible) that their main motive was 'to live in an own house or flat' (Bundesgeschäftsstelle Landesbausparkassen 2013: 26). In second place, the interviewees named building up of their old-age provision as a motive. In surveys conducted between 2008 and 2011, the LBS also determined which housing type was the most popular among the respondents. The single-family dwelling (with or without granny flat) led clearly with 59 percent compared to the terraced house (15 percent), the condominium (22 percent), and other variants (four percent) (Bundesgeschäftsstelle Landesbausparkassen ibid.: 17). Not surprisingly, renting an accommodation did not appear in these studies, neither in the questions nor as a possible answer. In the same survey, the building society contract turned out to be the most popular starter saving form for home buying with 41 percent of responses, beating even the saving balances of banks with 39 percent (ibid.: 31). It is striking how derogatory the depiction of living in rented accommodation compared to living in a private property is. Looking at the homepage of another major German building society, a further aspect emerges: When visiting the homepage of the German building society *Schwäbisch Hall* in early 2018, the slogan 'break up with your landlord' is the first eye-catching headline. Presupposing the recipient's approval, the advertisement also proclaims, 'Paying rent? No, thanks.' This implies that living in rented accommodation is worth less and, as it is mentioned further on, 'everyone dreams of their own home sooner or later':[1]

Figure 1: An advertisement for buying property suggests to end one's tenancy, using the semantics of an unhappy love affair (Bausparkasse Schwäbisch Hall AG, 2018).

In the following, I will present the findings of my research on these topics: What are the cultural ideals connected to renting and to home ownership respectively? To investigate this, I asked the very group that performs such ideals, i.e. people who invest in a building society contract to acquire a property.

Method and sample group

The sample group that I generated via snowballing within the regional framework of a research association that investigated the presence and the variants of the single-family home in northwestern Germany[2] included 15 qualitative interviews with 19 persons between April 2015 and July 2016.[3] I organised these conversations as narrative interviews (Spiritova 2014: 117 ff.). The duration of the interviews ranged from 37:50 minutes to 1 hour and 49 minutes. In all interviews, the topic at hand was both the personal story of Bausparen and the residence of the person in general. Before they moved to their own property, all persons interviewed either lived in rental accommodations or grew up in their parents' homes. Without me making a direct inquiry, most of the interviewees made a connection between these experiences as a central reason for their wish to become homeowners. I will now present four detailed results of the accounts and the semantics that surfaced in this sample group of people telling their stories of saving for their own property. The material indicates that imaginations about renting and home ownership are structured antagonistically. The interviewees are anonymised.

'Economising into one's own pocket' and the permanence of property

Already my first interviewee, Mrs. Hertel, replied to the question as to why she and her husband wanted to purchase a house as followed:

> 'We simply don't want to gift a landlord money. We prefer to economise into our own pocket.' (Interview Hertel Family, 25 August 2015)

Mrs. Hertel refers to the rental payment as a gift to the landlord. For her, it is basically a payment without a lasting value. In her understanding, renting is not paying for accommodation but giving away money, a financial loss. The purchase of property, on the other hand, seems to be a rational and forward-looking way of 'economising into one's own pocket'. Therefore, she describes two modes of proceeding, which are either positively or negatively accentuated: while renting only benefits the landlord, living in one's own property is understood as 'economising' – although the money is also spent. Here, the term 'economising' implies the rational use of capital for one's own benefit now and in the future. Mr. Hertel added in connection with his wife's statement:

> 'Well, it's mainly the rent that is our concern. Even though it's not high, it is a cost block that is gone as soon as it is paid. And, as they say, a mortgage means to economise into one's own pocket for 30 or 40 years. This is similar to renting, but it is to ensure that we will get a home for our ourselves.' (ibid.)

The cost block, as which the rent is described, is understood to be re-invested fully into the own property. As such, Mr. Hertel compares the building loan to the rent. The decisive difference between these forms of payment is the understanding of mortgage not as an expense but as an investment of the family's money. Furthermore, the mortgage is not perceived as debt. The idea of a direct conversion of rent into property skips the intermediate step of the loan with all costs involved, which in Germany can be provided by a bank or a building society, and which must be paid back with interest. This indebtedness is not part of this family's home ownership story, it is hidden behind a form of 'debt amnesia', as Adiana Soaita and Beverly Searle (Soaita and Searle 2016) coined it. In their research on home ownership in the UK, they observed

> 'the normalisation of debt in the UK, which feed into the unspoken, tacit knowledge of homebuying. As shown in other studies, our participants simply saw mortgage debt as a good form of debt or even no debt at all: "in this country, having a mortgage is seen as saving, really"' (Soaita and Searle 2016: 1098).

Payment-related costs also disappear in the case of the interviewed German houseowners behind the idea of investing into 'one's own pocket'. The importance of *economising* is also indicated by repeating this statement at the end of the interview. To the open question of whether the family would like to add anything to our conversation, Mrs. Hertel replied:

> 'Well, you have to speed up somehow in life. You simply have to consider whether it's worth it or not. And our main priority is a permanent house, to economise into our own pocket.' (ibid.)

With the notion of the permanent house, a second dichotomy is being communicated: the permanent house vs. unpredictable renting. Paying rent is once again understood as losing the family's wealth. The lasting house, on the other hand, implies a sustainable investment in the family's future. The statement, expressed both at the beginning and at the end of the interview, marks the importance of this perception for the desire for own property. The ideal of the lasting house has also been observed in another realm of the housing sector. In her study on advertising prefab house design, Julia Gill detected the ideal of consistency (*Beständigkeit*) (Gill 2010: 180 f.).[4] She interprets such an orientation as an antipode in a world of consumption characterised by accelerated product and consumption cycles. Unlike most everyday objects, buyers expect and imagine home ownership to fulfil lasting values. Gill (2010: 184) points out that in the German case, where the acquisition of a home is in fact and as a cultural preference done once in a lifetime, longevity combined with the preservation or even an increase of the property value is much desired. Other interviewees used the same or a similar phrase to explain and rationalise the purchase of property. For example, the White family:

'Well, we are a couple since 1996, and after two or three years it was clear that we would move in together. We first considered renting a flat and started to view several flats. But then we discarded this idea. Why should we give the money to a landlord? We better look for our own house.' (interview White family, 21 December 2015)

This statement marks the start of the family's history of living together and once again presents the central argument against renting an apartment. Paying rent is not understood as a payment for a received service or good, but as giving away money to a landlord, basically a gift without any return. In a later statement, Mr. White adds:

'Well, it cannot be denied: The rent that the landlord gets is better paid to the bank as a monthly obolus, and then after 15 to 20 years we are able to say, "Now this is our own property." Meanwhile, I changed my view a little bit, since after 20 years, a house naturally is in need of repair.' (ibid.)

Unlike the Hertel family, the White family is aware of their financial dependence on the bank until the loan is repaid. Their conception is not focused on economising into their own pocket, because they refer to the monthly mortgage as redemption they pay to the bank. They understand that the house is not part of their assets until the debt is repaid in full. However, they also understate and revalue these redemptions as doing the bank a small courtesy, since they call it 'a monthly obolus'. This term indeed trivialises the costs for a house that, in fact, are not small amounts of money or even a voluntary donation, as the meaning of the Greek word obulus (*a small coin*) suggests, but are a high and legally binding financial engagement. At the same time, Mr. White seems to be aware that property does not exist forever and causes significant maintenance costs. Such maintenance costs were a blind spot in all other interviews, and in the other interviewees' perspectives concerning the ideals connected with own property and renting. Similarly, Mr. Schneider described the idea that the money paid for rent was ultimately lost, while a loan is supposed to multiply the value of the property in the long run:

'Well, I know this from my past. I grew up with the idea that someone [...] who lives in rented accommodation will pay rent until the end of his life. And the one who buys a house will pay back the loan for thirty years. One day, the redemption will be completed and then the person will pay less than for living in rented accommodation. This is especially favourable when one's income decreases in old age. Maybe it is my background that made me do it this way.' (interview Mr. Schneider, 26 August 2015)

In Mr. Schneider's story, owning a property is much cheaper in the long run than renting it. However, this description leaves out a fundamental precondition to make this calculation add up in the end: a lasting or even rising property value, and stable or rather decreasing maintenance costs.

The understanding that residential property is to be acquired for the purpose of old-age or retirement provision is not just one of the central selling strategies of German building societies since they were invented, but was lately raised anew by asset-based welfare policies that unfold as 'responsibilisation', i.e. as individualising risks of any kind: 'Home ownership is increasingly being regarded as a proven remedy against life's uncertainties. It is not so much the state that helps to protect individuals against biographical vicissitudes, but individuals have to rely on themselves for their social security and are themselves responsible for their asset development' (Heeg 2013: 7 f., author's translation). Guarantees and benefits that the Fordist welfare state also in its West German variant offered to its citizens now turn into offers that the individual can buy or rather consume, and that consumer-citizens have to pay for (Blank et al. 2012: 168). One important element in this recent view of social security as private asset management is residential property. Mr. Schneider's argument ties in with the dynamics of responsibilisation. Planning for his old age when his income will decrease is based on owning a house that he expects to cause lower costs than paying rent. It is telling that this consideration is also made without mentioning any element of social security that comes from public authorities.

As other research yielded, such accounts and semantics are nowadays widely shared in countries with a great variety of welfare regimes. Thus, Christian Poppe et al. (2013) in their case study on 'The role of homeownership in the financing of everyday life', based on group interviews in Norway, Denmark, and the United Kingdom, conclude that 'people see homeownership as attractive and become owners rather than tenants for a number of financial as well as more profound social reasons. In all countries, financial motives tend to be mentioned first and are also what the focus group participants commonly formulate as the main conclusion of the discussion on why they have become homeowners' (Poppe et al. 2013: 6). Common opinions that this research documents are 'views like "it is cheaper to buy than to rent", "it is a good investment", and "it is better to pay to oneself than wasting money on rent to somebody else"' (ibid.).

Figure 2: An advertisement that suggests that owning a house is not costlier than paying rent and simultaneously equates house with ownership and flat with renting (National Association of German Building Societies, around 1930).

The idea of economising into one's own pocket has been used as a marketing strategy by Bausparkassen since the beginning of the twentieth century. A setting copy for an advertisement campaign of the National Association of German Building Societies states, for example: 'Every month you pay 40 or 50 Marks or more, in the end you own nothing. Thus, in about 30 years you will have spent 15,000 to 25,000 Marks just on rent. For the same amount you could be a homeowner!' (author's translation) It is also telling that such campaigns equated renting with small flats and owning with small houses surrounded by a garden:

Today, the homepage of the LBS building society offers a rent calculator, which invites visitors to enter their monthly rent (between 50 and 2,000 euros) and the number of years they have already lived in an apartment (LBS 2017). If, for example, the visitor selects 700 euros rent and 25 years, the homepage calculates: 'That's the amount of rent you gifted: 210,000 euros.' Obviously and consequently, the better option is to buy a house. To be successful, advertising has to match the cultural values and ideals of potential customers. The drastic wording ('to gift') fits in with the before mentioned conceptions, and vice

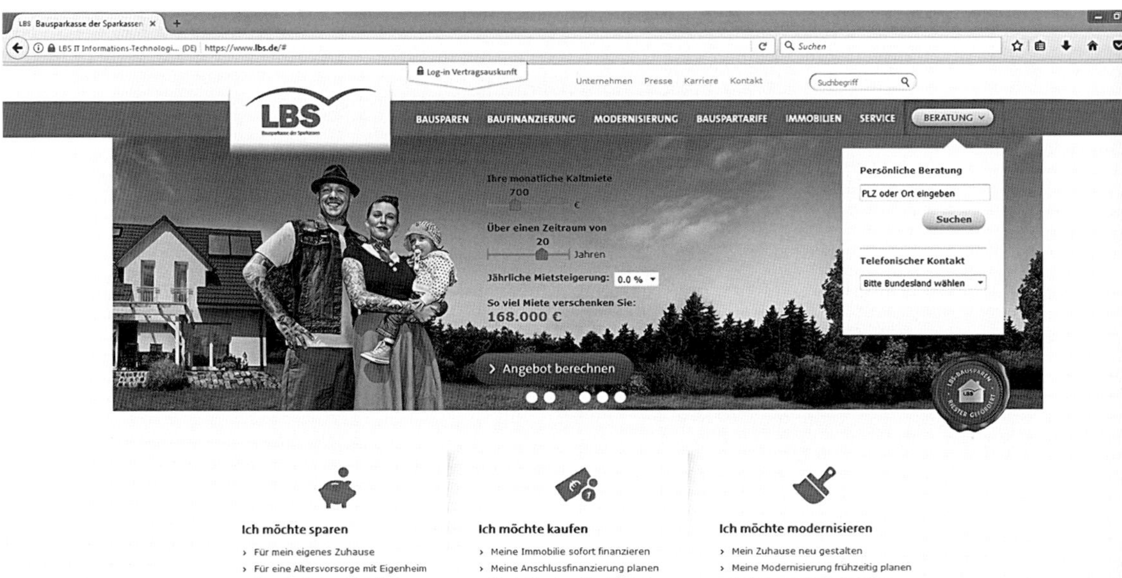

Figure 3: The LBS Building Society's 'Mietrechner' (rent calculator) equates paying rent with gifting or wasting money (LBS Westdeutsche Landesbausparkasse, April 2018).

versa. Rental payments are characterised as a gift to the landlord and a waste of the tenant's wealth. In contrast to this waste of money, the LBS calculator presents loan payments as money that could be saved without any sacrifice. The resulting obligations towards banks or building societies and related costs are not part of the equation. The provision of living space and the administrative services of the landlord are completely neglected in this calculation.

Making the housing preference plausible

Another striking point in the interview material can be found in the interviewees' housing-related biographical history. Almost all interviewees agreed with the idea of renting as a temporary solution. At this point I have to mention that this dominant preference of home ownership as a way of living is most likely based on the composition of the sample: most of the interviewees live in a suburban or rural area. They either grew up in their parents' properties or they lived with their parents in rented accommodations. Mrs. Hertel, for example, continued in the context of the above discussed quote:

> 'We simply do not want to gift money to a landlord. We would like to economise into our own pocket. We are used to that from our families. My parents as well as your (addressing her husband) parents live in a single-family home. We don't know anything else, and therefore this has always been our aim for the future.' (interview Hertel family, 25 August 2015)

The Hertels adopted a positive attitude towards being a houseowner from their parents, and both internalised home ownership as the ideal way of living. Life as a houseowner is therefore the only lifestyle imaginable for the young family, and it is clearly described as an 'aim for the future'. Although the Hertels lived in a flat in the same house as their landlord at the time of the interview, this form of living vanished in the representation of their housing history. It merely had the status of an intermediate step between the past and their imagined future life in their own property. The Hertels also discussed the possibility of receiving financial support from their families to buy a house. In their study on 'young adults' pathways into homeownership', Oana Druta and Richard Ronald discovered, beyond other things, that

> 'homeownership is a uniquely suitable way for families to ensure continuity, particularly of social status. Owned homes are physical objects difficult enough to squander, but easy enough to tap into when needed. Thus, while allowing the older generation to keep wealth in the family, it enables the younger generation to engage in responsible consumption.' (Druta and Ronald 2016: 14)

While the Hertels report that they see their parents' example as a role model, they also concede that they try to ensure a continuity of social status and wealth by owning a single-family home. Growing up in each partner's parents' house is thus presented in the accounts as a plausibilisation of the own housing preferences. Very similar to the Hertels, Mrs. Schwenker also described growing up in her parents' house as a formative experience in her biography:

> 'I had a room of my own. I have two siblings, I am in the middle, and we all had a room of our own. This was self-evident for me, and it was common practice in my circles, too. It also was common practice that all my friends grew up in a house, in a private home, and not in a rented one. Later, when I got to know other ways of living, I really appreciated what was self-evident in earlier times.' (interview Mrs. Schwenker, 5 July 2016)

Although Mrs. Schwenker mentioned in a previous part of the interview that she used to live in two different rented apartments with her siblings and her parents, both of these phases vanished behind the experience of growing up in a private property, which she characterised as a common practice in her circles. Living in rented apartments became a sort of exotic and different 'way of life', and her own past became too unimportant to be mentioned. She even characterised her former peer group as people living in a private home, and not 'some rented ones'. Her childhood Mrs. Schwenker told of in the interview began when she had her own room in her family's house, so that she developed a deep and positive connection to this 'way of life'. Mrs. Schwenker adopted this draft for her own living ideas:

> 'I grew up with this idea because my parents lived that way. In my parents' environment, the families, meaning siblings of my parents with their families, all have their own property. That was normal and natural for me. Well, at some point the own home will happen. With a partner, children, whatever.' (interview Mrs. Schwenker, 5 July 2016)

These experiences led Mrs. Schwenker to take it for granted that her own home would eventually *happen*. The idea of becoming a homeowner was strongly connected to the idea of founding a family. The house therefore included not only the partner, but also children, which would complete the living and housing ideal. Mr. and Mrs. White, who both grew up in a rural environment, told a similar story:

> 'Well, we always saved for this purpose, to acquire a housing property. One that is ours. Renting is only a temporary solution, if at all. But in fact, this was never an option for us as an aim in life, to create a situation where we live in rented accommodation. It should always be home ownership. This has also been the case in our family, my parents had housing property, the farmstead.' (interview White family, 21 December 2015)

The desire to become a homeowner is again described as an 'aim in life'. Renting is only, if at all, a temporary solution and cannot be imagined as a biographically plausible aim. The basis for this view in nearly all interviews is the parents' home ownership. The White family sees the explanation for their attitude in their rural origin. Most of the interviewees regard their parents' way of living as a smart strategy that is understood as a successful model for their own life. Therefore, these experiences, including the negative attitude towards renting, are appropriated by the next generation. This devaluation of renting is an especially interesting finding of the interviews, because it was not included in the list of questions and was in all cases brought up by the interviewees themselves. This reflects the interviewees' strong appreciation of home ownership and their negative appraisal of renting. This trait has also been documented in various research on housing preferences: Poppe et al., for example, found very similar 'social inducements' in their study on Norway, Denmark, and the UK:

> 'One is tradition and social status; buying is the way "we" get a home. Not only getting a home, but also "knowing that it's yours" is a goal in life. The influence of the parents and other family members are often mentioned as a reason for ending up as homeowners. Thus, social heritage and learning from one's social environment appear as important triggers.' (Poppe et al. 2013: 7)

Designing the living space: *freedom of choice vs. dependencies*

Another characteristic of the interviewees' stories is a dichotomy of dependence vs. self-determined lifestyle and the freedom of choice. Mr. Hertel, for example, explained why he and his wife were looking for a house to purchase at the time of our interview:

> 'You simply have more space. Here, we live in a rented flat. And that's okay. But if we want to change something architecturally, putting in an additional wall or something like that, we don't want to discuss this with the landlord.' (interview Hertel family, 25 August 2015)

Living in a self-owned house is connected to the idea of being free to design the living space according to one's own wishes. Renting, on the other hand, is understood as being dependent on someone else's decisions. The freedom of living in a rented accommodation is mostly ignored: not having to deal with certain liabilities, like, for example, communicating with municipal authorities. The basic difference between rents and costs of buying is the positive attitude towards the idea of freedom, which, in this understanding, living in a rented flat cannot ensure. The idea of achieving freedom, which the Hertel family associates with home ownership, was also highly important for the White family:

> Mrs. White: 'I mean, we never lived in rented accommodation, and here we can do what we like. We do not have to ask anybody beforehand. This would not be possible in a rented flat.' Mr. White: 'Well, if we would consider tearing something down.' Mrs. White: 'Some walls, or whatever.' Mr. White: 'Perhaps we would need to ask the building authority or a structural engineer, but nobody else. If we both agree to do that, then we could do that.' (interview White family, 21 December 2015)

Renting serves as a symbol of other-directed living. Living in one's own property, on the other hand, in this case a secluded farmstead in a rural area, is understood as a fully self-determined form of living. Mostly independent from external influences, the capacity to act in terms of designing the property is believed to lie exclusively in the hands of the homeowners. This kind of freedom is considered impossible in rented flats or houses. Again, these findings are also reported by Poppe et al. in their comparative study on Norway, Denmark, and the UK. They report that in their interviews another 'frequently mentioned set of motives for going into homeownership is related to freedom: as an owner, one can do whatever one pleases to the home, like decorating, improving its standards, and in other ways facilitate commonplace lifestyles and identities as individuals and families' (Poppe et al. 2013: 7). Interestingly, despite these ideas of freedom connected to one's own house, not all Westphalian interviewees have characterised home ownership as a gain in freedom of choice. Besides the only briefly mentioned aspects of property organisation and management, the home was also regarded as a high financial burden and a restriction regarding the freedom of choice, for example in the case of Mrs. Schwenker:

> 'What discourages me is the financial burden for a very long time. You can't say after two years: Oh well, somehow, I do not like the house anymore. I will move. With renting, I have this flexibility. Home ownership is such a big commitment for a long time.' (interview Mrs. Schwenker, 5 July 2016)

First and foremost, there are financial considerations which she believed to be a significant argument against home ownership. These have been understood to be a long-term commitment. At the same time, living in a rented place is providing possibilities of flexibility, especially when it comes to changing one's place of residence or work. Being a homeowner is binding both financially and locally. For Mr. Schneider, the security – compared to a lease contract – was a weighty argument for property. When asked what constitutes good living for him, he answered:

> 'On the one hand, you can live in the house for a long time, so to speak. You don't have to be afraid that you have to move out after three months. This can happen in a rented apartment, even if you have a contract.' (interview Mr. Schneider, 25 August 2015)

A rented apartment is considered something that cannot offer security, not even by contract. The fear of losing his housing space due to actually arbitrary termination by the landlord leads in his perception conversely to the positive emphasis on long-term living in a private home. A similar viewpoint was reported by Mrs. Schwenker. When asked about arguments that support the idea of becoming a homeowner, she not only voiced her scepticism mentioned above, but also pointed out benefits of home ownership:

'One important point is: It is a security for retirement. And, of course, it is nice to own something So, here in my rented flat, sure, I have the feeling that this is mine somehow. But my landlord could someday announce his own needs and terminate the contract. Owning a home is a security.' (interview Mrs. Schwenker, 5 July 2016)

For her, too, the loss of the rented accommodation is a dread, against which the central thought manifests itself: A rented flat is not an asset and is principally terminable at any time. Both Mr. Schneider and Mrs. Schwenker expressed the fear of a termination by the landlord as the central negative aspect of renting accommodation. Additionally, Mrs. Schwenker mentioned another positive value of ownership as such. For her, owning something is a value in itself. Similar observations, albeit in relation to the residential property market in the UK, have been made by Susan Smith, Beverly Searle, and Nicole Cook. They state:

'housing wealth is celebrated as a "feel-safe" resource. Portrayed as a shield, comfort zone, blanket, buffer or tool, it is hard to overstate the sense of security conferred on study participants by the possession of home assets. Particularly for established middle-aged owners [...] it is difficult to overrate "the comfort of knowing that you've got something that you can fall back on".' (Smith et al. 2008: 87)

These results find their parallel in the ideas of Westphalian middle-class homeowners. The own home is regarded by the interviewees as a stone manifestation of security and safety. Protection against the termination of the rental contract by laws and politics, on the other hand, were not an argument which played any role in the interviewees' accounts. However, none of them had ever been confronted with such a situation. In cultural respects, home ownership is equated with security, while rental housing is perceived as insecure and dependent on others. The possibility of losing the rented apartment was therefore in these cases communicated as an argument for buying a house.

Emotional investments: lifeblood and nest-building

In addition to costs and considerations of freedom and dependency, some interviewees also discussed another investment that would also influence their attitude towards renting or ownership: emotions. Mrs. Hertel explained:

'Well, it is simply a consideration whether we want to invest a lot of money and lifeblood (Herzblut) into our rented flat, or if we want to safe it and therefore have the chance to do this for ourselves in the future in our own home. Permanently.' (interview Hertel family, 25 August 2015)

Besides a lot of money, Mrs. Hertel mentioned a non-material currency: lifeblood (*Herzblut*). Living and designing one's own home result in a personalised product with more than only economic value. A comparable investment in a property that is only occupied for a rent is not among the ideals of the respondents. The investment of lifeblood is sensible only in one's own property. Mrs. Meier, who was able to buy a previously rented house after living there for a few years with her husband, also discussed a similar idea. With the acquisition, new considerations began to arise, which clearly differed from those when living in rented accommodation:

> 'After we purchased the house, we had the possibility to realise all those ideas that we had discussed earlier. But when you live in rented accommodation you don't do this. You don't invest your money into something that is not yours. We didn't do it because the house was in need of repair. It was mainly a beautification, an enhancement. And maybe a bit like building a nest. One that you like. Adding something of your own, you know? To make it nice for yourself.' (interview Meier family, 23 June 2016)

For Mrs. Meier, conversions and adjustments to the house were related to her relationship to the property. The beautification, as she put it, would pay off only if the house belonged to herself. Only own property thus makes possible the realisation of living concepts. Following the pattern of interpretation of economising into one's own pocket makes adjustments seem to be a waste of money as the results would not become part of one's own possessions. Living in rented accommodation is therefore understood as a restricted form of life, because renovations or beautifications would require the permission of the landlord. The image of nest-building brings beautification processes into a poetic connection with natural habitation processes. In his *La poétique de l'espace*, Gaston Bachelard dedicated a whole chapter to the nest as a symbol and the spatial ideas connected with it. He gives the image of the nest a particularly intimate note: 'A nest, like any other image of rest and quiet, is immediately associated with the image of a simple house' (Bachelard 1994: 98). The metaphor of nest-building therefore includes the desire for security and intimate well-being, which is accompanied by the desire to return to one's home: 'It is the natural habitat of the function of inhabiting. For not only do we *come back* to it, but we dream of coming back to it, the way a bird comes back to its nest.' (Bachelard 1994: 99) Furthermore, Bachelard emphasised: 'An intimate component of faithful loyalty reacts upon the related images of nest and house' (Bachelard 1994: 99). With the image of nest-building, Mrs. Meier described both the beautification work on her own home and a cautious attempt to create security for her family. The implementation of their own ideas in the case of the Meier family took place incrementally, so that they gradually adapted the house. The house, the garden, and the entrance area, which the family successively rebuilt after buying the house, document this appropriation. The appropriation processes also imply a do-it-yourself aspect associated with the desire to own a home. Silvana Rohner in her research on 'dream houses' in the US aptly stated that 'then as now a modern and large house with possible do-it-yourself views is part of the suburban dream and shapes it' (Rohner 2012: 57). Similar observations have been made by Julia Gill in her study on advertising prefab houses. Individualising these mass products is a central feature of the prefab market:

> 'The high importance of the "individual" design of the home is reflected in the promise of prefab house manufacturers that they will help their clients build their tailor-made dream house based on their personal wishes and ideas, because as a status symbol, the home has above all the task to represent the uniqueness of its owner's personality' (Gill 2010: 165).[5]

Both in the case of Mrs. Meier and the appropriation of the occupied house, and in the context of the individual design of the tailor-made prefab dream house, the house itself is understood to express the owner's personality. Mrs. Meier calls this *adding something of your own and to make it nice for yourself.* Living in rented accommodation, on the other hand, stays connected to the idea of living in the property of someone else.

Conclusion

My sample group indicates an antagonistic perception of renting and home ownership. While renting is understood as gifting money to a landlord and therefore wasting money, being a houseowner, on the other hand, is seen as a rational way to 'economising into one's own pocket'. To amortise a mortgage is not regarded as being indebted, but rather as part of a circular exchange that in the end brings back the paid instalments to the person who spent them. Only one family in the sample group communicated the awareness that the house is not really the family's property until the loan is fully payed back. Being a houseowner is widely characterised as a lasting and worthier way of housing.

The interviewees stated that this attitude towards home ownership has been adopted from their parents' example. Growing up in a private home is widely accepted as a role model and a 'way of life'. Episodes in which the family had lived in rented accommodation disappear behind the main plot of the biography: growing up in self-own property. Renting, on the other hand, has, at best, been described as a temporary solution.

Finally, renting and home ownership are believed to offer different ways of expressing oneself. Renting is imagined as dependence on someone else's decisions. Home ownership, on the other hand, is believed to give freedom of choice. The house manifests the personality of its owner, which is reinforced by connecting the house with strong emotions. Living in rented accommodation, however, is disdained as living in the property of someone else.

Acknowledgements

Research for this article has been done within the research network 'A House and its Objects between Family Life, Resource Management and Museum', director: Elisabeth Timm (WWU Münster, Seminar for Folklore Studies / European Ethnology), funded by the German Federal Ministry of Education and Research (programme 'The Language of Objects – Material Culture in the Context of Social Developments') 2015–2018, www.hausfragen.net (accessed 28 April 2019), funding code 01UO1504B.

References

Bachelard, G. (1994), The Poetics of Space (Boston: Beacon).

Blank, F., Ewert, B., and Köppe, S., 'Leistungsempfänger, Bürger oder Konsumenten? Nutzer in der Sozialpolitik', WSI Mitteilungen 65(3), 168.

Bollnow, O. (2011), Human Space (London: Hyphen Press).

Bundesgeschäftsstelle Landesbausparkassen (2013), LBS-Wohneigentumsstudie 2013 (Meckenheim: DCM Druck).

Bundesstiftung Baukultur (2017), Baukultur Report 2016/2017 City and Village (Berlin: Medialis).

Druta, O. and Ronald, R. (2016), 'Young adults' pathways into homeownership and the negotiation of intra-family support: A home, the ideal gift', Sociology, 1–17.

Ellerbrock, K.-P. (2017), 'Konsumentenkredit und "Soziale Marktwirtschaft": Zum Wandel des Sparkassenbildes und des geschäftspolitischen Denkens in der Sparkassenorganisation – Das Beispiel der Stadtsparkasse Witten', Westfälische Forschungen 67, 293–317.

Gill, J. (2010), Individualisierung als Standard. Über das Unbehagen an der Fertighausarchitektur (Bielefeld: transcript).

Heeg, S. (2013), 'Wohnen als Anlageform: Vom Gebrauchsgut zur Ware', Emanzipation 3(2), 5–20.

Helbrecht, I. and Geilenkeuser, T. (2010), 'Homeownership in Germany: Retirement strategies of households in a tenant society', Teorija in praksa 45(5), 975–993.

Helbrecht, I. and Geilenkeuser, T. (2012), 'Demographischer Wandel, Generationeneffekte und Wohnungsmarktentwicklung: Wohneigentum als Altersvorsorge?', Raumforschung und Raumordnung 70(5): 425–436.

Landesbausparkasse LBS Homepage (2017), Mietrechner, https://www.lbs.de/ (accessed 11 October 2017).

NRW.Bank (2014), Wohnungsmarkt Nordrhein-Westfalen – Analysen. Wohnungsmarktbericht NRW 2014. Schwerpunkt: Entwicklung von Kauffällen und Preisen (Düsseldorf: NRW.Bank).

Poppe, C., Collard, S., and Jacobsen, T. (2013), The role of homeownership in the financing of everyday life. Financialisation at the household level (Oslo: Sifo).

Redensek, Jeannette (2017), 'Zur Rezeption des Bauernhauses durch die Architekten der Moderne in Deutschland um 1900', Zeitschrift für Kulturwissenschaften 1, 49–71.

RegioWoB OWL (2011), Wohnen in Ostwestfalen-Lippe. 1. Regionaler Wohnungsmarktbericht (Borgentreich: Conze Druck).

Rohner, S. (2012), 'Real Estate – Selling the suburban home. Vermarktung eines Traumhauses', in I. Tomkowiak (ed.): Little boxes all the same? Suburbia. Gelebt – gedacht – inszeniert (Zürich: Institut für populäre Kulturen), 49–58.

Schulz, C. (2006), 'Zur Sozialgeschichte des Wohneigentums', in: Schwäbisch Hall-Stiftung (ed.): Kultur des Eigentums (Berlin/Heidelberg: Springer), 369–376.

Smith, S., Searle, B., and Cook, N. (2008), 'Rethinking the risks of home ownership', Journal of Social Policy 38(1), 83–102.
Soaita, A. and Searle, B. (2016), 'Debt amnesia: Homeowners' discourses and the financial costs and gains of homebuying', Environment and Planning A 48(6), 1087–1106.
Spiritova, M. (2014), 'Narrative Interviews', in C. Bischoff, K. Oehme-Jüngling and W. Leimgruber (eds.): Methoden der Kulturanthropologie (Bern: Haupt), 117–130.
Statista (2016), 'Bausparkassen – Statista-Dossier', http://de.statista.com/statistik/daten/studie/38105/umfrage/bausparsumme-der-bausparkassen-in-deutschland (accessed 23 August 2018).
Wagner-Douglas, I. (2005), 'Sonnenschein und Schlaufuchs. Werbebilder der Bausparkassen', in Haus der Geschichte Baden-Württemberg (ed.): Zuteilungsreif. Bausparer-Geschichten aus dem Südwesten (Stuttgart: Haus der Geschichte Baden-Württemberg), 104–111.
Wischermann, C. (1997), 'Mythen, Macht und Mängel: Der deutsche Wohnungsmarkt im Urbanisierungsprozeß', in J. Reulecke (ed.): Geschichte des Wohnens Bd. 3: 1800-1918. Das Bürgerliche Zeitalter (Stuttgart: Deutsche Verlags Anstalt), 335–502.
Ziereis, B. (2005), 'Bausparen im Kino. Der Bauspar-Spielfilm zwischen Unterhaltung, Information und Werbung', in Haus der Geschichte Baden-Württemberg (ed.): Zuteilungsreif. Bausparer-Geschichten aus dem Südwesten (Stuttgart: Haus der Geschichte Baden-Württemberg), 112–121.

Illustration credits

Figure 1 with kind permission of Bausparkasse Schwäbisch Hall AG: Screenshot of the landing page 'Mach Schluss mit Deinem Vermieter': https://www.schwaebisch-hall.de (accessed March 2018).
Figure 2 with kind permission of Wirtschaftsarchiv Baden Württemberg, Stuttgart: Setting copy for an advertisement campaign of the National Association of German Building Societies, around 1930.
Figure 3 with kind permission of LBS Westdeutsche Landesbausparkasse: Screenshot of the building society's front page 'Mietrechner': https://www.lbs.de (accessed April 2018).

Endnotes

1 As historical research has documented, German savings banks in general since the 1950s and until the 1970s have changed their strategies from fostering parsimony and economy to selling consumer loans within a modern consumer society (Ellerbrock 2017 using the example of the municipal savings bank Witten in North Rhine-Westphalia). The data used in this article hint to a more recent development that also advertises a mortgage or home loan as something to fulfil consumers' wishes.

2 See the chapters by Cantauw, Caplan/Wagenknecht, Caplan, Flamme/Walter, and Wagenknecht in this volume for further results from this research association; cf. also the latest updates of its publications on www.hausfragen.net.

3 The average age of the interviewees was around 40. While the youngest interviewees were in their early twenties and still searching for a suitable home, the oldest couple was in their early eighties and owned several properties. In total, six women and 13 men were interviewed. Almost all interviewees described themselves as middle class, mostly with an academic background. Three persons classified themselves as property owners. The sample group was generated through newspaper calls. In four cases, interviews took place in my office, while the other eleven interviews took place in the interviewees' homes.

4 See Gill in this volume on that.

5 Translation: Smigla-Zywocki. Original: 'Die hohe Bedeutung der „individuellen" Gestaltung des Eigenheimes spiegelt sich im Versprechen der Fertighausunternehmer, ihren Kunden zum maßgeschneiderten Traumhaus nach ganz persönlichen Wünschen und Vorstellungen zu verhelfen, denn als Statussymbol hat das Eigenheim vor allem die Aufgabe, die Einmaligkeit der Persönlichkeit seines Besitzers zu repräsentieren.'

Single-family houses as urban mines – terra incognita of resource management

Sabine Flamme
Gotthard Walter

Background

Since industrial modernity, the single-family home has been one of the central places of private consumption and thus one of the most important anthropogenic resource deposits of our time. In Germany, the number of single-family homes has risen to around 15.7 million by 2016, making it the most common form of home and real estate ownership among private households. Around a quarter of households in Germany are located in a single-family house (Statista 2018).
If we look at the single-family house from the point of view of resource efficiency, the type of construction, mobility as well as living and use are decisive for determining the consumption of resources along its life cycle. In the following, we present results of our research project on the development of resource management in a single-family home and the associated or included circular economy.

Increasing global demand for resources

Global demand for raw materials is growing unabated and is estimated to at least double over the next thirty years (SRU 2016). A decoupling of economic performance and resource consumption has hardly been successful so far. In addition, new technologies, for example for electronic equipment, for modern steel grades, or for high-performance concretes, require new raw materials in larger quantities. Due to a natural or artificial shortage of raw materials, raw material prices will rise in the medium and long term. The extraction of raw materials also sets large quantities of other unused materials in motion, which have to be mined in order to reach the desired resources. For example, 99 Mg[1] of overburden is produced during the production of 1 Mg of copper (SRU 2016).

The associated land consumption can lead to significant changes in the ecosystems affected and to a loss of local biological diversity as well as to drastic changes in the water balance and the landscape. In terms of resource consumption, the construction sector is of enormous importance worldwide. In Germany alone, approximately 550 million Mg of natural mineral materials such as sand and gravel are mined annually and used to produce new building materials (BBS 2017). This consumes about 4 ha/d (= 14 million m^2/a)[2] of land.

Further ecological effects are the enormous energy requirements for the production of building materials, such as cement, and the associated greenhouse gas emissions. In 2012, global cement production was responsible for around 8 percent of the greenhouse gas CO_2 emitted (55 percent of this is caused by the deacidification of limestone and 45 percent comes from the fuel). With the rapidly growing global demand for housing and infrastructure, especially in the Global South, this figure is currently forecast to rise to around 20 percent by 2050 (Winnefeld 2017).

Buildings as anthropogenic mines

The increasing use of resources means that more and more raw materials are tied up in short-lived or long-lived products, thus creating anthropogenic stocks at various levels. In this context, the term 'urban mining' is often used as a supplement to classical circular economy.[3]

The relevant distinguishing feature when considering urban mines – in the sense of a life cycle analysis – is the period of the resource's release, that is the period of time for which the raw materials used in consumer and production goods are bound (resource conversion cycle) (Flamme et al. 2013). A distinction is made between short-term urban mines, such as electrical appliances, and long-term urban mines, such as buildings. Current estimates (Schiller et al. 2015) show that in Germany around 28.2 billion Mg of material is by now tied up in buildings, grid-bound infrastructure, building services as well as in capital and consumer goods due to the permanent build-up of inventories (see fig. 1). Per capita this corresponds to 341 Mg of material, including 318 Mg of mineral materials, 4.3 Mg of metals, primarily steel, but also approximately 100 kg of copper, 4.3 Mg of wood, and 3 Mg of plastics. By far the largest

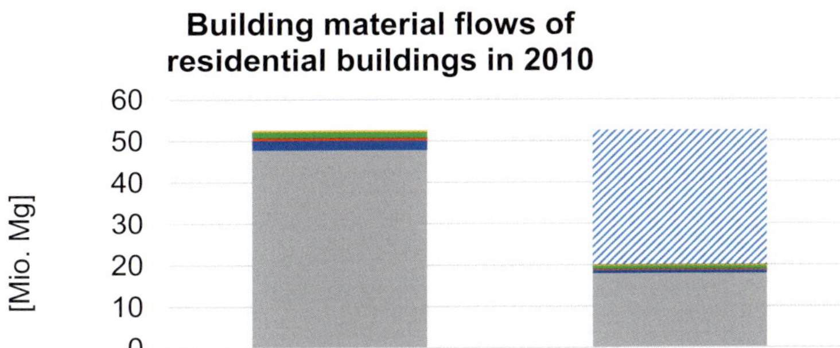

	Input	Output
stock increase		32.5
others	0.3	0.3
timber	1.5	0.8
plastics	0.6	0.2
metals	2.4	0.8
mineral materials	47.8	18

Figure 1: Building material flows for residential buildings in 2010 (own presentation according to Schiller et al. 2015).

part of the stock is located in the building sector. 55 percent of the stored masses alone are bound in residential and non-residential buildings. The remainder is included in underground engineering, which comprises infrastructures for transport, drinking water and wastewater, energy and information, and communication networks. In the long run, there will be an overall shift from portfolio growth to portfolio stagnation or reduction. Due to continuing internal migration, shrinking households, and the demographic decline in population figures expected in the long term until 2060, a much larger quantity of building materials – about one and a half times as much – will flow out of the residential building stock throughout Germany than will be added to it (Gruhler et al. 2011; Schiller et al. 2015). While mineral materials dominate the stock in buildings, metallic materials account for a far larger share in building services, capital goods, and consumer goods. In addition to ferrous metals, this applies above all to non-ferrous metals and, in smaller quantities, also to precious and special metals. If one considers the associated monetary raw material values, the pure material value of this anthropogenic stock can be estimated at around 1,300 billion euros, without demolition and disposal costs. 650 billion euros are accounted for by metals alone, about 150 billion euros each by plastics and wood, and about 350 billion euros by mineral and other materials (Schiller et al. 2015).

Determination of resource potentials in single-family houses

In the following, the consumption of resources and the anthropogenic stock are examined in more detail in connection with the residential form of a single-family house. To begin with, the different procedures for determining the potential of the building and the inventory are presented.

Building potential

Within the framework of the BMBF project, 'Private family households as urban mines – terra incognita of resource management', a total of fifty real estate descriptions of single-family houses from several property portals for the research area in Lower Saxony and North Rhine-Westphalia were initially analysed with regard to the following aspects:

- year of construction,
- size,
- equipment standard,
- used building materials,
- furnishings and utensils.

Furthermore, 843 single-family houses in North Rhine-Westphalia and 811 single-family houses in Lower Saxony were examined, which were built in the last ten years by Viebrockhaus, one of the largest prefabricated house manufacturers in Germany, in various designs. The following criteria were systematically evaluated on the basis of the documents provided by Viebrockhaus (Viebrockhaus 2016):

- type of construction,
- size,
- room layout,
- used building materials.

Since detailed data on the use of resources were available for these buildings, this evaluation formed the essential basis for the development of a model single-family house. The construction methods of solid house construction (with facing brickwork or external thermal insulation composite system) as well as timber frame construction were distinguished here. In addition, the masses of a single-family house from the 1950s were calculated on the basis of existing building plans and calculations for comparison purposes. The ecological footprint of the model single-family house was calculated using the ÖKOBAUDAT database of the Federal Ministry of the Interior, Building and Community (BMI) (BMI 2018). This database provides key data describing the ecological effects of construction materials and construction and transport processes. These are based on both generic data sets and company or association-specific data sets from environmental product declarations.

Based on DIN EN 15804 'Sustainability of buildings – Environmental product declarations – Core rules for the product category of construction products', the life cycle of construction materials and buildings is divided into life cycle sections ('information modules') A to D:

- Module A: Production phase (A1–A3)
  Construction phase (transport to site and building/installation) (A4–A5),
- Module B: Use phase,
- Module C: Disposal phases, including demolition and transport,
- Module D: Recycling, recovery, or reuse potential for the next product system.

Since only information on the process modules A1 to A3 is obligatory for all manufacturers of construction products and therefore only the corresponding information is available in ÖKOBAUDAT for these modules, only the *manufacturing phase* was considered for calculating the footprint of the various components.

With regard to the building materials of mass relevance here, such as minerals, this phase also plays a decisive role in the overall life cycle in terms of ecological effects. According to the data available in ÖKOBAUDAT, there is considerable potential for relief (e.g. through recycling) in the further life cycle stages (modules C and D) for components made of wood or metal. However, especially for module D, there are still significant data gaps, or the data supplied by manufacturers have to be checked for plausibility first. If the corresponding data are available in validated form, only a consideration of the entire life cycle is conclusive for calculations in the form described above.

Three common parameters were selected from the large number of potential environmental impacts, which can be used to illustrate the respective ecological effects:

- the primary energy demand from the total renewable and non-renewable primary energy demand (PERT+PENRT) in MJ.
- The value of the primary energy demand for the components and materials considered contains the primary energy required for production and includes the total primary energy demand of all upstream process chains. The primary energy demand is assessed in the categories of renewable and non-renewable and stated in the unit MJ. Renewable energy sources include biomass, solar radiation, geothermal energy, hydro and wind power. Non-renewable primary energy describes the energy available from naturally occurring energy sources (e.g. hard coal and lignite, oil, natural gas, and uranium).
- The use of freshwater resources (FW) in m^3. This parameter includes the fresh water consumption for the production of a substance.
- Global warming potential (GWP) in kg CO_2 eq.
  Global warming potential describes the contribution of a trace gas to the anthropogenic greenhouse effect. The value is not given as an absolute value but as carbon dioxide equivalent, in kg CO_2 equivalent units. This means that all relevant emissions are related to their potential greenhouse effect in relation to carbon dioxide.

Potential inventory

The originally planned complete survey of single-family houses, including the inventory, is, in addition to the associated high expenditure of time, a considerable encroachment on the privacy of the residents. Despite the best field contacts in the research consortium and several suggestions for adapting the recording instruments, no volunteers could be won for a corresponding survey. The following alternative approaches were used instead:

- evaluation of photo-documentations of real estate description. The real estate descriptions mentioned above were systematically evaluated using their photographic documentation with regard to the identifiable furnishings and decoration. Therefore, in addition to the number, the dimensions of the identifiable furniture were also estimated on the basis of empirical values, and the respective volume of the piece of furniture was calculated as a result.
- development of volume-mass functions for different furniture groups Based on the analysis of a furniture store catalogue, volume-mass functions were calculated for fifty furniture groups (e.g. tables, shelves, cabinets), which were used as a basis for determining the inventory mass (see fig. 2).

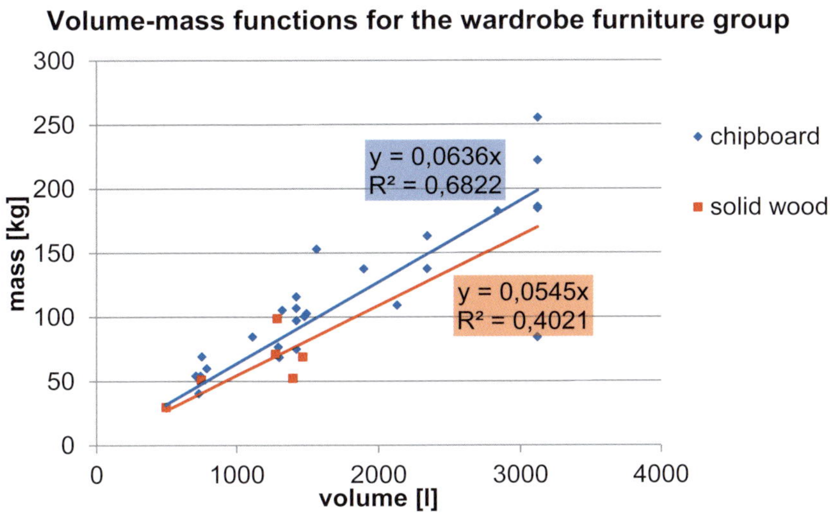

Figure 2: Volume-mass functions for the wardrobe furniture group (example).

- evaluation of statistical data.
  In particular, the stock of electrical appliances can be determined comparatively well by using official statistics (including DESTATIS) showing the degree to which households are equipped with such appliances.

On the basis of these complementary approaches, an estimation of the material flows in the single-family house in relation to material groups was carried out. Two different equipment standards were used as a basis:

- standard configuration:
  selection of furnishings based on real estate description evaluation and statistical data;
- upscale configuration:
  additional furnishings (including electrical appliances) and high-quality furniture (e.g. higher proportion of solid wood).

Due to the variety of materials used in the inventory (e.g. types of plastic), a qualitative classification and not a calculation of the ecological footprint was carried out for the inventory.

Results

Mass flows

Based on the evaluation of the real estate descriptions and the catalogue of the prefabricated house manufacturer, a model single-family house was calculated with the following characteristic values: 1.5-storey construction, without basement, and a living space of approx. 165 m² (spread over ground floor and upper floor; see fig. 3).

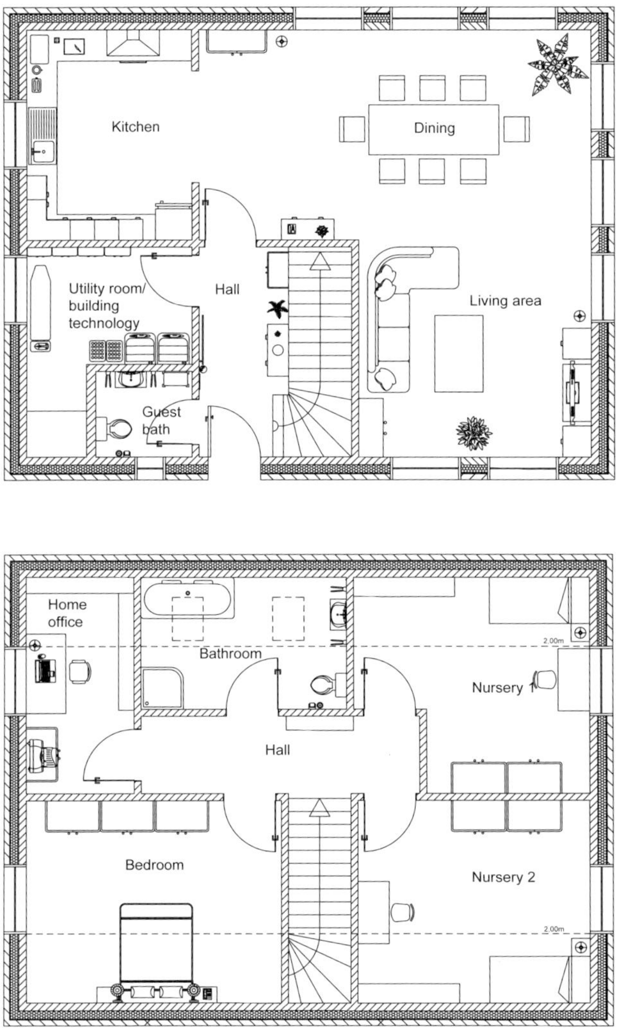

Figure 3: Room layout in the model single-family house.

In this model single-family house, considering the different construction methods, between 115 and 221 Mg of material are used in total, which are divided between the different trades as shown in figure 4.

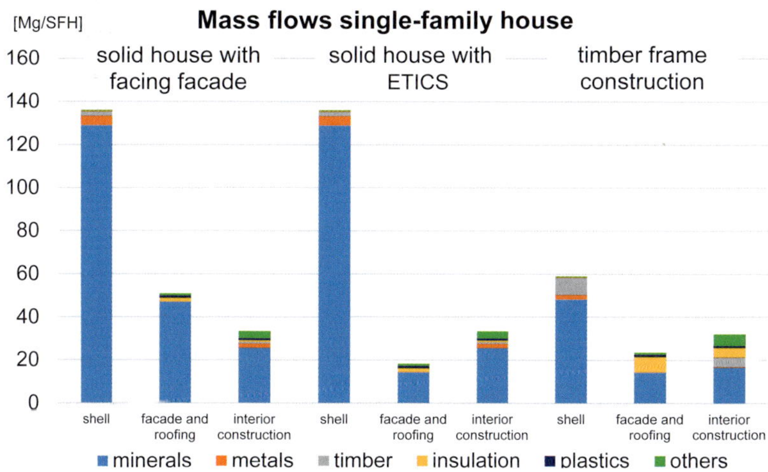

Figure 4: Mass flows in the model single-family house.

As expected, mineral building materials (e.g. concrete, plaster, tiles), especially in solid construction, account for the largest proportion (approx. 90 percent by weight). The mineral fractions still account for 69 percent by weight for timber-frame structures. For the 1950s single-family house, which was examined for comparative purposes, the proportion of these fractions is around 95 percent.

The other fractions, such as metals, wood, and plastics, play a subordinate role in the mass of solid houses. The wood, (wood fibre) insulation, and other fractions accounting for 11 percent, 10 percent, and 6 percent by weight are additionally relevant for the house in timber frame construction. The latter fraction mainly contains gypsum plasterboard used for interior finishing.

Comparing these results with the quantities calculated on the basis of building documents and calculations for a residential house of comparable size from the 1950s, it shows that, due to the significantly higher mineral content, this house with approx. 520 kg/(m^3 of enclosed space) has a value 20 percent higher than the model single-family house in solid construction.

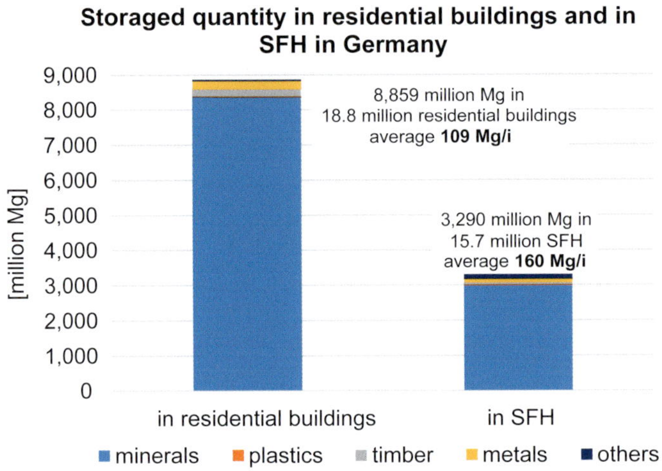

Figure 5: Stored quantity in residential buildings and in single-family houses.

Projected for Germany, around 3.3 billion Mg of material would be tied up in the 15.7 million single-family houses (see fig. 5). This corresponds to around 37 percent of the total stored volume of 8.8 million Mg in residential buildings in Germany (Schiller et al. 2015). With a specific material quantity of around

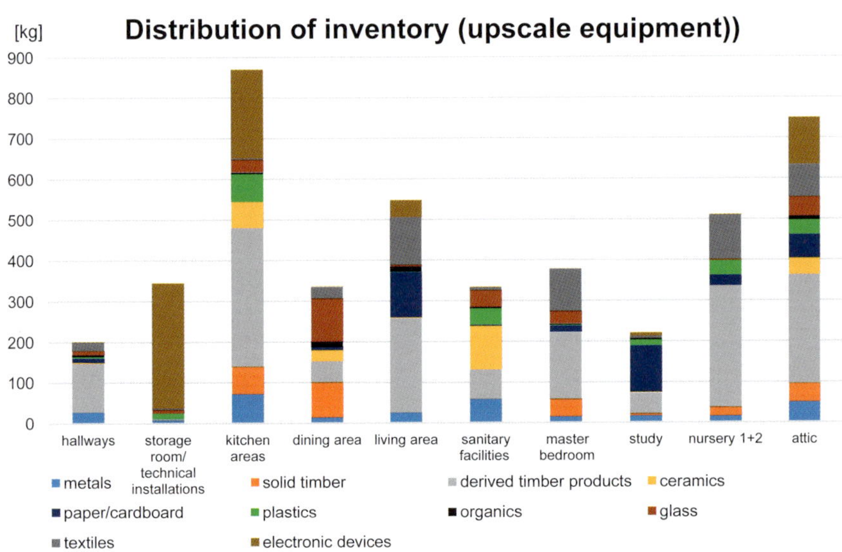

Figure 6: Distribution of inventory (upscale equipment).

160 Mg/(inhabitants in single-family houses), this value is around 77 percent higher than for inhabitants of apartment buildings (around 90 Mg/inhabitants in multi-family houses) and 47 percent higher than the average value for all residential buildings in Germany (around 109 Mg/inhabitants in residential buildings).
The amount of inventory, on the other hand, is comparatively low at 3.5 Mg in a single-family house with basic equipment and 4.5 Mg in a single-family house with upmarket equipment. The largest quantities can be found in the kitchen or in the storage rooms, such as the attic and in the basement, with 20 or 15 percent of the total quantity (see fig. 6).
The inventory consists mainly of wood/wood materials (approx. 1.9 Mg/ single-family house) and electrical appliances (approx. 700 kg/single-family

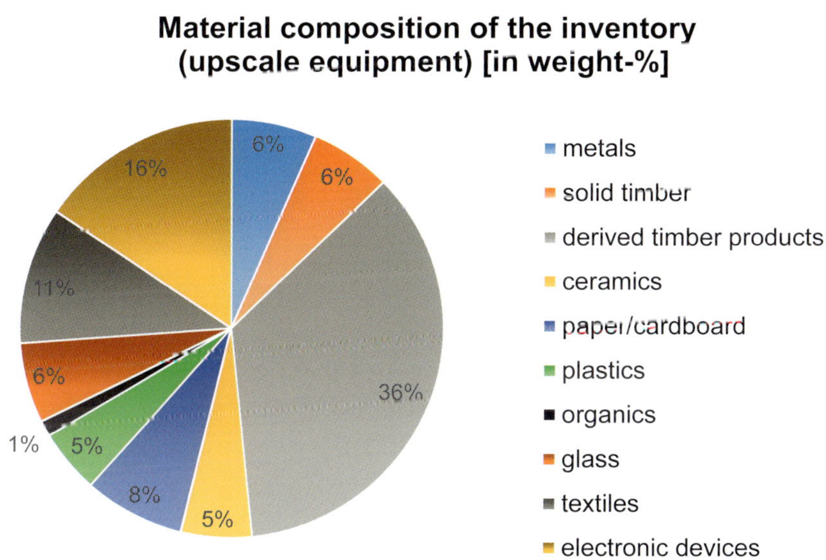

Figure 7: Material composition of the inventory (upscale equipment).

house), with no significant difference between basic and upmarket equipment regarding the composition (see fig. 7). The latter value is also supported by a Europe-wide study which identifies a specific quantity of electrical and electronic equipment 'in use' of around 300 kg for each German citizen (ProSum 2017).

Ecological footprint

Based on the determined material masses of the model single-family house built using different construction methods, the environmental impacts were calculated for the individual material groups and the building as a whole. The parameters of *primary energy demand* and *global warming potential* are influenced to varying degrees by the different building materials. Due to the high

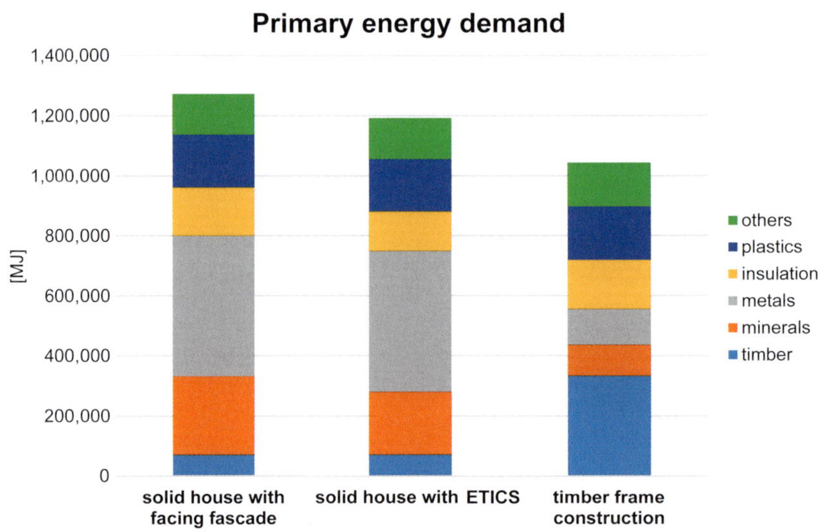

Figure 8: Primary energy demand in a model single-family house.

mass content and the specific factor, minerals (approx. 90 percent volume content and 20 percent primary energy demand) and metals (3 percent volume content and 37 percent primary energy demand) are mainly responsible for the determined environmental impacts (see fig. 8). The wood fraction reduces the environmental impact from all other fractions in the global warming potential parameter in all construction methods. Due to the high proportion of wood, this reduction is highest for single-family houses in timber frame construction with around 45 percent of the CO_2 equivalent. This leaves a quantity of 71 or 76 Mg of CO_2 equivalent for the solid house and around 22 Mg of CO_2 equivalent for the timber-framed house (see fig. 9). These quantities correspond to CO_2 emissions of an average car travelling around the world fourteen or respectively thirteen times.

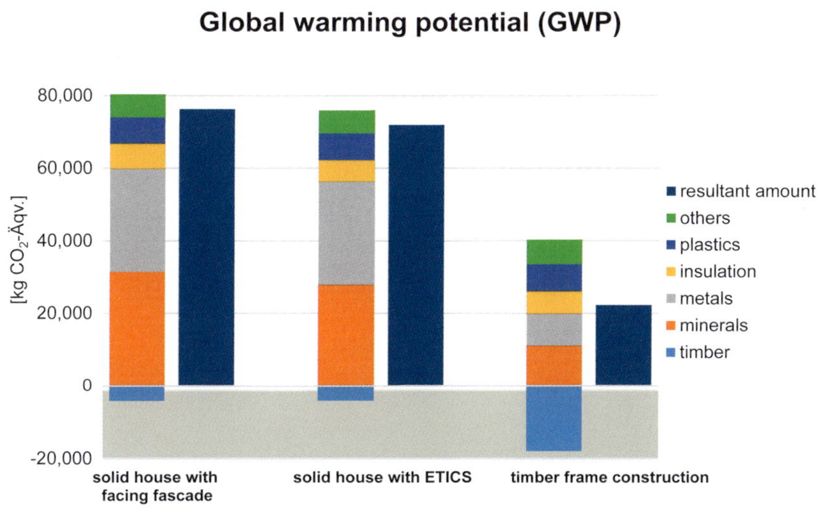

Figure 9: Global warming potential in a model single-family house.

More than 94 percent of the *fresh water resources* parameter results from the wood fraction. The single-family house in timber frame construction has, due to the significantly higher proportion of wood, a water consumption of approx. 28,000 m^3, which is five times higher than with other construction methods.

Qualitative/quantitative classification of the inventory

In order to be able to better classify the quantities determined in the context of the project as inventory in single-family houses, the following comparative values are helpful:

- The volume of around 70 million Mg calculated for the total inventory of single-family houses corresponds to twenty-eight times the annual volume of bulky waste produced in Germany (2.5 million Mg/a).
- At approx. 29.4 million Mg, the total volume of the relevant wood and wood materials fractions contained therein is approximately three and a half times as large as the annual volume of waste wood for disposal in Germany (approx. 8 million Mg/a).
- The annual plastic consumption in Germany (approx. 10 million Mg) is three times higher than the plastic quantity of 3.3 million Mg in the inventory of single-family houses.
- The precious and special metals in the inventory, especially electrical and electronic equipment, have a high monetary value. The stock of

around 10 Mg calculated for the precious metal gold in single-family houses alone has a value of around 350 million euros.

Conclusion

The resource stock calculated for the model single-family house underlines the importance of an efficient use of anthropogenic stocks in order to be able to cover the continuously increasing demand for resources. With a share of around 10 percent of the stock of around 28.2 billion Mg of material calculated for Germany, relevant quantities and thus resources are tied up in single-family houses, which could potentially be put to further use. An important prerequisite for this is further knowledge of the quantities, qualities, and the respective release dynamics of these materials.

In addition to these substances, which are bound to the building for the long term, other relevant resource sources that are mainly available in the short term exist in the single-family house. For example, the stock of electrical and electronic equipment with important functional metals and semiconducting metals of high economic relevance in households in Germany has increased to approx. 300 kg per inhabitant. And the smartphones the house contains now have a gold content that exceeds the concentration in natural mines by a factor of twenty-five to thirty (ProSum 2017). This potential will also continue to increase as a result of increasing mechanisation and must therefore be taken into account.

Acknowledgements

The project 'Private households as urban mines – terra incognita of resource management' focuses on the development of resource management in a single-family home and the associated or included circular economy research network 'A House and its Objects between Family Life, Resource Management and Museum', funded by the Federal Ministry of Education and Research Program (The Language of Objects – Material Culture in the Context of Social Developments), www.hausfragen.net, funding code 01UO1504C.

References

BBS (2017), 'Zukünftige Nachfrage nach Steine-Erden-Rohstoffe bis 2035', bbs-Zahlenspiegel 2017, www.baustoffindustrie.de/fileadmin/user_upload/bbs/Dateien/Downloadarchiv/Konjunktur/Zukuenftige_Nachfrage_nach_Steine-Erden-Rohstoffen.pdf (accessed 7 February 2019).

BMI (2018), ÖKOBAUDAT Informationsportal nachhaltiges Bauen, http://www.oekobaudat.de/ (accessed 20 August 2018).

Flamme S. and Walter, G. (2013), 'Das Rohstoffpotenzial durch Urban Mining', in: Ressourceneffizienz – Der Innovationstreiber von morgen, RKW Kompetenzzentrum (Frankfurter Societäts-Medien GmbH), 260–279, ISBN-10: 3899813057.

Gruhler, K. et al. (2011), Auswirkungen des demografischen Wandels auf das Stofflager und die Stoffflüsse des Wohngebäudebestandes. Deutschland 2050 (Stuttgart: Fraunhofer IRB).
ProSum (2017): Prospecting Secondary raw materials in the Urban mine and Mining wastes, http://www.prosumproject.eu/ (accessed 20 August 2018).
Schiller, G. et al. (2015), 'Kartierung des anthropogenen Lagers in Deutschland zur Optimierung der Sekundärrohstoffwirtschaft, Forschungskennzahl 3712 93 316', UBA-Studie 83/2015, 2015.
SRU (2012), Sachverständigenrat für Umweltfragen, Umweltgutachten: Verantwortung in einer begrenzten Welt, (Berlin: Erich Schmidt Verlag), ISBN 978-3-503-13898-2.
Statista (2018), Anzahl der Einfamilienhäuser in Deutschland in den Jahren 2001 bis 2016, Anteil privater Haushalte im Besitz eines Einfamilienhauses in Deutschland, Verteilung der Bevölkerung in den Ländern Europas im Jahr 2015 nach Art der Wohnung, https://de.statista.com/statistik/daten/studie/39010/umfrage/bestand-der-einfamilienhaeuser-in-deutschland-seit-2000/ (accessed 20 January 2018).
Viebrockhaus (2016), Das Zuhausehaus, Katalog.
Winnefeld (2017), 'Reaktivität synthetischer Alumosilikat-Gläser unter alkalischen Bedingungen', presentation on 16 November 2017 at the workshop: Massenreststoff als Rohstoffquelle, Bundesanstalt für Materialforschung und prüfung, Berlin, unpublished.

Endnotes

1 Mg is the scientific and international designation for the otherwise frequently used unit.
2 This corresponds to an area of around 2,000 football pitches.
3 The scientifically misleading use of the term 'mine' in this context is to be understood as a metaphor that places the idea of value creation in the foreground.

Modern traditions: the modernist apartment and the detached single-family house in early post-war conceptions of the ideal home in West Germany[1]

Johanna Hartmann

This article deals with the idea and the spatial configurations of the ideal home in West Germany during the late 1940s and early 1950s. Related to the housing shortage following the war, this was a historical period when the space of the home experienced a particular significance in public debates and became remarkably visible in the media. But beyond reconstruction efforts, the home in mid-century West Germany appears at the centre of a very broad discourse, not only regarding the aim to provide everybody with accommodation, but rather to supply them with a space in which, through performing the rituals and practices of modern home life, they could be integrated into the envisaged 'modern' society. At the same time as houses, streets, and cities were reconstructed, a massive amount and variety of domestic advice media appeared, educating people on how to furnish and decorate their homes, how to perform domestic tasks, and, more generally, how to live at home.[2] More books then ever were published on interpretations of the ideal new home in the 1950s (Pollak 2005: 30).

The post-war discourse on the issue of the home probably found its most striking manifestations in a number of home and housing exhibitions that took place in several West German cities during the early post-war years, featuring the 'new home' and explaining everyday domestic life.[3] The first significant home exhibition after World War II was *'neues wohnen'* ('new living') by the German Werkbund in Cologne in 1949 (fig. 1 and 2). Many more exhibitions on the home and on the design of everyday objects followed in West Germany over the next decade. That was before the issue of how to live at home would eventually be interpreted as a question more of individual taste than of public

dwb
neues wohnen
werkbundausstellung
KÖLN 1949
vom 14. Mai
bis 3. JULI
Messehallen KÖLN DEUTZ

Figure 2: Installation view of the *'neues wohnen'* Werkbund exhibition, Cologne 1949. Source: Rheinisches Bildarchiv Köln, rba_L000006_41.

education in the 1960s. The exhibitions ranged from rather small temporary presentations by local and regional actors and institutions to huge undertakings like the famous housing exhibition *Interbau Berlin 57* which received international attention for its modern residential buildings that are still existent and lived-in today. Like the *Interbau*, some exhibitions invited their visitors inside new residential buildings that had just been finished, where some of the flats had been fully furnished and equipped as show homes. Other shows took place in exhibition halls that were big enough to set up entire small show homes inside them, where people could peek inside the rooms or even enter them to experience the spaces and objects of modern home life as close as possible. In all of these exhibitions, the interior of the home was presented as the intimate space in which the West German society was supposed to restore itself after the war. Despite of their differences in size and style, the post-war home exhibitions seem to have been connected by a certain discourse in which the design

Figure 1: Poster for the *'neues wohnen'* Werkbund exhibition, design by Jupp Ernst, 1949. Source: Werkbundarchiv Museum der Dinge, Inv. Nr. O12388.

of the home and society's morality became closely interlinked. In the displays, which not only consisted of furnished interiors but also offered programmatics in form of exhibition catalogue texts, as well as a variety of accompanying images, the home functioned as the base of a future in which modern architecture and functionalist design 'complement (and even help create) rational, "enlightened" postwar citizens' (Betts 2004: 8).[4] Interestingly though, besides presentations of the modern home with all its references to classic modern architecture (light rooms, wide windows, and open floor plans), the exhibitions nearly always featured an opposite spatial concept as well: the small detached single-family house of traditional architecture complete with a shingle covered slanted roof. Whereas the furnished show homes at the exhibitions mostly took shape as modern apartments to be understood in multi-storey buildings ready to house the masses after the war, the figure of the small detached single-family house often showed up in accompanying media such as drawings and texts. Even though the exhibitions hardly presented the traditional house as an actual spatial solution, its appearances in images and texts by no means were only incidental side notes. Quite the contrary, I want to argue, the figure of the small detached house played a crucial part in the narrative of post-war modern living in West Germany. On the following pages, I would like to discuss the modernist apartment and the detached single-family house as different but closely interrelated spatial conceptions of the early post-war ideal home. In a close reading I will focus on one exhibition, '*neues wohnen*' ('new living') in 1949, which, although in many regards quite unique, was exemplary for the post-war discourses on the modern home regarding its overall spatial figures on display.

The Werkbund's presentation of a 'new living' in 1949

On 14 May 1949, the *Deutscher Werkbund*, the association of leading German designers and manufacturers who over the next decade would become one of the main protagonists in post-war discussions about how to arrange domestic space and how to teach domesticity to a broad audience,[5] opened the exhibition '*neues wohnen*'. For three weeks, tables and chairs, armchairs and sofas, beds and shelves, cupboards and kitchen units were shown along with a range of wallpapers, textiles, crockery, cutlery, and various other everyday utensils, all displayed in one of the big halls of the Cologne Trade Fair Centre (fig. 2). The idea of the show was to school the aesthetic sensibilities of potential consumers of new concepts of housing and interior design. 'Our aim is an honest "New Living"!' declared the *Deutscher Werkbund* in a leaflet (Deutscher Werkbund 1949b). As it was only four years after the end of the Second World War and housing in Europe still was in critically short supply, the 'new living' was anything but a private matter. Indeed, it was unquestionably political, as attested by the opening addresses of four public figures, recorded in the exhibition catalogue: Robert Görlinger, mayor of Cologne, Willi Suth, chief municipal director of Cologne, Eduard Schalfejew, vice to Ludwig Erhard, economic director of the British-American zone, and Erik Nölting, minister of economic affairs in the Federal State of North Rhine-Westphalia.

> 'The legacy of wartime, the horror of endless streets of bombed-out housing, confronts us with significant and pressing tasks, such as no generation has ever had to deal with before.' (Schalfejew 1949) 'Today, given the ruins of war and the prospect of comprehensive reconstruction, the Werkbund philosophy is more relevant than ever [...] and one turns therefore to both manufacturers and consumers in the hope of leading both to a higher standard of living.' (Görlinger 1949)

The exhibition proposed to address the housing needs of 'the man in the street' to provide a home for 'the multitudes who have lost all they had' and who 'should not have to make do with the meagre resources of emergency aid' (Görlinger 1949); and, first and foremost, to provide for 'the family'. These notional figures served to formulate a sense of 'we' in post-war society: a 'we' upon whom 'hard times in the past [had] also forced downsizing and thrift' (Nölting 1949). Hence, the exhibition should 'show that apartments fitted out even by simple means can provide versatility and home comforts', said August Hoff, the director and professor of the *Kölner Werkschulen* (Cologne Art & Craft Schools) who was responsible for planning the exhibition in collaboration with Heinrich König and Erich Köllmann (Hoff 1949).

The organisers of the show had originally planned to provide several small temporary flats in order to introduce the audience to the spatial dimensions and arrangements of modern living. But as this plan could not be realised, however, owing to a lack of funds (cf. König 1949: 291), most of the furniture pieces were shown in groupings distributed over the exhibition area. Ultimately, a mock-up of only one apartment type was installed: the '*Wohnung für das Existenzminimum*' (apartment for someone with a very low income), designed by Jupp Ernst and Josef Lucas. And since hopes of installing a variety of types had been quashed, this sole exemplar found itself all the more prominently in the (rather critical) public eye.

The modernist apartment

Whereas later West German housing exhibitions tended to show enclosed domestic environments as cosy, comfortable, and protective spaces, the main exhibit of this early show in Cologne was a very minimalistic installation that seemed rather fragmental and quite frugal as a home. The set-up was to be precise, not in fact an apartment. Instead, visitors found themselves looking at a kind of booth, open on three sides and minimally furnished with a very few items indeed. This '*Existenzminimum* apartment' was not so much an apartment as a fragmentary suggestion of a living space, a structure that could hardly be read as a concrete solution to the post-war housing shortage.

Interestingly enough though, with its name, the '*Wohnung für das Existenzminimum*' referred to the primary theme of the Frankfurt CIAM (*Congrès Internationaux d'Architecture Moderne;* international conference on modern architecture), where in 1929, under the directorship of Ernst May, debate had revolved around 'the most practicable floor plan for the smallest possible apartment' (Moser and Giedion 1979: 36). Unlike this conference and its subsequent public presentation of selected floor plans, the presentation twenty years later with the same title did not show any floor plans. Still, to choose the same title was an explicit expression of commitment to the programme, planning debates, and stipulations of the *Neues Bauen* architectural movement; and the revival of the '*Existenzminimum* apartment' seemed in 1949 a wholly reasonable and also admirable way to pare things down to essentials.

On an aesthetical level, the poster of the exhibition articulated a significant link to the spatial conceptions of the *Neues Bauen*. The poster's modernist graphics suggest a modern living space, filled with only two statement pieces and the surrounding landscape that becomes part of the interior through transparent walls and big window openings. Portrayed in an extreme central perspective, the space draws the viewer's gaze first inside and then out again into an exterior space to the rear of the visual frame that is almost completely dominated by a large tree. The poster not only functioned as a visual connection to the 1920s architecture avant-garde, it also provided instructions on how to approach and understand the main exhibit of the 1949 show. Designed also by Jupp Ernst, one of the two architects of the '*Existenzminimum* apartment', the graphical image articulated the spectator's ideal perspective on the exhibited show home and demonstrated how the spectator's view was to be navigated through the modern interior into framed green outdoors. Accordingly, the show home in the exhibition hall as well provided both features, the marked standpoint from where the audience was supposed to look into

Figure 3: The *'Existenzminimum apartment'* at the *'neues wohnen'* Werkbund exhibition, Cologne 1949. Source: Rheinisches Bildarchiv Köln, rba_057117.

the installation, as well as the framed nature. Two photographs of the exhibition, both in possession of the *Rheinisches Bildarchiv* (Rhine Picture Archive) captured the set-up.[6] One presents a sweeping vista of the installation in its broader spatial setting in the trade fair hall seen from above (fig. 2). The clearly structured shot explicates a part of the route pursued by exhibition visitors up to the point (at the bottom of the image) where they come upon the show apartment. Even though the image shows two visitors looking into the mock-up, it lets assume yet another position from where the apartment was to be seen and understood: Between two vertical laths at the left verge of the installation, a high, narrow, organically shaped table – or possibly a bar or counter, given its height – appears to indicate where visitors should stand to gain an optimal view of the *'Existenzminimum* apartment'. On this table, as can be seen when the image is enlarged, stood two 3D architectural models, one of an urban multi-storey apartment block, the other of a single apartment, probably to be understood as an enlarged section of the multi-storey building next to it. Standing behind the counter with these two models in front of them, visitors were supposed to read the '*Existenzminimum* apartment' they were looking into as a new urban housing type within the broader context of post-war architecture.

The second photograph reveals what viewers would focus from their standpoint behind the counter (fig. 3). Very similar as with the poster, the viewers' gaze would be drawn through the minimally furnished interior and only come to rest, almost frontally, on some branches (in a vase) that are framed by a window-like construction mounted on a sideboard. This frame is so inconspicuous as to appear at first glance to be merely a further means of stabilising the installation. Yet on closer inspection, it becomes clear that it functions as a minimal yet highly effective sign to articulate a view onto a garden or other green open space. Hence, the narrative created by the spatial-pictorial interconnections of poster and show home articulated a modern minimalistic apartment in a well-organised urban but green context, an ideal that clearly refers to the reconstruction concept of the so called '*aufgelockerte, gegliederte und durchgrünte Stadt*', the well-structured and green city scape (Göderitz et al. 1957; Reichow 1948; see Durth/Sigel 2010 on how this concept conveyed the German war planning by the Nazi regime).

The detached house

Up to here, I have explicated the '*Existenzminimum* apartment' as a modern, urban space with clear references to some of the most prominent features of the architectures of *Neues Bauen*, such as big glass openings providing a light interior, or the flat roof signalling the rejection of traditionalist architectural forms. I now aim to show that the same ideal home also included an opposite spatial concept: an enclosed space with clear references to the detached single-family home. Like I did in my analysis of the poster and the frame-like construction inside the show home, I will again discuss one piece of media (the exhibition catalogue) and one particular element of the show home's interior (the carpet). I will begin with the latter.

With its ornamental pattern that seemed like a unique contrast to the otherwise minimalist furnishings, the centrally situated carpet may strike some as a remarkable testimony to nineteenth-century bourgeois interiors. However, it had an important function on several levels for the apartment shown here. Firstly, it served in the exhibition – the aim of which was, after all, not only to familiarise

Figure 4: Cover page of the catalogue of the '*neues wohnen*' Werkbund exhibition, design by Hans Leistikow 1949. Source: Werkbundarchiv Museum der Dinge, Inv. Nr. D3916.

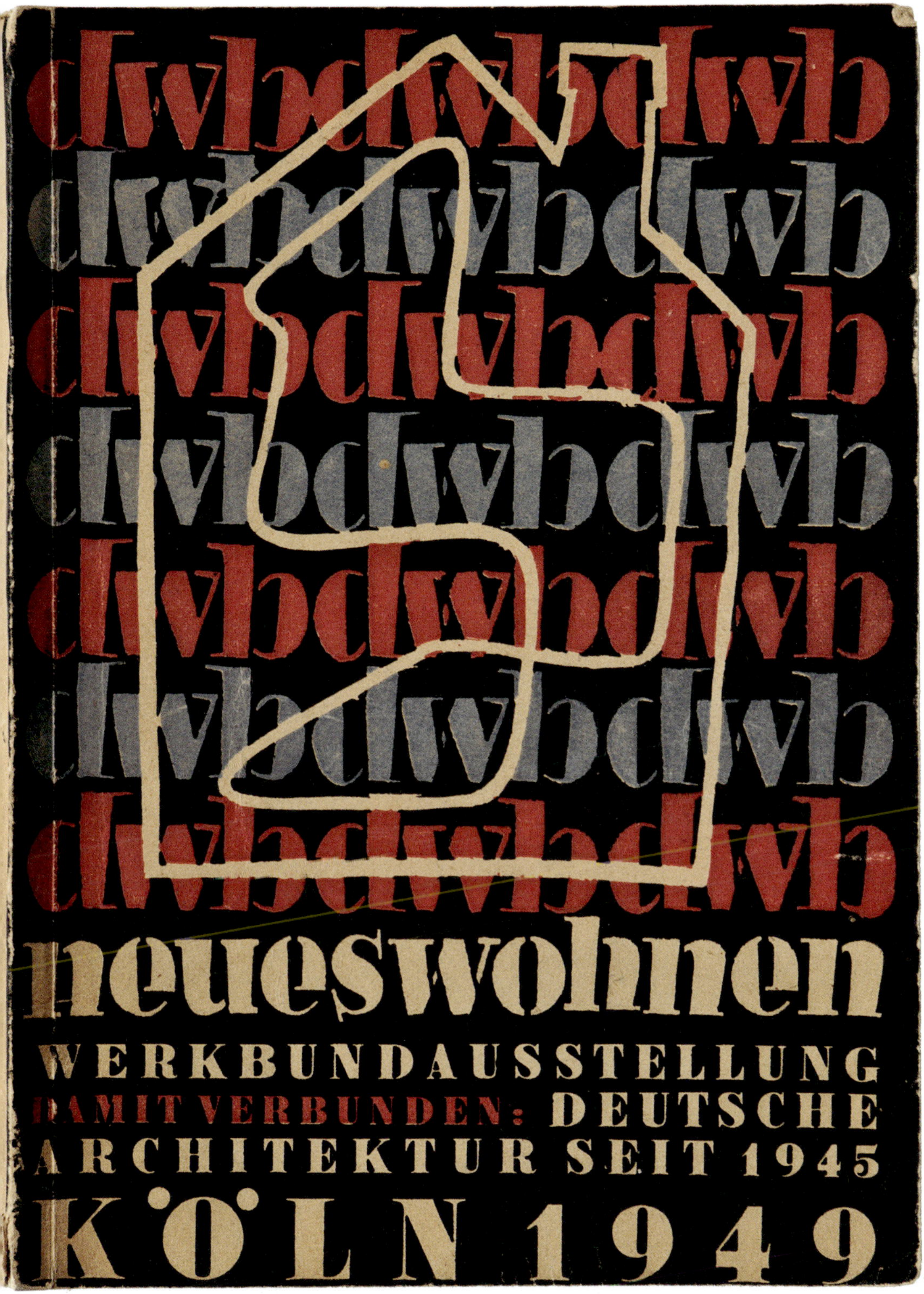
neueswohnen
WERKBUNDAUSSTELLUNG
DAMIT VERBUNDEN: DEUTSCHE
ARCHITEKTUR SEIT 1945
KÖLN 1949

visitors with modern furniture but also to school their appreciation of good old items that are 'impeccably designed and [...] remain objects of utility and beauty for all time' (Schmitt 1949: 35) – as an example of how items of 'timeless and enduring quality' (ibid.) might be combined with modern furnishings. Secondly, the Werkbund was concerned to present an apartment that would be not only as minimally furnished as possible but also identifiable as a 'home'; and this evidently would require some 'home comforts'. The Persian carpet in this underlaid both: the modern furnishings and the notion of a comfortable home. Here was an object whose haptic and warming physical qualities in combination with its winding yet strictly geometric floral patterns could take the 'cold edge' (Herck 2005) off a modern interior décor. In my view, however, its third and most essential function was to articulate an enclosed, self-contained space within the open-ended '*Existenzminimum* apartment'. The geometric floral pattern of the carpet is modelled on the Persian garden that – given its primary focus, the basin and water fountain set amid vegetation oriented to the four points of the compass – is emblematic of universal harmony. Michel Foucault numbers such garden in 'which the whole world comes to enact its symbolic perfection' among the heterotopia, since it – and likewise the carpet modelled on it and woven quasi as 'a sort of garden that can move across space' – is 'capable of juxtaposing in a single real place several spaces, several sites that are in themselves incompatible' (Foucault 1986: 25 f.). In the fragmentary show apartment at the Cologne exhibition the carpet did precisely that: in the mock-up, which eschewed offering orientation via a floor plan, the rectangular textile foundation was a stabilising element inasmuch as it provided a basis for the furnishings; and it also turned the construction of thin wood laths, mere suggestions of walls, minimal furnishings, and non-delimited dimensions into an apartment. Even if the carpet here may be presumed to have been 'fake Persian' (Günther 1994: 22), its pattern nonetheless formulated an all-encompassing whole that rooted the fragmentary character of the installation in an image of self-contained and consummate space.

The topos of the inherently consummate space that is demarcated from exterior space and oriented inwards, to its own centre, was further reinforced by a medium destined for public exposure, namely Hans Leistikow's cover design for the exhibition catalogue: a sketchy but unbroken outline of a house with a pitched roof and a chimney, centrally positioned and almost filling the entire page (Deutscher Werkbund 1949a). Whereas the poster presented '*neues wohnen*' as a modern, open-plan concept in the tradition of *Neues Bauen*, the catalogue gave it the form of a traditional, small, pitched-roof house, evoking the figure of the detached home for a single family (fig. 4). The catalogue may well have been a rather small and relatively thin little book but it was the exhibition's primary publication, besides the poster. The image of the house here is significant because it not only adorns the cover of this prominent medium but is also the sole illustration in the entire exhibition catalogue. We are hence clearly instructed to read the pitched-roof house as a space of '*neues wohnen*'.

Interestingly, this house is furnished – with a piece not at all to be expected in such architecture: A second unbroken line within the house traces a cantilever chair. While the pitched-roof house was hardly what the reader might expect from '*neues wohnen*' – a term written consistently in lower case, incidentally, which made it all the more modern – the cantilever chair within this classic type of house was clearly a shorthand for modernism. It cited the items of steel furniture pioneered by Mart Stam, Marcel Breuer, and Mies van der Rohe: items that had become emblematic of a new, modern, and progressive lifestyle in the late 1920s, and subsequently gained traction as 'status symbols of a modern, open-minded upper class' (Fischer 2016: 17). As neither the house nor the chair were actually on display in the exhibition, the catalogue illustration operated programmatically at a meta-level. It harmoniously fused two markers that had hitherto connoted opposing factions in the fields of architecture, furniture design and housing theory. The link of these signs served several purposes. The crucial point to any inquiry into the spatial figures foreseen for '*neues wohnen*' was that the cantilever chair as the modern furniture per se served to connote the modernity of the small house. With this piece of furniture, the catalogue's cover illustration presented the small house with its pitched roof and chimney as a – symbolic, not concrete – spatial and theoretical figure of modern '*neues wohnen*'.

The home of the poor

The pitched-roof house announced the form and style of '*neues wohnen*' not only on the cover of the catalogue but also in one of its articles, which explained in more detail how the cover illustration was to be read. It was the printed version of architect Rudolf Schwarz's opening address at the exhibition, and it is the only text in the catalogue without a title, which suggests it was of overarching significance or perhaps even some kind of manifesto (Schwarz 1949). But the interest of this article lies above all in the fact that, amongst all the catalogue contributions written about the exhibition's various aspects and sections, primarily about objects designed for the home, it alone focuses on the space in which 'new living' should unfold. In Schwarz's text, the ideal living space crops up not under the name '*Existenzminimum* apartment' but as something like the 'home of the poor'. Its inhabitant, here, is not a solitary person but a family that has found a home within the house. In evoking the figure of the 'home of the poor' to address a type of housing equipped only with the bare necessities of life, Schwarz sought to underline not so much the functionality of the space but the fact of being compelled to accept spatial and material constraints. This might well prompt a reflection on humanitarian ethics. The 'home of the poor' motif upgrades the simple lifestyle into a timeless, mythical, and romanticised place, where lack itself serves to highlight what is truly essential:

> 'Privation purifies and tests every object, narrowing it down to just what it should be: a bed, a table, a kettle. All of these simple things [...] arrive at pure design in the home of the poor, and are no more embellished than their use.' (Schwarz 1949: 18)

Living space – which here is morphed from the apartment into the small house then into the very essence of humankind – is charged with a quasi-religious significance that, however, in lauding simplicity, makes the figure of the poor and modest house appear neutral and therefore normal. The '*Existenzminimum* apartment' as a downsized type of housing for the new generation hence by no means disappears from the narration; on the contrary, it is made clear that the mock-up prominently displayed in the exhibition was to be read not (only) as an architectural response to the housing shortage but also as a model concept that might prompt aesthetic and ethical inquiry into what '*neues wohnen*' means, respectively could or should mean.

Schwarz borrowed the 'home of the poor' figure from a poem by Rainer Maria Rilke, who therein describes it as an enclosed space within which precisely those 'simple', 'natural' things in life, such as shells or pebbles, are appreciated as they would be in 'the hand of a child' and reveal their singularity (Rilke 1903).[7] Schwarz drew here on the imagery of a poet familiar to most Germans on account of a quite other house – that in the line 'He who has now no house will ne'er build one'; and who, owing to this lack, so the poet, 'restless [and] solitary [...] will rove.' (Rilke 1902)[8]

In connecting the spatial figure of the house with *Heimat* (in its sense of native home or homeland) and a space of intimacy whose perfection lies in its very simplicity, Schwarz anticipated that phenomenological preoccupation with the spatial figure of the house undertaken only a few years later by Gaston Bachelard in his *La poétique de l'espace* of 1957. There, Bachelard wrote: '[...] our house is our corner of the world. As has often been said, it is our first universe, a real cosmos in every sense of the word. If we look at it intimately, the humblest dwelling has beauty.' (1984: 4) Bachelard's topology, which was rooted in the phenomenology of poetic images and pursued an expressly visual interest, was a compilation of dreamed or fantasised notions of a 'happy space' that he identified especially in the figure of the house and its metaphorical counterparts, namely natural habitats such as the nest and the shell. Although Bachelard names no particular form of inhabitable structure, he instead draws on terms such as enveloping, encompassing, the corner, and the simple cottage; and by characterising it as a familiar and familial home, simply crafted yet complete with a cellar and an attic, he conjured in the mind's eye the detached house with its own pitched roof and history. It can be read on the same spectrum as the 'home of the poor', the figure Schwarz uses in order to link '*neues wohnen*' with an 'essentialising' concept of housing. The pitched-roof house on the exhibition catalogue's cover does not summarise a concrete plan, but rather names something in an (at least seemingly) universal image: a house, in Bachelard's sense of a 'happy space' of intimacy.

Interacting spatial configurations in the early post-war ideal home

The two very different spatial figures with which '*neues wohnen*' was illustrated in Cologne – on the one hand, the small, detached house presented on and in the exhibition catalogue; on the other hand, the modern apartment in the multi-storey building that visitors were invited to read into the installation at the show – were shown in the exhibition's various means of presentation to be of equal value. The article by Rudolf Schwarz, in which the 'home of the poor' seems to be a romantically glorifying translation of the '*Existenzminimum* apartment', certainly set the two figures in relation to one another yet did not explicitly describe them either as identical or totally separate spatial structures. The small detached house and the apartment in a multi-storey block were each equally – and, I would argue, exclusively, in light of their complementarity and discursive superposition – publicised as examples of the '*neues wohnen*' theory, then seeking to broach viable architectural and interior design proposals for urban reconstruction as well as the notion of a modern private space.
The unremarked juxtaposition and medial interconnection of the two spatial figures, house and apartment, in the Cologne exhibition was no isolated incident. Similar trans-medial 'cross-fadings' occurred in several home exhibitions of the time, articulating an ideal that always included both spatial figures without pressing them in one design. The ideal of new living in the early post-war years simultaneously took shape as both, house *and* apartment; it was simultaneously presented to be traditional *and* modern, stable *and* versatile, closed *and* open, detached *and* part of a block, with a pitched *and* a flat roof;

a promise of privacy *and* of exposure to the public gaze. However, these contrasts in the articulation of *'neues wohnen'* were not by any means arbitrary. It is far truer to say that the two contrasting spatial figures were juxtaposed, combined, and superposed in various media in a way such as to present an ideal of living that precisely comprised both aspects. The small detached single-family house and the stylish apartment in a multi-storey building both acted as vital and complemental symbols in the two-part ideal of a *modern* home of *traditional* values. Where the modern apartment functioned as spatial figure for an awakening into a progressive modernity, the detached house symbolised, firstly, shelter as such and, secondly, traditional and conservative (family) values. Only the combination of both spatial configurations was able to articulate the ideal West German home in the early post-war years.

References

Albrecht, N. v. (2008), '"Die Gute Form". Wieder Ausstellen nach dem Krieg', in Werkbundarchiv – Museum der Dinge (ed.): Kampf der Dinge: Der Deutsche Werkbund zwischen Anspruch und Alltag (Leipzig: Koehler & Amelang), 97–99.

Bachelard, G. (1984), The Poetics of Space (translated by M. Jolas) (Boston: Beacon Press).

Betts, P. (2004), The Authority of Everyday Objects: A Cultural History of West German Industrial Design (Berkeley, CA: University of California Press).

Breuer, G. (2007), Das gute Leben: Der Deutsche Werkbund nach 1945 (Tübingen: Wasmuth).

Castillo, G. (2010), Cold War on the Home Front: The Soft Power of Midcentury Design (Minneapolis, MN and London: University of Minnesota Press).

Colomina, B. (1996), Privacy and Publicity: Modern Architecture as Mass Media (Cambridge, MA/London: MIT Press).

Colomina, B. (1999), 'Das Wohnhaus als Schaustück', in R. Ferguson (ed.): Am Ende des Jahrhunderts: 100 Jahre gebaute Visionen (Ostfildern-Ruit: Hatje), 126–165.

Deutscher Werkbund (1949a) (ed.): Werkbundausstellung Neues Wohnen. Deutsche Architektur seit 1945, 14. Mai – 3. Juli 1949 Köln, Westhalle und Staatenhaus der Messe, Köln, exhibition catalogue (Köln: Lang).

Deutscher Werkbund (1949b), Werkbund heute und Köln heute. Leaflet. Werkbundarchiv Museum der Dinge, Bestand Deutscher Werkbund, ADO 6-8/49.

Durth, W. and Sigel, P. (2010), Baukultur – Spiegel gesellschaftlichen Wandels. Studienausgabe (3 vols.) (Berlin: jovis).

Fischer, R. (2016), 'Vom Neuen Wohnen zur deutschen Wohnkultur? Mies van der Rohe und die Rezeption der Stahlrohrmöbel in den 1930er Jahren', in R. Fischer and W. Tegethoff (ed.): Modern Wohnen. Möbeldesign und Wohnkultur der Moderne (Berlin: Gebr. Mann Verlag), 13–69.

Foucault, M. (1986), 'Of Other Spaces' (trans. by J. Miskowiec), Diacritics 16(1), 22–27.

Göderitz, J., Rainer, R., and Hoffmann, H. (1957), Die gegliederte und aufgelockerte Stadt (Tübingen: Wasmuth).

Görlinger, R. (1949), untitled (opening address), in Deutscher Werkbund (ed.): Werkbundausstellung Neues Wohnen. Deutsche Architektur seit 1945, 14. Mai – 3. Juli 1949 Köln, Westhalle und Staatenhaus der Messe, Köln, exhibition catalogue (Köln: Lang), 9.

Grdanjski, M. (2007), '"Neues Wohnen" und "Deutsche Architektur seit 1945" – Werkbundausstellung Köln 1945', in W. Nerdinger (ed.): 100 Jahre Deutscher Werkbund: 1907/2007 (München: Prestel), 237–8.

Günther, S. (1994), Die fünfziger Jahre. Innenarchitektur und Wohndesign (Stuttgart: Deutsche Verlags-Anstalt).

Hartmann, J. (2010), 'Geordnete (Wohn)Verhältnisse. Geschlechterkonstruktionen im ausgestellten Wohnen der westdeutschen 1950er Jahre', Ariadne. Forum für Frauen- und Geschlechtergeschichte, 58, 40–45.

Hartmann, J. (2014), 'Möbel, Pläne, Körper. Lehrstücke des Wohnens in den 1950er Jahren', in I. Nierhaus and A. Nierhaus (eds.): Wohnen Zeigen. Modelle und Akteure des Wohnens in Architektur und visueller Kultur (Bielefeld: transcript), 39–55.

Hartmann, J. (forthcoming), 'Schooling the eye in modern home comforts. Spatial concepts in the "neues wohnen" ("new dwelling") exhibition of 1949', in G. Caramellino and S. Dadour (eds.): The Housing Project. Discourses, ideals, models and politics in 20th century exhibitions (Leuven: Leuven University Press).

Herck, K. van (2005), '"Only where comfort ends does humanity begin". On the "coldness" of avant-garde architecture in the Weimar period', in H. Heynen and G. Baydar (ed.): Negotiating Domesticity: Spatial Productions of Gender in Modern Architecture (London/New York: Routledge), 123–144.

Hoff, A. (1949), 'preface', in Deutscher Werkbund (ed.): Werkbundausstellung Neues Wohnen. Deutsche Architektur seit 1945, 14. Mai – 3. Juli 1949, Köln, Westhalle und Staatenhaus der Messe, Köln, exhibition catalogue (Köln: Lang), 16.

Holm, C. (2015), 'Bürgerliche Wohnkultur im 19. Jahrhundert', in J. Eibach and I. Schmidt-Voges (eds.): Das Haus in der Geschichte Europas. Ein Handbuch (Berlin: De Gruyter Oldenbourg), 233–254.

Keim, C. (1999), 'Die Frau auf der Corbusier Liege: Zur Konstruktion des Künstlersubjekts in Bildern moderner Weiblichkeit und modernen Möbels', in C. Bischoff and C. Threuter (eds.): Um-Ordnung: Angewandte Künste und Geschlecht in der Moderne (Marburg: Jonas), 69–83.

König, H. (1949), 'Werkbund Ausstellung Köln 1949, Neues Wohnen', Bauen und Wohnen, 4(7), 290–299.

Manske B. (2004), Wie wohnen: Von der Lust und Qual der richtigen Wahl: Ästhetische Bildung in der Alltagskultur des 20. Jahrhunderts (Ostfildern-Ruit: Hatje Cantz).

Moser, K. and Giedion, S. (1979), 'Das Programm des 2. Kongresses', in M. Steinmann (ed.): CIAM Internationale Kongresse für Neues Bauen. Dokumente 1928–1939, (Basel/Stuttgart: Birkhäuser), 36.

Nerdinger, W. (ed.) (2007), 100 Jahre Deutscher Werkbund: 1907/2007 (München: Prestel).

Nierhaus, I. (2004), 'WAND/SCHIRM/BILD: Zur Bildräumlichkeit der Moderne', in S. von Falkenhausen et al. (eds.): Medien der Kunst. Geschlecht, Metapher, Code (Marburg: Jonas), 122–132.

Nierhaus, I. and Nierhaus, A. (eds.) (2014), Wohnen Zeigen. Modelle und Akteure des Wohnens in Architektur und visueller Kultur (Bielefeld: transcript).

Nölting, E. (1949), untitled (opening address), in Deutscher Werkbund (ed.): Werkbundausstellung Neues Wohnen. Deutsche Architektur seit 1945, 14. Mai – 3. Juli 1949, Köln, Westhalle und Staatenhaus der Messe, Köln, exhibition catalogue (Köln: Lang), 15.

Oestereich, C. (2000a), 'Gute Form' im Wiederaufbau. Zur Produktgestaltung in Westdeutschland nach 1945 (Berlin: Lukas).

Oestereich, C. (2000b), '"Neues Wohnen". Die Kölner Werkbundausstellung von 1949', Geschichte im Westen 15(2), 49–65.

Pollak, S. (2005), 'Erlerntes Glück im Wohnen. Die Vermittlung einer neuen Wohnkultur der1950er Jahre aus genderspezifischer Sicht', in Land Oberösterreich/ Oberösterreichische Landesmuseen (eds.): Wie wir wohn(t)en. Alltagskultur seit 1945 (Weitra: Bibliothek der Provinz), 29–44.

Reichow, H. B. (1948), Organische Stadtbaukunst (Braunschweig: Westermann).

Rice, C. (2007), The Emergence of the Interior. Architecture, Modernity, Domesticity (London/New York: Routledge).

Rilke, R. M. (1902 [1996]), 'Herbsttag', in M. Engel and U. Fülleborn (eds): Werke, Kommentierte Ausgabe in vier Bänden, Band 1, Gedichte 1895 bis 1910 (Frankfurt/Main, Leipzig: Insel Verlag), 218.

Rilke, R. M. (1903 [1996]), 'Des Armen Haus ist wie ein Altarschrein', in M. Engel and U. Fülleborn (eds): Werke, Kommentierte Ausgabe in vier Bänden, Band 1, Gedichte 1895 bis 1910 (Frankfurt am Main, Leipzig: Insel Verlag), 249.

Schalfejew, E. (1949), untitled (opening address), in Deutscher Werkbund (ed.): Werkbundausstellung Neues Wohnen. Deutsche Architektur seit 1945, 14. Mai – 3. Juli 1949, Köln, Westhalle und Staatenhaus der Messe, Köln, ex. cat. (Köln: Lang), 13.

Schmitt, H. (1949), 'Schön – aber nicht teuer, unsere Dingwelt und die Forderungen unserer Zeit', in Deutscher Werkbund (ed.): Werkbundausstellung Neues Wohnen. Deutsche Architektur seit 1945, 14. Mai – 3. Juli 1949, Köln, Westhalle und Staatenhaus der Messe, Köln, exhibition catalogue (Köln: Lang), 31–35.

Schwarz, R. (1949), untitled (opening address), in Deutscher Werkbund (ed.): Werkbundausstellung Neues Wohnen. Deutsche Architektur seit 1945, 14. Mai – 3. Juli 1949, Köln, Westhalle und Staatenhaus der Messe, Köln, ex. cat. (Köln: Lang 1949), 17–19.

Sparke, P., Martin, B., and Keeble, T. (eds.) (2006), The Modern Period Room. The Construction of the Exhibited Interior, 1870 to 1950 (London: Routledge).

Wagner-Conzelmann, S. (2007), Die Interbau 1957 in Berlin: Stadt von heute – Stadt von morgen. Städtebau und Gesellschaftskritik der 50er Jahre (Petersberg: Imhof).

Werkbundarchiv – Museum der Dinge (ed.) (2008), Kampf der Dinge. Der Deutsche ‚Werkbund zwischen Anspruch und Alltag (Leipzig: Koehler & Amelang).

Endnotes

1 This article expands on Hartmann forthcoming, that article was translated by Jill Denton, and some of her elaborate work is still visible in this version.

2 It has to be noted, however, that domestic advice media was, of course, nothing new at that time. The construction of the domestic interior as the private space of the home has always been a practice of public concern and display as several theorists have shown (Colomina 1996, 1999; Holm 2015; Keim 1999; I. Nierhaus 2004, I. Nierhaus and A. Nierhaus 2014; Rice 2007; Sparke et al. 2006).

3 For research on some of the exhibitions see Albrecht 2008; Betts 2004; Breuer 2007; Castillo 2010; Grdanjski 2007; Hartmann 2010, 2014; Manske 2004; Nerdinger 2007; Oestereich 2000a; Wagner-Conzelmann 2007; Werkbund-archiv – Museum der Dinge 2008.

4 See also Oestereich's extensive research on the central discourse concerning the 'good form' in post-war Germany (Oestereich 2000a).

5 For information on the post-war activities of Deutscher Werkbund, see Breuer 2007; Nerdinger 2007; Wagner-Conzelmann 2007; Werkbundarchiv – Museum der Dinge 2008. Regarding the exhibition 'neues wohnen' see Oestereich 2000b.

6 The prints are part of a series of around twenty photographs, mostly well-lit and immaculately focused, that show installation views as well as individual exhibits of the 'neues wohnen' show. It is not known who took them. One can assume that the Rheinisches Bildarchiv commissioned them at the time as press material or for documentary purposes, in all probability from an in-house photographer. I am indebted to the staff of the Rheinisches Bildarchiv for this information, especially the archivist Evelyn Bertram-Neunzig.

7 It must be noted, however, that Schwarz misquoted Rilke (whether knowingly or not is unclear and anyhow of no relevance here), describing the home of the poor not,

like Rilke, as an altar shrine but as an everyday shrine and insofar he distanced himself somewhat from the sacralisation of this spatial figure, so rendering it more suitable for the secular Werkbund agenda.

8 Translated by Jessie Lemon, 1918. https://archive.org/stream/cu31924026255822/cu31924026255822_djvu.txt (accessed 29 March 2018).

Dream House Factories. What happened to the dream of the factory-made house?[1]

Julia Gill

For Le Corbusier, the development of ideal types for certain kinds of buildings, and their subsequent dissemination as standard types, was one of the most important tasks of architecture:

'It is necessary to press on towards the establishment of standards in order to face the problem of perfection. [...] A standard is necessary for order in human effort. [...] The establishment of a standard involves exhausting every practical and reasonable possibility, and extracting from them a recognized type conformable to its functions, with a maximum output and a minimum use of means, workmanship and material, words, forms, colours, sounds. Here we have the birth of style [...] Architecture is governed by standards. Standards are a matter of logic, analysis and precise study. Standards are based on a problem which has been well stated. [...] Standardization is imposed by the law of selection and is an economic and social necessity.' (Le Corbusier 1927: 123–127)

Out of the alliance between such cultural achievements and social responsibility grew, as if by itself, as the emergence of the Parthenon demonstrated, all the superior beauty – for Le Corbusier 'the overplus necessary only to men of the highest type.' (Le Corbusier 1927: 135–38) Le Corbusier argued here as a representative of a whole generation of architects who, at the beginning of the twentieth century – borne along by a still basically positive attitude towards progress, and against the background of a building industry still strongly stamped by craftsmanship –, looked upon the potential of industrialisation with downright euphoria. Convinced by the effectiveness of artistically planned interventions in the service of a freely developing society, he called for standards not only on technical and structural design considerations, but also on economic,

Figure 1–4: Single-family home area "Am Sonnenhügel", Berlin-Staaken.

social and – especially – design grounds. Through mass production, the house would finally be freed from ideological and sentimental ballast, and

> 'A house will no longer be this solidly-built thing which sets out to defy time and decay, and which is an expensive luxury by which wealth can be shown; it will be a tool as the motor-car is becoming a tool.' (Le Corbusier 1927: 244–245)

Yet thanks to prefabricated structures, our suburbs sprout ever more single-family houses which the visionary probably would have despised as sentimental and nostalgic, what he called 'le poème de l'été de la Saint-Martin' (Le Corbusier 1995: 197). The dream of the factory-made house became the dream house out of a catalogue. The goal of developing higher and at the same time cheaper housing standards (technical, construction, and design) has given

Figure 5–8: Single-family home area "Am Sonnenhügel", Berlin-Staaken.

way in the pre-fab[2] – as in all single-family houses – to eccentric individualisation. In this the possibilities are directed less towards the sculptural-spatial than towards formal aspects, and their architecture attempts, contrary to Corbusier's assumptions, not a rational language of forms but a predominantly tradition-rich repertoire of styles. Thus, we find Le Corbusier's assumption that pre-fabs would free the house from its ponderousness and piety in order to yield to new, pragmatic, and sober buildings of surpassing beauty, turned on its head.

While it appears that high and partially normalised quality standards have long been desired and demanded (no vendor fails to refer to the quality seal on his products), house buyers didn't and don't want to identify themselves with a standardised house architecture which expresses seriality and prefabrication. As a result, consistently high-quality standards can establish themselves only on a technical basis, while on the design level there is no investment in creatively sophisticated ready-made houses, but rather above all in an (apparently) larger creative freedom for the client. The pre-fab customer today could, as stated by the vendor advertisements, design his own home freely according to his own wishes.

Out of this ambition arises – in connection with urban planning that gives precedence to isolated plots over, for example, densely built-up areas with their correspondingly higher need for coordination – a discrepancy between the creative drive of the individual and the public interest, since our built environment as a habitat and a component of our culture must possess defined spatial and design qualities. Exactly this public interest is what Le Corbusier consciously implied in his demand for an environment designed according to his ideas, and which he considered to be on a par with economic and social considerations.

The conflict of interest between individual and society was vividly elucidated by Sigmund Freud in his essay *Civilization and its Discontents* in 1930 (German original: 'Das Unbehagen in der Kultur', Freud 1994). Freud used the term *Unbehagen* (which can also be translated as uneasiness, discomfort, or anxiety) in his text for what we feel in the face of a cultural achievement whose gains are inextricably bound with a lack of happiness. According to Freud, this discontent, so defined, lives in all of us. It comes from an 'indelible core of cultural hostility', based on 'the recognition that every civilization rests on a compulsion to work and a renunciation of instinct and therefore inevitably provokes opposition from those affected by these demands' (Freud 1968: 8). Out of this insight arose the question for Freud of how much individuality a culture could allow – and vice versa: how many concessions a culture can exact from the individual.

Applying Freud's structural model of the personality to the cultural community, the creative impulse and the wish to design one's own home as an individual one on the drives side oppose the demands of society and the built environment on the cultural side.

Standard dreams

The success of the commercial ready-made family house cannot be explained strictly by quantifiable factors like cost and secure completion dates or high construction and material standards. On the contrary, the industry had and has to battle here against various reservations (cf. Allensbach 2005). There

are probably additional needs being addressed that architects are no longer trusted to meet. And indeed, the concern that architects are primarily interested in their own dreams is not entirely plucked out of thin air.
Data on the state of these needs give cause to reflect on the design and marketing of pre-fabs. Informed by the insights that culture theories offer, the ready-made house since the 1990s indeed has developed from an appropriately priced house for everybody into a high-end product that counters status anxieties. With the offer of an all-in-one place comes a comprehensive consumer-oriented marketing concept: from the idea of buying a house in a supermarket, through offers like colour, style or *feng-shui* counselling, to promotional offers like a weekly dream house lottery – with friendly help from celebrities. For example, the Swabian firm *Exnorm* put two *Sissi* designs on the market in 1998 to honour Empress Elisabeth of Austria's death centenary. In 2001, Hanse-Haus advertised the football club *FC-Bayern-München-Haus*, in club colours. And the firm Viebrockhaus has worked with the fashion and jewellery designer Jette Joop for years (cf. Gill 2010: 79–83). The development of such strategies is based on the insight that in buying one's own house an entire life plan and style of living is implied (cf. Bourdieu 2002: 41). Consequently, the marketing of ready-mades is less and less about value for money and increasingly about intangible and hardly quantifiable promises of happiness: quality of life, *joie de vivre*, and lifestyle. Thus, the objectives underlying the ownership of a single-family pre-fab – for example self-determination, living close to nature, economic security, and self-expression – lose some of their rationality and increasingly take on the character of compensatory projections. And so, the appeal to Freud is in this respect not random. Between the poles of need and projection, drive and culture, individual and society, what interests us is which images will convince the customers.
Actually, the fulfilment of the dream house, which in the vendors' advertisements is so urgently communicated, already wipes away the memory of the pre-fab's mass-produced origins. Likewise, the latitude in production, which is enabled by newest applications of CAD and CNC technologies and developed with precisely this in mind, allows for differentiated offers while maintaining serial production. They individualise standard solutions – and standardise individuality. Nonetheless, pre-fab house offers generally appear to be strangely uniform. Why is that?

Standard images

Imposed by standards and zoning requirements to realise the maximum floor space on a minimum plot of land, and due to a combination of always similar use specifications in pre-fab houses, a limited number of typological possibilities arise. Their formal differentiation must operate within a broadly intelligible and therefore hardly individual vocabulary, if they are to satisfy the various fantasies and, at the same time, generally addressable requirements of representation that have always been bound up in having one's own home.

Living in one's own home combines concrete advantages like adaptability to individual needs, protection against the tyranny of landlords, and economic security – especially in old age – with features such as independence, freedom, and autonomy. With connotations of such conservative values as reduced consumption, frugality, discipline, labour, and long-term planning, owning a home is valued as an appropriate expression of a successful biography, as studies show (cf. BBR 2001: 19 f.). At the same time, owning a single-family house demonstrates individual success in life and upward social mobility, and thus fulfils the function of a status symbol. Nonetheless, through the increasing prevalence of home ownership, for which the pre-fab as both product and driver is largely held responsible, the representative function is no longer exclusive. This sets the representation of social distinction as a secondary mechanism in motion. The initially low-cost house nowadays has to appear bigger and more expensive to assert the owner's financial potency and to pretend a higher level of social status (cf. Bourdieu 1987: 120–125 and 500–513).

The advertising promises used by vendors to help their clients to acquire the customised dream house of their individual wishes and imaginations additionally aim at these representational needs. They flatter the need of potential customers to express a public image of the uniqueness and significance of their person. At the same time, the ever-increasing number of variants on offer supply the customer with numerous possibilities for identification.

Thus, the imagery of the structures activates clichés – whether *Alpine* or *Norddeutsch*, *Mediterranean* or *Scandinavian*, *Modern* or *Ecological* – which are for their part standardised and constantly reproduced in all areas of advertising. These images illustrate dream worlds, from Mediterranean flair and cool ambience to fantasies of castles and gardens inhabited by rich and beautiful celebrities. Furniture magazines and catalogues, newspapers, guidebooks, promotion films, and media of all kinds similarly spread such images. We see television productions like Inga Lindström and Rosamunde Pilcher films, *Der*

Landarzt (The Country Doctor) or *Das Schloss am Wörthersee* (The Mansion on the Wörthersee), or soap operas devoted to the lives of well-off Californian, Texan, or Italian dynasties. Cooking shows, arranged around highly polished kitchen blocks, set the standard for the new feel-good home. Numerous decoration soaps, broadcast over various channels many times a day, serve the awakened yearnings, as installation advisers with a part to play in the family fate, give practical tips and instructions on how to realise these dream worlds within the owner's own four walls (cf. Gill 2010: 87–91).

Standard components

The handcrafted and the industrially manufactured product are distinguished from each other above all by the opposite meaning and valuation of, respectively, the primary, actual function and the secondary, symbolic function. Such a paradigm change is also significant for the commercialisation of the ready-made single-family house, which transforms the owned home into a product, and construction into a service – in the eyes of most vendors a step which they look back upon with pride. However, this forces them into an increasingly systematic application of the product form in order to remain competitive within a steadily growing market (cf. also Baudrillard 2001: 16).

The prerequisite of this competitiveness is to match the production and distribution conditions of other industries, for example the automobile, furniture, or garment industries. From the start, these fell under the heading of mass customisation. Here, mass production and customisation are bound together in a way which can be understood as customised mass production, and means that, with an eye on the progress of technical development and under consideration of set parameters, an individualised garment, piece of furniture, or car can be as quickly and cheaply manufactured as if it was mass-produced. The distinction must therefore often focus on *nuances*[3]. Thus, for example, motorcar manufacturers offer an apparently endless palette of colours – in plain or double lacquer – as well as a wide variety of technical refinements and variations on the extra options. The consumer is soothed with the illusion that he is getting a unique model.

The transfer of these principles to ready-made houses means, thanks to the latest technology, that reasonably priced manufacture, based on industrialised and rational planning and building processes, no longer has to stand in the way of realising the individual builder-owner's wishes. In this way, the house manufacturer ostensibly offers the customer tailored products at moderate

prices, which heightens the attractiveness of the offer. At the same time, they can use the customer's information that steers the configuration process as input for the development of new products, essentially conducting market research and thus eventually profiting twice. Here, the internet offers the ideal interface between customer and vendor: company home pages do not always restrict themselves to information about the latest offer.
Interactive house configurators additionally enable potential house buyers to extend different floor plan suggestions with bay windows or winter gardens, select options like a gabled roof versus a hipped roof, and choose styles from classic to modern. Within a few seconds the customer can get a fixed price estimate with a visual simulation from top edge to base plate in 3D perspective.[4] The result often is an eclectic mix of distinct types, styles, and elements. These refer not only to the architecture of the house itself, but also the catalogue imagery of the firm, in which claims addressed only to architecture refer to the appearance, the flair of the house, the ambience of the home.

Standard language

Any marketing of the pre-fab product by catalogue or on the internet to anonymous customers must necessarily be general. The largest possible range of houses must be included in order to speak to the greatest number of potential buyers. Most vendors therefore refer to a broad selection of reference projects, which they nonetheless by no means want to be understood as readymades. Thus, the language commonly avoids any vocabulary that might evoke mass production or pre-fabrication and focuses on terms that might appeal to fantasies about taste (for example, style directions) and professional status (for example, draft proposal). The systematic listing of these offerings leads nonetheless back to the reality behind. Here, at the latest, doubts arise as to whether the advertised promises to tailor an individual dream house to every customer can be seriously und feasibly realised.
It is therefore perfectly understandable if vendors want to offer their clients help to orient themselves and identify possibilities in a very broad and highly diversified housing market. There are currently over 1,000 house models alone on the website for vendors listed by the *Bundesverband Deutscher Fertigbau*[5]. First, melodious names replace factual descriptions for the various building categories: a double-house becomes a *Duett*, a *Pasodoble* or a *Twin*, while a one-level retirement bungalow is sold under the label *Fifty5*. To make these attributes stand out in the crowd, further names are sought in order to

offer the client additional information about price categories and design directions. Key words associated with different lifestyles are often used, for example *Esprit*, *Ideal*, or *Sunshine*, or perhaps rather *Diamant*, *Prestige*, or *Royal*. Pointers to geographical-regional styles are also sought, from *Småland* and *Gomera*, to *York* and *Tirol*, to *Venezia* and *Florenz*. The vendors also pin great hopes on musical associations through house names such as *Jazz* or *Blues*, *Allegro* or *Forte*, *Ideenhaus Belcanto* or, finally, *Turandot*, *Othello*, and *Don Giovanni*. Such names should convey substance, purity, and exclusivity as well as Mediterranean ease and *La Dolce Vita* or a youthful outlook paired with Scandinavian pragmatism. Occasionally, this leads to results like *La Grande mit Wintergarten* (La Grande with winter garden), *Design Schupfholz* (which is a miniscule German settlement), or *Trendy Bielefeld* (a town in northwestern Germany whose name in jokes regularly symbolises not so trendy places in Germany). However, the arbitrariness of such names doesn't end here, but is intentionally connected to the established conceptual world of the consumer goods market. Thus, those names could easily be assigned not only to a variety of house models, but also to other products, like cars, exercise machines, and appliances, as well as deodorants, coffee, flour, and ultimately toilet paper (cf. Gill 2010: 99–103).

What happened to the dream of the factory-made house?

The context-free conception and presentation of the buildings in catalogues and on the internet corresponds ultimately to the lack of hierarchy of the accumulated structures and styles. With the re-entry into the sphere of the built reality, these stamp individual architecture with the character of the whole domain of single-family houses and transform the city and countryside into agonies of entropic urban sprawl. At the same time, the possible combinatorics of components adapted to structural engineering and thermal efficiency advances impassively. It fosters a *bricolage* of dreams – from which there is no awakening.

Thus, the freedom won in manufacturing is neutralised in a collage of boilerplate images – and nonetheless bought at a high price: indirectly by society and taxpayers through the spoiled landscape and high development costs, and directly by the buyer in whose interest all this supposedly transpires. On the one hand, the vendor pays entirely for the wishes of individualisation. On the other hand, a fashionable (facade) design rarely contributes to maintaining or increasing the value of a building. Investment in the largest possible standardised customised dream home on the smallest, cheapest possible plot of land is seldom worth it: the more eccentric the architecture and location, the lower the resale value. In the model home parks, out-of-fashion show houses are replaced when they no longer reflect the current trends. House owners don't have that option.

References

Allensbach Institut für Demoskopie (ed.) (2005), Image und Potentiale von Fertighäusern (Allensbach am Bodensee: Allensbach).

Baudrillard, J. (2001), Das System der Dinge. Über unser Verhältnis zu den alltäglichen Gegenständen (Frankfurt/Main: Campus).

Bundesamt für Bauwesen und Raumordnung (BBR) (ed.) (2001), Forschungen (Vol. 106). Hemmnisse der Wohneigentumsbildung (Bonn: BBR).

Bourdieu, P. (2002), Der Einzige und sein Eigenheim (Hamburg: VSA).

Bourdieu, P. (1987), Die feinen Unterschiede. Kritik der gesellschaftlichen Urteilskraft (Frankfurt/Main: Suhrkamp).

Le Corbusier (1927), Towards a new architecture (London: The Architectural Press).

Le Corbusier (1995), Vers une architecture (Paris: Flammarion).

Freud, S. (1994), 'Das Unbehagen in der Kultur', in A. Lorenzer and B. Görlich (eds.): Das Unbehagen in der Kultur und andere kulturtheoretische Schriften. Einleitung von Alfred Lorenzer und Bernhard Görlich (Frankfurt/Main: Fischer), 29–108.

Freud, S. (1991), 'Die Zukunft einer Illusion', in: A. Freud (ed.): Gesammelte Werke (Vol. 14). Werke aus den Jahren 1925–1931 (Frankfurt/Main: Fischer), 325–380.

Freud, S. (1968), 'The future of an illusion', in: J. Strachey (ed.): The standard edition of the complete psychological works of Sigmund Freud (Vol. 21). 'The Future of an Illusion', 'Civilization and its Discontents' and other works (London: Hogarth), 5–56.

Gill, J. (2010), Individualisierung als Standard. Über das Unbehagen an der Fertighausarchitektur (Bielefeld: transcript).

Herbert, G. (1984), The dream of the factory-made house. Walter Gropius and Konrad Wachsmann (Cambridge: MIT Press).

Illustration credits

Photos: Amos Fricke, 2012.

Endnotes

1 For the term and the concept of the 'factory made house' cf. Herbert 1984.

2 The terms pre-fab, factory-made house, and ready-made house will be used on the following pages for single-family houses of lightweight or solid construction which command a high degree of pre-fabrication and which are distributed by a house building company.

3 For the perception of the term cf. Bourdieu 1987.

4 E.g. https://haas-fertighaus.de/hauskonfigurator/; https://www.fingerhuthaus.de/haeuser/hausfinder/?gclid=EAIaIQobChMI6o_Fodyw3QIVRLTtCh1-3QkZEAMYASAAEgKa3PD_BwE; https://www.weberhaus.de/haeuser-finden/hauskonfigurator-starten/?google_campaign_id=7ef37d60-59cd-f175-c0cc-526f99083da9&gclid=EAIaIQobChMI6o_Fodyw3QIVRLTtCh1-3QkZEAAYAiAAEgK0QfD_BwE (all accessed 10 September 2018).

5 See https://www.fertigbau.de/ (accessed 7 February 2019).

Sunshine Boulevard, in the middle of nowhere: single-family homes and carports – advertising in the prefab industry in Germany

Anne Caplan

How to sell mass products as individual homes?

In a social situation in which markets address consumption as highly individualised and differentiated, how does one sell something prefabricated? This tension has accompanied the capitalist economy since the beginning of the 20th century, when Fordist production methods brought mass production and mass consumption together, reinforced by the welfare state. In this force field, the single-family house is a revelatory object of investigation since in an international comparison, home ownership in (West) Germany is characterised by the fact that a house is 'a once-in-a-lifetime' purchase (this is a translation of a well-known building society slogan in Germany) and is treasured as an intimate family consumer commodity (Helbrecht/Geilenkeuser 2010). A one-off purchase at a very high price requires exceptional justifications, which can be both implicit and formulated. So how are prefabricated houses and other prefabricated buildings advertised in order to convey exclusivity and uniqueness, not in a luxury segment, but as mass consumer goods? The advertising for these products provides detailed information, provided that their content is not examined from an ideology-critical perspective but a cultural-analytical one. This was developed concisely in the media research of British Cultural Studies, in the context of which Richard Johnson characterised the segments of market research and advertising using the example of the motor car as 'capitalism's own cultural analysis', which always draws on a 'stock of public and private meanings', but at the same time adds something new and modified to this reservoir (Richard 2013: 27). Although it is a truism that advertising works with stereotypes, these stereotypes are not coincidental and by no means the ideological production of the economically powerful. Rather, in order to be appealing, they must resonate with people's desires. Therefore, numerous analyses of advertising have shown time and again that it is culturally profitable to examine sales images.[1]

Since the mid-20th century, the detached single-family house has functioned worldwide as an allegory of stability, family life and consumption.[2] How does the ready-made sector address the claims to represent an individuality associated with a detached house in the countryside? Which ideals of family, house, nature, living and mobility can be found here? Which of these do we already know from history, and which accents are new? In order to examine these questions, current prefabricated building advertisements were examined exemplarily for the current article. On the one hand, the analysis will lead us into familiar realms of cultural ideals of nature and family; on the other hand, it will lead to new sales arguments that react to the more recent horizon of limited resources. Another essential finding is that, when it comes to making offers to consumers, the heterosexual gender order still proves to be a tried and tested expression of ways of life and living. Spaces are strictly dichotomously gendered, or a dichotomous gender world is spatially articulated. All in all, the advertising visualises an idea of privacy that no longer needs public space as a counter image.

The single-family home as a form of promoted dwelling since the 19th century – auto-mobility as a form of 'approach road'

How close-knit stability and control in a detached house are regarded is not only a diffuse feeling among friends and enemies of single-family homes but rather the result of political decisions. Since the 19th century, free-standing detached houses have been promoted by socially conservative and also nationalist currents of the Homestead Movement (Heimstättenbewegung) on the one hand; as well as by socialist-utopian concepts based around the Garden City concept in modern architecture. But due to the wars and the economic situation, this form of life and living could only be turned into reality in a few exceptional projects. This changed in West Germany and in the Federal Republic after the Second World War when the watchword was reconstruction. Supported by housing legislation and the economic upswing, the suburban single-family home became a realisable dream and a prime place of consumption, especially for workers and the lower middle class (Staub 2009:

156). The goals associated with the policy of promoting owner-occupied housing have apparently also proved to be true, since sociological housing research in the last decade of the old Federal Republic of Germany revealed a decreasing but still prevailing correlation between conservative electoral decisions and home ownership (Häußermann/Küchler 1993).
The prerequisite for the success of single-family house policies in Germany, however, was first and foremost the motor car. It was only motorised individual transport that made it at all possible to populate suburban areas and commute on a daily basis to work in the towns and cities, and later to transport children to leisure and educational facilities. In addition, motor car manufacturing was one of the central pillars of economic growth. A number of different federal governments used the promotion of motorised private transport as an economic policy measure. A veritable guarantee of mobility to the 'little house in the countryside' was therefore provided comparatively late (namely between 1971 and 1985), once again by a law on the extension of federal trunk roads.[3] This decision must be seen in the context of the 1966/67 recession and the 1975 and 1982 oil crises. The infrastructure thus created was decisive for the development of a commuter culture between the city and suburbia. Klaus Voy and Werner Polster have characterised this process as a 'home-automobile culture' (Polster/Voy 1993b: 293), which combined housing, leisure and travel in a historically specific way.
The home and the car became material milestones in people's biographies (ibid.). While a home of one's own represents stability, constancy and rootedness, a car symbolises mobility, flexibility and freedom. The fact that the car and the house nevertheless constitute a vital symbiosis is partly due to the fact that both convey modern ideals of individualisation and privacy (ibid.: 344). Above all, mass production and the associated reduction in the price of consumer goods made the long-term 'production of privacy' and the 'democratisation of luxury' possible (ibid.: 341). In the context of the Cold War, consumer freedom and consumer intensity were symbols of the free world with its promise of infinite growth, while renunciation and frugality were identified with non-freedom and 'communism'.[4]

The twin significance of prefabs: modern consumption and/or stopgap solutions

In terms of building history there is evidence of a linear shift from half-timbered houses to the mass production of timber-frame constructions as part of technical innovations at the beginning of the 19th century (Spohn 2007: 155).[5] Historically older is the depreciation of half-timbered and timber houses, a fact that has been proven since the middle of the 16th century. Until the mid-19th century, wood, the predominant building material, had repeatedly led to devastating fires, especially in densely built-up cities (Walberg/Arbeitsgemeinschaft für zeitgemäßes Bauen e.V. 2015: 59 f.). This contributed to brick houses being regarded as more stable and durable, while fire-prone wooden houses were subject to high fire insurance in the wake of emerging requirements for fire protection. As a result, these houses were also at a disadvantage when it came to acquiring mortgages (Junghanns 1994: 28).[6] At the beginning of the 20th century, prefabricated construction received a new boost from Fordist production methods (standardisation, typification, assembly line production) and the development of new materials like reinforced concrete and steel – processes that boosted the production of houses and dwellings as well as cars. The avant-garde in architecture and design was fascinated by the new potentials and also explicitly established a link between the house and the car. In 1920, Le Corbusier developed his Citrohan assembly house (based on the Citroën automobile group, the first company to introduce assembly line production in Europe) (Ågren/Wing 2014: 10).[7] Prefabricated houses were not only coveted, they also carried with them that part of housing history that had to do with storage, lodging and makeshift accommodation. Under the pressure of the housing shortage after the First World War, pioneers of prefabricated construction such as Peter Behrens, Walter Gropius and Gustav Lilienthal had already begun to apply cost-cutting methods of industrial construction. However, since the standardisation and rationalisation of automated pre-production was primarily realised as publicly funded small housing construction for needy families, prefabricated houses were not only synonymous with cost minimisation, but also with poverty (Junghanns 1994: 68). The use of prefabricated elements for military barracks and provisional homes additionally supported the connotation of prefabricated houses as makeshift solutions (Vorwig 2014: 307).

In turn, the boom in the prefab industry after the Second World War (Staub 2009: 160)[8] enabled low-cost production, which could also be afforded by middle and low-income households in the post-World War II reconstruction period.[9] This also symbolised modern consumption (Vorwig 2013; 2014), and uniformity. The industry experienced a boom phase from the early 1960s onwards. Steelmaking corporations like Krupp and Hoesch as well as shipping and commodity enterprises like Kaufhof AG and Neckermann entered the market (Vorwig 2014: 311). The prefabricated parts industry experimented with new residential concepts and synthetic houses as well as spatial cell construction methods and meta-city construction systems (Vangerow-Kühn 1984: 27 ff.). Ultimately, the recession in the construction industry in 1974/75 and the 1976 Housing Modernisation Act put an end to experimental ideas of industrialised construction and promoted a guiding architectural idea of 'conservation renewal' (Schäfer 1999: 115).

To date, prefabricated houses have not been able to prevail over solid construction. According to a representative Emnid survey commissioned by the BHW Bausparkasse in 2011, 37 percent of those surveyed preferred custom-built houses designed by an architect, 27 percent preferred to build their own house and only 19 percent preferred a prefabricated house.[10] This is also reflected in the supplier market. Disregarding their size, the number of enterprises in the building trade in the Federal Republic of Germany shows an unbroken dominance and demand for solid constructions. The Statistical Yearbook 2016 (Sector 23, Building) revealed that in June 2015 there were a total of 18,720 building enterprises in Germany of which 575 were companies building prefabricated housing (Statistisches Bundesamt 2016: 568). This profile is based on an employment ratio of 241,233 persons in building construction and 9,378 employees in precast construction. Whereas in building construction the share of skilled workers and master craftsmen in the workforce is 59.6 percent, and thus higher than their share in precast construction (52.9 percent), in the precast sector the share of business employees (29.3 percent) is higher than in building construction (20.5 percent) (ibid.). This suggests that distribution and marketing in the prefabricated parts sector require comparatively more effort than in building construction, where the proportion of employees is higher in the skilled trades and production.

The sample used in the present study

After the promises of growth in the modern oil industry had bottomed out, and the demands of the ecology movement had moved (under the term 'sustainability') into specifications of spatial, urban and traffic planning as well as building legislation, new social and cultural perceptions arose for the private home in the countryside. Although there was no individual standardisation in production, it was an excellent process for resource efficiency and resource conservation. This is where this study begins. As indicated above, images and texts produced by precast manufacturers had to argue against a long history of the cultural devaluation of precast construction (Junghanns 1994: 28, 68 f.; Gilbert 1984: 19, 161, 218). What relationships can be discerned from the long, culturally ambivalent significance of prefabricated construction? To what extent do traditional or changed images of privacy, family and consumption play a role in the sale of residential housing and the associated automobility? Does a line of tension emerge between industrialised construction and manual production, and what role does resource efficiency play in the advertising language of precast manufacturers? The empirical basis is the print advertising of the precast concrete industry in the housing and carport sector: a sample of a total of ten catalogues[11] published between 2014 and 2017 by four prefabricated house manufacturers in Germany and three carport manufacturers.[12] From the sample of researched print advertising produced by the precast concrete industry in the housing sector, the catalogues of Heinrich Meyer Werke (HM Carport)[13] and Gussek Haus[14] were selected for detailed analysis. Here, the selection of print advertising was based on the use of the same stock image in both catalogues. In order to examine the question of how the manufacturers dealt with the fact of pre-production, and which advertising strategies were applied to counter this fact, the empirical material was analysed in terms of content in the light of Visual Culture Studies, with image and text being treated equally.

Between wood and pixels: traditional craftwork instead of industrialised production methods

Both HM Carport and Gussek Haus advertise with photorealistic renderings of their products (cf. figs. 1 and 2). Here the dream of the house or carport is exaggerated by a fictitious photorealistic computer simulation. By contrast to photos taken from stock image portals, which also appear in the catalogues, the depicted scenes never actually occurred. The renderings are visual 'dream castles' made of pixels that cannot be viewed, touched or even inhabited anywhere in reality. However, photorealistic renderings offer the possibility of depicting a building in a realistic manner, which makes them an important means of presenting products to potential buyers.
The first thing that catches the eye is that the sun is always shining in both catalogues. The sky is blue. Unpleasant elements like appliances and garbage cans in the carport catalogue or untidy, dirty interiors in the prefab catalogue are consistently avoided. On the one hand, this is not surprising when it comes to advertising. On the other hand, it is no accident when it comes to detached houses. After all, small, clean, bright detached houses in a summery ambience had already been the visual advertising medium used by the building societies and Homestead Movement (Ziereis 2005), while single-family homes in US suburbs had become both an instrument and an expression of a racially

Figure 1: Heinrich Meyer-Werke Breloh GmbH & Co. KG (2014), Carports, p. 46.

Figure 2: GUSSEK HAUS, Franz Gussek GmbH & Co. KG (2017), Boulevard, p. 9.

divided society (and also made famous around the world via cinema and TV) (Harris 2013: 272). Even if the depiction discussed here shows a fixed building, it is nothing more than a theoretic study of options. A depiction helps to make a building realisable, but it always stays immaterial. At that point we see in a specific way, that only the 'dream of a house' is being sold. This dream is more important in the presentation than a building that really exists: 'No houses but homes' (Kriese/Scholz 2012: 293).
CAD renderings are based on a frame model of horizontal and vertical lines in which objects can be drawn in the structure by adding individual anchor points. Robert Ågren and Robert D. Wing have examined the development of CAD technology in the immediate context of the precast industry. In particular, the industrialisation of design required for precast buildings required innovation processes in the areas of planning and manufacturing. For example, the quick connection system invented by Konrad Wachsmann and further developed by Fritz Haller made it possible to erect a prefabricated house in just a few hours (Ågren/Wing 2014: 13). Ågren and Wing formulate the thesis that here the multiple configuration possibilities in a three-dimensional symmetrical axial connection system already point to the concept of a modular grid, which can also be found in today's CAD and 3D programmes (ibid.). In this context,

Figure 3: Heinrich Meyer-Werke Breloh GmbH & Co. KG (2014), Carports, p. 74/75.

it is interesting to note that computer visualisations in the viewed material produced by the precast industry are no longer a production method, but rather an aesthetic strategy with which a product can be quickly brought to the attention of the buyer. The 3D animations here are no longer part of the technical or creative production, but rather a setting for individual customer wishes, which make the buildings appear as unique pieces. HM Carport's advertising material even shows half-timbered carports as rendered simulations, with the manufacturer's note 'Tradition past and present' (cf. fig. 3). While construction was historically linked to a specific contract until the 20th century, even when prefabricated construction principles were used like those in half-timbered buildings, prefabricated building companies today produce for an anonymous market (Spohn 2007: 155). It is precisely this anonymity that is obscured in the visual and linguistic combination of timber framing and prefabricated construction – prefabricated construction is presented as a traditional and individually crafted product.
Amongst others, HM Carport advertises with a high-quality photo series showing impressions of the hand-made production of a 'half-timbered carport' (cf. figs. 4, 5 and 6). In contrast to the idealised, bright and clean renderings and staged photos of the prefabricated houses and carports, the atmosphere

Figure 4: Heinrich Meyer-Werke Breloh GmbH & Co. KG (2014), Carports, p. 2/3.

Figure 5: Heinrich Meyer-Werke Breloh GmbH & Co. KG (2014), Carports, p. 72.
Figure 6: Heinrich Meyer-Werke Breloh GmbH & Co. KG (2014), Carports, p. 70/71.

in this series seems dark and untidy, almost mystical, with material, wood shavings and tools lying around. Here, the light entering from the top left through a shining window is far too diffuse for a real working process but is reminiscent of the atmosphere in a Gothic cathedral.[15] In his comments on light in art, Hartmut Böhme recognises that the industrialisation and digitalisation of society has established a rationality of production and abstraction that is no longer primarily based on materiality (Böhme 1997: 7). If we now transfer this train of thought to the present series of pictures, the spirit shining through the window here does not illuminate abstract elements but rather physically tangible craftsmanship.

The series is accompanied by statements such as: 'Half-timbered carports, because real manual work is priceless' (Heinrich Meyer-Werke Breloh GmbH & Co. KG: 70), 'Here, tried and trusted carpentry is the solution for realising your building project' (ibid.: 73), 'We use our decades of experience in this traditional discipline' (ibid.). HM Carport equates the traditional with the tested and the authentic and emphasises not innovation but continuity. The advertising example also hints at the principle of uniqueness inherent in a work of art: 'Half-timbered carports are one-off productions geared to the customers' individual wishes and site conditions' (ibid.), 'Everything is produced and assembled by hand, each carport is unique' (ibid.). It is characteristic that the entire catalogue begins with a picture from the half-timbered carport series. The image shows a man cutting wood in a dimly lit hall. The whole scene is provided with the slogan 'Everything here has always been handmade' (see fig. 4). HM Carport thus transfers the advertising motif of a single photo series for a specific handmade product to the entire range and underscores this by presenting itself as a family business with a long history:

> 'Everything started 175 years ago in Bispingen in the Lüneburger Heide. It was here that master carpenter Hans Christoph Meyer founded his company, which has been passed on from father to son ever since, now in the sixth generation.' (Heinrich Meyer-Werke Breloh GmbH & Co. KG: 86)

Here, industrial rationalisation achievements in precast element manufacturing[16] are countered by presenting the company's tradition of craftsmanship. By contrast, Gussek Haus sets a different accent. The company combines the idea of craftsmanship with regionality, pioneering spirit and, since the company was founded in 1951, this is also linked to the idea of reconstruction and growth, which is reflected in formulations such as 'our hands at work' (GUSSEK HAUS, Franz Gussek GmbH & Co. KG: 5), 'There is nothing good unless you do it yourself' (ibid.: 67).

> 'We are convinced that the high-quality work of our employees, their love of perfection and their open-mindedness towards new techniques and future-oriented technologies also have something to do with the region where we feel at home. The living environment between lush meadows and green forests, healthy air, the serenity of the people and their friendly and harmonious coexistence are obviously fertile breeding grounds for genuine, high-quality work. Craftsmanship, a sense of quality, an eye for excellent workmanship and a feeling for the responsibility each individual bears towards our customers have allowed our company to expand over the decades and made it in demand today.' (GUSSEK HAUS, Franz Gussek GmbH & Co. KG: 7)

Here, Gussek Haus uses themes like nature, tradition, region and sustainability. But the specifics of precast production are neither named nor emphasised. Although the company describes itself as open to 'new techniques and future-oriented technologies', it locates these thematically between 'lush meadows and green forests' and emphasises its own 'sense of responsibility' (ibid.), which according to the advertising text is also reflected in a long company tradition. Similar to the tension that appears here between serial production and manual work, as well as between industry and nature, the advertising images produced by the precast industry on stability and regional roots also reveal an antithetical image of flexibility and adaptation options. Among other things, HM Carport uses the house as an allegory to illustrate the stability of one of its products:

> 'The illusion of a traditional building is based on the striking roof shape. Here, the observer recognises familiar forms and connects them with stability and security.' (Heinrich Meyer-Werke Breloh GmbH & Co. KG: 51)

Text modules used by HM Carport refer to material properties: Text modules used by HM Carport emphasise material features like stability, anchorage and durability: 'Powerfully dimensioned support beams' (Heinrich Meyer-Werke Breloh GmbH & Co. KG: 17), 'Stable construction' (ibid.: 23), and 'Above-average solid construction' (ibid.: 84). At the same time, the manufacturer contradicts stability and fixation/durability with flexibility in the form of adaptation and individualisation options: 'Expand the use of your carport' (ibid.: 23), 'Many individualisation options' (ibid.: 7), 'Adapt each model entirely to your preferences' (ibid.). A similar approach can be found at Gussek Haus. Statements like: 'This is how we combine the advantages of timber frame construction and solid brick-on-brick facing façade construction' (GUSSEK HAUS, Franz Gussek GmbH & Co. KG: 35), 'the "solid brick", i.e. massive image of facing façade construction touches the emotional needs of many prospective builders' (ibid.) are countered by statements such as: 'Finally, the icing on the cake is the unique flexibility of prefabricated house construction' (GUSSEK HAUS, Franz Gussek GmbH & Co. KG: 49).

Idealised social relationships in the family and spatialised gender orders: the nuclear family

The birth of the first child is an occasion for many couples to build or buy a suburban family home.[17] So it is no surprise that the proportion of children's pictures in the Gussek Haus advertising material (a total of 49 photos) is relatively high in relation to 77 photos of adults.[18] If we follow the pictures presented in the advertising catalogues examined, the target group of people interested in building consists of white, handsome, healthy heterosexual

Figure 7: Heinrich Meyer-Werke Breloh GmbH & Co. KG (2014), Carports, p. 86/87.

Figure 8: GUSSEK HAUS, Franz Gussek GmbH & Co. KG (2017), Boulevard, p. 14.

couples in their mid-thirties to mid-forties with two children, usually a boy and a girl. Both Gussek Haus and HM Carport focus on the presentation of stereotypical family images. What is significant here is that both companies even use the same stock image for product presentation (cf. figs. 7 and 8). This picture shows a blonde woman about 30 years old with two blonde children (a boy and a girl) roughly four to six years old. The group is happily smiling and lying in a hammock that seems to be on the edge of a deciduous forest. The picture is softly defined and avoids harsh contrasts. The golden glow featuring spots of light on the meadow and the foliage convey a warm, summery impression. There is neither a carport nor a house in sight. Stock images are images that can be overwritten with various meanings and can therefore be used in a variety of ways. Paul Frosh therefore also calls a stock image a 'generic image' (Frosh 2002: 172). Stock images are assigned keywords by the licensing picture agencies, and these follow social classifications as used by the advertising industry. In the case of the picture examined here, these could be, for example, at home, happiness, relaxation, family, garden, motherly love, cohesion, community, summer. The picture agencies mainly focus on familiar or desirable motifs:

> 'Their master discourse is rhetoric, not science, their institutional context advertising, not journalism; and they employ realist representational codes only insofar as they reproduce the familiar "real" and allow for the rhetorically effective projection of values and desires associated with its depiction.' (ibid.: 176)

Stock photography draws sharp distinctions and addresses subjective experiences of identity, social status, advancement and knowledge (ibid. 180). In 1996 superdiverse population groups, the elderly and people with disabilities, for example, were subsumed in the Image Bank catalogue into the category 'One World'; while the white middle class was marked and presented as individuals in the category 'People' (Frosh 2001: 641). In the sample analysed here, all family members shown are blonde or dark-haired, but always white.[19]

The house as a sign of economic success guarantees privacy and uniformity not only in terms of security and family seclusion, but also in terms of class and diversity.

Men do carports, women do care

The gender order of the families shown here is also stereotypical. It is noticeable that HM Carport shows considerably fewer people in its product catalogue than Gussek Haus (ratio 6 to 126 illustrations featuring people).[20] The men depicted here are visualised in close relation to the carport with regard

Figure 9: Heinrich Meyer-Werke Breloh GmbH & Co. KG (2014), Carports, p. 72.

Figure 10: Heinrich Meyer-Werke Breloh GmbH & Co. KG (2014), Carports, p. 11.

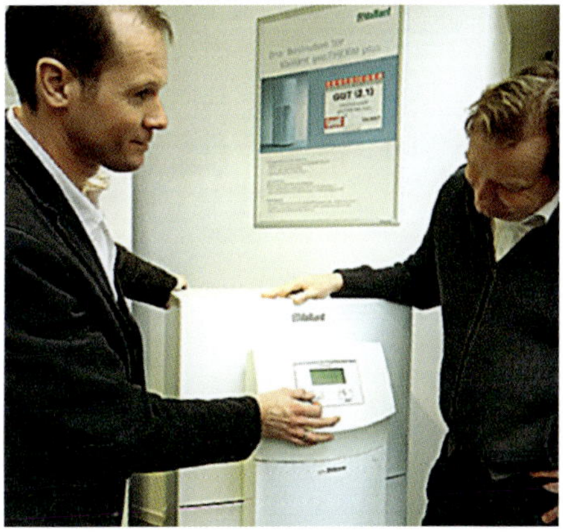

Figure 11: GUSSEK HAUS, Franz Gussek GmbH & Co. KG (2017), Boulevard, p. 20.
Figure 12: GUSSEK HAUS, Franz Gussek GmbH & Co. KG (2017), Boulevard, p. 65.
Figure 13: GUSSEK HAUS, Franz Gussek GmbH & Co. KG (2017), Boulevard, p. 64.

to planning, material procurement and construction (cf. figs. 9 and 10). The only woman in the carport catalogue is shown lying in a hammock with two children in a leisurely and relaxing situation (see fig. 7 above). From the point of view of the carport dealer, it is evident that the man is portrayed as the decision-maker or doer, while the woman plays a supportive role in childcare. In the Gussek Haus catalogue, too, the women shown are predominantly involved in household tasks, whilst the men are working in the office or involved in manual work or looking at plans and talking shop (cf. figs. 11, 12 and 13). Both catalogues exclusively use the generic masculine in their texts: for example 'Mitarbeiter[n]' (Heinrich Meyer-Werke Breloh GmbH & Co. KG: 10), 'Bauinteressenten' (GUSSEK HAUS, Franz Gussek GmbH & Co. KG: 35) and 'Bauherren' (ibid.: 7).

The fact that the prefabricated house manufacturer uses considerably more people to illustrate his product than the carport manufacturer may also be due to the fact that many references to home-making processes controlled by women can be found in home advertising. Everyday activities in and around the house are staged – situations like playing with the children, cooking, housework and socialising (cf. figs. 14, 15 and 16).

In the prefabricated house catalogue, men are presented in a few pictures as dedicated fathers. This can be seen, among other things, in a kitchen scene between three persons (cf. fig. 17). Thanks to the arrangement of the persons in relation to one another and the setting of the single-family house, the viewer can assume that the persons are father, daughter and son. Father and son have their arms lying on the worktop in front of them, and their bodies leaning towards each other. The daughter can be seen in the background between the two male protagonists. She is depicted in the background, shielded by the male bodies. The kitchen table is misappropriated as a drawing table. Although the father is not involved in cooking a family meal, he is portrayed as an actor participating in family life. The change of the male role in the family context from 'protector' to 'provider' (Williams Barnes 2013: 101) is shown here in the care of the children, but without the man taking over specific household activities. At the same time, an ideal of family togetherness is seen, which integrates the man more strongly into representations of leisure time within the home:

> 'However, the togetherness promoted by social critics, represented in magazines and on television [of the 1950s, author's note] was not so easily achieved. [...] Togetherness was intended to allow couples to obtain fulfillment through the joining of the family, eliminating the strict separate spheres where women were expected to dedicate time and labor to their home and children and men worked outside the home.' (Patton 2013: 148)

Figure 14: GUSSEK HAUS, Franz Gussek GmbH & Co. KG (2017), Boulevard, p. 24.
Figure 15: GUSSEK HAUS, Franz Gussek GmbH & Co. KG (2017), Boulevard, p. 56.
Figure 16: GUSSEK HAUS, Franz Gussek GmbH & Co. KG (2017), Boulevard, p. 32.

Figure 17: GUSSEK HAUS, Franz Gussek GmbH & Co. KG (2017), Boulevard, p. 12.

While Elizabeth Patton was already observing the depiction of 'togetherness' on TV and in print media in the post-war years of the USA, such depictions were not yet commonplace, especially in post-war house advertising in Germany. Contemporary depictions of people, e.g. in building society advertising, still referred in this genre to women and children (often playing in the garden or on the terrace) in accordance with the bourgeois gender order, while the man was out of sight earning the money to finance the dream home (Wagner-Douglas 2005: 106). In family-centred advertising in the house building sector, the focus has now shifted towards focusing on everyday family situations in which a dedicated father participates.

It is striking that the pictures in the carport catalogue mainly show men, while the prefabricated house catalogue shows almost as many men as women. In the prefabricated house catalogue, women can also be seen negotiating with their own family and with building consultants (cf. fig. 18). Here, the woman is visible as an administrator or mediator between inside the home and outside. Providing for the family, home-making and the associated role as a consumer allow women to move from the domestic to the public sphere.

Figure 18: GUSSEK HAUS, Franz Gussek GmbH & Co. KG (2017), Boulevard, p. 64.

Wives are shown in reproductive work or care activities in the privacy of the home, or together with husbands when purchasing in the exhibition and sales centre of the prefabricated house manufacturer, whilst husbands are also portrayed alone as earners/breadwinners in their professional/outside work. In the carport catalogue, the process of planning and buying is uncoupled from the domestic female sphere. Here, women are not visualised as participants. There is a clear separation between 'male business and female home spheres' (Miller 1991: 266),[21] which also appears in the catalogue texts: 'By experienced craftsmen's hands' (Heinrich Meyer-Werke Breloh GmbH & Co. KG: 9), 'Expert graduate engineers and structural engineers (*Ingenieure und Statiker*, male forms only) process your building application professionally' (ibid.: 11), 'Our employees (*Mitarbeiter*, male form only) are happy to come to your home' (ibid.: 10). Compared to the family-centred prefabricated house catalogue, the carport catalogue is also much more technical. Serial details and production processes are discussed in detail:

> 'In order to guarantee the load-bearing capacity of the carport, the roof construction is reinforced with a load-bearing capacity of 85 kg/m² up to a load-bearing capacity of 165 kg/m². A wooden roof made of stable 21 mm thick Softline profile boards serves as the basis for waterproofing and greening. Alternatively, the roof can be sealed with a 1.0 mm thick PVC foil.' (Heinrich Meyer-Werke Breloh GmbH & Co. KG: 37)

A dichotomous gender order can be seen not only in the language but also in the allocation of the sexes to the buildings: men are at the carports, women in the kitchens and, as can be seen in the following chapter, accompanied by girls, in the garden.[22]

The private paradise – the (girls') garden and living in natural surroundings

The examination of the advertising material on hand has shown, among other things, that houses are depicted from the rear, i.e. from the garden area, which cannot be seen from the outside. The prefabricated house manufacturer thus joins a tradition that conveys the ideal of bourgeois intimacy or privacy with the image of the garden. The moment of an 'inner-directed [...] self-absorption' (Sennett 1977: 5) is reinforced by the fact that the depicted properties are all shown in isolation, independent of any direct neighbourhood: as if they existed not only in their respective gardens, but also outside the context of a street or settlement. The single-family houses are depicted on the edge of a forest or on a green meadow. Visualisations of neighbouring houses are rare in the entire sample, especially in the prefabricated house catalogues:

'you try to make intimate and local the scale of human experience – that is, you make local territory morally sacred. [...] Love of the ghetto, especially the middle-class ghetto, denies the person a chance to enrich his perceptions.' (ibid.: 295)

By contrast, the situation is somewhat different in the carport catalogues. Here, there are more and more photographs in the entire sample showing the products in real surroundings and linked to their respective houses. Since the 1950s, there has been evidence of visualisations on green field sites, for example in building society advertising (Wagner-Douglas 2005: 107). Julia Gill (2010: 93) notes that such subjects also suggest a multi-optional feasibility

Figure 19: Heinrich Meyer-Werke Breloh GmbH & Co. KG (2014), Carports, p. 41.

Figure 20: GUSSEK HAUS, Franz Gussek GmbH & Co. KG (2017), Boulevard, p. 53.

according to which the building can be adapted to any environment. Thus, the residents are seen as owners who have the freedom to build their own home in almost any natural environment. The depictions of prefabricated houses in green surroundings, flowering landscapes and far away from any civilisation convey an idyllic yearning for a private, secluded life in nature. The overall arcadian impression is reinforced by blue skies and sunshine as well as softened images and golden light effects. Christoph Baumann (2016: 253) links the 'Arcadian' with the 'retreat into the private' and 'happiness in the small', factors which became established among the bourgeoisie especially during the Biedermeier period of the 19th century. It is interesting to note that in the sample all the representations of persons in the garden are female. To be more precise, only girls can be seen. Sunken in thought, they enjoy fresh flowers and sun-drenched green spaces. Here, the garden presents itself as a place of cultural development, private relaxation and pleasure.

Figure 21: GUSSEK HAUS, Franz Gussek GmbH & Co. KG (2017), Boulevard, p. 2.
Figure 22: GUSSEK HAUS, Franz Gussek GmbH & Co. KG (2017), Boulevard, p. 28.
Figure 23: GUSSEK HAUS, Franz Gussek GmbH & Co. KG (2017), Boulevard, p. 6.

In art and literature, the garden functions as an allegory for femininity. The garden gate is thereby interpreted as the threshold to growing up.[23] The garden as an agency of knowledge and civilisation belongs, as an idea, to industrialisation.[24] The advertising material presents us neither with simple country life nor with self-sufficiency romanticism,[25] but with the house and garden as consumer goods. The garden does not fulfil an economic function but is presented as a place of pleasure and recreation with childlike female connotations. Luxurious, tidy gardens with pools, exclusive garden furniture and sumptuous, frequently blossoming plants indicate the prosperity of their affluent owners.

My home is my castle – luxury and the single-family home

The Gussek Haus catalogue title 'Boulevard', (originally a French word indicating a magnificent avenue), and designations such as 'Ulmenallee, Lindenallee or Kastanienallee' (Elm Avenue, Lime Avenue and Chestnut Avenue) are an exclusive and natural choice for Gussek Haus. From 1765 onwards, so-called 'Lustalleen' (*pleasure avenues*) consisting mainly of elms, oaks and linden trees were planted in the Dessau Garden Kingdom irrespective of manor houses and aristocratic residences (Peters 2008: 25). The fact that Gussek Haus product names are so closely modelled on the 'Lustallee' may be a coincidence, but the fact is that 'avenues' convey the idea of aristocratic palace gardens, stately villas, representation and luxury. Jürgen Peters notes that, in the 18th and 19th centuries, avenues were created as landscape elements for traffic-related reasons (Peters 2004: 105). Streets lined with trees were used to structure stately upper-class residential landscapes, not only as visual axes but also for representational purposes, thereby underscoring a feudal claim to power (Peters 2008: 17).

The word 'Allee' originates from the French word 'aller' (*to go*) and might be translated as 'alley'. Since classical avenues were not residential streets but traffic routes between individually located seats of power, Gussek Haus uses such designations to reposition its prefabricated houses in the countryside, as if the nearest neighbour lived at least a carriage ride away. Gussek Haus equips its single-family mansions in gardens and terraces with expensive designer furniture like the Eames Plastic Chair. Modern classics appear in the furniture sector, especially among those manufacturers of prefabricated houses who market high-quality catalogues and want to differentiate their products from prefabricated, low-priced mass-produced goods in order to position them in the luxury segment. Here, in addition to the Gussek company, Büdenbender's catalogue products should also be highlighted from the sample. Among other things, the company relies on the Barcelona Chair by Mies van der Rohe (1929) in its catalogue of architect-designed houses to present houses such as 'Flaviano – Exclusive[26] Architekten-Villa mit Penthouse' (Büdenbender Hausbau GmbH: 4) or 'Molveno – Exceptional, spacious family house' (ibid.: 11).[27]

Figure 24: GUSSEK HAUS, Franz Gussek GmbH & Co. KG (2017), Boulevard, p. 17.
Figure 25: GUSSEK HAUS, Franz Gussek GmbH & Co. KG (2017), Boulevard, p. 15.

Figure 26: Heinrich Meyer-Werke Breloh GmbH & Co. KG (2014), Carports, p. 16/17.
Figure 27: Heinrich Meyer-Werke Breloh GmbH & Co. KG (2014), Carports, p. 47.

Although furniture like the 'Plastic Chair', which appears in many illustrations in the Gussek catalogue, once corresponded to modular concepts – they were the first serially produced plastic chairs and underscored this by interchangeable baseframes for the seat shells and inexpensive industrial production – such furniture is used here (similar to the prefabricated house) as an allegory of style and luxury. Their character stands above the image of functionality. Lush, partially flowering plants, pools and ponds underline the Gussek company's claim to exclusivity, while at the same time emphasising the financial accessibility of the dream homes depicted:

> 'Many components, extensions and conversions can be realised at a later date, so that you do not have to overburden your current house budget unnecessarily.' (GUSSEK HAUS, Franz Gussek GmbH & Co. KG: 49)

Here, living in a detached house not only becomes a dream come true, but also a personalised 'memorial during one's own lifetime' (Kaschuba 2007: 5):

> 'With the further development of house forms lifestyles are becoming increasingly important alongside the design of the living areas. [...] As with computers, it is apparently the peripheral facilities that are also important today in the single-family home. For they multifunctionalise and gentrify the object of desire: my home as a spatially designed "second self".' (ibid.: 3)

The integration of hobby rooms into the house and every conceivable option for leisure activities makes 'leaving this ideal world' superfluous and encourages familial control in one's own home (Pollak 2005: 32). In order to enhance its serially titled product range (AC, DC, NC, OC, PC, SC, FC), which can be considered as a reference to prefabrication, HM Carport relies on images of current luxury cars and vintage cars under its carports. The HM carport, which according to the manufacturer is supposed to 'protect your heartthrob' (Heinrich Meyer-Werke Breloh GmbH & Co. KG: 27), thus becomes an object of distinction in order to adequately display ownership made visible in the form of the car: 'The sweeping carports of the AC series break the visual monotony of conventional constructions and offer a refreshing view of your car.' (ibid.: 15) By contrast, depictions of houses in building society advertisements in the 1960s did not yet include cars or garages. This was due to the fact that the motor car was initially regarded as a rival to building society savings (Wagner-Douglas 2005: 107). Today, however, car ownership and house purchase are no longer economically mutually exclusive but rather mutually dependent. This advertising survey presents a home of one's own and its peripheral facilities as a personal design and consumption space in which the nuclear family can develop in protected privacy.

Conclusion: detached desires, society out of sight

While prefabricated construction in production and design was coveted at the time of its creation as a twin promise of cost reduction on the one hand and technical feasibility on the other, these aspects play at best a subordinate role in the promotion of products in home construction. Instead, manufacturers present their industrialised goods as a craft tradition in a family business and as unique items placed in the luxury goods segment with the help of various accessories like designer furniture, vintage cars and distinguished product names. Lush, flowering gardens with pools or ponds also play an important role. The advertising material for potential buyers presents the house from the back and thus as a private matter. Urban and social neighbourhood contexts are not part of the sales strategy. A public space in the form of a street side is visually non-existent in the catalogues. To build and own a house thus manifests itself as a private matter and as something highly personal. The privacy aspect also emerges in the form of the visualised remoteness of the respective family from social and economic connections: Adolescent girls play within the shelter of the garden – even without neighbour's children, the man's workspace is outside the living area, and the interior of the house becomes a comfortable world of well-being thanks to the woman's maternal care.

The political debates on housing forms still visualised urbanity as a contrast in late 19th century social issues (for example in building society advertising in the early 19th century).[28] But in the visual world of single-family houses today there is not even a negative representation of urban or public features. In fact, there is no form of public sphere at all in the advertising images. The private space stands for itself and is connected with nothing but 'nature'. This 'depoliticized withdrawal' (Sennett 1977: 296) into the private sphere is precisely the force field that has regularly confronted local authority planning – which for some years has been devoted to the development of old single-family house areas of the 1950s to 1980s in small towns and rural areas. Owners are considered difficult to address in matters concerning development projects, as they claim their building environment is a private matter.

Acknowledgements

The research for this article has been done within the research association 'The Flow of Things or Private Property? A House and Its Objects between Family Life, Resource Management and Museum', led by Elisabeth Timm (WWU Münster, Seminar for Folklore Studies/European Ethnology), funded by the Federal Ministry of Education and Research (BMBF) programme 'The Language of Objects: Material Culture in the context of Social Development', www.hausfragen.net, funding code 01UO1504A. The article was originally published in German (Caplan 2018) and translated by Roy Kift.

References

Ågren, R. and Wing, R. D. (2014), 'Five Moments in the history of industrialized building', Construction Management and Economics 32(1–2): 7–15.

Bärnthol, R. (2011), 'Ein „grünes Zimmer" – Wohngärten der 1960er Jahre', H. May and M. Eigmüller (eds.), Siedlung, Architektur, Wohnen. Umbruchzeit. Die 1960er und 1970er Jahre auf dem Land (Bad Windsheim: Fränkisches Freilandmuseum), 275–282.

Baumann, C. (2016), 'Die Lust am Ländlichen – Zur Persistenz und Variation idyllischer Ländlichkeit', Informationen zur Raumentwicklung 2: 249–259.

Böhme, H. (1997), 'Das Licht als Medium der Kunst. – Über Erfahrungsarmut und ästhetisches Gegenlicht in der technischen Zivilisation', in M. Schwarz (ed.): Licht, Farbe, Raum. Künstlerisch-wissenschaftliches Symposium (Braunschweig: Verlag Leporello), 111–137. https://www.hartmutboehme.de/media/Licht_4piqEXd.pdf (accessed 7 March 2018).

Bourdieu, P. et al. (1998), Der Einzige und sein Eigenheim, erw. Neuausgabe der Schriften zu Politik & Kultur, 3 (Hamburg: VSA).

Bundesministerium der Justiz und für Verbraucherschutz, Gesetz über die soziale Wohnraumförderung (Wohnraumförderungsgesetz – WoFG) §1 Abs. 2 Nr. 2, 13.09.2001. https://www.gesetze-im-internet.de/wofg/BJNR237610001.html (accessed 7 March 2018).

Deutsche Säge- und Holzindustrie Bundesverband e.V. (2018), Der Cluster Forst und Holz: mehr Beschäftigte als die Automobilbranche, http://www.saegeindustrie.de/sites/branche.php (accessed 7 March 2018).

Bundesverband Deutscher Fertigbau e.V. (2018), GUSSEK HAUS – Schöne (H)Aussichten. http://www.fertigbau.de/mitglieder/fertighaushersteller/gussek.html (accessed 7 March 2018).

Caplan, A. (2018), 'Sunshine Boulevard, in the middle of nowhere: Einfamilienhäuser und Carports – die Werbebilder der Fertigteilproduktion in Deutschland', kommunikation@gesellschaft, Journal für alte und neue Medien aus soziologischer, kulturanthropologischer und kommunikationswissenschaftlicher Perspektive 19: 1–31.

Driessen, K. (2010), 'Akteure, Beweggründe, Triebkräfte der Suburbanisierung', in H. Pechlaner and M. Bachinger (eds.): Lebensqualität und Standortattraktivität. Kultur, Mobilität und regionale Marken als Erfolgsfaktoren (Berlin: Erich Schmidt Verlag), 215–228.

Frosh, P. (2001), 'Inside the image factory: stock photography and cultural production', Media, Culture & Society 23: 625–646.

Frosh, P. (2002), 'Rhetorics of the Overlooked. On the communicative modes of stock advertising images', Journal of Consumer Culture 2(2): 171–196.

Gilbert, H. (1984), The Dream of the Factory-Made House. Walter Gropius and Konrad Wachsmann (Massachusetts: MIT Press)

Gill, J. (2010), Individualisierung als Standard. Über das Unbehagen an der Fertighausarchitektur (Bielefeld: transcript).

Grunow, D., Schulz, F. and Blossfeld, H. P. (2007), 'Was erklärt die Traditionalisierungsprozesse häuslicher Arbeitsteilung im Eheverlauf: soziale Normen oder ökonomische Ressourcen?/What Explains the Process of Traditionalization in the Division of Household Labor: Social Norms or Economic Resources?', Zeitschrift für Soziologie 36(3): 162–181.

Harris, D. (2013), Little white houses. How the postwar home constructed race in America (Minnesota: University of Minnesota Press).

Häußermann, H. and Küchler, M. (1993), 'Wohnen und Wählen. Zum Einfluss von Hauseigentum auf die Wahlentscheidung', Zeitschrift für Soziologie 22(1): 33–48.

Helbrecht, I. and Geilenkeuser, T. (2010), 'Homeownership in Germany. Retirement Strategies of Households in a Tenant Society', Teorija in Praksa 47(5): 975–993.

Johnson, R. (2013, FE 1985), 'Was ist überhaupt Kulturanalyse?', in F. Januschek (ed.): Politische Sprachwissenschaft. Zur Analyse von Sprache als kultureller Praxis (Opladen: Westdt. Verlag), 23–70.

Junghanns, K. (1994), Das Haus für alle. Zur Geschichte der Vorfertigung in Deutschland (Berlin: Ernst & Sohn).

Kaschuba, W. (2007), 'Das Einfamilienhaus: Zwischen Traum und Trauma? Beobachtungen zur versteinerten Sofaecke', Archithese 37(3): 18–21, http://www.kaschuba.com/texte/Einfamilienhaus.pdf (accessed 7 March 2018).

Kemeny, J. (1981), The Myth of Home Ownership. Private versus Public Choices in Housing Tenure (London: Routledge).

Klinger, C. (2009), 'Zwischen Haus und Garten. Weiblichkeitskonzepte und Naturästhetik im 18. Jahrhundert', in C. Holm and H. Zaunstöck (eds.): Frauen und Gärten um 1800. Weiblichkeit–Natur–Ästhetik (Halle Saale: Mitteldeutscher Verlag), 12–36.

Kraftfahrtbundesamt, Bestand an Kraftfahrzeugen und Kraftfahrzeuganhängern in den Jahren 1960 bis 2017 nach Fahrzeugklassen, http://www.kba.de/DE/Statistik/Fahrzeuge/Bestand/FahrzeugklassenAufbauarten/b_fzkl_zeitreihe.html?nn=652402 (accessed 7 March 2018).

Kriese, U. and Scholz, R. W. (2012), 'Lifestyle Ideas of House Builders and Housing Investors', Housing, Theory and Society 29(3): 288–320.

Leonard, L., Perkins, H. and Thorns, D. (2004), 'Presenting and Creating Home: The Influence of Popular Building Trade Print Media in the Construction of Home', Housing, Theory and Society 21(3): 97–110.

Lersch, P. M. (2014), 'Geburten und die Wohnraumversorgung von Familien: Anpassungen der Wohnung im zeitlichen Verlauf / Childbirth and Room Stress among Families: Housing Adjustments over Time', Zeitschrift für Soziologie 43(2): 131–149.

May, H. and Rodenberg, M. (eds.) (2013), Der Reichswald. Holz für Nürnberg und seine Dörfer (Bad Windsheim: Fränkisches Freilandmuseum Bad Windsheim).

Miller, R. (1991), 'Selling Mrs. Consumer: Advertising and the creation of suburban socio-spatial relations, 1910–1930', Antipode 23(3): 263–301.

Morris, M. S. (1996), "Tha'lt be like a blush-rose when tha' grows up, my little lass": English cultural and gendered identity in *The Secret Garden*, Environment and Planning D: Society and Space 14: 59–78.

Münter, A. H. C. (2011), 'Wanderungsentscheidungen von Stadt-Umland-Wanderern in vier Stadtregionen. Regionaler Vergleich der Muster und Motive, Informations- und Wahrnehmungslücken sowie Beeinflussbarkeit der Wanderungsentscheidung', (PhD diss., TU Dortmund, Fakultät Raumplanung).

Patton, E. (2013), 'Spaces of Masculinity and Work', in E. Patton and M. Choi (eds.): Home sweat Home. Perspectives on housework & modern relationships (Lanham: Rowman & Littlefield), 147–167.

Peters, J. (2008), 'Funktion und Ästhetik – Kulturgeschichte der Alleen in Preußen. Beitrag zum Tagungsband "Arnsberger Umweltgespräche"', in Landesarbeitsgemeinschaft Naturschutz (ed.): Alleen im Spannungsfeld von Verkehrssicherheit und Landschafts- und Umweltschutz, 17–110.

Peters, J. (2004), 'Alleen und Pflasterstraßen als kulturelles Erbe. Entwicklungsgeschichte und heutige Bedeutung am Beispiel der Mark Brandenburg', UVP-report 18(2+3): 105–109.

Pisani, S. (2014), 'Ich-Architektur. Das Haus als gelebte Vita und Alter-Ego', in S. Pisani and E. Oy-Marra (eds.): Ein Haus wie ich. Die gebaute Autobiographie in der Moderne (Bielefeld: transcript), 9–40.

Pollak, S. (2005), 'Erlerntes Glück im Wohnen. Die Vermittlung einer neuen Wohnkultur der 1950er Jahre aus genderspezifischer Sicht', in A. Euler (ed.): Wie wir wohn(t)en. Alltagskultur seit 1945 (Weitra: Bibliothek der Provinz), 29–44.

Polster, W. and Voy, K. (1993a), 'Die Automobilisierung der Bundesrepublik', in K. Voy, W. Polster and C. Thomasberger (eds.): Gesellschaftliche Transformationsprozesse und materielle Lebensweise. Beiträge zur Wirtschafts- und Gesellschaftsgeschichte der Bundesrepublik Deutschland (1949–1989) (Marburg: Metropolis), 323–337.

Polster, W. and Voy, K. (1993b), 'Eigenheim und Automobil – Materielle Fundamente der Lebensweise', in K. Voy, W. Polster and C. Thomasberger (eds.): Gesellschaftliche Transformationsprozesse und materielle Lebensweise. Beiträge zur Wirtschafts- und Gesellschaftsgeschichte der Bundesrepublik Deutschland (1949–1989) (Marburg: Metropolis), 293–351.

Pryce, G. and Oates, S. (2008), 'Rhetoric in the Language of Real Estate Marketing', Housing Studies 23(2): 319–348.
Richards, L. (1990): Nobody's Home. Dreams and Realities in a New Suburb (Melbourne: Oxford University Press).
Schäfer, I. (1999), OKAL – Pionier im Fertighausbau 1928–1998. Eine Studie zur Wirtschaft- und Technikgeschichte (OKAL Lauenstein: Salzhemmendorf).
Scheffold, J. (2011), 'Stereotype Eigenheimarchitektur durch Bausparen?', in H. May and M. Eigmüller (eds.): Siedlung, Architektur, Wohnen. Umbruchzeit 1960er und 1970er Jahre auf dem Land (Bad Windsheim: Fränkisches Freilandmuseum Bad Windsheim), 99–106.
Scheidegger, T. (2009), 'Der Boom des Bäuerlichen, neue Bauern-Bilder in Werbung, Warenästhetik und bäuerlicher Selbstdarstellung', Schweizerisches Archiv für Volkskunde 105: 193–219.
Schimek, M. (2004), Zwischen Anspruch und Wirklichkeit. Staatliche Einflussnahme auf das ländliche Bauen: Das Land Oldenburg zwischen 1880 und 1930 (Münster: Waxmann).
Seidl, E. (ed.) (2005), "Zuteilungsreif": Bausparer-Geschichten aus dem Südwesten. Ausstellungskatalog (Stuttgart: Haus der Geschichte Baden-Württemberg).
Seiter, E. (1990), 'Different Children, Different Dreams: Racial Representation in Advertising', Journal of Communication Inquiry 14(1): 31–47.
Sennett, R. (1977), The Fall of Public Man (New York: Alfred A. Knopf).
Simon, K. (2005), Fertighausarchitektur in Deutschland seit 1945 (Oberhausen: Athena).
Spohn, T. (2007), 'Gebäude für die Translozierung ab Fabrik – der Fertigbau im 20. Jahrhundert', in F. Kaspar (ed.): Bauten in Bewegung. Von der Wiederverwendung alter Hausgerüste, vom Verschieben und vom Handel mit gebrauchten Häusern (Mainz: Zabern), 155–172.
Statista, Bruttoausgaben der Wirtschaftsbranche "Häuser und Bauen" für Werbung (TV, Print, Radio, Online) im Jahr 2008 in Millionen Euro nach Produktgruppen. https://de.statista.com/statistik/daten/studie/1732/umfrage/werbeausgaben-der-wirtschaftsbranche-haeuser-und-bauen-im-jahr-2008/ (accessed 7 March 2018).
Statistisches Bundesamt (ed.) (2016), Statistisches Jahrbuch, Bereich 23 Bauen. Wiesbaden, https://www.destatis.de/DE/Publikationen/StatistischesJahrbuch/StatistischesJahrbuch2016.pdf?__blob=publicationFile (accessed 7 March 2018).
Staub, A. (2009), '"Einmal im Leben". Rooting the "Little Man" to Conservative Values in Postwar West Germany', in M. P. Berg and M. Mesner (eds.): After Fascism. European Case Studies in Politics, Society, and Identities since 1945 (Münster: LIT-Verlag), 153–177.
Staub, A. (2017), 'Von Stunde Null bis Tempo 100. Das Einfamilienhaus und die "Amerikanisierung" westdeutscher Wohnideale in der Nachkriegszeit', Zeitschrift für Kulturwissenschaften 1, 73–97.
Vangerow-Kühn, A. (1984), Die Fertighaus-Bauindustrie in der Bundesrepublik als Modell für Rationalisierung durch Industrialisierung im Bauen (Stuttgart: Fraunhofer IRB).
Vorwig, C. (2013), 'Marktplatz Rheinland – Eine neue Baugruppe im LVR-Freilichtmuseum Kommern', rheinform. Informationen für die rheinischen Museen 01: 25–30.
Vorwig, C. (2014), 'Fertighausbau im 20. Jahrhundert anhand ausgewählter Beispiele', in C. Heuter, M. Schimek and C. Vorwig (eds.): Bauern-, Herren-, Fertighäuser – Hausforschung als Sozialgeschichte. Eine Freundesgabe für Thomas Spohn zum 65. Geburtstag (Münster: Waxmann), 301–321.
Vorwig, C. (2014), 'Bungalow und Wohncontainer. Neues Bauen im LVR-Freilichtmuseum Kommern am Rande der Gegenwart', in S. Elpers and A. Palm (eds.), Die Musealisierung der Gegenwart. Von Grenzen und Chancen des Sammelns in kulturhistorischen Museen (Bielefeld: transcript), 123–146.
Wagner-Douglas, I. (2005), 'Sonnenschirm und Schlaufuchs. Werbebilder der Bausparkassen', in E. Seidl (ed.): "Zuteilungsreif": Bausparer-Geschichten aus

dem Südwesten. Ausstellungskatalog (Stuttgart: Haus der Geschichte Baden-Württemberg), 104–112.
Walberg, D. and Arbeitsgemeinschaft für zeitgemäßes Bauen e.V. (eds.) (2015), Massiv- und Holzbau bei Wohngebäuden. Vergleich von massiven Bauweisen mit Holzfertigbauten aus kostenseitiger, bautechnischer und nachhaltiger Sicht. Kiel, http://www.dgfm.de/uploads/media/ARGE-Kiel-Studie-Massiv-Holz-08-01-2015.pdf. (accessed 7 March 2018).
Williams Barnes, N. (2013), 'Making Easier the Lives of Our Housewives', in E. Patton and M. Choi (eds.): Home sweat Home. Perspectives on housework & modern relationships (Lanham: Rowman & Littlefield), 89–105.
Zachmann, K. (2008), 'Küchendebatten in Berlin? Die Küche als Kampfplatz im Kalten Krieg', in M. Lemke (ed.): Konfrontation und Wettbewerb. Wissenschaft, Technik und Kultur im geteilten Berliner Alltag (1948–1973) (Berlin: Metropol), 181–205.
Ziereis, B. (2005), 'Bausparen im Kino. Der Bauspar-Spielfilm zwischen Unterhaltung, Information und Werbung', in E. Seidl (ed.), "Zuteilungsreif": Bausparer-Geschichten aus dem Südwesten. Ausstellungskatalog (Stuttgart: Haus der Geschichte Baden-Württemberg), 112–117.

Sources

Heinrich Meyer-Werke Breloh GmbH & Co. KG, 2014, Carports, 05/14.
GUSSEK HAUS, Franz Gussek GmbH & Co. KG, 2017, Boulevard. https://www.gussek-haus.de/fileadmin/user_upload/Newsroom/Mediathek/Blaetterscripte/Haeuser/Boulevard-2017-05/index.html (accessed 16 March 18).
Büdenbender Hausbau GmbH, 2014, Architektenhäuser. Edition 2014–03.
Thank you for the permission to publish the catalogue images in this article: Heinrich Meyer-Werke Breloh GmbH and Franz Gussek GmbH.

Endnotes

1 See also (among others) Scheidegger (2009) on rural aesthetics/idylls in advertising.

2 For an extensive examination see also the regulation theory perspective of home-ownership societies in USA and Australia by Kemeny (1981) and Richards (1990).

3 Georg Leber, the Minister of Transport of the Federal Republic of Germany (1966–1972), called for 85 percent of the population to live less than 10 km from the nearest motorway (Polster/Voy 1993a: 330).

4 The private household, and especially the kitchen, were politically embedded places that were supposed to convey the vision of a US-American European policy in times of the Cold War (Zachmann 2008: 187 f.).

5 'In the early 19th century, timber frame construction was introduced in the United States of America as a further development of half-timbered construction. Standardised planks (made possible by the emergence of steam-driven sawmills) were manufactured using blunt connections to nail them to walls and ceilings. The advantages of this method of construction were less material, quicker building progress, and standardised working processes. (Walberg/Arbeitsgemeinschaft für zeitgemäßes Bauen e.V. 2015: 9).

6 On state influence (among others in fire prevention) in building, see Michael Schimek (2004).

7 Simon (2005: 240) used the example of the Citrohan assembly house to investigate how type designations from the automobile industry were transferred to the prefab sector. This form of identification was intended to enable a high degree of recognition and thus an effective brand structure. Arno Vangerow-Kühn (1984: 110) also refers to the development of brand-name products in the

prefabricated house sector, something that can be ascribed to the quality of serial production and in-house material testing.

8 See also Schäfer (1999: 61–64, 80–81, 88).

9 'The prefabricated house played a special role in postwar German housing. Off the silver screen, it was often the most feasible form of single-family housing for the lower classes, due to its cost-efficient construction methods and guaranteed price.' (Staub 2009: 160)

10 https://www.postbank.de/postbank/pr_bhw_pdextra11_umfrage_lust_am_bauen.html (accessed 7 March 2018).

11 The companies publishing the advertising materials examined for prefabricated houses were: Büdenbender Hausbau GmbH: Netphen-Hainchen, GUSSEK HAUS, Franz Gussek GmbH & Co. KG: Nordhorn, Partner Haus Fertigbau GmbH & Co. KG: Medebach, Danhaus GmbH: Flensburg-Handewitt. The companies publishing the advertising materials examined for carports were: Heinrich Meyer-Werke Breloh GmbH & Co. KG: Munster, Siebau Raumsysteme GmbH & CO. KG: Kreuztal, Carport-Schmiede GmbH & Co. KG: Bad Zwischenahn.

12 In 2007 and 2008, the housing and construction sector invested almost 50 million euros in advertising (TV, print, radio, online). The smallest sums were spent on advertising outdoor facilities (0.5 million euros) and prefabricated houses and houses (5.8 million euros). At 10 million euros, the construction supply sector was targeted almost twice as highly as prefabricated houses and houses (Statista 2008).

13 The wood processing plants of the Heinrich Meyer works in Munster and Bispingen can be allocated to the German sawmill and wood industry. The branch includes carpenters and timber construction companies as well as prefabricated builders. The German Sawmill and Wood Industry Association (Deutscher Säge- und Holzindustrie Bundesverband e.V.) states: 'In terms of employees and turnover, the forestry and timber industry is one of Germany's leading industries. The industry has more employees than the motor vehicle or electrical industry. The sector employs almost one million people, comprises around 160,000 companies and achieves an annual turnover of around 114 billion euros. [...] Apart from a few large companies in the wood-based materials, pulp and paper industries, the timber industry mainly consists of medium-sized companies. These include sawmills, the timber trade, the furniture industry, packaging and prefab industries, as well as carpenters and joiners. Most of them are owner-managed family businesses located in structurally weak rural regions. Thus, the timber industry is of special importance for the regional economic structure and its labour market' (Deutsche Säge- und Holzindustrie Bundesverband e.V. 2018).

14 The Bundesverband Deutscher Fertigbau e.V. (Federal Association of German Prefabricated Buildings) provides the following information on Gussek Haus: 'Founded in 1951 by Franz Gussek and managed by the third generation, the family-run company with headquarters in Nordhorn, in the county of Bentheim, can look back on a success history of almost 65 years. With an annual turnover of around 80 million euros and around 390 highly qualified employees, the GUSSEK Group is one of the top suppliers in the prefabricated house industry.' (Bundesverband Deutscher Fertigbau e.V. 2018).

15 See also gothic cathedrals as a 'medium of light' (Böhme 1997: 7).

16 'The entire house building/production process is broken down into a chain of manageable individual activities. The work of most employees is narrowly restricted. The individual activities can be carried out by unskilled workers after a short training period under the guidance of specialists. This increases productivity.' (Vangerow-Kühn 1984: 100).

17 This is in accord with the observations in the rest of the catalogues in the sample: While the prefab house brochures show especially families with kids and men at work, the carport catalogues are barely showing persons.

18 Ellen Seiter has noted for the US American market: 'Picturing children allows advertisers to call up rich, cherished associations: nostalgia, love, the fullness of the future, the comfort of home, the pleasures of family life.' (Seiter 1990: 31)

19 In her study on the 'racial representation' of children in US advertising, Ellen Seiter stated that intimate family scenes in private space always show a clear racial separation, with black children appearing exclusively in public spaces: 'Victoriana is a vision of inside, an inside safe, protected, insular. [...] In general market-advertising, African-American children never appear in the space of domestic fantasies, never share in these utopian visions of "home".' (Seiter 1990: 35) Following Dianne Harris, a stereotyping of potential house buyers emerges, which prefers white people and presents them as economically potent. Concerning US-American single-family houses of the 1960s, she notes: 'For those who were leaving behind blue-collar and/or immigrant backgrounds, the house became a potent symbol of acceptance and an instrument of aspiration to a broader range of opportunities. [...] Little proclaimed whiteness, class stability, and citizenship quite like a house of one's own in the suburbs.' (Harris 2013: 21)

20 This corresponds with the observations in the other catalogues in the sample: While the prefabricated house brochures increasingly show families with children, and men at work, the carport catalogues hardly show people at all.

21 Miller's study refers to a special historical situation: the early 20th century was marked by enormous urban growth in the USA. Not only were fewer services available in the suburbs, they were also rather unattractive as places of work for domestic staff. At the same time, technologies developed that (also) made domestic work easier. Thus, the suburban household was no longer simply organised by women or delegated to employees, but managed by the women themselves, while the men commuted to work in the cities. For the Federal Republic of Germany, traditionalisation processes have been observed in relation to the course of marriage and the domestic division of labour. See Grunow et al. (2007).

22 Similar gender orders have also been documented for other places. In a study on print advertising in the construction industry in Christchurch/New Zealand, Lorraine Leonard et al. write: 'Today men and women are pictured in the kitchen and other 'domestic' settings but there is still a strong tendency to characterize some parts of the homes as feminine and others masculine. Certainly, in outdoor spaces such as garages, and in advertising for DIY products, text and images were often imbued with a masculine flavor. Women predominate in flower gardens, kitchens and bathrooms.' (Leonard et al. 2004: 106)

23 'In Biblical tradition, symbols of closure and architectural inaccessibility and solidity were often metaphors for a woman's body. The garden enclosed, the sealed fountain, and the closed gate were equated with female virginity.' (Morris 1996: 67)

24 In this context, the house and garden not only formed a refuge for family privacy as a bulwark for anonymising the modern state, but also a 'last reserve of nature' in which humans constitute themselves (Klinger 2009: 18). Thus, the garden in England at the beginning of the twentieth century also fulfilled a civilising function: urban gardens of the working class and school gardens were intended to turn girls into good mothers and to help boys find work (Morris 1996: 60 f.).

25 Bärnthol (2011: 278) notes that today's kitchen gardens are becoming an aesthetically distinctive element in relation to the 1960s residential garden, which still sought to hide these areas.

26 Büdenbender uses a French spelling here to convey the claim to exclusivity. This possibility of distinction through French also refers back to the past, namely to the time when French was the language of the European courts. Julia Gill (2010: 102) also points out that French designations as advertising terms convey exclusivity.

27 Gwilym Pryce and Sarah Oates have studied the importance of language in real estate advertising. Their analysis of real estate advertisements for the Strathclyde

conurbation in Scotland between 1999 and 2006 shows that the use of emotive vocabulary increases in advertising material for high-prices houses. Under 'emotive' they understood descriptions of 1. Originality (words such as 'character', 'natural', 'individual', 'original', 'unique'), 2. Ambience (words like 'bright', 'charming', 'deluxe', 'pleasant', 'elegant'), 3. Prestige (vocabulary such as 'exclusive', 'executive', 'up-market', 'successful' and 4. Excitement (words like 'amazing', 'breathtaking', 'fantastic', 'incredible'). (Pryce/Oates 2008: 15 f.). See also Pierre Bourdieu et al. (1998: 54 f., 85) on language in house advertising.

28 See, for example, the building society film 'Menschen im Schatten, Menschen im Licht' (1934), which contrasts life in gloomy urban rented housing blocks with that in bright housing estates in green surroundings (Ziereis 2005: 114).

California dreaming in West German suburbia: modernist bungalow architecture and its middle-class aspirations

Carola Ebert

Since the 1960s, modernist bungalows have become a ubiquitous suburban building type in West German cities. From the early 1950s onwards, a large number of architectural projects contributed to the rise of the single-storey *Bungalow* with a flat, mostly cantilevering roof (fig. 1) that developed into the iconic post-war modernist house. During the 1960s and 1970s, numerous *Bungalow* projects in commercial housing schemes and as part of large housing estates turned this building type into a mass commodity. This era came to an end in the early 1980s, when rising property prices made the construction of single-storey buildings largely unaffordable, and when the reduced formal vocabulary of the modern bungalow no longer conformed with contemporary popular taste and architectural trends, which focused more on the traditional pitched-roof image of a 'house'.

This chapter on the West German modernist bungalow draws on the author's research of 64 *Bungalows*, which were built and published throughout West Germany between 1952 and 1969.[1] It gives an overview of findings with regard to the *Bungalow*'s etymology, its formal characteristics, location, and siting, which are analysed in relation to the typology's cultural connotations and its representation in architectural and popular press.

Figure 1: Exterior view, Haus Nieaber, 1958, Bad Salzuflen (Reinhard & Sander architects).

The West German modernist bungalow

While the German term *Bungalow* until today suggests an Anglo-American genealogy, the relationship between this German phenomenon and its international references is less straightforward. The architecture of this single-storey flat-roofed modernist typology does not refer to the American bungalow with its Arts and Crafts architecture, large roofs, shingle-clad facades, and rustic stone bases – a typology which originated in California and became a national icon between 1880 and 1920. Contrary to what the Anglo-American imagination associates with the terminology, *Bungalows* in Germany are inextricably connected to architectural modernism. Etymologically, the Anglo-American term acquired new architectural references in post-war West Germany.[2] Until the late 1940s, the word bungalow had been a technical term in Germany, used to describe foreign buildings, e.g. colonial architecture in the tropics, US-American housing, or English country houses. It was only from the 1950s onwards that the word was used in everyday language and with regard to local buildings. It acquired the new, more general meaning of 'country house, summer house' (Pfeifer et al. 1993: 184; author's transl.). At the same time, the word *Bungalow* came to be associated with the modern architecture of contemporary houses in Germany and abroad whose characteristic features were large glass panes, cantilevering flat roofs, and wall slabs extending to the exterior. Architecturally defining for the modernist *Bungalow* were modern Californian houses – even if none of these houses were called bungalows in the USA: the homes by the Viennese architect Richard Neutra, who had emigrated to the USA in 1923 (Drexler et al. 1982; Hines and Neutra 1982), and those of the Californian Case Study House programme (McCoy 1962; McCoy and Singerman 1989), model homes, conceived to embody a new way of life in a sunny climate using most recent construction methods.

In West Germany, contemporary literature called Neutra's American houses 'Neutra-Bungalows', and praised them as 'dream houses of modern mankind' and 'the most contemporary and technically most accomplished form of [the bungalow]' (Betting and Vriend 1959; author's transl.). *Modern California Houses*, Esther McCoy's overview about the Case Study House programme (McCoy 1962), was tellingly titled *Wohnbau auf neuen Wegen. Musterhäuser und Bungalows* (New Ways in Housing: Model Homes and Bungalows) in German in 1964 (McCoy 1964). The use of the term *Bungalow* in these and other West German publications (Mitlug 1959; Trost 1961; 1965; Swiridoff and Steingräber 1967) reveals the architectural-semantic difference between the English term 'bungalow' and the German *Bungalow*. It also highlights how quickly the German term had become closely associated with the modern single-storey single-family house. Until today, for German lay and architectural audiences alike, a *Bungalow* is a modernist flat-roofed house; modern post-war Californian houses are *Bungalows;* and the true 'American bungalow' is in fact a house by Richard Neutra – whereas some English-speaking authors quite rightly use 'like a Case Study House' (Wainwright 2014) to account for these connotations which are different and unexpected for an English-speaking audience.

The German *Bungalow* is thus particular in its modernity and somewhat at odds with a globalised architectural culture whose terminology it uses. In his seminal publication *The Bungalow. The Production of a Global Culture*, Anthony King established the bungalow as a generic type across the globe and across centuries (King 1984). His use of the word subsumes different building types, which are culturally specific, and he refers to architectural characteristics as well as socio-economic aspects. However, socio-economically, the situation King describes for bungalow boom times in Great Britain in the 1890s or in the USA at the turn of the twentieth century was largely similar

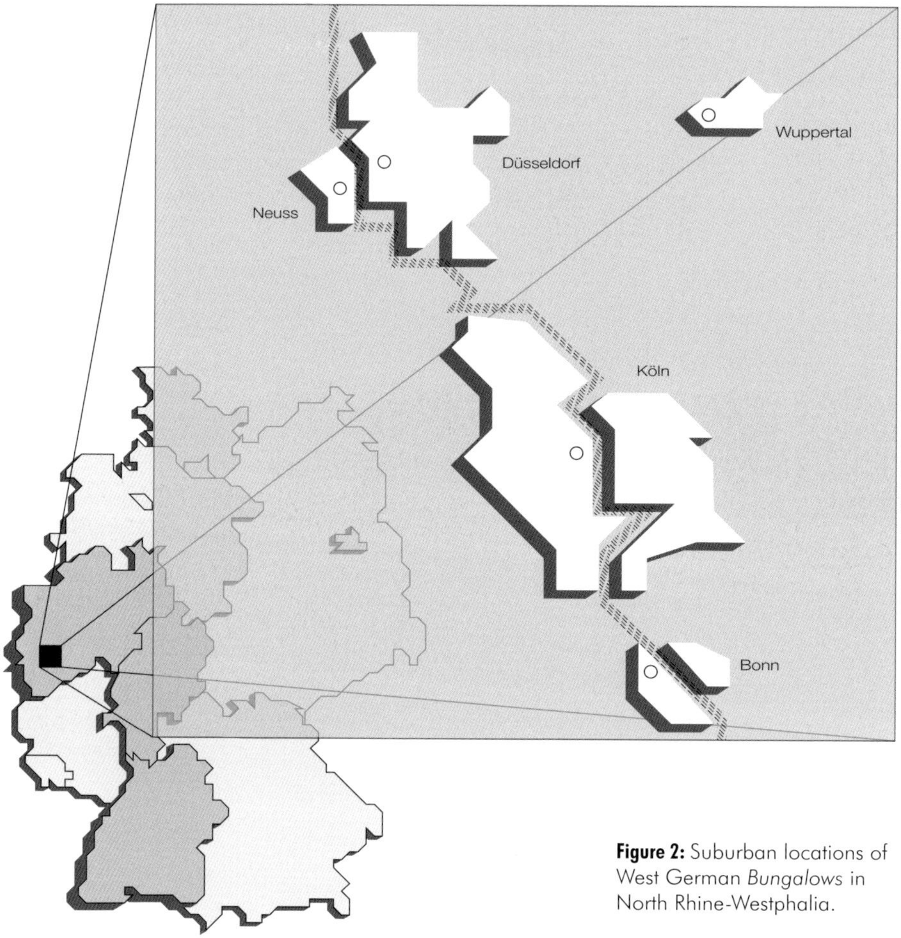

Figure 2: Suburban locations of West German *Bungalows* in North Rhine-Westphalia.

to that in post-war West Germany. In England in the late eighteenth century, the Industrial Revolution and mercantile profits from the colonies provided the historic background to the bungalow's growing influence as purpose-built holiday dwelling. Over the next century, the countryside changed from agricultural production to recreational consumption, and the bungalow became a sought-after dwelling for the countryside and expanding suburbs. Similarly, in West Germany the rise of the *Bungalow* coincided with increasing economic prosperity. Due to the growth dynamics that became popular as the *Wirtschaftswunder* – the economic boom during the late 1950s and 1960s –, new suburban areas on former farmland, city edges, and in the countryside near the city developed (fig. 2). Surplus capital met an interest in contemporary lifestyles, recent construction techniques, and holiday homes in the countryside. Additionally, a new housing law aimed at raising the amount of property ownership and single-family houses by encouraging potential buyers with fiscal ameliorations (Zweites Wohnungsbaugesetz 1956).

Figure 3: View from the living room towards the garden, Haus Gessler, 1953, Stuttgart (Klaus Gessler).

California dreaming

Whether in architectural magazines, design weeklies, or coffee table books like *Landhaus und Bungalow* (Trost 1961), from the mid-1950s onwards, the *Bungalow* is omnipresent in professional and popular publications alike. The examples shown in these publications range from simple prefabricated box *Bungalows* and compact *Bungalows* in housing estates to a large number of architect-designed single-family homes, grander modernist villas for industrialists, and the most famous German *Bungalow*, the so-called *Kanzlerbungalow* (Chancellor's Bungalow). Modern bungalow architecture, with its Californian inspirations of living comfortably with nature due to recent building technologies, became the housing ideal of the *Wirtschaftswunder* decades.

> 'The highest happiness of the young prospering generation was the bungalow, in which the architect's art of "capturing the warming, healing, and exhilarating light" could unfold particularly well. [...] In a home "generously filled with light" one felt "almost on holiday".' (Glaser 1997: 231; Glaser cites contemporary magazines; author's transl.)

The *Bungalow* is thus not just a modern house in close contact with its 'privatised landscape' (Ebert 2012b; author's transl.). It signifies a casual, practical, and – by combination of all these traits – holiday-like home environment. A good decade after the war, young West German architects built these home environments with simple technologies and materials on cheap building plots – with predominantly Californian references but also referring to concurrent contemporary developments in Scandinavia, Belgium, the Netherlands, etc.

Haus Gessler was one of the first modernist bungalows completed in West Germany. In 1952, architect Klaus Gessler built the house at the age of twenty-six for his family on a sloping 1,000-square metre site in the city of Stuttgart, located in south-western Germany (fig. 3). A magazine article described the exceptional impact of its living room and the close relationship with the outdoors:

> 'A wide glass facade, from floor to ceiling and ten metres long, generously opens up the living room towards the garden. Four large glass panes, held by uncoated aluminium frames, can slide horizontally, and thus complete the unity of living room and garden.' (Schirmer 1953: 53; author's transl.)

The article explains in great detail how the 'low building volume' is united with the exterior space, and how the spaces of the 'living room and garden merge in a way that the garden [...] becomes almost tangible and attains a corporeal presence' (Schirmer 1953: 48; author's transl.). Using the spatial and abstract terminology of architectural modernism, these descriptions illustrate an important motif of *Bungalow* architecture; the interlacing of the garden and the interior by way of architectural elements that create semi-defined outside spaces with room-like qualities in between. In his study of inter-war housing, Andreas Vetter coined the conceptual term *Pseudoraum* to describe these ambivalent or intermediary spaces between in- and outdoors (Vetter 2000: 26-32). The way *Bungalow* architecture shapes this interlacing between exterior and interior portrays both its Californian post-war inspiration – and how the Californian modern houses in turn were heirs to the European ideas of *Liberated Dwelling* in the 1920s and 1930s (Giedion 1929; 2018).

Another example for the close spatial and atmospheric connection between the interiors and the garden (and another example of an architect's building designed for himself) is Günther Balser's 'Bungalow-Haus' (N.N. 1956: 992), built in 1956 in Frankfurt am Main. The meandering shape and narrow span of the plan bring almost every room into direct contact with the garden (fig. 4): 'Everywhere the garden's greenery looks into the house through floor-to-ceiling windows.' (F. 1957: 184; author's transl.). The living room, an almost separate pavilion underneath a thin flat roof with a large overhang (fig. 5), is fully glazed and opens up towards the southern garden and to the outdoor swimming pool. Balser's endeavour that the *Bungalow* should convey

Figure 4: Interior view of the living room, Haus Balser, 1956, Frankfurt am Main (Günther Balser).
Figure 5: Exterior view of the living room, Haus Balser.

the feeling of 'constantly being on holiday in your own home' (Balser 1959: 276; author's transl.) seems to have been achieved, according to Gia Balser who reported decades later that – between the agave in the living room and the banana tree outside – her and her husband's friends always felt 'just like in California' (Balser and Balser 2012; author's translation).

The significance of modern architecture in West Germany

Descriptions of *Bungalows* in contemporary media and from a historical perspective equally praise the accomplishments of architectural modernism – especially the intense interplay of interior and exterior spaces facilitated by large glass windows and the cantilevered roof. This strong focus on modern architecture's successes and achievements has largely shaped how *Bungalow* architecture is perceived in (West) Germany until today. Yet it also has to be seen in the context of the threefold significance that modern architecture in general acquired in West Germany after 1945. In the 1950s and 1960s, modern architecture came to signify, firstly, the *Bundesrepublik*, West Germany as a young nation, secondly, its connections to Germany's democratic past during the Weimar Republic, and, thirdly, the *Westbindung*, the close relationship with the USA and other Western political allies during the Cold War.

Barbara Miller Lane has shown how the fact that, from the 1930s onwards, German National Socialists 'saw architectural styles as symbols of specific political views' (Lane 1968: 2) was a result of politicised architectural debates about the Bauhaus or flat-roofed housing schemes, which had already established this connection during the Weimar Republic. During the 1920s, the flat roof had become the symbol of the new style. It had ignited a debate about the new, modern architecture between its proponents – who understood the new style as the expression of a modern industrial age and democratic values – and its adversaries – who wanted to safeguard preindustrial times and estatist society along with traditional building types and forms.

Because architecture had carried such strong political connotations from the Weimar Republic through the National Socialist regime, architectural discourse in post-war West Germany inherited an intense political symbolism, and modern architecture became an aesthetic embodiment of the West German return to democracy after 1945. Transparent, modernist, and flat-roofed, the *Bungalow* expressed its Californian references and the new *Bundesrepublik* as eloquently as it referred to the Weimar period. Like modern architecture in general, it was understood to construct the visual narrative of the historic 'break'

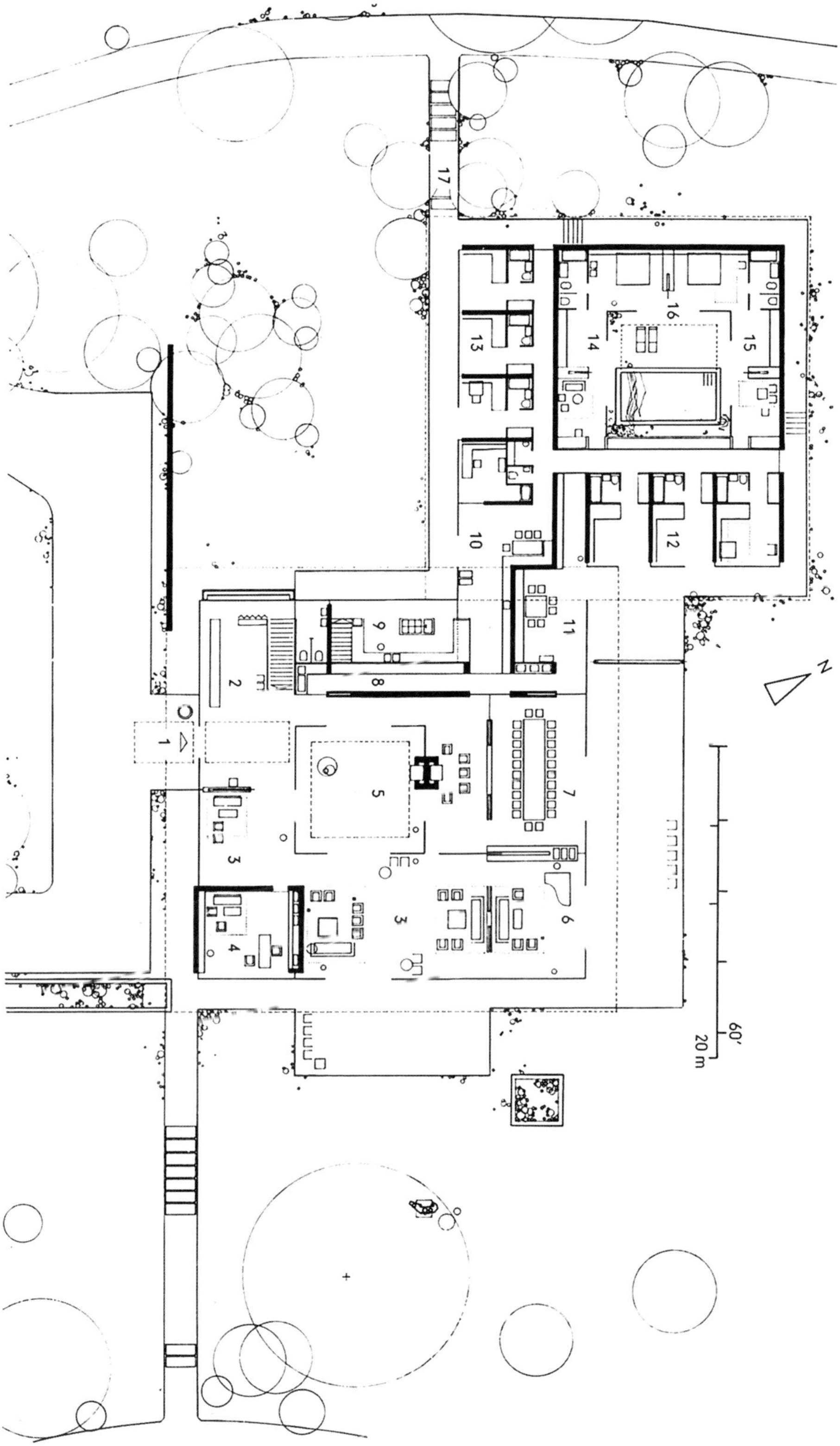

Figure 6: Plan, Kanzlerbungalow, 1964, Bonn (Sep Ruf). Literature on the Chancellor's Bungalow mostly addresses the open-plan reception area in the larger pavilion (below), and overlooks the different spatiality and the residential character of the smaller pavilion (above), where the chancellor lived.

with the National Socialist past and the reconnection with the 'democratic' *Neues Bauen*, the modern architecture of the Weimar period. In its references, post-war modernism in West Germany thus oscillates between the contemporary, transatlantic context of Americanisation, modernisation, and political alignment with the West, and the German tradition of the Weimar period. These connotations are especially vivid in the *Kanzlerbungalow*, built 1963-64 in Bonn, as a prestigious residence and reception building for the West German Federal Chancellor by architect Sep Ruf. It is interesting how popular criticism of its modern architecture addressed Americanisation, for example, when the *Kanzlerbungalow* was derided as a 'Hilton for beginners' or a 'cross between an aquarium and an American drugstore' (N.N.1967, 160; Koppetsch 2009, 60; author's transl.). Architectural authors, on the other hand, keep referring to the same historical periods – the 'modern tradition' since the 1920s (Pehnt 1970: 50; author's transl.) and the 'Bauhaus tradition' (Riese 1986: 73; author's transl.) – and praise the *Kanzlerbungalow* for how it connects 'moral meaning' with 'the human longing for freedom and prospect' (Knoll 1965: 6; author's transl.). The political and moral impetus of modern architecture in post-war West Germany is heightened by repeated references to the 'defamation of modernism during the National Socialist regime' (Nerdinger 2008:

Figure 7: Street view, Haus Dr. W., 1959, Hanover (Hans Klüppelberg).

26; author's transl.; cf. Riese 1986: 73; Swiridoff and Steingräber 1967: 53). While the residential character of the building is embodied so clearly in the *Kanzlerbungalow*'s name and layout (fig. 6), the corresponding literature rarely addresses it as a home. Instead and beyond this example, *Bungalow* publications reveal the effort to integrate modern houses into the grand narrative of architectural modernism, including its political significance in West Germany.

A Janus-faced building typology

Images and interpretations of *Bungalows* focus on the way in which the living space opens up towards the garden and the surrounding landscape. But while the garden sides are featured widely and mostly illustrate modern architecture's radical transparency, most street facades (often unpublished) present a rather different image (fig. 7). The morphological analysis of *Bungalow* architecture reveals that a Janus-faced disposition is a fundamental trait of this building typology (Ebert 2014; 2016). The way in which modern bungalows unite two different conceptions of space within a strictly orthogonal configuration is one of the most important features of the *Bungalow* typology. The much-acclaimed openness of the living space is juxtaposed with a second, equally modern, but completely different spatial configuration: the functional, cubicle-like arrangement of small, individual rooms that line up along a private hallway and whose spatial seclusion results in an altogether different, more closed facade. In contemporary publications, however, this aspect was superseded by the many depictions of the *Bungalow* as an open, transparent, and modern pavilion.

Within modern architectural discourse, the way *Bungalows* were visualised and conceptualised had a strong influence on its interpretation. This phenomenon is most tangible in analyses of Paul Schneider-Esleben's *Haus Riedel*, which was built between Düsseldorf and Wuppertal in 1953 (fig. 8). Heinrich Klotz, for example, argued that the house reveals 'the influence of Mies van der Rohe', pointing to the 'interplay of walls and glass surfaces' and the 'walls [that] jut – or "shoot" – out', which had replaced the 'facade with traditional window openings' (Schneider-Esleben and Klotz 1987: 10; cited after Ebert 2014, transl. Jesse Coburn). Rolf Beckers' analysis of Schneider-Esleben's work takes up a similar line of argument. Beckers traces the 'unusual floor plan' back to 'Mies van der Rohe's country house projects of the twenties', and interprets it as an 'attempt to realize a free floor plan like the one that Mies van der Rohe perfected with the [...] Barcelona Pavilion', in which 'a horizontal

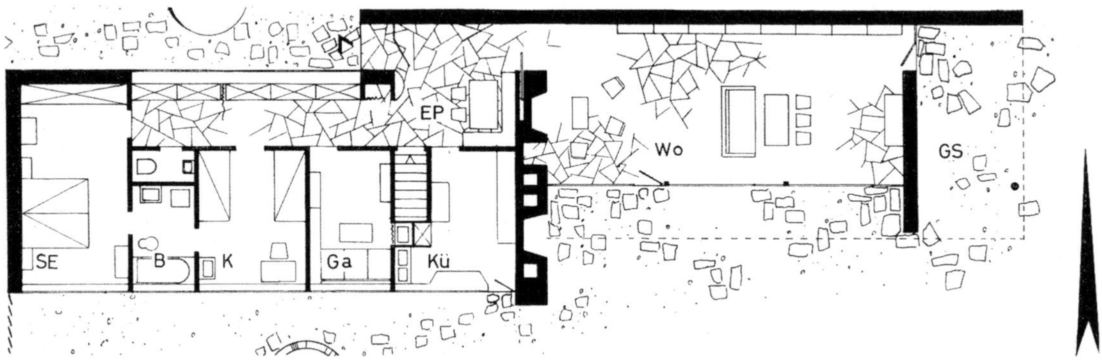

Figure 8: Plan, Haus Riedel, 1953, Haan (Paul Schneider-Esleben).

spatial system was articulated [...] merely through free-standing walls' (Beckers 1995: 110; cited after Ebert 2014, transl. Coburn).

In comparison to the Miesian projects that Beckers takes as points of reference, *Haus Riedel*'s floor plan presents neither a pavilion nor a spacious modernist villa, but a compact single-family home of 120 square metres, in which the *Bungalow*'s dual spatial concept is well articulated. Schneider-Esleben's design mediates between the openness of the living room and the small, individual rooms by dividing the bungalow with a massive brick wall. This vertical break integrates the deep living room facade – a floor-to-ceiling glass wall underneath a cantilevered roof – with the flat street-side facade finished with wood panelling in front of the kitchen, bathroom, and bedrooms. Beckers sharply criticises the compartmentalisation of this wing of the building (which the architect himself had praised for its efficiency and practicality (Schneider-Esleben 1954: 674)) and complains that the house 'as a whole, does not consistently adhere' to the logic of Miesian modernism (Beckers 1995: 110; cited after Ebert 2014, transl. Coburn).

This pointed example demonstrates how in West German twentieth century architectural discourse unambiguity and the modernity of architectural motifs became central features of interpretation. *Bungalow* architecture was subsumed under the grand narrative of the rise of modern architecture with all its implications – national and international, political and aesthetic. Manifold similar statements make evident that the early modern architectural historiography prioritised the inclusion of *Bungalows* into the canon of modern architecture over allowing for any of the complications arising from addressing their status as a private residence, and a middle-class home at that.

The *Bungalow's* middle-class aspirations

Even though it may not have been addressed in architectural discourse, the status of the *Bungalow* as a middle-class house is apparent in both contemporary literature and cultural history. An analysis of West German *Bungalows* with regard to their size, price, and clientele (Ebert 2016, 228–39) showed that the majority were family homes for owners with middle-class occupations like salesmen, architects, doctors, scientists, and lawyers. An average family bungalow had a floor area of about 140 square metres on a plot of approximately 1,000 square metres. Even though, architecturally, West German *Bungalows* may be understood as a continuation of 1920s and 1930s European residential modernism, the circumstances of their realisation are fundamentally different. Instead of a well-to-do upper-class elite who could furnish avant-garde projects like Mies van der Rohe's *Haus Tugendhat* with noble and very expensive materials, post-war *Bungalows* were middle-class family homes for clients in more modest circumstances.

The *Bungalow's* luxury is more spatial, based on layout and design, than purely material. Here, it once more references its underlying Californian dream, and – in doing so – it also displays its inherent middle-class aspirations. Most Case Study Houses, for example, had been designed with educated or artistic middle-class families in mind, as Dolores Hayden has argued (Hayden 1989). And with regard to Neutra's work and clients, Thomas Hines distinguishes between the early work for a wealthy upper-class elite and the post-war work for 'the middle-class majority that made up the public of most of the mid-century modernists' (Hines and Neutra 1982: 254). Even though in West Germany Neutra's houses were often perceived as upper-class residences, there are many references to his middle-class clients and their 'often very limited financial means' (Wandel-Hoefer 1989: 180; author's transl.). Neutra himself had been, as Beatriz Colomina has pointed out, interested in the topic of the small, affordable private house for his entire life (Colomina 1999: 154). He asserted: 'It's not with the wealthy that the future of contemporary architecture lies [...]. It is with the people in the middle. They are the ones who can afford to be uninhibited [...].' (Hines and Neutra 1982: 257)

In *The modern American house: spaciousness and middle-class identity*, Sandy Isenstadt investigates how modern architecture was employed to achieve a sense of spaciousness in small modern houses – 'designers claimed they could endow the small house with "an impression of airy space far beyond its actual dimensions" and well ahead of its actual costs' (Isenstadt 2006: 4). The clients' desire for spaciousness '[e]xplicitly, almost heroically, in conflict with

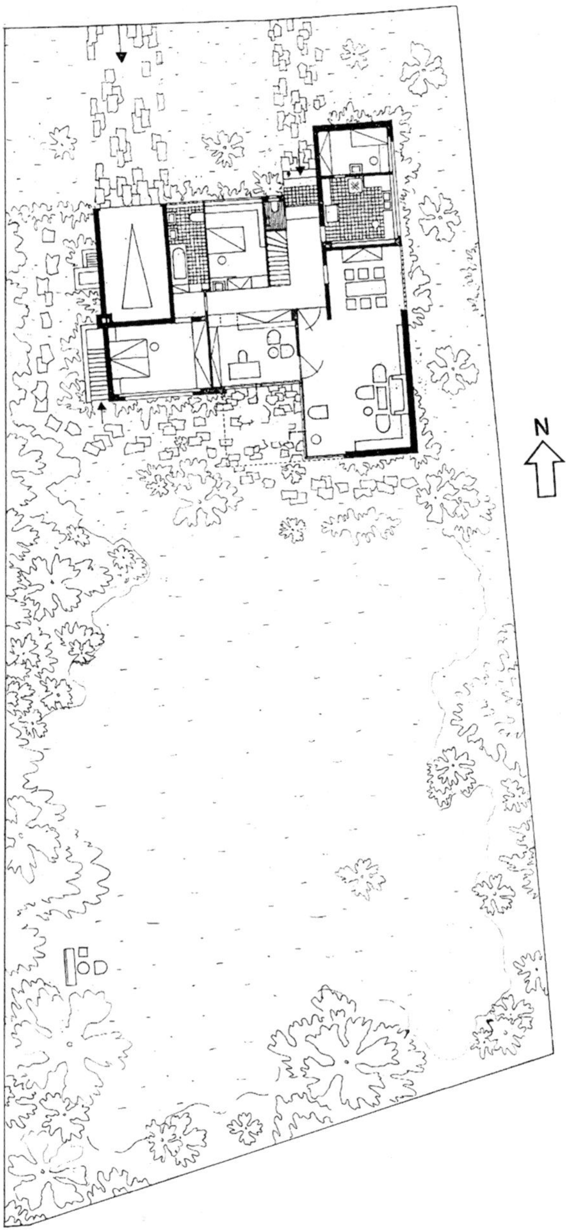

Figure 9: Site plan, Haus Keil, 1955, Meerbusch near Dusseldorf (Bernhard M. Pfau).

actual dimensions [...] was founded on the tension between spatial aspirations and financial limitations' (Isenstadt 2006: 6). For Isenstadt, the fixation of the small modern house on the close contact to the garden and the landscape is always class-specific.

> 'Spaciousness in small places, in other words, is an artefact of middle-class design culture: an enhancement of a middle-class family's most valuable possession – its house – promoted in vehicles of consumer culture like magazines and pitched often as a discounted way to acquire the visual trappings of greater wealth.' (Isenstadt 2006: 7)

German sociologist Helmut Schelsky characterised the middle-class society by the fact 'that broad circles turn away from matters of the society at large, become disinterested in the public sphere, and withdraw into the private realms of work and family' (Schelsky 1955: 237; author's transl.). And the *Bungalow* exhibits a striking synchronicity of social and spatial retreat into suburbia *and* into privacy, which seems to be a direct physical expression of Schelsky's more psychological conclusion.

The architect's ability to 'maximise spaciousness' not only applied to the relationship between house and garden, but also to the siting of the house itself (fig. 9). Whilst opening up towards the 'privatised landscape', the same *Bungalows* that are portrayed as transparent pavilions in the media cut themselves off completely from their suburban surroundings.[3] They display closed facades towards the street and are placed at the edge of their plots, maximising private views and minimising visibility. As has been said about *Haus Balser*, it is 'thus, from the garden, that the [Bungalow] wants to be perceived: embracing and shielding its own piece of land, closed towards the world beyond, but open to the sun' (F. 1957: 188; author's transl.). While the first, obvious Californian dream lies in the close connection to the outdoor area, a second one can be identified in exactly this spatial economy of maximising views and minimising space, which had been ignored in twentieth century architectural discourse. It is here that the West German modernist *Bungalow* reveals its true nature as a middle-class house.

References

N.N. (1956), 'Bungalow-Haus in Frankfurt', Bauwelt 47 (42); 992–993.

N.N. (1967), 'Kanzlerbungalow: Richtiges Haus', Der Spiegel 21 (17).

Balser, G. (1959), 'Eigenheim eines Architekten in Frankfurt/M.', Deutsche Bauzeitschrift 7(3), 276–280.

Balser, G. and Balser, G. (2012), unpublished interview.

Beckers, R. (1995), Der Architekt Paul Schneider-Esleben (Weimar: VDG).

Betting, W. and Vriend, J. J. (1959), Bungalows: Deutschland, England, Italien, Holland, Belgien, Dänemark (Darmstadt: Müller-Wellborn).

Colomina, B. (1999), 'Das Wohnhaus als Schaustück', in R. Ferguson and S. Emerson (eds.), Am Ende des Jahrhunderts. 100 Jahre gebaute Visionen (Ostfildern-Ruit: Hatje Cantz), 126–165.
Drexler, A., Hines, T. S., and Neutra, R. (1982), The architecture of Richard Neutra from international style to California modern (New York: Museum of Modern Art).
Ebert, C. (2009), 'Into the great wide open. The West-German modernist bungalow of the 1960s as a psycho-political re-creation of home', Multi. The RIT Journal of Plurality and Diversity in Design 2(1), 35–51.
Ebert, C. (2012a), 'Moderate Modernism for the Middle Classes. The West German Modernist "Bungalow" and the Ideal of a Prosperous "Levelled Middle Class Society" in Post-war Germany', in H. Heynen and J. Gosseye (eds.), Proceedings of the 2nd International Conference of the EAHN (Brussels: VWK), 579–584.
Ebert, C. (2012b), 'Privatisierte Landschaft. Westdeutsche Architektenbungalows 1952–1959 zwischen kalifornischem Traum und (nicht-)städtischer Realität', dérive. Zeitschrift für Stadtforschung 47, 18–23.
Ebert, C. (2014), 'Pavilionizing the bungalow. A recurring motif in (West) German architectural history', ARCH+ 217, 48–51.
Ebert, C. (2016), 'Entspannte Moderne. Der westdeutsche Bungalow 1952–1969 als Adaption eines internationalen Leitbilds und Symbol einer nivellierten Mittelschichtsgesellschaft', (PhD diss, Universität Kassel, Kassel).
Ebert, C. (2018), 'Architecture and politics in West Germany 1952–69. The political symbolism of the modernist bungalow', unpublished conference paper, SAH Annual International Conference.
F., O. (1957), 'Eigenheim des Architekten Günther Balser in Frankfurt', Architektur und Wohnform 66(5), 183–188.
Giedion, S. (1929), Befreites Wohnen (Zurich: Füssli).
Giedion, S. and Geiser, R. (eds.) (2018), Sigfried Giedion: Liberated Dwelling (Befreites Wohnen) (Zurich: Lars Müller).
Glaser, H. (1997), Deutsche Kultur. Ein historischer Überblick von 1945 bis zur Gegenwart (Bonn: Bundeszentrale für politische Bildung).
Hayden, D. (1989), 'Model Houses for the Millions: Architects' Dreams, Builders' Boasts, Residents' Dilemmas', in E. McCoy and H. Singerman (eds.), Blueprints for modern living. History and Legacy for the Case Study House (Los Angeles: Museum of Contemporary Art), 197–212.
Hines, T. S. and Neutra, R. (1982), Richard Neutra and the search for modern architecture (New York: Oxford University).
Isenstadt, S. (2006), The modern American house: spaciousness and middle-class identity (New York: Cambridge University Press).
King, A. D. (1984), The Bungalow. The Production of a global culture (London: Routledge & Paul).
Knoll, H. N. (1965), 'Wohn- und Empfangsgebäude für den Bundeskanzler in Bonn', glasforum. Architektur, Raumkunst, Gebrauch 15(3), 6–15.
Koppetsch, J. (2009), 'Der Kanzlerbungalow in der öffentlichen Diskussion', in Wüstenrot Stiftung und Stiftung Haus der Geschichte der Bundesrepublik Deutschland (eds.), Kanzlerbungalow (Munich: Prestel), 50–63.
Lane, B. M. (1968), Architecture and politics in Germany, 1918–1945 (Cambridge, Mass.: Harvard University Press).
McCoy, E. (1962), Modern California houses. Case study houses 1945–1962 (New York: Reinhold).
McCoy, E. (1964), Wohnbau auf neuen Wegen. Musterhäuser und Bungalows – ihre Planung, Konstruktion, Bauausführung und Wirkung (Ravensburg: Maier).
McCoy, E. and Singerman, H. (eds.) (1989), Blueprints for modern living. History and Legacy for the Case Study House (Los Angeles: Museum of Contemporary Art).

Mittag, M. (1959), Kleinsthäuser, Ferienhäuser, Bungalows. 160 Beispiele kleiner Eigenheime, Wochenendhäuser, Gartenhäuser, kleiner und mittelgroßer Ferienhäuser aus dem In- und Ausland (Gütersloh: Bertelsmann).
Nerdinger, W. (2008), 'Sep Ruf – Moderne mit Tradition', in W. Nerdinger, H. Böhm, and S. Ruf (eds.), Sep Ruf 1908–1982. Moderne mit Tradition (Munich: Prestel), 20–27.
Pehnt, W. (1970), Neue deutsche Architektur 3 (Stuttgart: Hatje).
Pfeifer, W., Braun, W. and Zentralinstitut für Sprachwissenschaft (1993), Etymologisches Wörterbuch des Deutschen (2nd ed.) (Berlin: Akademie).
Riese, H.-P. (1986), 'Glashaus im Verborgenen', in Deutsche Architektur nach 1945. 40 Jahre Moderne in der Bundesrepublik (Stuttgart: DVA), 73–75.
Schelsky, H. (1955), Wandlungen der deutschen Familie in der Gegenwart: Darstellung und Deutung einer empirisch-soziologischen Tatbestandsaufnahe (Stuttgart: Enke).
Schirmer, E. (1953), 'Ein Wohnhaus ohne Konzessionen', Architektur und Wohnform 62 (2), 47–55.
Schneider-Esleben, P. (1954), 'Ebenerdiges Wohnhaus bei Düsseldorf', Bauen und Wohnen 9(12), 673–674.
Schneider-Esleben, P. and Klotz, H. (1987), Paul Schneider-Esleben: Entwürfe u. Bauten 1949–1987 (Braunschweig: Vieweg).
Swiridoff, P. and Steingräber, E. (1967), Der Bungalow. Wohn- und Empfangsgebäude für den Bundeskanzler in Bonn (Pfullingen: Neske).
Trost, K. (1961), Landhaus und Bungalow. Beispiele moderner Eigenhäuser im In- und Ausland mit einer Einführung (Frankfurt/Main: Ullstein).
Trost, K. (1965), Bungalows (Berlin: Ullstein).
Vetter, A. K. (2000), Die Befreiung des Wohnens. Ein Architekturphänomen der 20er und 30er Jahre (Tübingen: Wasmuth).
Wainwright, O. (2014), 'Venice Architecture Biennale: the top 10 pavilions', The Guardian, 6 June.
Wandel-Hoefer, R. (1989), 'Zur Architektur Richard Neutras – Eine Analyse seines theoretischen Werkes und der Umsetzung in seinen Bauten', (PhD diss., TH Darmstadt, Darmstadt).
Zweites Wohnungsbaugesetz (1956).

Illustration credits

Figure 1: (1960) Deutsche Bauzeitschrift DBZ 8 (9), 1096.
Figure 2: © Carola Ebert, Visualisation by StuhlR.
Figure 3: (1954) Bauen und Wohnen 9 (6), 287.
Figure 4: (1960) Die Kunst und das schöne Heim 58 (11), 425.
Figure 5: Trost, K. (1961), Landhaus und Bungalow. Beispiele moderner Eigenhäuser im In- und Ausland mit einer Einführung (Frankfurt am Main: Ullstein), 86.
Figure 6: Pehnt, W. (1970), Neue deutsche Architektur 3 (Stuttgart: Hatje), 51.
Figure 7: (1960) Deutsche Bauzeitschrift DBZ 8 (6), 710.
Figure 8: Hoffmann, K. (1955), Neue Einfamilienhäuser (Stuttgart: Hoffmann), 74.
Figure 9: N.N. (1957), Bauen und Wohnen 12(3): 89.

Endnotes

1 The chapter thus contains ideas and text passages published by the author in related articles and online publications (Ebert 2009, 2012a, 2012b, 2014, 2016, 2018).
2 Due to the different status of the single-family house and individual home-ownership in East Germany, the word referred to a modern weekend home, a *Datscha*, in the GDR.
3 See Caplan (this volume) on such isolated views of today's announcements of prefab houses in Germany.

Two homes: revisiting a French type of dwelling

Sophie Chevalier

The majority of French people – across a wide range of social groups – have a double residential project: their first home serves as the main residence, often in a big city like Paris, and a second home is located in the countryside or a small town and is used mainly for holidays. Most of the latter are inherited, but some are bought. In this contribution, I look at how people invest in these second homes and manage the two types of dwelling (Chevalier 1999, 2002, 2004). More recently (Chevalier, Lallement and Corbillé 2013), I studied foreign secondary residents in Paris[1] and how their presence has influenced the city's transformation (Chevalier and Lallement 2014a; 2014b). I also contrasted them with Parisians and Provincial French with a second home in Paris. Research on residents in Paris over the years has revealed several types of middle-class people: those who spend their working lives in Paris but, when they retire to the countryside, retain a small Parisian apartment for use by themselves and younger family members; and those who work in the regions, but buy a *pieds-à-terre* in Paris for their own occasional use, but more often for their children (when studying in Paris, for example). There is a social aspect of these residential strategies, with secondary homes not only involving kin, but also friends. I begin by sketching the general context with some quantitative indicators; then I turn to how rural homes relate to the main urban residence. Then I touch on the situation of those who keep *pieds-à-terre* in Paris, whether they are French or foreign. Finally, the practice of maintaining a secondary residence is related to the French kinship system, allowing for variations between regions and historical periods.

Some numbers

In 2017 (Arnold 2017), Metropolitan France had nearly 35 million households, of which four out of five were the main residences, more than a tenth were secondary residences and nearly a tenth were empty. The most striking feature of the last twenty years is the rise in vacant dwellings. We should note that 58 percent of main households are owner-occupied; and around 40 percent are rented, of which 17 percent are social housing. 56 percent of French dwellings are houses, close to the EU average; main and secondary residences do not differ in this respect. Collective dwellings – apartment blocs – have been growing in each category but more so for secondary homes. In fact, since 2013, collective dwellings have been built faster than individual homes. After falling significantly in the 1990s, the proportion of secondary residences has been growing slightly in the last decade and these are located mainly in the countryside and small towns (population under 100,000). In the long run, their number varies markedly from one decade to the next. This reflects fluctuations in the national economy since secondary homes depend on the balance of household income and expenditure. Foreign secondary residents vary for similar reasons, with the share of individual nations fluctuating over time. The price of prestigious buildings is affected accordingly (Chevalier, Lallement et Corbillé 2013: 32ss).

A home in the country

Since the 1950s, most urban French households, irrespective of social class – as the same statistical sources show – own or aspire to own a secondary residence in the country. They intend to keep or buy such a home, not necessarily to live there. In this two-home project their urban quarters serve as their main residence, but their house in the country symbolises 'the family'. The latter may be considered – in most cases – as a materialisation of family identity. This could be called 'anchoring the lineage in a materialized space' as Annette Weiner (1985) described property relations in traditional Maori society of New Zealand. The phenomenon of city-dwellers keeping two homes is related to France having been a latecomer to industrialisation (compared with Britain, for example). In 1945, the French peasantry still represented half the national population, but the countryside emptied quite quickly after that (Mendras 1971; Weber 1976). This social transformation, however, was not a matter of small landed property being replaced by big landlords. France has a long tradition of a landed peasantry and the idea of owning land is shared by most French people. Only recently has production declined sharply in the countryside, leaving behind what is now largely a recreational landscape. But, unlike their nineteenth-century Swedish counterparts (Frykman and Löfgren 1987), the French bourgeoisie did not take up romantic love of nature (see Thomas 1983 for England). Strindberg's depiction of a bourgeois summer paradise in the countryside is typically Swedish, but it has no parallel in the French two-home project. For most French city dwellers, the countryside is a place filled with memories of people who share a rural past of smallholders and inherited property. Their ties to the countryside are closely linked to family history; home there is then family residence and the material core of their identity.

In my Paris suburban case study, carried out during the late eighties and early nineties (Chevalier 1996; 1998; 2002), many of the inhabitants kept a house where they or their parents grew up, often inherited from their family. This is not limited to that social group. The majority of my informants were the first generation to come from the countryside to work in manufacturing industry around Paris. Many were over 50 years old. Their ties with the countryside were still lively and close.[2] Kinship identity was a strong feature of their rural family home and sometimes included extended family members.

Their secondary residence was where they anchored inter-generational ties of descent. They often kept or bought a second residence, but not necessarily to live there. Some married couples maintained separate country residences, if they came from different regions. Preference and pragmatic reasons could influence the choice to buy: geographical proximity – for easy reach at weekends or for short holidays or just to be by the seaside. Some bought old property whether or not they had historical family ties to a region.

> Thérèse is from an aristocratic Breton family. In a conflict with her brothers, she and her sister were disinherited. Some years ago, she bought a place in Vendée, South of Brittany. Even though this was not the region she grew up in, it is nearby. She is very attached to the area and would never buy a house in the South of France, for example. She spends all her holidays in this house, and last year her elder daughter was married there.

The function of a rural residence is to be a meeting point for family members of different generations and a symbolic anchorage in material space, whether owned solely or jointly. It is always painful to sell a residence of this kind, especially if it has been in the family for generations, since it is often seen as being common, not private property. The longer the residence has been in the family, the harder it is to let go. The upkeep of these family homes can be expensive, and this, too, may lead to conflict between kin.

> Alice is the only daughter of a middle-class family who lives in the Paris suburbs. Her mother is still alive but disabled. She inherited the original home of her father's farming family, not far from Paris, where she has never lived herself, having only spent holidays there. She still has kin in this area. She has visited the house sometimes with her husband and daughters; it does not have central heating and its comfort level is very basic. Recently, she had to take out a loan to repair the roof which was collapsing. She is entertaining the idea of selling it.

> Mrs L.'s case is quite similar. She is an old lady who worked her whole life in a Nanterre factory. She owns a big family house as jointly-held property with her brothers and sisters in the Ardennes. The property is in poor condition, because it suffered damage in both World Wars. Although no family member could ever afford to repair it, they decided to keep it with all the furniture. No family member ever spent holidays in this house: there are few modern comforts (no heating system, for example). Nevertheless, Mrs L. frequently spoke of 'her' house and gave lively descriptions of its antique family furniture.

If a house is inherited with its furniture and decorative objects, these are rarely moved to the main residence, since they are taken to form a whole with the dwelling itself. For example, a sideboard from Brittany is too big to get into most Paris flats, but in any case, it is symbolically attached to the rural dwelling. This rooted décor then becomes an object of transmission strategies, since its value is long-term, not for everyday use.

Attachment to place conflicts with a familiar Western distinction between moveable and immovable property, for the furniture of the family residence becomes an immovable part of the building. In her reanalysis of the Maori case described by Marcel Mauss (1990) in *The Gift*, Annette Weiner (1985: 210) designates some objects as 'inalienable wealth', meaning movable objects that become immovable because they cannot be detached from their origins. They belong inherently to their original owners and are imbued with affective qualities as a result; they bring past time into the present. Weiner distinguishes, for this traditional society, two kinds of inalienable possessions: those that should never circulate and others that under some circumstances may be given out on loan (1985: 210–212).

The French family residence functions much as sacred Maori bones and stones do that are believed to 'anchor' a lineage to a particular locality, physically securing descendants' ancestral rights (1985: 211). In the French case, one can use the housing market to create as many 'bones' as one likes. With rural family property, some objects are on loan between generations. Time plays a fundamental role in this: the process of 'anchoring' is necessarily long-term. In France, the long-term embodiment of a lineage in material culture is focused especially on the family home. Houses and objects contain the lineage in time. Some, perhaps many secondary residences embody the ideal of continuity and security that binds the generations together over time.

A *pieds-à-terre* in Paris

In another study (Chevalier, Lallement and Corbillé 2013), we looked at foreign middle-class owners or renters of accommodation in Paris. This is related to, but different from another trend whereby French retired couples sell their main residence in Paris in order to combine country living with a smaller flat in the capital. Foreigners who settle in Paris for economic reasons are a different matter. Owning secondary homes has been studied by sociologists, anthropologists and geographers quite often in the countryside, by the sea or in the mountains, but not often in cities. The number of secondary residences in Paris was about 80,000 in 2011, comprising both national and foreign owners. For some French households, at a stage in the life cycle, the city dwelling can become their second residence and the country home their main one.

> When Monelle and André retired, they made a rural secondary home in Burgundy their main residence and kept their large Paris apartment, the mortgage on which they had paid off their mortgage, for their own and their children's families' use. Now they are contemplating selling their Paris flat to buy a smaller one nearby using the rest to develop their rural home.

There is not only one type of secondary residence in Paris. You can find the whole range from a studio where one sleeps on the couch to a big apartment used as a family home when the owners lived in Paris. A lot depends on how secondary and primary homes are used in relation to each other. Most secondary residents owned a principal residence in the countryside, and some of them had a number of homes, in addition to the one in Paris, including a holiday home outside of the city, by the sea or in the mountains. The fact that the Paris flat was often just one of several homes makes use of the term 'secondary' somewhat problematic. In fact, their socio-economic profile, behaviour and attitudes are not unlike those of foreign secondary owners, some of whom had several homes around the world. What distinguished French from foreign secondary residents in Paris is that they keep or buy one appartment mainly for family reasons, whereas foreigners tend to leave their family out of it. Some of them buy an apartment in Paris that their children can use as students. There are parallels with some French.

> When Caroline retired as a researcher, she sold her small house in a gentrified area of Paris and converted her second home in Brittany, where she was born and which she later inherited from her parents, into her main residence. With the proceeds from her town house, she bought out her sister from the family home and purchased a small studio in Paris which she uses to visit her daughter and granddaughter.

> Dominique and Maurice, a lecturer and doctor, live in a small town in Eastern France where they own a big house. When their oldest child decided to study in Paris, they rented an apartment; when their second child also moved to the capital to study law, they bought a larger apartment for the two children. They visit them from time to time and enjoy the good life in Paris. The wife recently bought a small house by the sea shore with some inherited money.

Parisians who switch their main residence to the countryside are usually middle class and in their late fifties; they do so when they retire or after their children left home. Provincials at a similar stage of life buy a studio or small flat mainly mainly to be used by children studying in Paris.

> Franco, an Italian professor, bought a Paris apartment in his fifties, which he and his wife visit as often as they can. In addition to his apartment in Milan, he co-owns a family residence by the sea. When in Paris, they go cycling with Italian friends who also have homes there.

> Hillary and her husband, both in their fifties, bought a flat on a timeshare basis with four other American couples parallel to the Champs Elysees. Children are not allowed to use the flat. The purchase was made through

a New York realtor. For most of the owners the flat is just a financial investment. Hillary and her husband are the only ones who use it regularly. She prepares these visits in advance from her home in Los Angeles, buying concert and exhibition tickets online.

Both foreign and French secondary residents get up to similar things in Paris: It is a city of culture, with convenient access to museums, theatres, cinemas, etc. They try out new restaurants, sampling national cuisines that don't exist where they normally live. The city is also a fabulous market place, the 'shopping capital of the world', as the town council and tourist buses claim – with its department stores and specialist shops for food, fashion and luxuries. For an event like a wedding, secondary residents may buy clothes there that are not available at home. The big difference between the two groups' attitude to Paris is kinship and especially the role of children in family decision-making. As with rural secondary homes, for French couples the meaning of a Paris apartment is often part of a family strategy, to take advantage of access to the capital as a political, economic and cultural centre in a country that remains Jacobin to a substantial degree with the best educational opportunities. It usually pays off to have a 'foothold' in Paris.

In contrast, children play almost no part in the movements of foreign couples: buying an apartment is normally a project of a couple, with no children involved. This distinguishes a Paris flat from a home in the countryside and, of course, from an inherited family house.

Conclusions

This practice of keeping two homes with the focus on being grounded in the countryside is a fundamental aspect of French kinship. The family house – inherited or bought – anchors the descent system in material space and contrasts sharply with other European systems of neolocal residence – of which the British are the prime example – which tends to cut the later stages of a married couple's life cycle off from other generations.

French secondary residents often have a Parisian residential project as a way of keeping their lineage's toehold in the capital of what is still a highly centralised country. They may either keep an apartment in Paris when they no longer have to work there or they get hold of one from a provincial base. This practice of dual residence in city and countryside allows people to combine several lifestyles that elsewhere might be available only to the relatively rich.

Secondary residents move between different spaces, but they always refer to one of them as the main one, as home. They maintain ties with different places at once. They live in two or several localities – they are 'multi-local': they feel at home in a number of places to which they are attached in different ways, but always as citizens within France itself. This contrasts with foreign secondary residents for whom Paris is often a 'world' in itself, detached from the rest of France. In Paris they have no territorial roots or sense of local citizenship. But they pay their taxes back home.

My international study of secondary residents in Paris provides a comparative framework for exploring the issue of movement and stability: the two always go together in varying combinations. And of course, this practice of combining principal and secondary residences can only be understood comparatively within a wider context of political and economic history at the national and ideally global levels. I have principally tried here to identify a particular French kinship pattern based on dual residence for a wide range of income levels.

References

Arnold, C., (2017), Le parc des logements en France au 1er janvier 2017, INSEE Focus, n°103.

Barou, J. and Prado, P. (1995), Les Anglais dans nos campagnes (Paris: L'Harmattan).

Chevalier, S. (1996), 'Transmettre son mobilier? Le cas contrasté de la France et de l'Angleterre', Ethnologie Française XXVI(1), 115–128.

Chevalier, S. (1998) 'Destins de cadeaux', in S. Chevalier and A. Monjaret (eds.): Les cadeaux: à quel prix? Ethnologie Française XXVIII(4), 506–514.

Chevalier, S. (1999), 'The French Two-Home Project. Materialization of Family Identity', in I. Cieerad (ed.): At home. An anthropology of domestic space (New-York: Syracuse University Press), 83–94.

Chevalier, S. (2002), 'The Cultural Construction of Domestic Space in France and Britain', SIGNS: Journal of Women in Culture and Society, 27(3), 847–856.

Chevalier, S. (2004), 'A propos de la constitution de la sphère privée et publique', in S. Chevalier and J.-M. Privat (eds.): Norbert Elias et l'anthropologie. 'Nous sommes tous si étranges …' (Paris: Editions du CNRS), 151–158.

Chevalier, S. (2012), 'Material Cultures of Home', in The International Encyclopedia of Housing and Home, (Amsterdam: Elsevier), 222–229.

Chevalier, S., Lallement, E. and Corbillé, S. (2013), Paris résidence secondaire. Enquête chez ces habitants d'un nouveau genre (Paris: Belin).

Chevalier, S. and Lallement, E. (2014a), 'La "parisianité" comme patrimoine partagé. La ville, ses résidents secondaires et son mythe', in C. de Saint-Pierre (ed.): La mise en jeu du patrimoine dans la configuration de la ville d'aujourd'hui, (Rennes: Presses Universitaire de Rennes), 73–87.

Chevalier, S. and Lallement, E. (2014b), 'La résidence secondaire à Paris: un exemple de multirésidentialité à l'heure de la globalisation', in P. Hamman, M. Blanc, C. Duchêne-Lacroix, T. Freytag and C. Kramer (eds.): Questionner les mobilités résidentielles à l'aune de la multilocalité, (Strasbourg: Néothèque), 323–336.

Frykman, J. and Löfgren, O. (1987), Culture Builders. A historical anthropology of middle-class life (London: Rutgers University Press).

Mauss, M. (1990), The gift: form and reason for exchange in archaic societies (New York/ London: Norton).

Mendras, H. (1971), La fin des paysans: changement et innovations dans les sociétés rurales françaises (Paris: Armand Colin).
Munn, N. (1970), 'The Transformation of Subjects into Objects in Walbiri and Pitjantjatjara', in R. Berndt (ed.): Australian Aboriginal Anthropology, (Nedlands: University of Western Australia Press), 141–163.
Thomas, K. (1983), Man and the natural World. Changing Attitudes in England 1500–1800 (London: Penguin Books).
Weber, E. (1976), Peasants into Frenchmen: the modernization of rural France, 1870–1914 (Stanford: Stanford University Press).
Weiner, A. (1985), 'Inalienable wealth', American Ethnologist, XII(2), 210–227.

Endnotes

1 There are numerous studies on foreign secondary residents located in the countryside; see the pioneer's one Jacques Barou and Patrick Prado (1995).

2 In the Parisian suburb that I investigated, more than half of my sixty informants possessed a second home.

From rooms to houses: multi-family and single-family houses among the Minangkabau in Sumatra, Indonesia

Marcel Vellinga

Introduction

The first known use of the adjective vernacular in relation to architecture dates back to the early eighteenth century. In his *Glossographia Anglicana Nova* (1707), Thomas Blount refers to the term vernacular as 'Proper and peculiar to the House or Country one lives in'. The *Oxford Dictionary of English* (2003) traces the etymological origin of the term vernacular to the Latin *verna*, meaning 'home born slave'. From early on, therefore, the concept has been associated with a notion of belonging to a home or a place, be it a house, a region or a country. The use of the term in the field of linguistics to denote a dialect, that is 'a particular form of a language which is peculiar to a specific region or social group' (Oxford English Dictionary 2003) attests this association. Vernacular architecture is an architecture that belongs to and in a particular part of the world. No matter how it has later been defined (as an 'architecture of the people', an 'architecture without architects' or an 'architecture of the everyday'), the notion that vernacular architecture is rooted in a specific place has always been one of its defining features. Paul Oliver's *Encyclopedia of Vernacular Architecture of the World* (1997), which is structured on a regional basis and comprises some 1,400 entries that describe the vernacular traditions specific to particular places and cultures, perhaps most emphatically exemplifies this view. The discourse on vernacular architecture that established itself in the late nineteenth century and that burgeoned in particular during the second half of the twentieth century confidently perpetuated this perceived close connection between places and the vernacular forms of architecture that were encountered in them. Most studies published during this period analysed vernacular architecture as geographically and culturally distinctive building forms that belonged to a distinct locality. Vernacular architecture was seen to constitute the authentic architecture of a region, rooted in local community, tradition and environment, and expressive of the cultural identity of a region and the people that inhabited it (Upton and Vlach 1986; Oliver 1997). The corollary of this assumption was that any architectural deviation or transformation of what was deemed to be the local vernacular was often described and explained in terms of cultural contamination or loss, and was generally attributed to the influence of impersonal and culturally hegemonic processes like industrialisation, modernisation or globalisation. Indeed, vernacular architecture, representing locality, culture and tradition, was often used to critique such processes and more specifically the way in which contemporary architectural practice was intricately entangled with, if not subservient to them. More often than not, the vernacular was represented as vulnerable to, if not an actual victim of such outside forces (Upton 1993; Vellinga 2011).

The confidence with which earlier generations of scholars expressed the close relationship between locality, culture and vernacular architecture is no longer present at the beginning of the twenty-first century. For one thing, rapidly changing environmental, economic and cultural contexts have had a major impact on vernacular traditions all around the world. In many places, processes like climate change, urbanisation, migration, technology transfer and conflict (to name but a few) have fundamentally altered the hitherto presumed axiomatic notion of 'one place, one culture, one form of vernacular architecture'. Increasingly, vernacular architecture appears to be diverse and hybrid rather than singular and pristine, combining functions, meanings, forms and materials that in the past may have been seen to be culturally distinct. At the same time, new understandings of analytical concepts such as culture, tradition and locality have challenged the assumptions underlying earlier definitions and representations of vernacular architecture, as well as the notion that radical architectural change is a manifestation of cultural decline and the result of autonomous external forces.

Paying more attention to the role of human agency, recent studies have begun to explore the ways in which vernacular traditions actively transform, overlap, combine and amalgamate because of the deliberate intentions and actions of people (Vellinga 2005). Vernacular architecture, it is increasingly recognised, is a dynamic process directed by human agency, rather than a static product. One of the consequences of the earlier static notion of vernacular architecture as rooted in place and tradition is that new, 'modern' forms of architecture that have sometimes emerged alongside or instead of traditional forms because of changing environmental, social or economic contexts have often been ignored. Once more, such architectural forms are commonly regarded as symptoms of cultural contamination or decline; alien or foreign building types that are not part of the true vernacular tradition and that are thus not worthy of attention. This chapter will focus on one example of this tendency in western Sumatra, Indonesia, where the traditional vernacular multi-family house of the Minangkabau people has slowly but surely been replaced by small single-family houses.

Although the latter now completely dominate the western Sumatran architectural landscape, they have received little to no academic attention. Studies of Minangkabau vernacular architecture focus almost exclusively on the iconic traditional multi-family house (the *rumah gadang* or 'large house'). The chapter will show how this tendency to favour the multi-family house over the single-family house limits our understanding of the use and meaning of either and ultimately achieves nothing but the perpetuation of a popular image of Minangkabau vernacular architecture that does not represent the realities of the twenty-first century. The chapter will conclude that the single-family houses are the products of conscious decisions and choices on the part of the Minangkabau. They represent a new phase in a continuously evolving cultural tradition and as such should be regarded as a new form of vernacular architecture that belongs as much to and in western Sumatra as the traditional multi-family house.

A popular image

The vernacular architecture of the Minangkabau people constitutes one of the most distinctive building traditions in Indonesia. The traditional multi-family house with its characteristic roof spires, floor elevations and colourful woodcarvings is particularly well-known today, and has become one of the key symbols of Minangkabau cultural identity, both inside and outside of Indonesia. Nonetheless, despite its relative fame and prominence, Minangkabau vernacular architecture has not been subject to much research. A small number of studies was published during the late nineteenth and early twentieth centuries and today provide valuable, albeit incomplete historical records (Verkerk Pistorius 1871; Van Hasselt 1881). However, up until the late 1980s, when Indonesian vernacular architecture in general began to receive more interest,

Figure 1: Minangkabau traditional multi-family house (*rumah gadang*), Lima Kaum, West Sumatra, 2014.

comparatively little was known about the building tradition. The studies that were published around the turn of the twentieth century tended to focus solely on the architectural form, construction and layout of the multi-family houses. Interest in the use and meaning of the houses and the social composition of the families that owned them was very limited. More recent work around the turn of the twenty-first century has paid more attention to such social and symbolic aspects, but in general tends to corroborate a stereotypical popular image that does not represent current realities (for example Ng 1993; Pak 1997; Asri 2008; Doubrawa, Lehner and Rieger-Jandl 2016).

The key architectural elements of the popular image of Minangkabau vernacular architecture are the raised floors of the multi-family houses, the distinctive sweeping spires of the thatched roofs, the floor extensions annexed to the sides of the buildings and the presence of colourful decorative woodcarvings on the façades (fig. 1). In spatial terms, the image emphasises the rectangular floor plan of the houses, which consists of a variable number of bays that contain small compartments at the back that are used as bedrooms and/or storage spaces for the members of individual households, which commonly comprise the members of one nuclear family (that is, a mother, father and children). The front part of the houses consists of an open communal space that is used by all households that use the house for everyday activities like cooking and socialising, as well as for ritual events like weddings and funerals. The members of a matrilineal descent group communally own the houses. The houses thus constitute multi-family homes that house the members of several nuclear families, consisting of a conjugal couple and their children, all of whom belong to the same descent group. However, only the women actually live in the houses. The husbands only visit the house of their wives at night, while the men of the descent group that owns the house (the sons and brothers of the women) sleep in the house of their wives. The size and design of the house is determined by the socio-political affiliations of the matrilineal descent group that owns and inhabits it (Ng 1993; Pak 1997; Asri 2008).

Despite the persistence of this popular image, it is clear that there is in reality much more historical and regional variety than the image allows for. Historical research by Jeffrey Hadler (2008) has shown that the Minangkabau have lived in multi-family houses since at least the early nineteenth century. At the time the houses appear to have been dispersed in small clusters surrounded by rice fields, but because of wars and Dutch colonial policies, they were mostly concentrated in nucleated villages and small towns by the 1860s. These nineteenth century multi-family houses did not necessarily take the form of the Minangakabau *rumah gadang* as it is popularly known today, however. Dutch colonial writings indicate that there were at least ten different Minangkabau house forms in the nineteenth century (Verkerk Pistorius 1871; Van Hasselt 1881). The *rumah gadang* with the sweeping roof spires that has now become synonymous with Minangkabau vernacular architecture was just one of those house types, which was pro actively selected and promoted by the Dutch colonial government for political purposes, even though it was historically not found in all parts of West Sumatra (Hadler 2008).

More recent research in the late twentieth century has found at least four different house types, as well as much regional diversity in terms of settlement form and symbolic meanings associated with, for example, the roof design, floor elevations and woodcarvings. Perhaps more importantly, it has also found significant variation in terms of the use and inhabitation of the houses (Vellinga 2004). The popular image associates the *rumah gadang* with a matrilineal descent group that comprises various nuclear households, and presents the house as the exclusive communal domain of the women of those households. In some parts of West Sumatra, however, another social grouping that is reminiscent of Lévi-Strauss' (1982) 'House societies' and that comprises the members of the matrilineal descent group plus their in-married husbands, occupies a much more central position. It is the members of this group (called a *rumah*, literally 'house'), rather than just the matrilineal descent group, who are responsible for the construction and maintenance of the building and that use the house on a day-to-day basis, both for everyday and ritual purposes. In other parts of West Sumatra, the popular image also appears incorrectly (or in any case outdated), as *rumah gadang* are today frequently inhabited by the members of one household only (often an elderly couple or a young family with small children), rather than by a number of families together (Vellinga 2004).

The contemporary popular image of Minangkabau architecture is thus selective and incomplete. Not only does it prioritise one specific house type, which it erroneously present as the only 'true' Minangkabau house; it also tends to exclude a range of other architectural types, including field huts, meeting houses, mosques, single-family houses and rice barns (although the latter are sometimes included). Effectively, it simplistically equates one group of people (the Minangkabau) with one territory (West Sumatra) and one specific building

Figure 2: Minangkabau Culture Documentation and Information Center (PDIKM), Padang Panjang, West Sumatra, 2014.

type (the *rumah gadang*), ignoring the meaningful historical and regional diversity of Minangkabau sociality, culture and architecture as it does so. Nonetheless, despite its reductionist and essentialist nature (or perhaps rather because of it) the image of the *rumah gadang* has become a pre-eminent symbol of Minangkabau ethnic and cultural identity, alongside other key constitutive symbols of 'Minangkabauness', such as the distinctive matrilineal kinship system, the prominence of Islam and the importance of entrepreneurship (Kahn 1993). From at least the early 1980s onwards, the image of the Minangkabau house has been represented and promoted through a range of media including publications, design guidance, museums and cultural theme parks, souvenirs, music, novels, currency, websites and, most recently, social media (fig. 2). Like the Dutch colonial government in the nineteenth century, the Indonesian government, tourism industry and media have actively appropriated the *rumah gadang* as the one and only 'true' Minangkabau house (Vellinga 2003).

One of the first authors to comment on this contemporary appropriation of the Minangkabau house was Tsuyoshi Kato (1982). Writing in the early 1980s, Kato noted how the Minangkabau vernacular tradition found itself in a paradoxical state of revival and decline. On the one hand, the *rumah gadang* was clearly emerging as a key symbol of Minangkabauness, its image being progressively put forward to support a rapidly growing (and increasingly international) tourism industry and to represent Minangkabau culture and identity vis-à-vis the many other ethnic groups in Indonesia. As part of this concerted promotion effort, the government actively promulgated the construction of new public buildings that incorporated elements of traditional Minangkabau design. Throughout West Sumatra, and especially in the provincial capital of Padang, many new public and commercial buildings (ranging from government offices to banks and from hotels to petrol stations) were crowned with the distinctive Minangkabau spired roof and adorned with traditional colourful woodcarvings (Colombijn 1994). In addition, in one or two cases, brand-new traditional-style houses were built, albeit that their function (museum or cultural theme park) and materiality (concrete, cement and zinc) was distinctly non-traditional. At the beginning of the 1980s, the *rumah gadang* had become the symbol *par excellence* of Minangkabau cultural identity.

On the other hand, Kato noted, despite this symbolic prominence, it was clear that many of the traditional *rumah gadang* were no longer maintained or used. In many parts of West Sumatra, especially in the so-called Minangkabau 'heartland' (*darek*) around the towns of Bukittinggi, Payakumbuh and Padang Panjang, large numbers of houses had been abandoned or dilapidated, if they had not already been demolished. Many were

Figure 3: Small single-family house, Pariangan, West Sumatra, 2014.

neglected and derelict or, if they were still in use, were inhabited by small numbers of people only, often elderly couples or elderly single women, or in some cases young nuclear families with limited means. Instead of the multi-family *rumah gadang*, Kato noted, the ubiquitous house type in West Sumatra at the beginning of the 1980s were so-called 'small houses' (*rumah kecil*); contemporary, more 'modern' looking buildings, roughly cubic, made of brick, cement or concrete and with simple gabled roofs, that housed single households rather than the members of large matrilineal descent groups (fig. 3). The omnipresence of such single-family houses has only increased since the early 1980s, as more and more small houses have been built during the last 40 years or so, leaving more and more *rumah gadang* partly inhabited or deserted.

From rooms to houses

Despite the fact that they are nowadays omnipresent in West Sumatra, the 'small' single-family houses have never received much scholarly attention. Their emergence and popularity appears related to a process of family nuclearisation that has been observed among the Minangkabau from at least the late nineteenth century onwards. Nuclearisation in this instance refers to the process whereby single households, made up of a conjugal couple (a husband and wife) and their children, assume an increasingly important position in daily life vis-à-vis the larger multi-family matrilineal descent groups that comprise the members of several nuclear families. As noted before, in the traditional context (represented in and perpetuated by the popular image), various nuclear households lived together in one multi-family house, with each conjugal family having its own dedicated bedroom at the back. The women were all directly related (that is, they were daughters, sisters or cousins and all part of the same descent group) and to a large degree shared and pooled resources. In this traditional context, the members of the matrilineal descent group (the women plus their brothers) collectively built and maintained the houses. The husbands of the women visited their wives at night, but invested their labour and money in the house of their mothers and sisters, that is to say, their own descent group (Prindiville 1985; Van Reenen 1996).

In the contemporary context, however, the vast majority of nuclear families has left the multi-family houses to move into their own single-family homes, which they will have built themselves once their financial situation allowed it, albeit often with the help of other relatives and professional builders. In contrast to the traditional situation, a husband now commonly builds a house together with his wife, rather than just for his sisters. This process, which has been referred to as a move 'from rooms to houses' (Prindiville 1985: 42), has been observed in West Sumatra since at least the early twentieth century. It appears related to an increased desire for levels of privacy, comfort, prosperity and convenience that the traditional social organisation and *rumah gadang* could not offer.

The date that this process of nuclearisation took off and the speed by which it proceeded differed per region, depending on when the area concerned was incorporated into the global cash economy. Thus small houses have long been present in the heartland areas around Bukittingi and Payakumbuh (areas that have been integrated into the international political economy since colonial times), where they are today found in large numbers (Tillema 1926). In other regions in the so-called borderlands (*rantau*), which remained relatively isolated until well into the twentieth century, the traditional multi-family houses remained in use for longer and small houses began to emerge somewhat later on. By the 1980s, however, the single-family homes were well and truly established in those areas too, while at the beginning of the twenty-first century they have become the dominant house form all over West Sumatra; and indeed, Indonesia more generally (Hanan 2017).

Figure 4: Traditional *rumah gadang* surrounded by small houses, Pariangan, West Sumatra, 2014.

The single-family houses in West Sumatra may be said to 'symbolise the dreams of home, prosperity and social status' of the Minangkabau in much the same way that they do so elsewhere (Timm, this volume). Nonetheless, the process of nuclearisation that enabled their emergence and proliferation and to which they in turn contribute has often been described and analysed in negative terms. The increased importance of nuclear families vis-à-vis the traditional matrilineal descent groups, so clearly symbolised by the numerical dominance of single-family houses over the traditional multi-family houses, has frequently been taken to reflect a process of cultural erosion that will ultimately lead to the disappearance of the unique matrilineal kinship system and, with it, Minangkabau culture (including its distinct vernacular architecture). The fate of the matrilineal system has been an anthropological concern since Dutch colonial times, with fears that it cannot co-exist with Islamic and Western values and lifestyles (both of which tend to be more patrilineal), resulting in regular predictions of its demise (for a critical discussion of these predictions see Kahn 1976; Prindiville 1985). Despite such fatalist prognoses, however, the matrilineal system is still in place at the beginning of the twenty-first century and forms a prominent constituent of a distinctive, creative and dynamic Minangkabau culture that uniquely combines traditional elements with Islamic and Western (and increasingly global) features. Instead of symbolising its demise, the single-family house is an inseperable part of this culture.

Figure 5: Traditional *rumah gadang* with modern extension, Rao Rao, West Sumatra, 2014.

The single-family houses are easier and cheaper to build than the traditional multi-family ones, allow for more privacy and are generally regarded as more 'modern' and 'up-to-date'. Incorporating modern conveniences (electricity, plumbing) and dedicated functional spaces (bathrooms, kitchens), they are seen to provide a better quality of life than the traditional buildings that commonly lack such facilities. They also allow for more individualisation in terms of size and materiality, exterior and interior design, and furnishing and decoration. Despite all this, however, it is evident that they do not necessarily reflect a disbandment of the matrilineal descent groups to which their owners belong. The small houses are normally built on land owned by the descent group, often in close proximity to the traditional *rumah gadang*. In many instances, this results in very compact clusters of small single-family houses, inhabited by close relatives (sisters, daughters, cousins), surrounding one or more traditional multi-family houses (fig. 4). Throughout most of the twentieth century, the spatial organisation of the small houses was reminiscent of that of the traditional houses, with an open hall generally flanked by a number of individual bedrooms (Vellinga 2004). In some instances, they were inhabited by the members of two or more nuclear families, as sisters shared the same house built by their parents. In more recent decades, as more and more single-family houses have been built and the buildings become larger and more architecturally diverse (due at least in part to an increased exposure to

urban architectural precedents), more variation in spatial layout has begun to emerge. The social cohesion of the matrilineal descent groups is still strong, however, with single-family members commonly continuing to share resources and activities like looking after the children, cooking and entertaining.
The spatial separation caused by the single-family houses has thus not led to a complete break-up of social cohesion. Nor has it meant that the traditional *rumah gadang* have entirely lost their significance in social life. In many instances, the old houses are still inhabited, if only because some of the descent group members (normally elderly people or young families with limited means) cannot afford to move into a single-family home. However, even if they are no longer inhabited, the multi-family houses may in some cases still be used for ceremonial purposes, for instance to celebrate a birth or wedding or to conduct a funeral. In such instances, the members of the matrilineal descent group continue to look after the houses, even if they are uninhabited. Sometimes the houses are modernised or renovated (commonly using contemporary materials and technologies) or have new extensions (for instance, a new kitchen or bathroom) added to them (fig.5). Nonetheless, in most cases it would appear that *rumah gadang* have been left to dilapidate and collapse, not so much because of the emergence of the single-family homes, but because of the high costs of maintenance, the lack of comfort, the associations with the past and poverty, or a combination of all those factors together. The same goes for some of the other traditional buildings, most notably the rice barns (*rangkiang*) and meeting halls (*balai*).

Old and new vernaculars

To an extent, then, the traditional Minangkabau house may be said to be in a state of predicament. However, as noted, this predicament is not so much caused by the process of nuclearisation as such, but by a combination of social, economic and environmental pressures. Although 'modern' materials such as corrugated iron were first introduced in the region during the late nineteenth century (Kahn 1993), the vast majority of *rumah gadang* were built using natural materials (timber, bamboo, rattan, palm-fibre thatch) well into the twentieth century. Those materials were all sourced locally and assembled using traditional mortise and tenon technologies that required no plans or blueprints, but that were dependent on the skills of an expert master builder. Although some houses in remote areas were still built in this way during the 1990s (Vellinga 2004), in most parts of West Sumatra the rapidly increasing integration into the global cash economy meant that new materials (corrugated iron, concrete, cement, zinc) had begun to replace traditional ones by the mid-twentieth century. Not only were the new materials cheaper, they were also easier to obtain and required less technical expertise to work with. As a result, by the end of the twentieth century, traditional master builders were hard to find anywhere in West Sumatra, and with them the knowledge and skills needed to build and maintain the traditional *rumah gadang* had largely disappeared.

A major contributor to this process has been the deforestation of Sumatra. Although regional variation exists and accurate figures are hard to come by, research shows that the primary forest cover on the island has been nearly

Figure 6: 'New vernacular' house, Balimbing, West Sumatra, 2014.

halved between 1990 and 2000 alone (Arunarwati Margono et al. 2012). Media reports in 2013 suggested that the Sumatran rainforest is predicted to have mostly disappeared by 2030 (The Guardian 2013). In the course of half a century, most of the woodlands have been felled by multinational companies to make way for palm oil and acacia plantations, as well as coal, copper and gold mines. Apart from the catastrophic impacts on the local biodiversity and global climate change, as well as the conflicts and human rights abuses that come with the (often illegal) forced dispossession of land, the process of deforestation has meant that the timber that was traditionally used to build and maintain the *rumah gadang* is no longer available today. During the 1990s, the rainforests had almost completely disappeared in the heartland regions of West Sumatra, but isolated patches of forest that could supply suitable timber were still present in small parts of the eastern borderlands. In 2018, suitable timber to build a house in the traditional manner is unlikely to be found anywhere in the region, a situation that has contributed to a further decline of the building tradition.

Because of all those social, economic and environmental changes, the use of fired brick, cement and concrete for building construction has become ubiquitous. Many of the single-family houses that were built throughout the early and mid-twentieth century were still made of timber, even though most had corrugated iron rather than thatched roofs. By the 1980s, timber had been almost completely replaced and was only used for roof structures, door and window frames and, in more remote regions, structural systems. Not only are manufactured materials such as brick and concrete cheaper to procure and easier to use, they are also regarded as more modern. Nonetheless, their environmental qualities are much poorer. Their manufacture uses more energy and causes more pollution than the procurement of the traditional natural materials would have done, and their impact on the inhabitants' health seems more detrimental. The concrete ground level floors in particular seem to have an impact on the prevalence of joint pains and rheumatism. The brick and concrete houses also appear to be more vulnerable to the impacts of the various environmental hazards that the region is prone to, such as landslides and floods (both of which are likely to increase as a result of the deforestation) and earthquakes. The latter in particular at times have had a devastating impact on the single-family houses. Although the *rumah gadang* are not invulnerable to those impacts either, anecdotal evidence indicates that the damage is overall less significant or catastrophic. Despite those shortcomings, the single-family houses today completely dominate the West Sumatran architectural landscape. The traditional *rumah gadang* are still present, but are effectively islands in an ocean of single-family homes. The latter are almost invariably made of manufactured materials, while the traditional timber building know-how and skills appear to be as good as obsolete. Increasingly, the 'small' single-family houses are turning into large mansions that display an eclectic mix of architectural styles that seems far removed from traditional Minangkabau architectural design. In some instances, however, the houses make up an extension of a traditional *rumah gadang*, while in other cases, their design resembles that of the traditional multi-family house, complete with all its distinctive design features: the floor extensions, the raised floor, the colourful woodcarvings and, most importantly, the sweeping roof spires (fig. 6). Such 'new vernacular' single-family houses were first observed in the late 1970s (Kato 1982). Their emergence may have been influenced by the construction of similar traditional-style museum buildings in Jakarta and Padang in the mid-1970s. Whatever their origin, from the 1990s onwards, those new vernacular single-family houses constructed of manufactured materials such as concrete, cement and zinc, but made to look as if they had been built traditionally, have proliferated. At the same time, more unashamedly modern *rumah gadang* that expose the new materials while maintaining a traditional style have also been built. More often than not, those new vernacular buildings comply with the popular image known from the media, exemplified most expressly by the replica Minangkabau royal palace in Pagaruyung.

The construction of privately owned new *rumah gadang* emerged around the time when traditional Minangkabau roofs began to adorn major public buildings in West Sumatran towns and cities. This phenomenon, mentioned earlier on, has been explained as an attempt by the central Indonesian government under President Suharto (1966–1998) to domesticate and control Minangkabau ethnic sentiments (Colombijn 1994; Schefold 1998). The policy undoubtedly benefited the emerging international tourist industry at the time, but also fostered local cultural consciousness. The expression of 'Minangkabauness' became a source of pride, and many Minangkabau people privately began to use the image of the *rumah gadang* to pronounce their connection to West Sumatra and Minangkabau culture (for instance by adding a miniature spired roof to their mailbox). The new vernacular single-family houses were one expression of this sentiment. Many of them were built with remittances sent back home by Minangkabau people who had emigrated to other parts of Indonesia or abroad. Others were built by members of the local community who used the symbolism of the houses to appropriate positions of power (Vellinga 2003). Often, they were not used as actual houses, but stood as empty symbols of their owners' wealth and status. Following the collapse of Suharto's regime and the subsequent devolution of power to the provinces, this expression of cultural identity and pride, and with it the construction of new vernacular architecture, has been consolidated.

Like the more standard single-family houses, the new vernacular-style houses have commonly been regarded in negative terms, as examples of cultural erosion. Because they are built using modern manufactured materials and serve as single-family rather than multi-family houses, they are regularly said to lack authenticity. What is more, because they are often the result of conscious attempts to appear traditional, they sometimes have been described as fakes or simulacra: buildings that attempt to represent a popular image that in itself is already a representation, and reductionist and essentialist at that. The new *rumah gadang* are not 'real', as they are not truly traditional, but they are not completely modern either. They combine traditional vernacular forms and symbolism with modern, global materials and functions. In the eyes of some observers this means that, like the other single-family houses, they are not part of the Minangkabau vernacular tradition. In the eyes of others, however, including their owners, it is this combination of old and new that makes them powerful symbols of what it means to be a Minangkabau person in the twenty-first century: rooted in place and tradition, but simultaneously firmly established in an increasingly modern and globalised world (Vellinga 2003). From this latter perspective, the new buildings are as much part of the Minangkabau vernacular tradition as the old timber *rumah gadang* or the architecturally more eclectic small single-family houses.

Questions

In the eyes of many observers, both the 'small' and the 'new vernacular' single-family houses thus constitute a radical break with tradition. The former are thoroughly different from the traditional multi-family *rumah gadang* in terms of their design and materiality, and are commonly seen to embody a process of nuclearisation that in itself has often been regarded as a culturally erosive force because it involves the supposed disintegration of the traditional matrilineal descent groups. The new vernacular houses maintain the design features of the traditional multi-family house, but differ radically in terms of their materiality, use and meaning. Like the small houses, they are owned by individual households rather than entire matrilineal descent groups. However, as objectifications of the power, status and ambition of their owners, they are mostly not used as actual dwellings and seem to embody another form of cultural change, in which *nouveau riche* upstarts attempt to replace traditional authorities using their wealth and the symbolic power of consumer goods. In both cases, the standing of the houses is defined in explicit opposition to the popular image of Minangkabau vernacular architecture, which recalls a mythical time in the past when Minangkabau culture was traditional, authentic and untainted by outside, foreign influences, and houses (and other traditional buildings) with clearly defined and locally distinct design features formed an integral part of it.

No doubt influenced by the fact that they do not fit into this image, neither the small nor the new vernacular single-family houses have received much academic attention. As noted, most literature that deals with Minangkabau vernacular architecture simply perpetuates the well-known stereotypical popular image of the multi-family *rumah gadang*. It either makes no mention of the single-family houses at all and simply pretends that they do not exist (Navis 1984; Pak 1997; Asri 2008), or it acknowledges their existence (and indeed prominence) but then continues to pay little to no attention to them (Ng 1993; Doubrawa, Lehner and Rieger Jandl 2016). This tendency means that many questions related to the single-family houses in fact remain unanswered. For example, little is actually known about the composition of the households that build and occupy the small or new vernacular single-family homes. Clearly, the households are different from the matrilineal descent groups that are commonly associated with the traditional multi-family homes, but whether they always make up a nuclear family in the classic European sense (that is, one that consists of a father, mother and children), is not clear. Various studies of Minangkabau kinship and sociality have warned about a potential Eurocentric bias in the ongoing debates about the Impact of the nuclearisation process on the matrilineal system (Prindiville 1985).

Nuclear families dominate the popular imagination in the Western world (where they are often seen to be a 'natural' family type, even if they are not actually as common today as many people think they are) (Parkin and Stone 2004), but they do not necessarily constitute the only way to occupy a single-family home. Many other configurations are possible (elderly man and wife, single widow, brother and sister, single mother with adopted children, grandmother and grandchildren) and have in fact been observed among the Minangkabau, both in the single-family and the multi-family houses. As the traditional role of the *rumah gadang* as a multi-family home continues to diminish and as the single-family houses continue to multiply in number and grow larger and architecturally more diverse, it is not unreasonable to assume that the variation in household composition may remain significant, or even increase, as well.

Many other questions remain unanswered, too. Thus, little to nothing is known about the way in which the small houses are build. Neither the decision-making mechanisms during the design and construction stages, nor the division of labour during the construction process has been documented. No work has been published on how the construction, maintenance or improvement of the houses is financed or on how decisions about the location to build on are taken. Equally, it is not clear what planning regulations (customary or governmental), if any, need to be taken into account, or how the houses are passed on as part of the inheritance once the original owners pass away. Indeed, these are all questions that cannot truly be answered in relation to the traditional multi-family houses either because they are not a part of the popular image and have never really been addressed in the literature. One study that has paid attention to decision-making mechanisms and labour divisions during the construction process of a traditional multi-family house has shown that in-married husbands can play a more central role in the building and conservation of the *rumah gadang* than the popular image, which stresses the centrality of the brothers of the women of the house, allows for (Vellinga 2004). It shows that, in this respect at least, there may be more continuity between the multi-family and the small single-family houses than is often thought, although more research into, for instance, the ways in which the houses are inherited or what happens in case of a divorce is necessary to draw more than hypothetical conclusions.

The adherence to the selective and reductionist popular image of Minangkabau vernacular architecture that stresses the local rootedness and distinctiveness of the *rumah gadang* thus seriously hampers our understanding of both the multi-family and the single-family houses. Holding on to a fixed and essentialist image of what Minangkabau vernacular architecture is (and is not) results in representations that do not always match social, economic or environmental realities, and that tend to see any changes to or deviations of the popular image (if recognised at all) as the result of cultural contamination or decline. Interestingly, the same may be said for the discourse on Minangkabau sociality, which is also based on static and essentially Eurocentric analytical concepts like matriliny, descent groups or nuclear families that may sometimes be more part of the imagination than (contemporary) indigenous reality (Kahn 1993). Janet Carsten (1997) has shown how kinship is not fixed but a process, ever changing over time, and how radically different concepts such as the hearth or shared substances (like food) may be more important determinants of what it means to be kin than descent or blood relationships. In a similar way, Vellinga (2004) has shown how Minangkabau multi-family houses are also processes that are built, maintained and ultimately taken down by the members of a group (a *rumah*) that is constituted through the shared involvement in exactly those activities. The house should thus be seen as an active objectification of this *rumah*, rather than as a static expression of the matrilineal descent group that it is commonly associated with in the popular image (see also Vellinga 2007).

It may be argued, in line with the anthropological discourse on kinship more generally (Parkin and Stones 2004), that in order to truly understand the meaning of Minangkabau vernacular architecture, any analysis should start with a recognition of indigenous concepts such as the *rumah* and the hearth, rather than etic concepts such as descent groups and nuclear families. It should also begin with an acknowledgement of the processual nature of Minangkabau architecture and kinship, both of which are not fixed and given but continuously (re)constructed as a result of human agency. Vernacular architecture is indeed often rooted in specific traditions and localities and expressive of the cultural identity of the people that inhabit the latter. However, this does not mean that either the architecture or the cultural identities concerned are static and fixed. Cultural traditions continuously transform in tandem with changes to social, economic and environmental contexts, driven by human intention and activity Architectural traditions are no exception to this. At the same time, households, families and kindred relationships continuously evolve, too, with new members added through birth or marriage and old ones lost through death or divorce. The results of such transformations can be radical (as in the case of the small single-family houses) or more subtle (as in the case of the new vernacular ones), but in neither case are they a manifestation of cultural contamination or decline caused by hegemonic outside forces. Rather, they arguably represent a new stage in the continuous evolution of a vernacular tradition that is not static or passive but actively developed and transformed by the Minangkabau in response to new circumstances, needs, opportunities and ambitions.

Conclusions

The association of vernacular architecture with distinct places is as strong today as it was at the time Blount published his *Glossographia Anglicana Nova*. However, the notion that the world is made up of numerous stable, bounded and homogenous cultures that each belong to a particular part of the world and that produce their own distinctive and pristine forms of vernacular architecture is no longer tenable. Cultural ideas, values and meanings, alongside the buildings and objects that embody them, are continuously transformed, borrowed, transmitted or amalgamated as a result of human interaction and give rise to ongoing processes of acculturation and hybridisation. This has no doubt been so throughout history, but is all the more apparent in a century characterised by an unprecedented level and pace of globalisation and cross-cultural interaction. To continue to ignore the dynamic nature of vernacular architecture and describe any deviations or transformations in terms of impoverishment, inauthenticity or loss results in the continuous perpetuation of stereotypical representations that are misleading, partial and out of touch with reality. In prioritising certain building types over others, they are also too exclusive and leave too many questions about both old and new vernaculars unanswered.

The case of the Minangkabau illustrates that an approach that acknowledges the dynamic nature of cultural traditions and that recognises the role of human intention and agency in their development may result in a more comprehensive understanding of the use and meaning of vernacular architecture. In contrast to the selective and reductionist popular image that has long been promoted by the Indonesian government, academics and the tourist industry, Minangkabau vernacular architecture comprises of more than just the traditional multi-family houses owned by matrilineal descent groups. Instead of the iconic *rumah gadang*, small single-family houses, of a very different design and materiality, and inhabited by households of different configurations, dominate the West Sumatran landscape at the beginning of the twentieth century. Rather than products of cultural erosion or contamination, these single-family houses are the result of conscious choices and decisions made by the Minangkabau, and accommodate new notions of privacy, comfort, prosperity and convenience. Like the 'new vernacular' single-family houses that have proliferated in the last forty years or so, they are not inauthentic, foreign or alien, but an integral part of a building tradition that continues to evolve in line with rapidly changing environmental, social and economic contexts. More research into their planning, design, construction, use and meaning is needed to move beyond the endless perpetuation of a stereotypical image of Minangkabau architecture that adds little to nothing to our understanding of this unique and distinctive building tradition.

References

Arunarwati Margono, B. et al. (2012), 'Mapping and monitoring deforestation and forest degradation in Sumatra (Indonesia) using Landsat time series data sets from 1990 to 2010', Environmental Research Letters 7(3), http://iopscience.iop.org/article/10.1088/1748-9326/7/3/034010/meta (accessed 7 February 2019).

Asri, S. (2008), 'Traditional houses and settlements in the Minangkabau heartland', in R. Schefold, P. J. M. Nas, G. Domenig and R. Wessing, R. (eds): Indonesian Houses: Survey of Vernacular Architecture in Western Indonesia (Leiden: KITLV Press), 101–116.

Blount, T. (1707), Glossographia Anglicana Nova: Or, a Dictionary, Interpreting such Hard Words ... as are at Present Used in the English Tongue, with their Etymologies, Definitions, etc. (London: Printed for D. Brown).

Carsten, J. (1997), The Heat of the Hearth: The Process of Kinship in a Malay Fishing Community (Oxford: Clarendon Press).

Colombijn, F. (1994), Patches of Padang: The history of an Indonesian Town in the Twentieth Century and the Use of Urban Space (Leiden: CNWS).

Doubrawa, I., Lehner, E. and Rieger-Jandl, A. (eds.) (2016), Village Architecture in Sumatra: A Comparative Study: Toba Batak, Karo Batak, Minangkabau (Vienna: IVA-ICRA).

Hadler, J. (2008), Muslims and Matriarchs: Cultural Resilience in Indonesia through Jihad and Colonialism (Ithaca: Cornell University Press).

Hanan, H. (2017), 'Tradition and modernisation in Indonesian Vernacular Houses', in S. R. Ju (ed.): *Southeast Asian Houses: Expanding Tradition* (Irvine: Seoul Selection), 25–54.

Kahn, J. S. (1976), '"Tradition", matriliny and change among the Minangkabau of Indonesia', Bijdragen tot de Taal-, Land- en Volkenkunde 132(1), 64–95.

Kahn, J. S. (1993), Constituting the Minangkabau: Peasants, Culture and Modernity in Colonial Indonesia (Oxford: Berg).

Kato, T. (1982), Matriliny and Migration: Evolving Minangkabau Traditions in Indonesia (Ithaca: Cornell University Press).

Lévi-Strauss, C. (1982), The Way of the Masks (Seattle: University of Washington Press).

Navis, A. A. (1984), Alam Terkembang Jadi Guru: Adat dan Kebudayaan Minangkabau (Jakarta: Grafiti).

Ng, C. (1993), 'Raising the house-post and feeding the husband-givers: The spatial categories of social reproduction among the Minangkabau', in J. J. Fox (ed.): Inside Austronesian Houses. Perspectives on Domestic Design for Living (Canberra: Research School of Pacific and Asian Studies), 116–139.

N. N. (2013), 'The Sumatran rainforest will mostly disappear within 20 years', The Guardian, 27 May, https://www.theguardian.com/world/2013/may/26/sumatra-borneo-deforestation-tigers-palm-oil (accessed 6 February 2019).

Oxford English Dictionary (2013) (Oxford: Oxford University Press).

Oliver, P. (ed.) (1997), Encyclopedia of Vernacular Architecture of the World (Cambridge: Cambridge University Press).

Pak, O.-K. (1997), 'Minangkabau', in P. Oliver (ed.): Encyclopedia of Vernacular Architecture of the World (Cambridge: Cambridge University Press), 1117–1118.

Parkin, R. and Stone, L. (eds.) (2004), Kinship and Family: An Anthropological Reader (Oxford: Blackwell Publishing).

Prindiville, J. C. (1985), 'Mother, mother's brother and modernisation: The problems and prospects of Minangkabau matriliny in a changing world', in L.L. Thomas and F. Von Benda-Beckmann (eds.): Change and Continuity in Minangkabau: Local, Regional and Historical Perspectives on West Sumatra (Athens: Ohio University), 29–43.

Schefold, R. (1998), 'The domestication of culture: Nation-building and ethnic diversity in Indonesia', Bijdragen tot de Taal-, Land- en Volkenkunde 154, 259–80.

Tillema, H. F. (1926), 'Indrukken van Menangkabau', Oedaya 3–8, 91–93.
Upton, D. and Vlach, J. M. (eds.) (1986), Common Places: Readings in American Vernacular Architecture (Athens: University of Georgia Press).
Upton, D. (1993), 'The tradition of change', Traditional Dwellings and Settlements Review 5(1), 9–15.
Van Hasselt, A. L (1881), Ethnografische Atlas van Midden-Sumatra, met verklarenden tekst (Leiden: Brill).
Van Reenen, J. (1996), Central Pillars of the House: Sisters, Wives and Mothers on a Rural Community in Minangkabau, West Sumatra (Leiden: CNWS).
Vellinga, M. (2003), 'The attraction of the house: Architecture, status and ethnicity in West Sumatra', in P. J. M. Nas and G. Persoon (eds.): Framing Indonesian Realities: Essays in Symbolic Anthropology in Honour of Reimar Schefold (Leiden: KITLV Press), 177–197.
Vellinga, M. (2004), Constituting Unity and Difference: Vernacular Architecture in a Minangkabau Village (Leiden: KITLV Press).
Vellinga, M. (2005), 'Engaging the future: Vernacular architecture studies in the twenty-first century', in L. Asquith and M. Vellinga (eds.): Vernacular Architecture in the Twenty-First Century: Theory, Education and Practice (London: Taylor and Francis), 81–94.
Vellinga, M. (2007), 'Anthropology and the materiality of architecture', American Ethnologist 34(4), 756 –766.
Vellinga, M. (2011), 'The end of the vernacular: Anthropology and the architecture of the Other', Etnofoor 23(1), 171–192.
Verkerk Pistorius, A. W. P. (1871), Studien over de Inlandsche Huishouding in de Padangsche Bovenlanden (Zaltbommel: Noman).

Illustration credits

Figure 1: Photograph: Erich Lehner, Technische Universität Wien, Austria.
Figure 2: Photograph: Erich Lehner, Technische Universität Wien, Austria.
Figure 3: Photograph: Erich Lehner, Technische Universität Wien, Austria.
Figure 4: Photograph: Irene Doubrawa, Technische Universität Wien, Austria.
Figure 5: Photograph: Irene Doubrawa, Technische Universität Wien, Austria.
Figure 6: Photograph: Irene Doubrawa, Technische Universität Wien, Austria.

Authors

Christiane Cantauw is a historian and anthropologist. She has been directing the Folklore Commission for Westphalia in Münster since 2005. Among her activities are encompassing projects in the field of digital humanities (funded by the Volkswagen Stiftung and the German Research Foundation) in which the visual, audio and manuscript collections of the Folklore Commissions have been digitised and made available for open access (2006–2013). From 2015 to 2018, she directed the project "As if made for us?! The path to home ownership?", funded by the German Federal Ministry of Education and Research. Since 2014, she regularly teaches graduate and undergraduate courses in social and cultural anthropology at the Seminar for Folklore Studies/ Cultural Anthropology at the University of Münster. Among her publications are: (2017), Von Häusern und Menschen. Berichte und Reportagen vom Bauen und Wohnen von den 1950er Jahren bis heute. Mit dem Bautagebuch von Rosemarie Krieger (Münster, New York: Waxmann).

Anne Caplan is a research associate in the Department of Sustainable Production and Consumption, Research Unit Innovation Laboratories at the Wuppertal Institute. Her research focuses on housing and home, participation and citizen science as well as urbanity and urban planning. From 2015 to 2018, she was Scientific Manager of the research association "The flow of things or private property? A house and its objects between family life, resource management and museum", funded by the German Federal Ministry of Education and Research (www.hausfragen.net). During this time, she realised and conceived various science communication formats for the contents of the research association. The calendar 'Park+Roll. Carports in Suburbia – von fliegenden Bauten und ruhendem Verkehr' created by a student project in cooperation with the MSD, Münster School of Design (Claudia Grönebaum), was awarded the Gregor Calendar Award in silver in 2018. Among her latest publications are: together with Katherin Wagenknecht (2018), 'Bauen oder kaufen? Eine qualitativ-vergleichende Studie zu Wohnpräferenzen in Einfamilienhausgebieten in Nordwestdeutschland', Forum Stadt 3, 259–273; and (2018), 'Design Research as a Meta-discipline', in: P. E. Vermaas and St. Vial (eds.): Advancements in Philosophy of Design (Berlin: Springer), 347–367.

Sophie Chevalier is Professor of Anthropology at the University of Picardie, France and Director of the "Habiter le monde" Research Centre. Her main interests are in economic life, consumption and leisure, cities and anthropology at home. She has carried out fieldwork in Paris and London on domestic material culture; in Bulgaria on exchange in a privatized economy with no money in the 1990s; and recently in Durban, South Africa after apartheid, on the new middle classes with reference to food and shared social spaces. Her recent books include: (2015, ed.), Anthropology at the Crossroads: The View from France (co-author, 2013), Paris, résidence secondaire, and (co-editor, 2013), Norbert Elias et l'anthropologie. She is co-editor of www.ethnographiques.org and on the editorial board of Ethnologie Française, Espaces et Sociétés, Home Culture and Social Anthropology/Anthropologie Sociale.

Carola Ebert is Professor for Interior Design, History and Theory of Architecture and Design at Berlin International University of Applied Sciences. Her research fields are the West German modernist bungalow, the theorisation of interior design, and teaching and learning in architecture and design. Her forthcoming and most recent publications are: (ed. 2020), Theorising Interior Design. Identity – Practice – Education; (ed. with E. M. Froschauer and Ch. Salge, 2019), Vom Baumeister zum Master. Formen der Architekturlehre vom 19. bis ins 21. Jahrhundert; (author, 2019), 'Inseln der Selbstreflexion. Drei Diskurse zur Architekturlehre im 21. Jahrhundert, in: ibid.; (with M. Sonntag, J. Rueß, L. Schilow and W. Deicke, 2018), Forschendes Lernen im Seminar. Ein Leitfaden für Lehrende (Berlin); as well as several publications related to her PhD thesis 'Entspannte Moderne. Der westdeutsche Bungalow 1952-1969 als Adaption eines internationalen Leitbilds und Symbol einer nivellierten Mittelschichtsgesellschaft'.

Sabine Flamme has been teaching material flow and resource management at the Department of Civil Engineering at Münster University of Applied Sciences since 2005. Since 2016, she has been speaker for the management board of the IWARU Institute for Infrastructure, Water, Resources and Environment, where she heads the Resources Working Group, which currently employs 15 scientists. Her research activities are currently focused on increasing added value in the field of urban mining. In this context, she supervises several research projects on material flows from anthropogenic deposits, on the development of recycling processes for building materials and constructions, and on new business models in the construction sector. She is a member of various working groups and has recently written numerous lectures and publications on the above-mentioned topics. In addition, she received the Urban Mining Award in June 2012 and is a founding member of IR Bau and re!source Stiftung e.V., respectively.

Julia Gill is an architect und architectural researcher in Berlin who teaches building design, construction and history at the Staatliche Technikerschule Berlin. Her main research issues are related to the conditions of production and appropriation of architecture, focussing on questions of individualisation and standardisation in affordable housing. She has taught at several universities and institutions, among them TU Braunschweig, RWTH Aachen, EPFL Lausanne, AZ Wien, Humboldt Universität zu Berlin and Universität der Künste Berlin. She is editor of the book series Forum Architekturwissenschaft (previously published Vol. 1 (2017), 2 (2018), 3 (2019) with Sabine Ammon, Eva Maria Froschauer and Christiane Salge. Her own publications include (2010), Individualisierung als Standard. Über das Unbehagen an der Fertighausarchitektur (Bielefeld: transcript); (2016), 'Edited Standards. A Plea for Greater Individuality in Standards', in W. Nägeli and N. Tajeri (eds.): Small Interventions. New ways of Living in Post-War Modernism (Basel: Birkhäuser), 115–118; and (2016), 'Germany's next Top-Modul', Bauwelt 28/29, 14–17.

Johanna Hartmann is a researcher in the fields of art history, architectural theory and gender studies. Her work centres on concepts of space, subjectivity, the body and gender in discourses of the home and city. She is working on a doctoral thesis on housing exhibitions and domestic advice media in post-war West Germany. Until July 2019, she was a lecturer and research assistant at the Institute for Art History – Film Studies – Art Education at the University of Bremen, working in association with the Mariann Steegmann Institute Art and Gender. Current publications include: (ed. together with K. Eck, K. Heinz and

Ch. Keim, forthcoming 2019), Wohn/Raum/Denken. Politiken des Häuslichen in Kunst, Architektur und visueller Kultur (Bielefeld: transcript); (with N. Jablonski, Ch. Schmitt, forthcoming 2020), '"Heile Welten" nach 1945: Heimat, Wohnkultur, Tourismus', in J. Gerstner, J. C. Heller and Ch. Schmitt (eds.): Handbuch Idylle. Traditionen – Verfahren – Theorien (Stuttgart: J.B. Metzler).

Folke Köbberling is an artist who develops models for interventions in urban space that transform existing structures and thus challenge routines of dealing with urban architecture in a subtle, often humorous way. She has been teaching artistic design at TU Braunschweig since 2016 and has realised projects and exhibitions together with Martin Kaltwasser, among others at Martin Gropius Bau and Haus der Kulturen der Welt (Berlin), at ZKM Karlsruhe, Lentos Museum (Linz) and Ruhrtriennale. Among her publications are: (2017), FULL STOP (Edition Metzel); (with Martin Kaltwasser, 2009), Hold it! The Art & Architecture of Public-Space-Bricolage-Resistance-Resources-Aesthetics (Berlin: jovis). See: http://www.folkekoebberling.de/.

Jakob Smigla-Zywocki has been a junior researcher at the University of Münster, Seminar for Folklore Studies/European Ethnology since October 2016, where he also teaches undergraduate courses in social and cultural anthropology. Before that he was a research assistant at the Folklore Commission for Westphalia in Münster in the research project "The Way to Homeownership". In parallel to his studies in modern and contemporary history and social and cultural anthropology at the University of Münster from 2010 to 2015, he worked at the Villa ten Hompel memorial site in Münster.

Elisabeth Timm has been holding the chair for cultural anthropology at the University of Münster since 2011. Her fields in research and teaching are family and kinship, theories of culture and the history of folklore studies. She is the general editor of the *Zeitschrift für Kulturwissenschaften* (transcript, together with Karin Harrasser) and of the Anthropological Journal of European Cultures (Berghahn, together with Patrick Laviolette). From 2015 to 2018 she directed the research association "The flow of things or private property? A house and its objects between family life, resource management and museum", funded by the German Federal Ministry of Education and Research (www.hausfragen.net). Among her latest publications are: (ed., together with Sonja Hnilica, 2017), Das Einfamilienhaus (thematic issue of the *Zeitschrift für Kulturwissenschaften*), and (2019), 'Die Ästhetik der Hysterie zwischen Ritual und Realie, ca. 1900. Kulturanthropologie und Wissensgeschichte einer Votivgabe', in

B. Herrmann (ed.): Anthropologie und Ästhetik. Interdisziplinäre Perspektiven (München: Wilhelm Fink), 55–95.

Inken Tintemann is a town planner who worked and graduated at the chair "Planungstheorie und Stadtentwicklung", held by Klaus Selle at RWTH Aachen. Her fields in research and teaching focused on needs and patterns concerning living and housing within different lifestyles and types of household. Among her publications are: City oder Suburb – Wohnoptionen für Familien im gesellschaftlichen Wandel: untersucht in Düsseldorf-Innenstadt und Neuss-Allerheiligen (Aachen: RWTH, 2015). Inken Tintemann is currently working for the municipality of Düren (North Rhine-Westphalia) where she is responsible for social town planning.

Marcel Vellinga is Professor of Anthropology of Architecture at Oxford Brookes University in the United Kingdom. Holding a PhD in Cultural Anthropology from Leiden University in the Netherlands, Marcel has extensive research and teaching experience in the fields of cultural anthropology and international vernacular architecture studies. Over the years, he has taught and published on a variety of topics including vernacular architecture, the anthropology of architecture, rural architectural regeneration, and tradition and sustainable development. Marcel is the Editor-in-Chief of the second edition of the *Encyclopedia of Vernacular Architecture of the World*, to be published by Bloomsbury Publishing in 2021.

Katherin Wagenknecht is scientific assistant at the Museum für Naturkunde in Berlin. She coordinates a project on citizen science, funded by the European Commission, aiming to explore and develop the infrastructure of citizen science on a European level. From 2015 to 2018, she was a junior researcher at the Seminar for Folklore Studies/European Ethnology (University of Münster), where she did research and analysis for the project 'Building a House for Us', funded by the German Federal Ministry of Education and Research, see www.hausfragen.net. Katherin Wagenknecht holds an MA in History and Sociology (Technical University of Darmstadt) and a BA in Cultural Studies (University of Leipzig).

Gotthard Walter studied civil engineering at the Münster University of Applied Sciences. He worked as a project engineer at the Münster University of Applied Sciences and from 1994 as head of department at the INFA Institut für Abfall- und Abwasserwirtschaft GmbH. Since 1999, he has been leading research assistant in the Resources Working Group at the Institute for Infrastructure, Water, Resources and the Environment at Münster University of Applied Sciences. His work focuses on the organisation and coordination of R & D projects in the field of material flow and resource management.

Johannes Warda currently holds a lectureship in history and theory of architecture at Erfurt University of Applied Sciences. As architectural scholar he has taught at the Bauhaus-Universität Weimar, the Akademie der Bildenden Künste Vienna and at TU Dresden. In 2014, as a grantee of the German National Academic Foundation, he received a PhD in architecture and historic preservation from Bauhaus-Universität Weimar. In 2017/18, he was Dresden Junior Fellow at TU Dresden and research fellow at the Leibniz-Institut für Geschichte und Kultur des östlichen Europa (GWZO) Leipzig. As a member of design collectives, he has been working on art and architecture projects, most recently on the Buchenwald Memorial (with pink tank). Recent publications include (2018), 'Das Ökohaus – ein technisches Denkmal?', in B. Weller and S. Horn (eds.): Denkmal und Energie 2019 (Wiesbaden: Springer Vieweg), 163–173; (2017), 'Keeping West Berlin "As Found". Alison Smithson, Hardt-Waltherr Hämer and 1970s Proto-Preservation Urban Renewal', in Á. Moravánszky and T. Lange (eds.): Re-framing Identities. Architecture's Turn to History 1970–1990 (Basel: Birkhäuser), 275–288; (2016), Veto des Materials. Denkmalpflege, Wiederverwendung von Architektur und modernes Umweltbewusstsein (Bosau: Wohnungswirtschaft heute).

Imprint

Cover: Anne Caplan and photo by Benjamin Widholm (single-family home in Germany/North Rhine-Westphalia, 2015)

Editorial team: Christiane Cantauw, Anne Caplan, Elisabeth Timm
Design and setting: Susanne Rösler, jovis
Lithography: Bild1Druck, Berlin

Printed in the European Union.

Bibliographic information published by the Deutsche Nationalbibliothek.
The Deutsche Nationalbibliothek lists this publication in the Deutsche Nationalbibliografie. Detailed bibliographic data are available on the Internet at http://dnb.d-nb.de.

jovis Verlag GmbH
Kurfürstenstraße 15/16
10785 Berlin

www.jovis.de

jovis books are available worldwide in select bookstores. Please contact your nearest bookseller or visit www.jovis.de for information concerning your local distribution.

ISBN 978-3-86859-543-7

Funded by

Bundesministerium
für Bildung
und Forschung

LWL
Für die Menschen.
Für Westfalen-Lippe.

WWU
MÜNSTER

EXTINCTA REVIVISCO.

Werner-Zeller-Stiftung
Stiftung für gesellschaftsbezogene Familienforschung
Seedammstraße 1 71229 Leonberg